# ANIMALS ALIVE!

# ANIMALS ALIVE!

## An Ecological Guide to Animal Activities

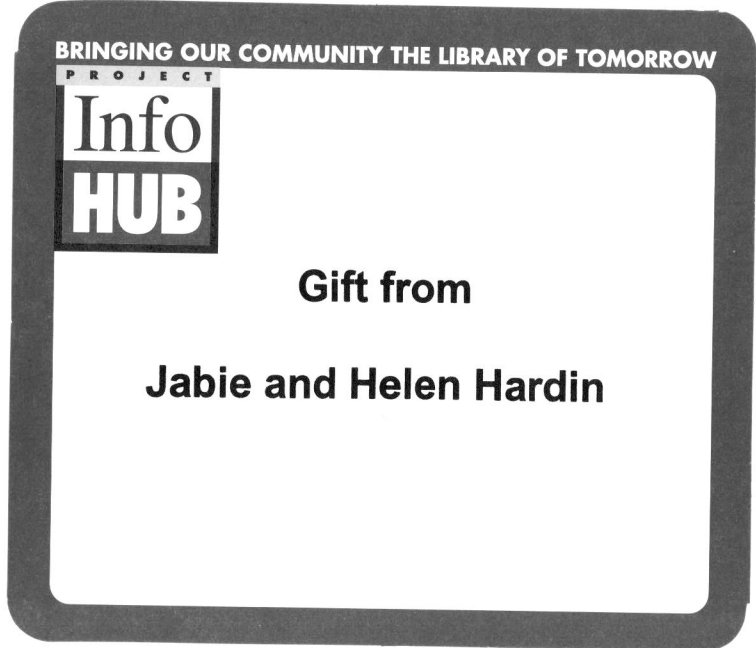

BRINGING OUR COMMUNITY THE LIBRARY OF TOMORROW

PROJECT

Info

HUB

**Gift from**

**Jabie and Helen Hardin**

## Dennis Holley

### Illustrated by Brian Payne

ROBERTS RINEHART PUBLISHERS

This book is dedicated to:

- My mother and father for buying me a microscope they couldn't afford and for their understanding about tadpoles and pigeons.

- My wife for her unending patience and support and for helping me pick up earthworms.

- My students, past and present, for teaching me far more than they will ever know.

"They are not our brethren. They are not our underlings. They are other nations, caught with ourselves in the net of life and time."

—*Henry Beston*

# CONTENTS

# PREFACE

*Study nature not books!* — Louis Agassiz

Agassiz's words admonish and remind life science educators to strive constantly to infuse students with the beauty, mystery, and wonder of nature. Teachers face tremendous challenges in developing new animal study programs or modifying existing programs so that they are interesting, educationally sound, environmentally wise, financially prudent, and noncontroversial.

*Animals Alive!* is designed to help teachers develop an inquiry-oriented program for studying the animal kingdom in which, whenever possible, live animals are collected locally, studied, and observed and then released completely unharmed back into their natural habitats. By careful selection and modification of the chapter questions, activities, and challenges in this book, teachers can plan, write, and conduct live-animal activities that students will find interesting and rewarding. These activities can be adapted to a wide range of ages and learning abilities, including upper elementary, junior high, senior high, and special education. With some adjustments, this program also could be used with lower elementary and even college-level students.

The sequence and content of this book are adaptable to most commercial textbook series and could be used to supplement your existing texts and laboratory materials. Some parts of the program could stand alone as self-contained units of study to enhance or demonstrate concepts about animals. This program does not attempt to cover all of the known animal phyla from sponges to mammals. Only phyla discussed in most commercial textbooks and/or phyla that lend themselves well to hands-on activities, easy collection, and simple, short-term maintenance are included.

*Animals Alive!* addresses the many concerns of life science teachers:

- **The need for educationally sound and interesting materials for teaching about the animal kingdom.** Students are interested in live animals and are motivated to learn from them. A spider in a jar brought from home by a student will generate more curiosity, observation, and critical thinking than any preserved specimen, elaborate plastic model, clever computer program, or action video program. Learning about the structure, adaptations and behavior of live animals and studying the nature of their habitats have much more relevance to students' lives and to the future of all living things.

- **The environmental soundness of methods and materials for studying the animal kingdom.** The major goal of life science education must be to develop and nurture a respect and concern for all living things and for our planet. Populations of many creatures once considered common, such as amphibians, are declining worldwide. Life science educators at all levels are expressing concern about the educational and environmental shortcomings of dissection, and many wish to reduce or eliminate dissections. The observe-and-release program utilizing live animals proposed here is an educationally sound and environmentally sane alternative to traditional dissection activities.

- **Possible exposure to harmful chemicals.** Concern is growing over the possible health hazards that chemical preservatives pose for teachers and students. Live-animal activities expose no one to toxic and possibly carcinogenic chemicals. The animals recommended for study in this program are nonpoisonous and nonaggressive. Students are likely to find these animals to be gentle, endearing creatures to which they can grow quite attached.

- **Legal or moral challenges to life science curriculums.** In recent years, legal actions and legislation have prevented individual students from being forced to dissect animals. At this point, only three states have imposed restrictions on the use of animals in the classroom by teachers. In California, students have the option to refuse to participate in any activity they feel would be "a harmful and destructive use of animals." In Florida, a student can be excused from the dissection of a preserved mammal or bird upon written request of a parent. A Pennsylvania law allows students to refuse to participate in dissection and requires that dissenting students be offered alternatives to dissection. State departments of education, listed in Appendix D, can provide information on current local restrictions. A curriculum such as this one, in which live animals are handled gently, studied respectfully, maintained safely, and released quickly, will lessen or eliminate any legal or moral problems associated with the study of the animal kingdom.

- **Shrinking or even vanishing of science budgets.** If all the animals recommended for study in this program are collected locally, the cost of the program is practically nothing. Even if some of the animals have to be ordered commercially, the cost of the program is less than it would be if similar preserved specimens were purchased for dissection. And if all of the animals are purchased commercially, the cost is less than one elaborate plastic model or several computer and video programs. The study of frogs illustrates the economics of the program. In its booklet, *Beyond Dissection*, the Ethical Science Education Coalition projects a cost of $573 to $1,609 to purchase 12 frogs per class for three classes of 24 students each over a three-year period. Collecting frogs locally costs little or nothing, discounting labor and trips to and from the collecting site. If live frogs are purchased, fewer will be needed than for dissection as each class can use the same frogs. For more savings, the same animals can be used at different grade levels.

- **Lack of experience in maintaining animals in the classroom.** The animals recommended for study in this program are kept temporarily and then released. There is no need to maintain permanent, ongoing collections of animals. As students and teachers gain more experience and confidence, they may want to keep some creatures year round. This book and the additional resources listed in Appendix F can help provide that experience and confidence.

- **Lack of space or equipment needed to keep and study live animals.** The common animals used in this program can be easily housed temporarily in sinks, jars, dish pans, plastic storage boxes, or aquaria. Animal housing containers often are found free or are very inexpensive to purchase. Some students and teachers have acquired all the aquaria they needed by running ads in the newspaper, asking for donations, and scouting out garage sales.

For observing the animals, microscopes, both compound and stereo dissecting types, would be ideal, but hand magnifiers will suffice in most cases. With or without equipment, students' eyes and inquisitive minds are the essential elements needed.

For collecting, safe and reliable transportation to and from collecting sites, appropriate clothing and footwear, suitable containers for transporting specimens, field guides for identification of invertebrate and vertebrate specimens collected (see Appendix F for some specific field guides available), and nets are needed.

- **The knowledge of where to collect live animals.** Students, their parents, fellow teachers, or friends who hunt, fish, boat, or hike are good sources of information. The state wildlife or natural resource authorities listed in Appendix C may be able to help. The animals used in this program are so common that usually just asking around will locate them.

- **Lack of time to collect and maintain live animals.** All of the recommended animals can be commercially purchased. Finding and taking the time to go collecting, however, has its own rewards in addition to free specimens. If students do the collecting, they gain experience in field work that is lacking in most life science curriculums. Once the specimens are in the classroom, students will gladly take care of them, learning and developing important skills in the process.

- **The support of parents and school officials.** Science education experts and current research tell us that the best curriculums today, and the curriculum trends in for the future, are based on teacher-generated materials that are inquiry oriented with many hands-on activities. That description fits this program exactly. Furthermore, the program is environmentally sane and financially prudent, and it eliminates legal or moral controversy.

Students are naturally curious about their planet and the living things around them. As life science educators, we are charged with channeling and shaping this wonder into knowledge of and respect for all living things. By treating the lowliest creature with the same care, concern, and even reverence as more complex creatures, we can show our students that all living things are precious.

The fate of many species and ultimately the quality of the environment itself may depend on people of all ages knowing about and caring deeply for the other creatures on this planet. It is my hope that this book will foster a better understanding of the amazing members of the animal kingdom and inspire its readers to treat these magnificent creatures and their habitats with care and concern.

This program has developed through many years of trying, failing, and much rewriting. Admittedly, it is still far from perfect. Therefore, I welcome your suggestions and would like to know about any new methods or materials you have developed for collecting, maintaining, and studying live animals.

I found that researching and writing this book made me a much better life science teacher. I hope the product of my efforts will do the same for you. Please contact me:

Dennis Holley
Roberts Rinehart Publishers
P.O. Box 666
Niwot, CO 80544

# PROCESS SKILLS TABLE

| Chapter | Observing | Measuring | Comparing Contrasting | Sequencing | Modeling | Predicting | Analyzing Reasoning | Drawing Conclusions | Experimental Design | Communication |
|---|---|---|---|---|---|---|---|---|---|---|
| 2 | S1, S6, F5, R4, In1 | S2, F3 | H2, H4, S2, In1 | R1 | H5, S1, R1, In2a, In3b | H4, H6, S4, R2, R3, In1 | H1, H2, H4, H5, H6, S3, S4, F1, F2, F3, R1, R2, R3, In1, In4a, In4b | In1 | S5 | H1, H2, H3, H5, S3, F1, F2, R1, R2, In1, In2a, In2b, In3b, In4a, In4b |
| 3 | S1, S2a, S2b, S2c, S2e, S2g, S2h, S5, S6, S7, B/R1, B/R2, B/R3, F4, F5 | H7, S2h, S3, S4, S7, B/R2, B/R3, F5, H7 | H2, S2d, S2h, S4, F2, F5, R2 | B/R4, R1 | H6, S1, S9, F3, In1b, In3b | H4, S7, S8, B/R2, B/R3, F5 | H1, H2, H3, H4, H6, H7, S2a, S2d, S3, S4, S6, S7, S8, B/R2, B/R3, F1, F2, F5, R1, R3, In3a, In4a, In4b | S2g, S7, S8, B/R2, B/R3, F5 | S6, S7, S8, B/R2, B/R3, F5 | H1, H2, H6, S4, S8, F1, R1, R3, In1a, In1b, In2a, In2b, In3a, In3b, In4a, In4c |
| 4 | S1, S2a, S2b, S2c, S5, S7, B/R1, B/R2, B/R3, B/R4, B/R5, F3 | H3, H7, S2, S3, S5, S8/H, S8, B/R9 | H2, S2c, S4, S6, F2, F4, R3 | S6, R5 | H5, S1, S8, R5, In4b | S2e, S7, B/R4, B/R5, F4 | H1, H2, H3, H4, H5, H6, S2a, S2e, S4, S6, S7, B/R4, B/R5, F1, F2, F4, R1, R2, In3a, In4a, In4c | S2e, B/R4, B/R5, F4 | S2e, B/R4, B/R5, F4 | H1, H2, H3, H4, H5, S4, S7, F1, In1a, In1b, In2a, In2b, In2c, In3a, In4a, In4c |
| 5 | H6, H7, S1, S2, S8a, S8d, S8f, S8h, S9, B/R2, B/R6, B/R7, B/R8, B/R9, R1 | H3, H7, S2, S3, S5, S8/H, S8, B/R9 | H2, S2, S3, S5, S8a, S8e, S8, B/R5, B/R7, F4, R3 | F2, R2 | H8, S8, S13, In2a | H7, S8h, B/R4, B/R6, B/R7, B/R8, B/R9 | H1, H2, H6, H7, H8, S8a, S8b, S8c, S8e, S8f, S8g, S8h, S9, S10, S11, S12, S13, B/R1, B/R2, B/R6, B/R8, B/R9, F1, F2, F3, R2, In2c, In3a, In4 | S8h, B/R2, B/R6, B/R7, B/R8, B/R9 | S4, S8h, B/R7, B/R8, B/R9 | H1, H4, H5, H8, S10, S11, S12, B/R5, B/R7, B/R8, F1, F2, In1a, In1b, In2b, In2c, In3a, In3b, In4 |
| 6 | S1, S2a, S2b, S2f, S2g, S2h, S2i, S2j, B/R1, B/R2, B/R4, B/R5, F3, F4, F4 | H6, S2e, S2i, S2j | H2, H6, S2c, S2i, S2j, B/R2, B/R3, F4, F5, R2, In3a | F6 |  | H6, S2h, B/R3, B/R4, B/R5, F4 | H1, H2, H5b, H5c, S2h, S2b, S2c, S2j, B/R4, B/R5, F1, F4, F5, R1, R3, In3b, In4a, In4b | S2g, B/R2, B/R3, B/R4, B/R5, F4 | S2g, B/R3, B/R5, F4 | H1, H2, H3, H5, S2g, S4, B/R1, B/R4, B/R6, F1, In1a, In1b, In2a, In2c, In3b, In4a, In4b |
| 7 | H7, S1, S4b, S4g, S4k, S4m, S4n, B/R3, B/R4, F2, F4, R2, R4 | H8, S4A, F2, F4, In3b | H1, H2, H7, H8, S1, S4d, S4m, B/R3, F1, F2, R1, R4, In1c, In1d, In3b, In4c | R5 | H3, S4b, S4c, S4f, S4m, B/R2, B/R3, F1, F4, In1a, In1d, In2a, In3b, In4c | H1, H6, H8, S4g, S4h, S4n, B/R2, B/R3, F2, F3, R3 | H1, H2, H5, H6, S4b, S4c, S4d, S4e, S4m, B/R1, B/R2, B/R3, B/R4, F1, S4n, In1a, In1b, In1c, In1d, In2a, In3b, In4a, In4c | H1, H6, S4h, B/R1, B/R4, F2, R3, In4c | H1, H6, S4h, B/R2, B/R3, F2, F3 | H1, H2, H3, H4, H5, H6, H7, S4d, S4m, S4n, B/R3, B/R4, S4k, S4m, B/R3, B/R4, F1, F2, F4, R1, R3, R4, In1a, In1b, In1c, In2a, In3b, In4a, In4c |
| 8 | H4, S1, S2, S3, S6, S7, S8, S10, B/R1, B/R2, B/R3, B/R6, B/R7, B/R8, F2, F3, F4, F5, R2, R3, R4, R5, In4 | H7, S7, S8, S10, S11, B/R1, B/R7, F5, In2a, In3a, In3b | H1, H4, S3, S4, S5, S6, S7, S8, B/R1, B/R2, F1, F2, F3, F4, F5, R1, R2, R3, R5, In1a, In1c, In3b, In4b | H6, S1, S3, S8, F2, R2, R4, In3a | H3, H5, H8, S4, S5, S6, S9, S12, B/R2, B/R4, B/R6, B/R8, F1, F2, F3, F6, R1, R2, R4, R5, In1c, In1c, In2c, In4b, In4c | H4, H5, H7, S8, B/R2, B/R3, B/R6, B/R7, B/R8, F5, R3 | H2, S3, S8, S9, S10, S11, S12, B/R1, B/R2, B/R3, B/R4, B/R6, B/R8, F2, F3, F4, F5, F6, R1, R2, R3, R4, R5, In1a, In4a, In4c | H4, S8, S10, B/R6, B/R7, B/R8, F3, F5, R2, R3, R5 | H4, S8, S10, B/R6, B/R7, B/R8, F5, R3, R5 | H1, H3, H8, S3, S6, S7, S8, S9, S10, S11, S12, B/R1, B/R3, B/R4, B/R6, B/R8, F1, F3, F5, F6, R1, R2, R3, R4, R5, In2a, In3b, In4a, In4c |
| 9 | H5, H6, H8, S1, S2, S4, S5, B/R1, B/R2, B/R4, B/R5, B/R6, B/R8, R4, In3b | S4, S5 | H1, H2, H6, S1, S3, S4, S5, S6, B/R4, B/R6, B/R7, B/R8, R5, R6, In1a, In2a, In3b | S4, R1, R4 | H1, H4, H5, S2, S3, S4, S5, S6, B/R4, B/R6, B/R7, B/R8, R5, R6, In1a, In2a, In2c, In4b, In4c | H4, H5, H7, S4, S5, S8, B/R2, B/R3, B/R6, B/R7, F4, F5, R5 | H1, H2, H4, H5, H6, H7, S1, S3, S4, S5, S6, B/R1, B/R2, B/R3, B/R6, B/R7, B/R8, F1, F2, F3, F4, F5, R1, R2, In2a, In2c, In4a, In4c | H7, S4, S5, B/R1, B/R3, B/R7, B/R8, F5, R6 | H7, S5, B/R3, B/R4, F5, R6 | H1, H2, H4, H6, H8, S1, S4, S5, S6, B/R1, B/R2, B/R6, B/R7, B/R8, F1, F2, F4, R1, R2, R3, R4, R6, In1a, In1b, In1c, In2a, In2b, In3a, In4a, In4c |
| 10 | H6, H8, S2, S3, B/R1, B/R2, B/R4, B/R5, B/R6, F2, R4, In3b | H5, S2, S3 | H1, H5, H6, S1, S2, S3, B/R1, B/R2, B/R4, B/R5, B/R6, F1, F2, R3, R5, R6, In1a, In1b, In3b | S2, R5 | H1, H2, H3, H4, H5, S2, S3, S4, B/R2, B/R4, B/R5, B/R6, F2, F3, F4, F5, R2, R3, R7, R9, In1a, In1c, In2b, In4a, In4b, In4c | H6, S2, S3, B/R2, B/R4, F3, F4, F5 | H1, H4, H5, H6, H7, H8, S1, S4, B/R1, B/R2, B/R4, B/R5, B/R6, F2, F3, F4, F5, R1, R2, R3, R4, R5, In1a, In2c, In3a, In4a, In4c | H8, S3, B/R1, B/R2, B/R3, B/R4, B/R5, B/R6 | H8, S3, B/R3, B/R4 | H1, H2, H3, H5, H6, H7, S1, S2, S3, B/R1, B/R2, B/R3, B/R4, B/R6, B/R7, F3, F4, F5, F6, R1, R2, R3, R4, R9, In1a, In1b, In3b, In4a, In4c |
| 11 | H6, H8, S2, S3, B/R1, B/R4, B/R5, B/R6, F2, In1c, In2c | H4, S2, B/R2, F6, R4, In3b | H1, H2, H3, H5, S1, S2, S4, B/R1, B/R2, B/R4, B/R6, F1, F2, R2, R3, In1b, In3b | S2, B/R3, F5, F6, R8, In3b | H1, H4, H5, H6, S2, B/R1, B/R2, B/R3, B/R4, B/R5, B/R6, B/R7, F2, F3, F4, F5, F6, R2, R3, R7, R9, In1a, In2c, In2d, In3b, In4b, In4c | H5, H7, S4, B/R1, B/R2, F3, R3, R5 | H4, H5, H7, H8, S1, S4, B/R1, B/R6, B/R7, F2, F3, F4, F5, F6, R1, R2, R4, R6, R7, R9, In1a, In2c, In3b, In4a | S4, B/R2, B/R5, R4 | H8, S4, B/R2, B/R6, F6 | H1, H2, H3, H4, H6, H7, H8, S1, S4, B/R1, B/R2, B/R4, B/R5, B/R6, F2, F3, F4, R1, R2, R4, R7, R9, In1a, In1b, In2c, In3a, In3b, In4a |
| 12 | H2, H3, H4, H6, H7, S1, S3, S4, S5, B/R1, B/R2, B/R3, B/R6, F1, F3, F4, F7, R1, R4, R5 | H4, H5, H7, S3, S4, S5, B/R2, B/R3, B/R5, B/R6, R4, R5 | H1, H2, H4, H5, H6, H7, S1, S2, S3, S4, B/R1, B/R2, B/R3, B/R4, B/R5, B/R6, F5, F6, F7, R1, R2, R3, R5, R6, In1c, In3a, In4a | S4, S5, B/R3, B/R4, B/R4, F5, F7, In2a | H1, H3, H4, H5, H6, H7, S2, S3, S4, S5, B/R2, B/R3, B/R4, B/R6, F2, F3, F4, F5, F6, F7, R2, R3, R7, R9, In1a, In1b, In2d, In3a, In4c | H5, H7, S4, B/R1, B/R2, F3, R5 | H1, H5, H7, S1, S2, S4, S5, B/R1, B/R2, B/R3, B/R5, B/R6, F2, F3, F4, F5, F6, F7, R1, R2, R4, R5, R6, In1b, In1c, In2a, In2c, In3a, In4d | H5, S4, S5, B/R2, B/R3, B/R4, F3, R1, R6, F6 | H5, H7, S4, B/R2, R5 | H1, H2, H3, H4, H6, H5, S1, S2, S4, S5, B/R1, B/R2, B/R3, B/R5, F2, F3, F4, F5, F6, F7, R2, R3, R6, In1a, In1b, In1c, In2a, In4a, In4c, In4d |

# 1. HOW TO USE THIS BOOK

Each chapter of this book investigates a major phylum of animals and is divided into sections dealing with classification, structure and habitat, collection of specimens, health and safety issues, teaching activities, and release of specimens.

## CLASSIFICATION

The classification methods used in this book are part of the five-kingdom classification system commonly used in life science education materials. Appendix A discusses this system in detail. Each phylum is classified into the major groups within the phylum, with both the scientific and common names for each group listed. Whenever possible, common names or descriptive phrases are used. Let the age and ability of your students dictate the use of scientific terms.

The chapters are arranged beginning with the animal groups simplest in structure and progressing to groups with more complex structure. This book deviates from the norm concerning the order of the first two phyla of upper invertebrates. Most textbooks consider the phylum Annelida to be more complex than the phylum Mollusca because annelids show segmentation similar to the arthropods and the vertebrates while mollusks do not possess segmented bodies. This ordering of complexity can be confusing to students because, in all aspects other than segmentation, mollusks clearly are more advanced than annelids. However, these chapters can be used in any order, in part or in full, to fit any approach: phylogenetic, systematic, ecological, or a modified combination.

## STRUCTURE AND HABITAT
## COLLECTION OF SPECIMENS

Background information on body structure; feeding; reproduction; habitat; and economic, social, environmental, or medical importance provides a general description of the entire phylum and the specific classes within the phylum.

The timing of collection activities is important in areas where winter conditions may preclude collecting or releasing live animals. Early spring and late fall in such areas may also present problems. Many animals have not yet made an appearance in early spring, and in late fall they may be secluding themselves in preparation for winter. Late spring and early fall present the best opportunities for collection and release in areas with severe winters.

Collecting requires safe and reliable transportation to and from collecting sites, appropriate clothing and footwear (wading boots would be ideal), and buckets or suitable containers for the transport of specimens. A high-quality fine-mesh dip net and insect sweep net, both with long, sturdy handles, are also invaluable. Such nets may be purchased from the suppliers listed in Appendix B or can be made.

Obtaining permission from the proper wildlife, health (see Appendix E), and school authorities is a necessary first step in collecting live animals locally. These authorities usually need to know what animals will be collected, approximately how many animals will be collected, how the animals will be maintained, and approximately when and where they will be released.

The sanctity of the animals' habitat should be preserved. Teachers and students should follow these rules: Do not disturb the area any more than necessary. Replace overturned rocks and branches, and leave the area as you found it. Collect the fewest specimens needed as the populations of many creatures are being reduced in the name of science through overcollection.

The health of specimens is of prime importance. Place the animals in suitable containers and get them from the field to the classroom as soon as possible, being careful to avoid extremes of temperature, dryness, and loss of oxygen. Anyone who collects—teachers, students, parents, or others—should have permission from proper authorities, understand the correct procedures for collecting in an ecologically sound manner, and fully appreciate the health requirements of the animals being collected.

People who live in large urban areas or in areas with great climate extremes may find it impossible or impractical to collect all or any of the animals suggested for study in this book. Commercial purchase of live specimens may be necessary. Appendix B lists the names, addresses, phone numbers, and pertinent information for firms that sell live animals from stocks that they maintain at their own facilities. Since these firms collect and maintain their own stocks, they usually can verify the exact species of any animal they ship, the origin of the animal, and the treatment of that animal prior to shipment. This information is vital for the proper release of the animal once the study is complete (see "Release of Specimens" in this chapter).

## MAINTENANCE OF SPECIMENS

Since the animals in this program must be maintained only briefly, elaborate equipment and involved methods are not necessary. Such common items as aquaria, jars, and dishpans work quite well as temporary housing.

All care and treatment of live animals is ultimately the responsibility of the teacher. Prior to collection or purchase, familiarize yourself with the maintenance requirements of the animal and be able to provide the following conditions as needed:

1. clean housing with adequate space
2. suitable food and clean water
3. appropriate light and temperature conditions
4. suitable exercise

Students will quickly volunteer to provide daily care for the animals. This can be a very beneficial experience for students, but take care to give such responsibilities only to those students whom you judge capable, and provide the selected students with adequate instruction on the handling and care of the animals.

Animals should not be left at school during vacations or times when school is not in session for extended periods. If adequate care cannot be maintained at school, the animal should go home with the teacher. Before sending any animal home for care by a student, make sure you can guarantee that the student will properly care for the animal and get parental and school permission beforehand.

Discourage students from bringing in abandoned or injured animals. If such an incident does occur, it could be used as a springboard for a discussion of the fate of animals in our society.

If necessary or desired, many of the animals recommended for study in this book can be kept for longer periods. The "Maintenance of Specimens" section of each chapter provides background primarily for short-term care and maintenance of animals in the classroom. Appendix F lists general and specific resources that could be of more assistance. Your local humane societies, zoos, veterinarians, and wildlife officials also can assist in creating a safe and humane animal experience in the classroom.

The health and safety of the students, the teacher, and the animals is a major consideration.

Certain diseases (zoonoses) can be transmitted from animals to humans. The transmission can be direct through bites, scratches, or physical contact or indirect through airborne organisms or insect vectors such as fleas, ticks, or mites. Teachers should be aware of some of the more common zoonotic diseases:

> *Lyme disease* is carried by the deer tick and transmitted to humans by the bite of that tick. Results can be fever, headache, and possible neurological and cardiac complications.
>
> *Pasteurellosis* (commonly called "snuffles") is carried in the oral and upper respiratory tract, especially in rabbits, and transmitted to humans by the bite or scratch of dogs or cats or the unhygienic handling of rabbit feces. Results are respiratory infections, usually of short duration.
>
> *Rabies* is a serious neurological disease that results in death by convulsion or progressive paralysis. It is carried by dogs and wild mammals such as skunks, raccoons, and bats. *Psittacosis* is carried in the dust from the feces or feathers of parakeets and pigeons and transmitted to humans by inhaling the dust. A variety of respiratory problems can result.
>
> *Salmonellosis* is carried on dogs, cats, mice, birds, amphibians, and reptiles (especially turtles) and transmitted to humans on food as a result of not washing the hands after handling these animals.
>
> *Ringworm* is carried by a wide variety of wild and domestic animals and usually transmitted to humans by direct contact. Results can be skin lesions.
>
> *Rocky Mountain spotted fever* is carried by ticks found on dogs and wild mice and voles and transmitted to humans by the bite of those ticks. Results can be a rash, headaches, and a high fever.

The animals recommended for study in this program pose no major health or safety threat to teachers or students if the following guidelines are followed:

1. Collect only animals that are healthy and free of obvious disease.
2. Provide proper instruction and equipment for safe observation and manipulation of the animal. Be aware of any local or state regulations in this regard. Some school districts now require students to wear protective gloves when handling any animal.
3. People handling an animal should wash their hands before and after contact. During contact, instruct students not to put their hands or anything that has touched the animal in their mouth and to keep their hands away from their face and eyes.
4. Report animal bites or scratches to the proper authorities and render necessary first aid. Keep the animal available for possible diagnostic testing.
5. Encourage students to report any allergies to animals they may have. Any rash or irritation that develops after an animal contact should be examined by a doctor.
6. Poisonous or stinging animals (some cnidarians, arachnids, insects, and reptiles) or aggressive biting animals (some insects, fish, reptiles, birds, and mammals) should not be brought into the classroom. Famil-

HEALTH AND SAFETY

iarize yourself and your students with such animals in your locale and be extremely cautious about deliberate contact with any of them.

7.  When collecting, be alert and cautious to avoid contact with poisonous plants and biting, stinging, or parasitic animals. Exercise extreme caution around water and other potentially dangerous areas.

8.  Even animals that appear to be healthy can become ill. Watch for changes in appearance, behavior, feeding, or breathing. If an animal appears ill, isolate it from other animals and remove it from the classroom. Consult a local veterinarian about the proper treatment of sick animals and the proper disposal of animals that die.

The chapter questions, activities, and challenges are designed to prevent animals from suffering pain or being deliberately exposed to microorganisms, radiation, extreme temperatures, or harmful chemicals. Do not modify the questions, activities, or challenges, especially those in the behavior/response category, in such a way that any animal's health or well-being is threatened.

Some students exhibit revulsion or fear of certain animals. Be sensitive to this fear and try to structure activities to break down unrealistic attitudes. You and other students may have difficulty understanding such attitudes and fears, but to the affected student they are quite real. Such situations provide an opportunity through compassion, understanding, and guidance to help the student develop a healthier and more realistic outlook toward that animal.

## TEACHING STRATEGIES

The facts, questions, and challenges in the "Teaching Activities" section of each chapter provide a base to develop process activities for studying live animals. The activities in this section are arranged into three categories:

1.  **Observation.** Students will observe and investigate the structure, movement, feeding, behavior/response, and reproduction/growth of the animal. The behavior/response category allows students to investigate how animals react to the environment around them. Such reactions are called taxes. Some of the various taxes animals exhibit are

    *geotaxis*—response to gravity

    *thermotaxis*—response to temperature change

    *galvanotaxis*—response to electrical currents

    *phototaxis*—response to light

    *magnetotaxis*—response to magnetic fields

    *hydrotaxis*—response to water

    *thigmotaxis*—response to touch or contact

    *chemotaxis*—response to chemicals

    *rheotaxis*—response to currents of air or water

2.  **Ecology.** Students will investigate the habitat and surroundings of the animal and discover its place in nature.

3.  **Integration.** At the end of each chapter students will be given activities to integrate what they learn about each animal group with other subject areas—writing, fine arts, social studies (history and geography), and societal/environmental issues. When possible, science-oriented math skills such as constructing and analyzing data tables and graphs, measuring, calculating, and problem solving have been incorporated into the chapter teaching activities rather than as a separate section at the end of each chapter. However, this book is not written to be fully integrated with any other subject area or any specific grade level.

The chapter questions, activities and challenges are designed to be used in hands-on experiences in which students are actively involved in scientific investigation. When possible, they follow an inquiry-oriented approach designed to develop the following science process skills:

1. **Observing.** Students will learn to better perceive objects and events.
2. **Measuring/graphing.** Students will learn to make, record, and display quantitative information.
3. **Comparing/contrasting.** Students will learn to identify distinguishing characteristics among objects or events.
4. **Sequencing.** Students will learn to put events in order.
5. **Prediction.** Students will learn to how to propose possible outcomes.
6. **Experimentation.** Students will learn how to design experiments to test their predictions.
7. **Analyzing/reasoning.** Students will learn how to explain the meaning and importance of data gathered or facts given. On occasion student data will be difficult to interpret ("muddy data"), and students will be frustrated. Use these situations to point out that in science things are seldom clear crystal clear. Trained scientists often disagree about how to interpret data from experiments.
8. **Drawing conclusions.** Students will learn to make general statements about particulars. If students are working with "muddy data," however, they may be severely limited in the logical conclusions they can draw from the data ("cloudy conclusions"). Again, explain that this is the nature of the fascinating enterprise we call science.
9. **Modeling.** Students will learn to construct physical or mental models.
10. **Communication.** Students will develop skills for conveying information in oral, written, or pictorial form.

The specific process skills developed during each chapter are shown in a table on page 4. Careful selection and appropriate modification of the chapter questions, activities, and challenges will allow you to control the length and depth of study as well as the proper blend of content and process skills to fit your exact goals and needs. In this book you and your students will be challenged to think scientifically, design experiments, and conduct scientific investigations.

The chapter facts, questions, activities, and challenges can be used in a variety of ways: laboratory situations, general class discussion, or small group discussion. The activities can also lead to independent student projects and creative homework assignments.

Although some factual background is necessary, try to maximize thinking and minimize memorizing. Let process lead to content when possible. For example, allowing students to first work with a live animal (process) and then discussing specific facts about the animal (content) will make the facts more understandable and relevant because students will have seen the animal live, up close, and in action.

Challenge your students to observe carefully, think creatively, and answer thoughtfully. Many of their observations and thoughts will not be clearly right or wrong. Try not to discount or discredit any student responses; build on them through investigative questioning until your students understand the point you are trying to make. If science is truly the search for truths, prove this to your students by allowing them to take many paths to those truths. As a life science educator, your challenge is twofold: to formulate questions that challenge your students to interpret, analyze, and think and to find the time to ask these questions in a life science curriculum already crammed with enough factual information to numb the mind.

One goal of this program is to develop an understanding and appreciation of the various habitats in which animals live. However, live animal activities in the classroom isolate the animal and do not allow students to appreciate the true nature of that animal's total existence. One way to correct this deficiency is to use as many visual aids as possible. Some appropriate visual aids are chalkboards, flat pictures, charts, transparencies, models, filmstrips, slides, movies, videos, laserdiscs, and appropriate television programs. Combining live animal activities with visual aids will give students a complete presentation of the nature of animals and their connection to wild places.

Not all students will be sensitive and kind at all times to the animals you are studying. Consider the possible problems uncooperative or disruptive students could cause and plan how you will deal with such problems if they arise. Make students aware of the plan and then enforce it evenly and fairly. If negative things happen, use your creativity to turn them into positive learning situations. Emphasize the sanctity of the tiny lives students hold in their hands.

## RELEASE OF SPECIMENS

The final phase of the program involves returning the animals back to suitable habitats unharmed. For the health of the animal and the sake of the environment, have a plan for what to do with an animal *before* you collect or purchase it.

If an animal was field-collected locally, release usually involves returning the animal to the collection site. Before releasing the animal, contact the appropriate school, health, and wildlife authorities, explain what you are going to do, and secure their permission.

If the animal was commercially purchased, proper and safe release poses some potential problems. Plan ahead! Contact your local wildlife or natural resource officials for authority to release the animal and for guidelines on where to release it. Contact the appropriate school and health officials and obtain their permission for release.

Before purchasing any animal, find out from the supplier the origin and exact species of the animal that will be sent and order only those animals that are native to your locale. Occasionally, due to shortages or to expedite timely delivery, suppliers may substitute. When ordering let the supplier know that you wish to be notified *before* any substitute animal is sent. These precautions are necessary to avoid releasing an animal into an unsuitable habitat or into a habitat where it might cause environmental problems. Even small common animals that appear innocuous can cause serious ecological damage. Regard any commercially purchased live animal as a potential ecological menace and don't create a problem in your area through carelessness or ignorance of proper release procedures.

The National Science Teachers Association and the biological supply firm Nasco both recommend that commercially purchased animals never be released into the wild under any circumstances. Other life science organizations and supply firms believe that release of properly identified animals into their normal range poses no ecological threat.

If a commercially purchased animal cannot be safely and humanely released, you must make provisions to permanently and properly care for that animal for the duration of its natural life. If a commercially purchased animal cannot be released and permanent arrangements cannot be made for its care, the animal should not be acquired.

# SECTION ONE: LOWER INVERTEBRATES

## 2. SPONGES

> **Kingdom:** Animalia
> **Subkingdom:** Parazoa (animals lacking definite symmetry and tissues)
> **Phylum:** Porifera
> **Classes:** Calcarea
> Sclerospongiae
> Demospongiae
> Hexactinellia

Sponge—plant or animal? The casual observer of today would easily make the same mistake as early biologists and misjudge the sponge (or its remains) to be a creature belonging in the plant kingdom. However, closer examination reveals that the sponge actually falls on the animal side of the sometimes fine line that separates the two kingdoms. Only at the microscopic level does the sponge reveal its true nature: a loosely organized colonial mass of animal cells clinging to a supporting framework of glasslike or lime splinters (called spicules) and/or stiff fibers (called spongin).

Most products sold today as sponges are synthetic, and even a natural sponge is nothing more than the cleaned, dried, and trimmed fibrous skeletal remains of the once-living animal. The variety of living sponges is truly amazing. Some are round, others are flat and crusty, and some are vaselike in shape. Some are gray or drab brown, but many are brilliant colors of red, orange, yellow, blue, violet, and even black. They range in size from a few centimeters (an inch or so) in diameter to giants more than 2 meters (7 feet) in diameter. Some reach heights of over 2 meters. Such gigantic sponges may be hundreds of years old.

Regardless of their size, shape, or color, all sponges are variations on a unique porous theme (Latin—*porous*, pore + *ferre*, to bear). The organization of a sponge is simple: a hollow cylinder closed at the bottom with a top opening called an osculum, or excurrent vent. The walls of the cylinder are composed of a jellylike material called mesenchyme. The mesenchyme is interlaced with supporting spicules and/or spongin fibers. Covering the outside are flattened epithelial cells; the inside is lined with collar cells. The wriggling flagella (hair-like projections) of the collar cells create water currents carrying food and oxygen into the deepest recesses of the sponge.

Slowly creeping amoebalike through the jellylike mesenchyme are the mesenchyme cells, which perform a variety of functions: secreting the skeleton, replacing cells that die or are damaged, and carrying food particles from one place to another.

Approximately 5,000 species of marine sponges live in the ocean from the intertidal zone at ocean's edge to abyssal depths miles down. Freshwater sponges number between 150 to 300 species, with approximately 27 species found in the lakes and streams of North America. Land sponges do not exist.

General Phylum
Characteristics

Sponges have no organs or systems of respiration, digestion, or excretion. Water brings in food and oxygen through the many openings in the sponge (called incurrent pores) and carries carbon dioxide and other wastes out through the excurrent vent(s) via water currents generated by the combined beating of the flagella of the collar cells.

Sponges are filter feeders. They pump water though their bodies and remove food particles in the process. Each cell feeds independently, engulfing minute organic particles, bacteria, algae, and protozoans. Some sponges obtain additional nutrients from photosynthetic green protists (algae) that live within them.

Although some sponges can change position very slowly, they are considered sessile (nonmoving) animals that permanently attach to surfaces in the water. Being unable to flee from predators, many sponges protect themselves with a bristly texture and strong chemicals. Some of these chemicals are toxic to small animals and can cause skin irritation and rash in humans.

Reproduction in sponges occurs asexually or sexually. One mode of asexual reproduction involves the sponges' amazing power to regenerate damaged or missing parts with ease. If a sponge is squeezed through a fine silk cloth and all its cells separated, the cells eventually creep back together (reaggregation) and regenerate into several new but smaller sponges.

Sponges also reproduce asexually by budding. Small branches or knobs break off the parent sponge and drift away to begin life on their own. All freshwater sponges and some marine sponges form internal buds called gemmules. A gemmule is a mass of food-filled mesenchyme cells surrounded by a thick coat strengthened with spicules. Gemmules are formed during unfavorable conditions such as drying or freezing and grow into new sponges when conditions become more favorable.

Sexual reproduction in sponges is similar to that in other lower aquatic invertebrates. Most sponges are hermaphrodites that form both sperm and eggs within the same body, but a few types are separate male or female individuals. In practically all sponges, the sperm are shed into the surrounding water through the excurrent vent(s) while the eggs are retained in the body. The eggs are fertilized as sperm enters the sponge with water currents. The fertilized egg develops into a swimming larva and makes its way out of the parent sponge. The larva eventually attaches to a surface and gradually changes into the adult form.

Specific Class
Characteristics

**Class Calcarea.** The calcareous sponges have a skeleton of calcium carbonate spicules. These sponges are all marine types and are found from the intertidal zone down to around 200 meters (660 feet).

**Class Sclerospongiae.** The coralline sponges were discovered on steep rocky slopes or in underwater caves only when scuba equipment made the marine environment more accessible to humans. Unlike other sponges, they have both silicon spicules and spongin fibers over a base of dense calcium carbonate.

**Class Demospongiae.** About 95 percent of all marine sponges and all freshwater sponges are in this class. They span the full range of sizes, colors, and shapes; they range from the intertidal zone to the abyssal depths in the ocean; and they are found in freshwater lakes and streams. Most have a combination of silicon spicules and spongin fibers in their skeletons.

**Class Hexactinellia.** This group is known as glass sponges because their silicon spicule skeletons form ornate jewellike objects when they are carefully cleaned and dried. They are most abundant in deep tropical waters.

—Humans have used the fibrous skeletons of certain sponges for bathing, mopping, and scrubbing since the Bronze Age. Overcollecting and fungus infestation decimated the natural sponge industry in the late 1930s and early 1940s, and since that time synthetic sponges have been developed. Natural sponges are still available and are preferred by certain artisans and craftsmen such as professional car and wall washers, leatherworkers, potters, silversmiths, and lithographers.

Sponges play an important role in their natural habitat as many creatures live on, in, or around sponges. Even though sponges may have a bristly texture and often produce strong irritating chemicals, they are fed upon by certain fishes, sea stars, and snails. The group of sponges known as boring sponges attach to the shells of mollusks and corals, tunneling down into them and eventually killing the animal inside. This is certainly detrimental to live mollusks and corals but can be beneficial in recycling the material in the shells and chambers of dead mollusks and corals.

Researchers recently have begun to study the chemicals produced by sponges. Their findings have created the possibility of new antibiotics to kill bacteria and fungi, new drugs to fight leukemia and certain viruses, and a possible aid against certain forms of arthritis.

A large marine sponge may be decades old. To collect such a sponge or its smaller cousins, one must tear or cut the sponge loose from its permanent ocean attachment or dig up the surface material on which the sponge is living. Too often, collected sponges are kept in makeshift marine aquariums where the conditions are far from ideal and then tossed back into the ocean at best or in the trash can at worst. Clearly, such methods are not environmentally prudent. If the sponge breaks down and dissociates and the water containing the dissociated clumps of cells is dumped back into the ocean, one has not technically killed the sponge or caused its death, but one certainly has caused the destruction of a thriving magnificent old individual creature. We have no right to do that, and no purpose is served by it. A better alternative is the use of freshwater sponges.

Freshwater sponges are found throughout North America. They are more common in northern and eastern lakes and streams than in southern and western ones. Although the specific factors that control the distribution of freshwater sponges are difficult to pinpoint, sponges are sufficiently broad in their distribution that many lakes or streams can be expected to contain at least some small specimens. In general, freshwater sponges will not be found in areas with frequent physical disturbances, high pollution levels, or turbid waters containing high levels of silt that can clog their feeding systems.

In cool climates, many species of freshwater sponges reach their mature size by late fall, when they begin to degenerate and eventually die. Overwintering gemmules will form new sponges the following spring. In warm climates, fall degeneration results in many small remnants that resume growth the next spring.

Freshwater sponges grow as brown, tan, or whitish-gray masses encrusted on rocks, logs, twigs, or parts of underwater plants in clean, slow-moving water. Only one species, Spongilla lacustris, has been found growing out of soft bottom sediments in standing water.

Collect freshwater sponges by carefully picking up by hand the substratum on which they are found. Cause as little disturbance to the collecting site as possible. Freshwater sponges are very fragile, so handle them carefully and transport them in pond water from the collection site. Several of the suppliers listed in

# The Importance of Sponges

# COLLECTION OF SPECIMENS

## MAINTENANCE OF SPECIMENS

Appendix B sell living freshwater sponges and gemmules, although their availablility may be seasonal.

Freshwater sponges kept in the classroom begin to degenerate after a short time but they are not dead, merely dissociated.

I have had success culturing freshwater sponges by placing them in a shallow glass dish with about 3 to 4 centimeters (1 to 1.5 inches) of clean pond water containing waterlogged twigs and some rocks. I gently aerate and cover the dish with a piece of glass to reduce evaporation. I keep the whole setup in dim light and disturb the sponges as little as possible.

At present, I have two such cultures established with the oldest being active for several years. I maintain the water level by periodically adding clean pond water. Approximately once a week I add to the dish a small pinch of flake goldfish food that I grind between my fingers to reduce the flakes to very small particles.

An interesting cycle of changes occasionally occurs in my cultures. During the summer months when my classroom is quite warm, the culture is merely a cottony mass of dissociated cells, fibers, and spicules on the bottom of the dish. As temperatures begin to cool in the fall, some of the cells occasionally form into small individual cylindrical sponges up to 1 centimeter long. By November the culture may have two to eight small but fully formed individual sponges, some with gemmules. By late winter, few, if any, individual sponges remain among the cottony mass. Early spring may see a few individual sponges forming again with total dissociation again by early summer. My students and I are quite interested to see if these apparent seasonal changes continue.

## HEALTH AND SAFETY
### Teachers

Some marine sponges such as the touch-me-not sponge contain toxic substances that can cause itching and burning followed by a rash if touched (another good reason for not collecting marine sponges!).

When collecting sponges from lakes and streams, follow good safety procedures around water regardless of its apparent depth. Be alert for possible contact with poisonous plants and biting or stinging animals.

### Students

Freshwater sponges present no health or safety risks for students. To be on the safe side, however, have students thoroughly wash their hands after contact with sponge culture dishes and the pond water they may contain.

### Sponges

Freshwater sponges are fragile, so handle them gently and transfer them from lake to culture dish to microscope slide carefully. Remember that sponges are totally aquatic and must be kept in water at all times. If they dry, they die. Use only clean pond or spring water on sponges, as city tap water may contain traces of chemicals that are harmful or fatal to them.

## TEACHING ACTIVITIES

Students can observe the overall mass of sponge growth with the unaided eye or a hand lens. To see the real details of sponge structure such as sponge cells, fibers, and spicules, however, a compound microscope with a magnification of up to at least 100X is necessary.

Whether you collect freshwater sponges or order them from a commercial supplier, they are usually encrusted on twigs or leaves. To observe live freshwater sponges, place a piece of the sponge mass on a depression slide or a well slide in several large drops of clean pond water. Have students examine the sponge through the compound microscope.

### Habitat

**H1.** *Sponge Habitat.* Have students respond to the question, What is the natural habitat of your sponge? (Answer: Freshwater sponges are found in lakes and streams attached to submerged rocks, sticks, and plant parts.)

**H2.** *Sponge Habitat Comparisons.* Have students respond to the question, In what other habitats might sponges be found? (Answer: Most types of sponges are found in the ocean from the intertidal zone to the abyssal depths.)

**H3.** *Land Sponges.* An explorer has returned from a remote area of the world proclaiming the discovery of the world's first known land sponge. Ask students to react to this claim. (Such a claim would certainly be false or inaccurate. Sponges must be totally immersed in water in order to survive. Without water flowing through and around them they cannot get food and oxygen and cannot rid themselves of waste products.)

**H4.** *Different Forms for Different Folks.* Some sponges exhibit different body forms depending on the surface they occupy. One freshwater type grows as fingerlike projections from soft bottom sediments but as an encrusting mat on sticks and rocks above the sediments. Ask students to speculate about why this sponge exhibits different forms on different surfaces. (The taller cylindrical form of sponge living in the bottom sediments is necessary to keep the sponge above the muddy sediments, which could clog the pores of the sponge and prevent water circulation.)

**H5.** *Walk a Mile in My Shoes.* Have students try to put themselves in the sponge's place by having them react orally or in written form to the following questions:

   a. Would you rather be a marine sponge or a freshwater sponge? Why? (Accept any reasonable answer but look for the idea that marine sponges may live decades or even hundreds of years while most freshwater sponges die in the cold of winter.)

   b. Would you rather be a sponge with long spicules or one with short spicules? (Long spicules have several benefits: They offer more protection from predators, they offer greater support to the entire body, and they are better than short spicules in keeping the pores from clogging.)

**H6.** *Muddy Water = No Sponges.* Have students imagine being on a field trip with the famous sponge expert, Dr. I. M. Porous. On the trip they come to a slow-moving stream that is very turbid with silt eroded from nearby farmland. Dr. Porous predicts they will find no sponges in the stream, and in fact they do not. Have students explain why sponges cannot survive in turbid, muddy water. (The mud and silt either bury the sponges or clog their pores, thus preventing water circulation.)

**S1.** *Sponge Structure.* Have students diagram and label a generalized sponge and its parts: osculum (excurrent vent), mesenchyme, mesenchyme cells, spicules, spongin fibers, epithelial cells, collar cells with flagella, and incurrent pores. (Note: Students will not be able to find all of these structures when viewing a piece or even an entire freshwater sponge through the microscope.)

**S2.** *Sponge Size Comparisons.* Have students compare and contrast the sizes of freshwater sponges to the sizes of marine sponges. (The height and diameter of freshwater sponges are measured in millimeters or a few centimeters. Marine sponges can be gigantic, with some over 2 meters [7 feet] in height and others over 2 meters in diameter.)

**S3.** *Sponge—One or Many?* Have students respond orally or in writing to the question, Is a sponge an individual or a colony, and why? (Biologists disagree on this question, so there is no definitive answer. Tell your students that you are looking for quality rather than correctness in the defense of their position regarding this question.)

**S4.** *Green Sponges?* The same species of freshwater sponge can be different sizes, shapes, and colors under different conditions. Many freshwater sponges growing on the upper surfaces of objects are green, but the same sponges growing on the undersides of objects are brown or tan. Have students speculate about the reason for this color difference. (The green color in some sponges is due to a green photosynthetic protist [algae] living in

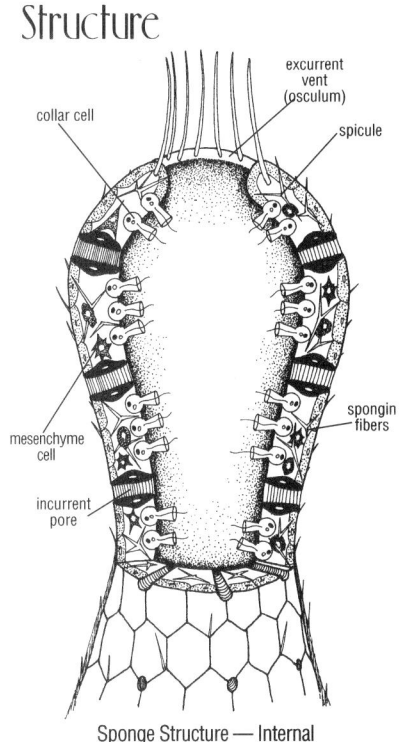

Structure

Sponge Structure — Internal

the sponge. For this algae to survive, light is required for photosynthesis. Hence only the sponges on the upper surfaces where light strikes them can support these protists.)

**S5.** *Sponge Regeneration.* Sponges have the greatest powers of reaggregation and regeneration of any animal. Reaggregation refers to the coming together of cells after they have been dissociated. Regeneration refers to the process by which missing parts grow back or old parts are replaced. In sponges, reaggregation precedes regeneration. As background, explain that the natural sponge industry collapsed in the late 1930s and early 1940s due to overcollection and the onslaught of a fungus that killed the sponges. **Challenge:** How can we use our knowledge of sponge regeneration to restock with commercial sponges areas that have been depleted by overcollection and fungal attack? Have students devise a way to meet this challenge. (One method that has been tried is to cut sponges into pieces and then allow the pieces to attach to rocks or bits of tile. The attached pieces are lowered to the bottom of the ocean, usually off the coast of Florida, and are harvested several years later.)

**S6.** *Sponges Come Together.* Reaggregation of sponge cells can sometimes be observed by using the following procedure:
a. Macerate a freshwater sponge into small pieces.
b. Place the sponge pieces in a fine porous cloth like silk or bolting cloth and squeeze the sponge pieces through the cloth into a small amount of clean pond water in a shallow dish.
c. Use a dropper or pipette to transfer clumps of filtered cells to a well slide. Observe these cells through a compound microscope under 100X to 400X magnification.
d. The clumps of cells should attach to the slide after several hours. During this time maintain the water level on the slide as necessary, being careful not to disturb the cells when adding water.
e. Once the clumps of cells have attached to the slide, submerge the entire slide in a shallow glass dish of clean pond water. Change the water in the dish carefully several times a day. Keep the dish in dim light at room temperature.
f. By carefully pulling up the slide and examining it through the microscope, students will see (if the cells cooperate) clumps of cells gradually coming together (reaggregation). Small individual sponges may form in several weeks.

**Feeding**

**F1.** *Sponge Food.* Have students respond to the question, What do sponges eat? (Answer: Sponge cells ingest minute organic particles, bacteria, algae, and protozoans.)

**F2.** *How Do Sponges Get Food?* Have students respond to the question, How do sponges eat? (Answer: Sponges are filter feeders. As water flows around a sponge due to natural currents and through the sponge due to currents induced by the beating of the flagella of the collar cells, it carries food particles with it. Individual sponge cells engulf food particles that bump into them. No matter how large the sponge, usable food must be small enough to be engulfed by a single cell.)

**F3.** *Fabulous Filter.* To successfully filter food, sponges must move large quantities of water through their bodies. A single sponge 10 centimeters (4 inches) high and 1 centimeter (0.4 inches) in diameter can pump around 23 liters (6 gallons) of water through its body every 24 hours. Have students calculate how long it would take a single sponge of that size to filter all the water in a standard 10-gallon aquarium.

---

a. Convert gallons to liters: 1 gallon = 3.8 liters, so
    10 gallons = 38 liters.
b. Set up the equation:
    $$\frac{24 \text{ hours}}{23 \text{ liters}} = \frac{x \text{ hours}}{38 \text{ liters}}$$
c. Cross-multiply: $23x = 24 \times 38 = 912$
d. To solve for $x$, divide both sides of the equation by 23:
    $$\frac{23x}{23} \text{ and } \frac{912}{23}$$
    Therefore, $x = 39.6$ hours

---

**F4.** *Is It Food Yet?* Do different types of sponges feed at different times? Have students analyze the following graphs and answer the questions that follow:

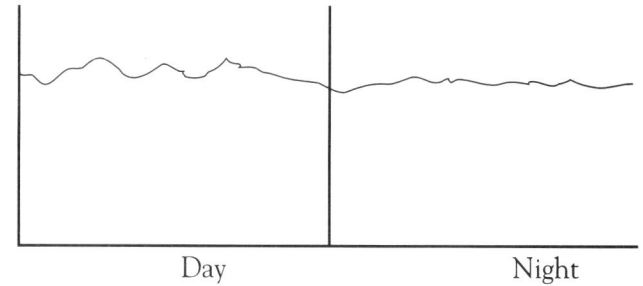

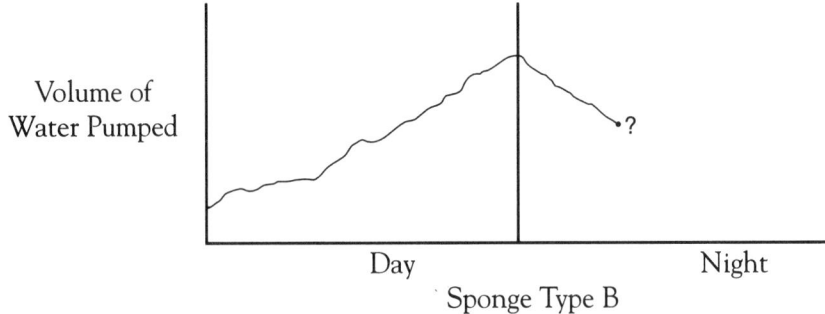

Sponge Type B

a. Which type of sponge shows a constant filtering rate not affected by day or night? (Type A.)

b. Which type of sponge shows a filtering rate greatest in late afternoon? (Type B.)

c. Why does the question mark appear in the graph of Sponge Type B? (No exact measurements are possible at night because shining a light on the sponge to take measurements causes the sponge to begin to start filtering again.)

**F5.** *Attack of the Hungry Encrusters.* The classic method used to observe the filtering action in sponges is to place finely powdered stain (dye) particles around a sponge. The colored particles will slowly pass into the sponge and a colored liquid will begin to stream out the excurrent vent(s). This method may work well with large marine sponges. If you live near the ocean, take your students on a field trip to the ocean, find a sponge, and try it out. Try it on freshwater sponges by placing the stain particles directly on the sponge. I have never had much success with this procedure on freshwater sponges, so I recommend another method, one I call "The Attack of the Hungry Encrusters," to show feeding action in freshwater sponges.

a. Have students examine, diagram, and describe dry flakes of fish food on a slide through a compound microscope at 100X magnification.

b. Submerge a microscope slide into a dish containing sponge culture. This works best if there is a mass of dissociated sponge material in the culture dish (usually freshwater sponges dissociate in a short time).

c. Float several large flakes of fish food on the water in the sponge culture dish. Gently tap the flakes until they sink. Use forceps to position the flakes on the submerged slide.

d. In a short time (8-10 hours) look for signs that the sponge cells are beginning to encrust the flake of fish food.

e. Have students periodically pull the slide carefully out of the sponge culture dish and examine it through the microscope to note changes in the fish food flake and the sponge cells. You should see the flake of food gradually disappear and the amount of sponge cells increase dramatically in a short time. In fact, after several days you may even see spicules that have formed in the cell mass encrusting the fish food. Do the sponge cells actually eat the disintegrating particles of fish food, or do they eat the bacteria and protozoans that are breaking down the fish food? I suspect both, but my students and I have not taken the time to thoroughly investigate this interesting behavior.

## Reproduction and Development

**R1.** *Sponge Reproduction.* Have students explain how sponges reproduce. (Answer: Sponges can reproduce asexually by regeneration, external and internal budding or gemmules. Sexual reproduction occurs when sperm and eggs develop inside the sponge. Most sponges are hermaphrodites and form both sperm and eggs inside themselves. Some sponges are separate

male or female individuals. Sperm are shed into the water and carried by currents into the body of another sponge where they fertilize the eggs located there.)

The fertilized egg develops into a swimming larva that eventually makes its way out of the parent sponge. The larva develops into the adult form in a series of steps, as the illustration shows. (You might scramble these drawings and have students put them in order.

**R2.** *Smoking Sponges.* Have students imagine that they are snorkeling in shallow tropical waters. Below them they see a large sponge with what seems to be smoke coming out of the excurrent vent. Have students speculate about what causes "smoking sponges." (Answer: Some sponges release sperm in such great quantity that it clouds the water and looks like smoke.)

**R3.** *Gemmules—Why and Why Not.* All freshwater sponges but only a few marine sponges form gemmules. Have students explain why. (Gemmules serve freshwater sponges as survival seeds in adverse conditions of drying or freezing. Marine sponges are not usually subjected to such drastic environmental changes and therefore have no need to form gemmules.)

**R4.** *Observe Gemmules.* Gemmules may be obtained in late fall from field-collected freshwater sponges or purchased from several of the suppliers listed in Appendix B.

The development of sponges from gemmules can be studied using the following method:

a. Carefully tease gemmules from the parent sponge using a fine needle or probe of drawn glass.

b. Transfer the gemmules to a well slide full of clean pond water. Have students examine the gemmules through a compound microscope, diagram them, and describe what they look like.

c. Cover the well slide with a cover slip and submerge the slide in a shallow dish of clean pond water or a dish of sponge culture. Once the slide is submerged, carefully remove the cover slip so that the gemmules are not disturbed and remain in the well. Cover the entire dish with a piece of glass or plastic and place it in dim light at room temperature.

d. Within several days the gemmules will attach to the slide. Within a week students will be able to observe the hatching of a gemmule and the beginning development of a new sponge. Have students make diagrams and write down descriptions of the development process as it proceeds.

**In1.** *Writing:* Give students small pieces of dried natural bath sponge and synthetic foam sponge. Have the students examine and test both sponges carefully, using whatever methods they choose. Ask students to write a report (individually or in groups) in which they explain which sample was the natural sponge and which was the synthetic sponge. Their report should include what observations or tests were conducted and what evidence they gathered to support their conclusions.

**In2.** *Fine Arts:*

a. Have students paint a picture of a sponge using a sponge (preferably a natural sponge).

b. Have students write a song or compose a poem entitled, "I'm Just a Lowly Sponge."

**In3.** *Social Studies:*

a. *History.* The controversy over whether sponges are plants or animals lasted until the first half of the nineteenth century. Ask students to explain in written form why it took so long to discover that sponges are animals. (With the unaided eye sponges appear stiff, nonmoving, unresponsive,

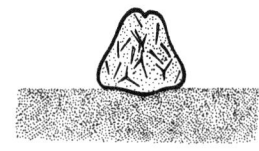

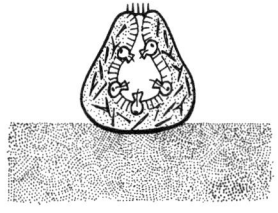

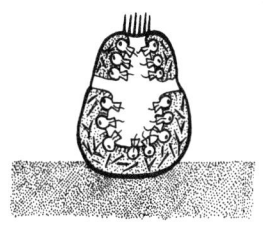

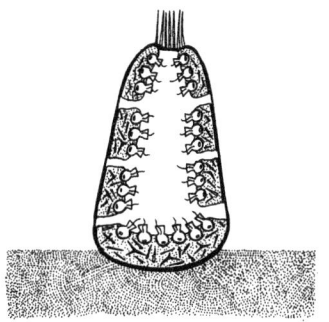

Sponge Larva Development

# Integration with Other Subject Areas

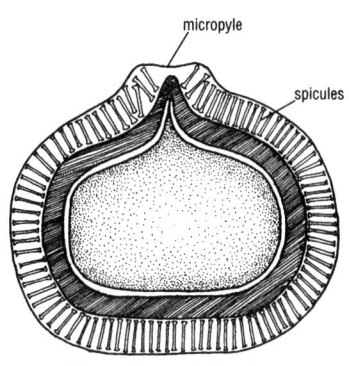

Sponge Gemmule Structure

and very plantlike. Only with better microscopes and techniques of microscopy did the true animal nature of the sponge become apparent.)

b. Geography. If possible, find references that show where commercial sponges were harvested in the past or are harvested today. Have students color in these areas on a blank world map. If your references are detailed enough, have students include tables showing how commercial sponge farming and harvesting have declined.

**In4.** *Societal/Environmental Issues:*

a. Have students respond either orally or in written form to the question, How can studying the reaggregation behavior of dissociated sponge cells be useful to humans? (Studying this type of cell behavior may yield information useful in research on cancer, the immune system, organ transplants, and other human health concerns.)

b. Have students respond either orally or in written form to the question, Why can sponges be thought of as biological apartment houses (or shopping malls)? (A. S. Pearse carefully picked apart a sponge the size of a kitchen sink and counted and classified all the creatures inside it. He counted 17,128 animals. Around 16,000 were one variety of shrimp, but many other kinds of animals were found, including several fish up to 13 centimeters [5 inches] long. This example shows that many animals live around, on, and in sponges.)

## RELEASE OF SPECIMENS

Place individual sponges or pour dissociated clumps carefully back into the approximate area from which they were collected or in shallow water of any lake or slow-moving clear stream.

# 3. CNIDARIANS

| | |
|---|---|
| **Kingdom:** | Animalia |
| **Subkingdom:** | Metazoa (animals with definite symmetry and distinct tissues) |
| **Phylum:** | Cnidaria (also called Coelenterata) |
| **Classes:** | Hydrozoa (hydroids) |
| | Scyphozoa (jellyfish) |
| | Anthozoa (anemones and corals) |

A cnidarian (or coelenterate) is a soft, gelatinous animal with a hollow bag or tube-like body (Greek—*koilos*, hollow + *enderon*, gut). The body has a single opening or mouth surrounded by slender, hollow tentacles covered with stinging cells (Greek—*knide*, nettle). The approximately 9,000 species of cnidarians are found primarily in ocean water; a few freshwater species also exist.

Many cnidarians go through two different stages in their life cycle. Each stage is characterized by a different body form. In the polyp form they somewhat resemble plants and are nonmoving (sessile). In the medusa form they are motile (mobile) with a bell-shaped body. Jellyfish go through both forms but spend most of their lives as medusa. Some cnidarians, such as the hydra and anemone, live only as polyps, and others, such as the Portugese man-o-war, live as mixed colonies of polyps and medusae.

Cnidarians have a definite body with distinct tissues, making them more advanced than the sponges. However, the body is hollow with no organs. The body wall consists of three layers: the epidermis (or ectoderm), the external layer of cells; the mesoglea, a jellylike material between the layers of cells; and the gastrodermis (or endoderm), the inner layer of cells.

Being only two cell layers thick, cnidarians have not been able to develop many complicated body systems. Water is the great provider, bringing food and oxygen and carrying away waste products.

**Digestive System and Feeding.** All cnidarians are carnivorous. They capture small invertebrates and fish by paralyzing them with the many stinging cells (nematocysts) on their tentacles. Each nematocyst is a tiny capsule with a coiled tube inside. Mechanical and chemical stimuli trigger the capsule to fire. Some nematocysts penetrate the prey and pump a paralyzing poison into it. The tentacles then move the paralyzed prey to the mouth area, where it is literally engulfed. Possessing only a rudimentary nervous system, the cnidarian cannot determine the best way to align the food so it works its elastic mouth around and over the food. It can swallow prey animals many times bigger than itself.

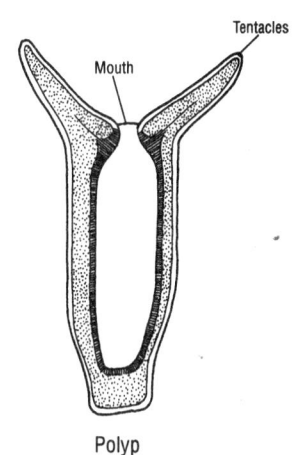

Polyp

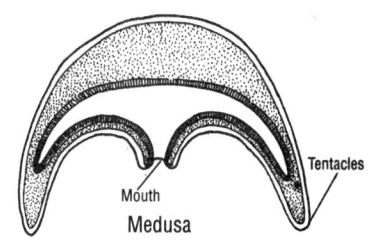

Medusa

Inside, some of the cells lining the hollow body cavity (gastro-vascular cavity) secrete enzymes that begin the digestion of the food. Other cells take in partially digested food and complete digestion. The nutrients are transported throughout the body by diffusion. Any materials that cannot be digested are passed back out through the mouth several hours later.

Many cnidarians have developed a symbiotic relationship with tiny photosynthetic protists. These protists use the carbon dioxide and other wastes from the cnidarian's cells to produce food and oxygen that the cnidarian can use. Many cnidarians depend on this relationship so much that they are green with protists and can live only in bright sunlight.

**Muscle System.** Cnidarians lack an organized muscle system, but the epidermal (ectoderm) cells can change shape when stimulated. Hence, cnidarian polyps can expand, contract, and move their tentacles by relaxing or contracting these epidermal cells, and the cnidarian medusae can open and close their bell-shaped bodies to propel themselves through the water.

**Nervous System.** Cnidarians lack a brain but possess a network of nerves called a nerve net. This nerve net spreads throughout the body and is most concentrated around the mouth. Both polyps and medusae have sensory cells in the epidermis that can detect chemicals and the touch of objects. In some medusae, sensory cells may be organized into structures called statocysts for maintaining balance and eyespots for detecting light.

**Circulatory System.** Cnidarians have no circulatory system. They depend instead on diffusion to move nutrients and oxygen throughout the body.

**Respiratory System.** Cnidarians possess no respiratory organs. They eliminate waste gases into and absorb oxygen from the water around them.

**Excretory (Urinary) System.** Cnidarians also lack excretory organs. They eliminate liquid wastes by diffusion directly through the body wall into the water around them.

**Reproduction and Development.** Most cnidarians can reproduce asexually or sexually. Polyps can produce new polyps by asexual budding. Many polyps also bud off of tiny medusae. When the medusae mature, they release sperm and eggs into the water. Fertilized eggs grow into ciliated larvae that swim around for a while before settling down, attaching, and changing into the polyp form so the cycle can begin anew.

**Class Hydrozoa (Hydroids).** This group has about 3,700 species, including the hydra, obelia, and Physalia (Portugese man-o-war). Most live in the ocean, but there are some freshwater types.

The unusual freshwater hydra has no medusal stage and exists as a solitary polyp. Each polyp is attached by a cuplike basal disk.

Obelia is a marine colonial hydroid with individual polyps living on an interconnected branching framework.

The Portugese man-o-war is actually a floating colony, with some polyps forming a large float bag and others digesting the food captured by the tentacles. The float may be 30 centimeters (12 inches) long with tentacles up to 20 meters (66 feet) in length. The nematocysts of the Portugese man-o-war can sting humans and have been known to be fatal. Swimmers and people walking along the beach where Physalia often wash up should take precautions to avoid them.

**Class Scyphozoa (Jellyfish).** This group has about 200 species. The true jellyfish exist primarily in the medusa stage. They are found mainly in the ocean, but some freshwater species do exist.

Jellyfish range in size from as little as 2 centimeters (0.8 inches) across to giants nearly 4 meters (13 feet) in diameter! The tentacles of the larger jellyfish may reach 40 meters (132 feet) in length.

Hydra

## Specific Class Characteristics

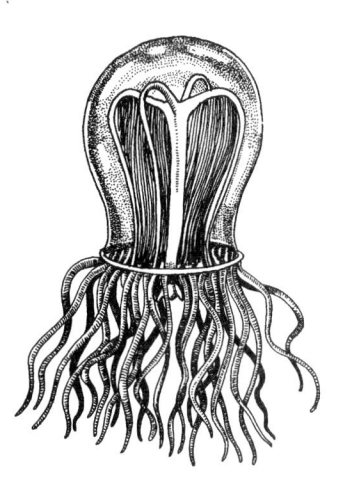

Jellyfish

Humans should also avoid contact with jellyfish, as such encounters can result in painful and sometimes fatal stings.

**Class Anthozoa (Anemones).** The 6,200 or so species of this group include the anemones and corals. All members of this group are found in the ocean, primarily in shallow coastal areas.

Like the hydra, they exhibit only the polyp stage in their life cycle. The anemones possess a baglike body topped with a whorl of large, stubby, hollow tentacles. Many anemones are brightly colored and were originally classified as plants (Greek—*anthus*, flower).

Anemones range in size from a few millimeters (a few tenths of an inch) in diameter to more than 1 meter (4 feet) across. Most of them average about 10 centimeters (4 inches) in diameter. Anemones attach by means of a large basal disk. They seem stationary, but they use mucal secretions to creep along on their basal disk at a pace of about 1 centimeter per hour.

Anemones range from the tidal zone to great depths in the ocean. Some shallow-water species depend heavily for food on photosynthetic protists that live inside them.

Corals grow primarily as colonies of polyps in shallow tropical ocean waters around the world. Some coral polyps secrete a rocky limestone container in which they live; these are called hard or stony corals. As a colony of stony corals grows, new polyps and more limestone is added. Countless millennia of such growth have produced huge rocky structures known as coral reefs.

Other types of coral polyps are the soft corals, which grow as fleshy-lobed or treelike colonies, and the horny corals, which have a hornlike framework.

The toxins of cnidarians make them beneficial to medical research. These powerful chemicals are being used to study nerve cell function and to track calcium in chemical reactions. They may also prove useful in treating cancer and arthritis.

Cnidarians also play a role in aquatic food chains, where they are aggressive predators and in turn are prey to sea stars, sea slugs, and some types of fish, turtles, and birds that are seemingly immune to their venom.

Jellyfish have flown into space aboard the shuttle to help humans study the effects of weightlessness on living things.

Corals and the reefs they build have been the most useful form of cnidarians to humans. We have utilized this resource in many ways—for food animals living around the reef, as building materials, filtering materials, jewelry, decoration, and for aquarium pets. The physical structure of the coral reef also provides a buttress against damaging wave action along our coastal developments. The

Anemone

## The Importance of Cnidarians

Coral

real value of coral reefs, however, lies in their importance to ocean ecology. On and in the rocky outcrops of the reefs lives a dazzling array of strange and wondrous creatures. Some reefs contain as much solid structure and as many living creatures as the largest human cities. These watery wonderlands of life are to be prized and protected not only for the practical and mundane products they yield, but for the preciousness of their beauty, diversity, and uniqueness.

The minireef aquarium, a microcosm of a coral reef, is the fastest-growing segment of the aquarium trade, with tanks ranging from tens to hundreds of gallons and costing from thousands to tens of thousands of dollars. The result has been the overcollection of selected species of fish and invertebrates (including certain anemones). Equally disastrous is the decline of reefs in many parts of the world due to the collecting of tons of live rock (dead coral encrusted with bacteria and an array of algae) and stony corals each year. Some experts predict that some of the most beautiful areas of Florida's reefs have less than ten years to live. Certainly collection is not fully to blame for the worldwide decline of reefs. Reefs are under assault from many human activities, such as deforestation, agricultural chemicals, industrial chemicals, sewage, fishing, and shipping, as well as, perhaps, climatic and oceanic changes. However, most experts agree that taking coral, live rock, fish, and invertebrates from reefs adds stress to a priceless ecosystem already battling for its existence.

Therefore, from an ecological standpoint, I urge you not to collect or purchase marine cnidarians. To do so further degrades declining oceanic ecosystems. It almost certainly dooms the individual animal collected, as marine cnidarians are very difficult to properly maintain in a classroom setting. All factors considered, it just makes sense to leave anemones, corals, and jellyfish where they are.

## COLLECTION OF SPECIMENS
### Jellyfish, Anemones, and Corals

### Hydra

The freshwater cnidarian known as hydra makes a good subject for investigating cnidarians in general. Hydra are abundant, easily collected (or relatively inexpensive to purchase), and fairly simple to maintain for short periods of time.

Collection involves gathering a large quantity of water plants from the edges of clean, permanent ponds, lakes, marshes, or slow-flowing streams. Hydra also may be found on sticks and stones in shallow water. Place plants, sticks, and stones in a container with water from the collecting site. On returning from the collection site, place the water plants, sticks, and stones and some of the water in white enameled pans or glass bowls set on white paper. Leave the pans or bowls undisturbed for several hours in a sunny location. The hydra usually detach and may be found on the bottom against the white background or even floating on the surface.

Pure cultures are available from the suppliers listed in Appendix B.

## MAINTENANCE OF SPECIMENS

Successfully culturing hydra for a great length of time requires diligent care and great patience. Hydra can be finicky about their surroundings and even with excellent care pass into a stage of decline called depression from time to time. Replacing the water with fresh spring or pond water may help lessen the severity of the depression.

Another problem with long-term maintenance can be providing food for the hydra. They are strictly carnivorous and have a hearty appetite for only live food.

For short-term study, place the hydra in a shallow glass container with water from the collection site. Keep the container at room temperature in diffused light. Containers should be lightly covered to reduce evaporation and to keep out dust and foreign matter. Plastic food wrap with small slits cut in it works well for this purpose. Hydra may be kept under such conditions without further care or feeding for several weeks.

Hydra may be maintained for several months without much attention by placing them in shallow, loosely covered glass bowls of pond water and putting the containers in a refrigerator at a temperature of around 10°C (50°F).

If you purchase hydra from commercial suppliers, detailed instructions for their care and maintenance will accompany the culture.

Many of the marine cnidarians are capable of stinging humans and causing painful burns or even death. The sea wasp jellyfish has a venom powerful enough to cause death in several minutes to a half-hour and has been blamed for fifty deaths among swimmers off Australia's north coast (another good reason for not collecting marine cnidarians!).

If you are collecting hydra from ponds and marshes, follow good safety procedures around water regardless of apparent depth of the water and be alert for possible contact with poisonous plants and biting or stinging animals.

Hydra pose no health or safety problem for students. While they possess stinging tentacles like marine cnidarians, hydra are far too small to pose any threat to students. However, it is a good precaution to have students thoroughly wash their hands before and after handling hydra containers and the pond water they contain.

Make sure the hydra do not dry out as they are being investigated. If they dry, they die. Maintain adequate water around them at all times on the microscope slide. Another concern is the quality of water used to maintain stock cultures and to bathe individual hydra during investigation. City tap water can contain traces of chemicals fatal to hydra. Use only clean pond or spring water on hydras. Finally, handle hydras carefully, as they have very soft bodies and damage easily.

To observe live hydras, use a dropper or pipette to transfer them to a depression slide or a well slide. These slides can be purchased from most scientific supply companies, or you can make your own well slides using ordinary glass slides. Make a ring of glue with a hot glue gun or a ring of clear aquarium sealer. Allow glue or sealer to dry and cure before using the slides.

A word of caution: Once you draw hydras up into a dropper or pipette, they can be difficult to get out. They have the annoying habit of attaching inside the dropper or pipette. Your students may find it as humorous as mine do to see you shooting water out of droppers onto the table, on their lab sheets, or even on them trying to dislodge hydras out of a dropper.

Hydras are so small that it is difficult to examine them with the unaided eye. Hand lenses offer only a marginally better view. Best results are obtained by viewing hydras through a compound microscope on low power (around 40X).

**H1.** *Hydra Habitat.* Have students respond to the question, What is the natural environment of the hydra? (Answer: Hydras are found in shallow fresh water attached to plants, sticks, and rocks.)

**H2.** *Cnidarian Habitat Comparisons.* Have students respond to the question, Where might other types of cnidarians might be found? (Answer: Mainly in ocean water but a few species are found in fresh water.) I have recommended not collecting your own marine cnidarians. However, to allow students to see live marine cnidarians, consider a field trip to a large commercial aquarium, a pet store, or a private residence where marine aquaria are kept. Such a trip could easily serve as the opener for a discussion on the conservation of coral reefs and the creatures found there. But would such a trip imply that collecting marine cnidarians is to be condoned? This is a question that you and your students will have to deal with before embarking on such an outing. Another possibility is the use of audiovisual materials to show marine cnidarians in their natural setting.

**H3.** *Green Hydra?* Depending on the species, hydras are white, brown, or green. Have students speculate about what causes the green color in green hydras. (Green hydras are colored by the presence of a symbiotic green protist in their inner cells.)

**H4.** *Green Hydra Light Preferences.* Ask students to predict what light intensity green hydras would probably prefer and have them explain why. (Green hydras seek brighter light intensities than other types. The brighter intensity seems to ensure adequate light for their protist "guest" to photosynthesize food for the protist and the hydra.)

**H5.** *Deadly Companions.* Despite their deadly stinging tentacles, anemones enjoy close relations with some other animals. Have students speculate about how and why certain creatures like the clownfish and some hermit crabs live around and even in anemones. (The clownfish secretes a mucous coating that does not provoke the stinging response, so it can actually spend time in the tentacles of the anemone. The anemone provides a haven from predators and a source of food particles. In turn, the clownfish drives away intruders and picks away dead tissue. Small anemones are often found attached to the borrowed mollusk shell that hermit crabs call home. The anemone offers protection to the crab and the crab reciprocates with stray bits of food.)

**H6.** *Walk a Mile in My Shoes.* Ask students to react orally or in written form to the question, Would you rather be a hydra, jellyfish, anemone, or coral, and why?

**H7.** *Hydra Graphs.* Have students analyze the following graph and attempt to answer questions.

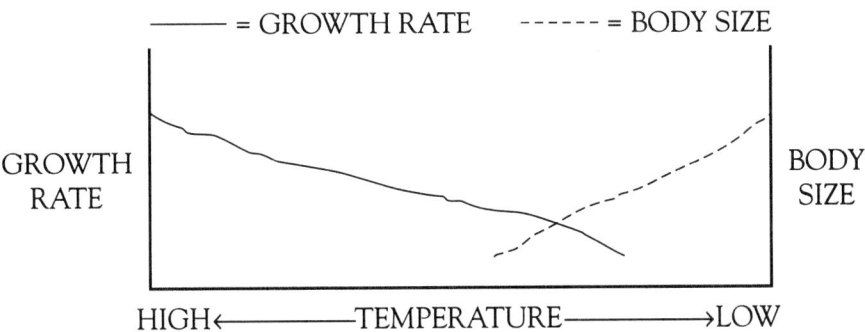

a. What is the relationship between reduction of temperature and growth rate? (When temperature goes down, growth rate decreases—a direct relationship.)

b. What is the relationship between reduction of temperature and body size? (When temperature goes down, body size increases—an indirect relationship.)

## Structure

**S1.** *Hydra Structure.* Have students diagram and label the hydra and its parts. Externally, whole specimen: mouth, tentacles, nematocysts (stinging cells), daughter bud, and basal disk. Internally, long section: epidermis (ectoderm), mesoglea, gastrodermis (endoderm), and gastro-vascular cavity.

**S2.** *Observe A Hydra.* Have students observe a live hydra carefully and answer the following questions:

a. Does the hydra have a head? (Answer: Technically, no.)

b. What type of symmetry (proportions) does the hydra illustrate? (Answer: Hydra show radial symmetry with each half looking as if it radiates outward from the center. More complex animals show bilateral symmetry, in which each half of the body looks nearly like a mirror of the other.)

c. What are the main divisions of the hydra's body? (The mouth and tentacles at one end, the body tube or stalk in the middle, and the basal disk on the other end.)

d. Hydras are not typical of the class Hydrozoa. Why not? (Hydras exist as separate individuals. Most hydroids live as colonies.)
e. Locate and describe the following body structures:
   1. tentacles
   2. mouth
   3. basal disk
   4. daughter buds (if any are present)
f. What is the structure of the nematocysts (stinging cells)? (A nematocyst is a minute rounded capsule containing a coiled tube. The nematocyst is contained within a parent cell called the cnidoblast—hence the phylum name *cnidaria* for these creatures. The nematocysts are most numerous on the tentacles and are grouped to form nematocyst "batteries.")

   Hydra have four kinds of nematocysts:
   1. Penetrants penetrate the covering of small animals and inject a paralyzing toxin.
   2. Volvents coil tightly around bristles or hair on the prey.
   3. Adherents, straight unarmed threads covered with sticky secretions, help anchor the tentacles for locomotion.
   4. Defendants kill or repel animals not acceptable as food.
g. What triggers the release of the nematocysts?

   Have students carefully touch the tentacles of a live hydra with a fine piece of drawn glass while viewing the hydra through a microscope. Students should see few if any nematocysts discharge because direct mechanical stimulation is not ordinarily an effective trigger. Placing certain chemicals such as vinegar or beef broth on a small piece of filter paper near the hydra will usually trigger nematocyst release. Control of nematocyst discharge is not fully understood, but both mechanical stimulation and chemical stimuli seem to be involved. This activity allows students to investigate thigmotaxis, response to touch, and chemotaxis, response to chemicals.
h. Count the number of tentacles on your hydra. How many are there? How does your hydra compare to other specimens? (Hydras have anywhere from six to ten tentacles.)

**S3.** *Hydra Length.* Have students devise a way to measure the length of a hydra. For its safety, however, the hydra must remain in the water on the slide. (Students could put a plastic ruler under the slide and align it with the body of the hydra, or they could put graph paper under the slide, determine the hydra's length in squares and then measure the squares.)

**S4.** *Cnidarian Size Comparisons.* Have students respond to the question, How does the size of the hydra compare to the size of jellyfish, anemones, and corals? (Hydras range from 5 to 30 centimeters [2 to 12 inches] long. Jellyfish range from about 2 centimeters [0.8 inches] in diameter to as large as 4 meters [13 feet] across; the larger jellyfish can trail tentacles up to 10 meters [33 feet] long. Anemones range from a few millimeters [a few tenths of an inch] in diameter to those over a meter [4 feet] across. Most corals are about the size of a pinhead.)

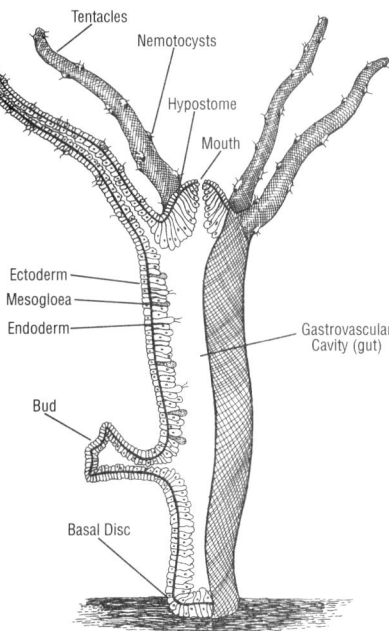

Hydra Structure — Internal

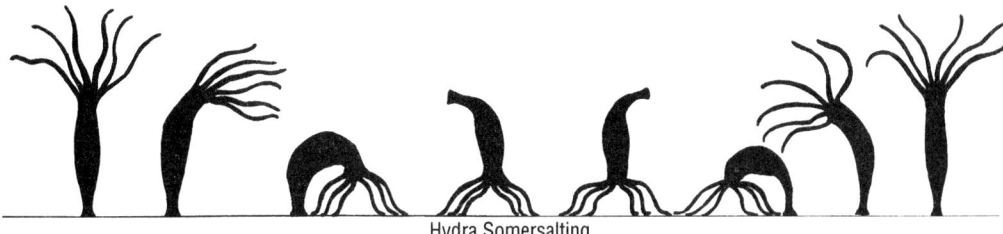

Hydra Somersalting

**S5.** *Hydra Movement.* Have students observe and describe how a hydra moves. The simplest mode of movement is a slow creeping on the basal disk. More rapid movement consists of a stepping motion with rests between steps, and a very rapid form of stepping called somersaulting sometimes occurs. Some hydras pull themselves up to an object with their tentacles, and sometimes they release and float free on an air bubble attached to the basal disk.

**S6.** *Hydra Basal Disk.* Have students observe the basal disk of the hydra. Gland cells in the disk secrete a sticky mucous by which the hydra attaches to objects in the water. As previously mentioned, hydras often attach to the insides of droppers and pipettes and are difficult to remove. Have students devise a way to conveniently and safely (from the hydra's standpoint) detach hydras from a culture dish and transfer them to a slide. (I have no easy answers. If you or your students come up with a good, reliable way of doing this, please let me know. Just remember that hydras are soft and easily damaged.)

**S7. Challenge:** *Can Hydras Regenerate?* Like sponges, hydras have amazing powers of regeneration. That is, they have the ability to grow back or repair missing or damaged portions of their bodies. To observe this phenomenon, have students place a microscope slide on an ice cube. Place a large drop of clean pond water on the slide and add a hydra. The cool temperature helps anesthetize the hydra. However, do not put the hydra directly on the ice or leave the slide on the ice too long, as either action could be fatal to the hydra.

Make scalpels by breaking a microscope cover slip into pieces or by heating and drawing out thin pieces of glass. Have students use their scapels to cut the hydra horizontally into three pieces: mouth and tentacles, body tube, and base. It would be ideal if students can make their cuts while viewing the hydra through a dissecting microscope. However, using a strong magnifier or hand lens and shining a bright light on the slide will suffice.

Put the cut pieces of the hydra in shallow dishes about half full of clean pond water. Loosely cover the dishes and keep them in dim light at room temperature. Use microscopes or magnifiers to make regular observations. Have students diagram the results.

Many good activities can be developed around hydra regeneration. For example, have students devise ways of testing the following problems:
a. Can hydras be induced to regenerate abnormally? (Vertical cuts through the mouth may result in two sets of tentacles.)
b. Which parts of a hydra regenerate most quickly?
c. What role does water temperature play in hydra regeneration?
d. What role does light intensity or color play in hydra regeneration?
In each case, have students predict what they think will happen before they begin. Have students construct appropriate data tables, charts, and graphs and ask them to draw conclusions from their data.

**S8. Challenge:** *Hydra Reassociation.* Hydras can reassociate as well as regenerate. That is, pieces of hydras placed in contact with each other fuse together and begin to grow. Through reassociation, one hydra may be grafted onto another hydra.

The ability of hydras to reassociate presents all kinds of interesting educational possibilities. For example:
a. Can students graft the mouth and tentacles of one hydra onto the body of another from which the mouth and tentacles have been removed?

b. Can students graft the mouth and tentacles from two hydras onto the tube of a third hydra from which the mouth, tentacles, and base have been removed—resulting in a hydra with a mouth and tentacles on each end?

You can have your students attempt any number of combinations. Remind them that the pieces must be in contact or very close proximity for reassociation to occur. Have students predict what they think will happen before they begin. Ask them to diagram their results.

**S9.** *Cnidarian Models.* Have students construct a model of a hydra, jellyfish, anemone, or coral. Students might use colored modeling clay or colored bread dough. The bread dough made from the following recipe is suitable for sculpting:

| | |
|---|---|
| 1 cup flour | 1 tablespoon vegetable oil |
| 1/2 cup salt | 1 cup water |
| 2 teaspoons cream of tartar | food coloring |

Stir all ingredients except the food coloring over medium heat until it becomes bubbly and rubbery. When the mixture cools, add food coloring and knead thoroughly. Use different colors of dough to make different body structures on the model. Store the dough in an airtight container in the refrigerator.

In this and each succeeding chapter of this book you and your students will be asked to investigate the behavior and responses of various animals. As you do so, consider how the actions of each animal relate to the following classifications of behavior:

- *Reflex*—simple behavior actions that are automatic responses to a stimulus
- *Instinctive behavior*—a series of complex, genetically determined behaviors
- *Learned behavior*—an instinctive behavior that an animal has modified based on past experiences

**B/R1.** *Jiggle Response.* Have students place a hydra in a drop of clean pond water on a depression or well slide. Instruct them to jiggle the slide and observe and describe how the hydra reacts.

This activity allows students to investigate thigmotaxis, or response to touch, contact, or movement. Hydras usually react negatively to movement by drawing in their tentacles and possibly balling up. Students might also carefully touch various parts of the hydra with a glass probe made by heating and drawing out glass into a fine thread. Use caution as hydras are delicate and can be damaged easily. Occasionally a hydra attaches to the probe and may be pulled out of the drop of water when the probe is removed; be sure to return it to water immediately.

**B/R2.** Challenge: *Are Hydras Sensitive to Light?* Have students devise a way to test this problem. This activity allows students to investigate phototaxis, or response to light. (One design would be to punch a small hole with a compass point in a piece of cardboard. Attach the cardboard to a flashlight, shine the spotlight on various parts of the hydra's body, and observe how it reacts.

Have students predict what they think will happen before they begin. Instruct them to keep data in appropriate tables, charts, or graphs and draw conclusions from their data.

By placing colored cellophane over the pinhole spotlight, interested, older, or more advanced students could also investigate whether hydras are sensitive to various colors.)

# Behavior/Response

**B/R3.** Challenge: *What Light Intensity Do Hydras Prefer?* Have students devise a way to test this problem. (One design would be to create a light gradient along a shallow glass container by placing a bright light at one end and covering the container with increasingly opaque materials until total darkness is achieved at the other end. Depending on the species, hydras tend to avoid either bright light or total darkness.

Have students predict what they think will happen before they begin; keep data in appropriate tables, charts, or graphs; and draw conclusions from their data.)

**B/R4.** *Anemone Disputes.* Cnidarians are not highly organized and complex animals, but they are more than docile, nonreactive bags of cells. They are aggressive predators, and some, like anemones, are fiercely territorial. Many species of anemones will attack other anemones that come too close. Interestingly, fights develop only between individuals of different genetic makeup.

Scramble the following steps in anemone territorial disputes and have students put them in the proper sequence:

Step 1. Anemones approach and touch tentacles.

Step 2. One or both anemones retreat.

Step 3. The anemones inflate their acrorhagi (small, inflatable bumps at the base of the tentacles armed with nematocysts) on the side facing their enemy.

Step 4. The anemones again approach, each trying to arch its body up over the other.

Step 5. The quicker anemone strikes and withdraws, leaving white fragments from the acrorhagi behind in the enemy's body. These fragments eventually will cause the body tissue around them to die and degenerate, possibly resulting in the death of the victim.

Step 6. The victor holds its ground. Its acrorhagi shrink to normal size, and it resumes feeding.

## Feeding

**F1.** *Hydra Food.* Have students respond to the question, What do hydras eat? (Answer: Hydras feed primarily on small aquatic crustaceans, but they will eat any small water plankter and even tiny fish, worms, and insects.)

**F2.** *Cnidarian Feeding Comparisons.* Have students compare and contrast what hydras eat with what jellyfish, anemones, and corals eat. (Answer: All cnidarians are carnivores that use nematocysts [stinging cells] to subdue and kill live prey. Corals eat mainly microscopic ocean plankton. Larger anemones eat small fish, crabs, sea stars, and some mollusks such as mussels. Large jellyfish eat primarily small fish or other open-water creatures.)

**F3.** *Hungry Hydra.* Ask students to visualize themselves as hungry hydras. Have them react to the following questions:

a. Would you remain attached and creep around slowly on your basal disk, or would you detach on a gas bubble and float? Why?

b. From a food-gathering standpoint, would you rather be a brown or a green hydra, and why? (Personally, I would rather be a green hydra because their green color results from the presence of a multicellular green protist that lives within their tissues and provides some nourishment. Brown hydra can survive up to 40 days without food, but green hydra can live up to 4 months without a meal.)

**F4.** *Observe Hydras Feeding.* Have students observe and describe the actual feeding behavior of hydras.

Most references suggest live Daphnia (water fleas) as a prey animal for hydras. I have had more consistent success using live Artemia (brine shrimp). Brine shrimp eggs can be purchased at pet shops, aquarium stores, or any of the suppliers listed in Appendix B. To hatch the eggs, mix eight level tablespoons of noniodized salt in a gallon of distilled water or 40 grams of noniodized salt in a liter of distilled water. Pour some of this mixture into a shallow glass dish and add the eggs. If possible, aerate with an aquarium pump to increase the percentage of hatching eggs. Loosely cover the dish. Hatching should begin in 24 to 36 hours.

Caution: Brine shrimp must not be added directly from the hatchery to a slide containing hydras. The salt water would be fatal to the hydras. Rinse the brine shrimp by pouring some of the water containing brine shrimp from the hatchery through a fine mesh cloth (I use a cloth fish net). Pour fresh water through the cloth, and then invert the cloth down into a container of fresh water. Let it stand for several minutes. Then shine a bright light on a small area near the surface of the container of rinsed brine shrimp. The swimming shrimp will congregate in the lighted area and may be removed easily with a dropper or pipette.

Place a drop of clean pond water on a depression or well slide and add live hydras. Add prey (rinsed brine shrimp) to the drop of water containing the hydras and have students describe the life and death struggle that results. Feeding action is best viewed through low power on a microscope. Using a strong magnifier with a bright light shining on the slide will give a limited but satisfactory view.

Hydras will sometimes swallow prey animals so fast that they swallow their own tentacles. However, the swallowed parts emerge later unharmed. My students and I have witnessed the struggle between a parent hydra and its daughter bud over the same prey animal. The struggle continued for nearly an hour, with the parent hydra finally winning.

**F5.** **Challenge:** *Will Bigger Hydras Feed Faster than Smaller Hydras?* Have students devise a way of testing this problem. (One design is to sort hydras by size on depression or well slides and add suitable prey animals. Remember to keep all variables except the size of the hydras constant—type of slide, amount of water on slide, number of hydras per slide, type and number of prey animals placed on each slide.

Have students keep data in appropriate tables, charts, and graphs and draw conclusions from their data.)

**R1.** *Hydra Reproduction.* Have students explain how hydra reproduce. (Answer: Hydras can reproduce both sexually and asexually in the polyp form. Hydras reproduce asexually by forming daughter buds during warm weather. A mature hydra with adequate food can produce up to two buds a day, with each bud maturing and beginning to reproduce in a week or less.

Sexual reproduction in hydras occurs in the fall. It may be triggered by lower temperatures, variations in food supply, or increased carbon dioxide concentrations from overcrowding or stagnation—no one is sure. Ovaries containing eggs and testes containing sperm develop in swellings on the body tube. Some hermaphroditic species produce both ovaries and testes on the same animal; others form either ovaries or testes only. In either case, sperm are released into the water, where they swim to and fertilize the egg. The fertilized egg, or zygote, grows and divides into a ball of cells, called an embryo, with a hard covering. The hard cover protects the embryo through the winter until it develops into a new hydra in the spring.)

**R2.** *Cnidarian Reproductive Comparisons.* Have students compare and contrast the reproduction of hydras with the reproduction of jellyfish and anemones. (Reproduction in jellyfish includes both medusa and

# Reproduction and Development

polyp forms. The adult jellyfish medusae release eggs and sperm into the water, where fertilization occurs. The fertilized egg grows into a ciliated swimming larva called a planula. The planula eventually settles to the bottom and begins to develop into a polyp. As the polyp grows it forms more medusae, which bud off and eventually develop into mature jellyfish.

Like hydra, anemones reproduce in the polyp form. Asexual reproduction is accomplished by literally pulling themselves apart. In some species fragments of the basal disk form tiny new anemones. Sexual reproduction occurs when eggs and sperm develop in the body cavity. The sexes may be separate or combined in hermaphroditic individuals. Egg and sperm are released into the water, where fertilization occurs. The fertilized egg eventually grows into a new anemone.)

**R3.** *Immortal Hydra?* Either orally or in written form, have students react to the following statement by Slobodkin and Bossert in the book *Ecology and Classification of North American Freshwater Invertebrates*: "It seems likely that hydra polyps are immortal." Slobodkin and Bossert continue: "All deaths in hydra can be assigned to such things as alteration in water quality or food supply, temperature shocks, starvation, and predation. There is no evidence for senesence (growing old; aging) in hydra."

The Pearses and Bushbaums, in *Living Invertebrates*, say that "individually identified hydras have been reported to cease budding and die after little more than two years. However, clones of hydras, reproducing only asexually, have been maintained for decades without showing any signs of decreased vigor as a total population."

## Integration with Other Subject Areas

**In1.** *Writing:*

a. Have students imagine they are the great forensic scientist, Dr. I. M. Baffled. A dead body has been brought to the crime lab. Witnesses say that the dead man was washed onto the beach barely alive. His last mumbled words before he died were "the wasp." His body shows no signs of injury or damage other than a series of large red welts on his back. Dr. Baffled must write a report to the police commissioner explaining what killed the man. (Answer: The man blundered into and was stung by one of the most venomous types of jellyfish, the sea wasp.)

b. Ask students to imagine that they are jellyfish. Have each student write a letter to a jellyfish friend describing an encounter with a human swimmer.

**In2.** *Fine Arts:*

a. Have students paint or draw a picture of a hydra, jellyfish, anemone, or coral and/or the habitat where these creatures live.

b. Have students write a song or compose a poem entitled "Ode to an Anemone" (or jellyfish or hydra).

c. Have students draw a cartoon showing a territorial dispute between two anemones.

**In3.** *Social Studies:*

a. *History.* Several names, such as hydra and medusa, used to describe cnidarians are also the names of legendary Greek monsters. Have students investigate this connection. (Most likely, someone with an active imagination and knowledge of Greek mythology looked at the tentacles of the tiny freshwater creature beneath the microscope and named it Hydra after the many-headed serpent slain by Hercules in Greek mythology. Each head of the Hydra was on a stalk, and each head grew back two more when it was cut off. Likewise, the trailing tentacles of the jellyfish probably reminded someone of the Gorgon monster,

Medusa, who had snakes for hair and was so hideous her very appearance turned people to stone.

These names are unfortunate because they give the false impression that these animals are evil, sinister monsters. In general, these creatures have more to fear from human activities than the reverse.)

b. *Geography.* If possible, find references that show the location of coral reefs worldwide. Have students color in reefs on a blank world map. Have students relate the locations of the reefs to water temperature. (Most coral reefs are found around 2100 kilometers [1,300 miles] on either side of the equator in warm seas.)

**In4.** *Societal/Environmental Issues:*

a. Have students analyze and react orally or in writing to the following statement: Coral reefs are the tropical rain forests of warm ocean waters.

b. Have students imagine that they have been called to testify before a United Nations committee convened to examine the pros and cons of banning all forms of commercial exploitation of coral reefs worldwide. Have students write a position paper in which they explain what they would say to this committee.

c. Have students react orally or in written form to the following statement: In 1966, Congress passed the Jellyfish Control Act, which appropriated nearly $5 million for studying ways to "control and eliminate jellyfish and other such pests from our coastal waters."

Hydra can be released safely back into unpolluted ponds, lakes, and marshes.

## RELEASE OF SPECIMENS

# 4. FLATWORMS

> **Kingdom:** Animalia
> **Subkingdom:** Metazoa (animals with definite symmetry and distinct tissues)
> **Phylum:** Platyhelminthes
> **Classes:** Tubellaria (planarians)
> Trematoda (flukes)
> Cestoda (tapeworms)

The lowliest of that large group of creatures we call worms are the flatworms. Because the flatworms have bilateral symmetry and definite organs, however, they are considerably more complex than the sponges and cnidarians discussed in preceding chapters.

Bilateral symmetry means that the body structures are arranged symmetrically on both sides of a central plane, with each half being more or less a mirror image of the other half. Bilateral symmetry is considered a mark of complex development in animals, and the animal groups discussed in this book from here on show this characteristic. Bilaterally symmetrical animals have a definite head called the anterior end, a rear called the posterior end, a top called the dorsal side, and a bottom called the ventral side.

In addition, flatworms, like more complex animals (and unlike sponges and cnidarians), are composed of three cell layers—ectoderm (outside), mesoderm (middle), and endoderm (inside)—that develop into true organs within the flatworm's body.

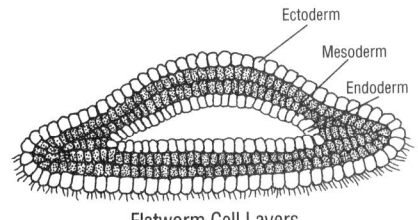
Flatworm Cell Layers

The body of a flatworm is soft, flat, and ribbonlike (Greek—*platy*, flat + *helminthes*, worm). The more than 10,500 species of flatworms are found in damp areas on land, in fresh water and ocean water, and as internal and external parasites on other animals.

**Digestive System and Feeding.** The planarians are free-living carnivores that prey on other small animals such as rotifers, nematodes, tiny crustaceans, and insect larvae. They also scavenge the dead bodies of larger animals if the opportunity presents itself. The mouth of the planarians oddly enough opens near the middle of the body out the ventral (bottom) side. A muscular tube called the pharynx protrudes out of the mouth for eating and is drawn back up into the body after feeding. The pharynx is connected to a highly branched Y-shaped intestine where the food is digested.

The digestive system of the flukes is similar to that of the planarians, but their mouth is on the anterior (head) end. Some flukes are ectoparasites living on the mouth, skin, gills, or other outside parts of fish, amphibians, and reptiles. Most flukes are endoparasites that feed internally on the body tissues and blood of their host animal.

Like the cnidarians, the planarians and flukes have digestive systems with only one opening. Food goes in and undigestible material is expelled through the same opening.

The tapeworms are all internal parasites of vertebrates. They are found primarily in the intestine of their host, where they attach to the intestinal wall by means of hooks and/or suckers. Tapeworms have no mouth or digestive system; they merely absorb the already digested food around them in their host's intestine.

**Muscle System.** The flatworms have true muscle cells and a well-developed muscle system. The especially mobile planarians have circular, longitudinal, and diagonal muscles within their body. Planarians do not swim freely but glide on objects in the water. This gliding motion is accomplished by muscular ripples moving from the head backward and flexing cilia (tiny hairs) on the bottom of the worm. Their way is smoothed by secretion of mucus from the bottom surface. Flukes do not exhibit a great deal of movement, and tapeworms move hardly at all.

**Brain and Nervous System.** The planarians have a small brain in the head end that is linked to the rest of the body by a ladder-shaped nerve—two longitudinal nerve cords running down each side with many cross connections. The planarians also have sense organs: eyespots on the head for detecting light and lobes called auricles protruding from the side of the head for sensing water conditions.

The flukes have a nervous system similar to that of the planarians, but they lack the sense organs of the planarians. The nervous system of the tapeworm is similar in structure to that of the other flatworms but is far less developed.

**Circulatory System.** Flatworms possess no circulatory system. They depend on diffusion to move nutrients and oxygen through the body. Such a system works only in animals that have a few cell layers and are not very thick. Therefore, while some flatworms can grow quite long (over 30 meters, or 100 feet), they are all very thin.

**Respiratory System.** Flatworms lack a respiratory system. They eliminate waste gases or absorb oxygen by diffusion directly through the body wall into or out of the water or fluids around them.

**Excretory (Urinary) System.** The flatworms do possess excretory organs. A pair of specialized tubes collect liquid wastes and expel them through pores on the body.

**Reproduction and Development.** Planarians reproduce asexually by literally pulling themselves apart behind the pharynx. Each part regenerates into a complete worm. Sexually, each planarian contains both male and female sex organs, but self-fertilization does not occur. Instead, two worms come together in opposing directions ventrally and exchange sperm, each fertilizing the eggs of the other. The eggs pass out of the body in an egg capsule, which holds both eggs and reserve food in the form of yolk cells. The planarians often fasten the egg capsules to the undersides of stones and logs in the water.

Flukes reproduce sexually in a manner very similar to that of the planarians. However, they produce about 10,000 to 100,000 times more eggs than the planarians. Some flukes lay so many eggs that the host's blood vessels containing flukes burst. The eggs of the fluke pass out in the sputum, urine, or feces of the host. Each fluke species has a succession of stages that must live in two or as many as four different host animals (including humans) to complete the life cycle. The life cycles of flukes are the most complex of any animal; only a few are fully understood.

Behind the "head" (called a scolex) of a tapeworm are a series of repeating segments known as proglottids. Each of as many as 4,000 proglottids contains both male and female sex organs. Tapeworms self-fertilize or cross-fertilize if other worms are present in the same host. Each proglottid may contain 100,000 eggs, and a single tapeworm is capable of producing more than a half billion eggs a year! The proglottids containing the eggs detach and pass out of the host's body in the feces or even crawl out of the host's anus under their own power. Like flukes, tapeworms go through different developmental stages in different hosts. A vertebrate is the final host of the adult tapeworm.

**Class Tubellaria (Planarians).** This group has about 3,000 species, with the common planaria being the most familiar. Most planarians live in the ocean, but some are found in fresh water and a few on land in damp areas. The freshwater planarians inhabit streams, ponds, and marshes and cling to the undersides of plants, rocks, and logs. They are about 1 to 2 centimeters (0.4 to 0.8 inches) long with a blunt, triangular-shaped head. The large eyespots on the head give them a comical cross-eyed appearance.

This group includes the first land animals we have encountered so far: the large Bipaliums, or land planarians. The Bipaliums were originally found in Asia but have been distributed around the world by commerce in tropical plants. They range in size from 1 to 60 centimeters (0.4 to 24 inches). Many of them are brightly colored. They have the unusual behavior of descending from leaves and branches by slime threads.

**Class Trematoda (Flukes).** This group has about 6,000 species, including the Chinese liver fluke, sheep liver fluke, and blood flukes. Flukes are thin, soft animals shaped somewhat like narrow elongated leaves. They usually have a sucker around the mouth and one or more suckers on the bottom surface. Flukes are about 1 to 2 centimeters (0.4 to 0.8 inches) long and are covered with a tough cuticle that resists the digestive enzymes of their host. All species are parasites, with some being external parasites (ectoparasites) and most being internal parasites (endoparasites) on all types of vertebrates as adults.

Flukes are a very serious health problem for humans in certain parts of Asia, Africa, and South America. Some endoparasitic flukes of humans are medically important:

*Intestinal flukes.* The larvae are passed to humans on water plants used as raw vegetables. In some parts of China, over half the population may be infested with these flukes.

*Liver flukes.* The larvae are passed to humans through raw or undercooked fish. Adult liver flukes may live in humans from 5 to 20 years.

*Lung flukes.* The larvae are passed to humans through raw or undercooked crabs and crayfish.

*Blood flukes.* The larvae burrow through human skin in water or are ingested from contaminated drinking water. Infestations by blood flukes cause a condition known as schistosomiasis (also called bilharziasis). Two hundred to three hundred million people may be infected by this one type of fluke, making it a world health problem second only to malaria.

**Class Cestoda (Tapeworms).** This group has about 1,500 species, including the pork tapeworm, the beef tapeworm, the dog tapeworm, and the broadfish tapeworm. The tapeworms are all internal parasites on vertebrate hosts. The body of a tapeworm consists of a scolex ("head") with suckers and/or hooks for attaching to the host animals connected to hundreds or thousands of sections called

# Specific Class Characteristics

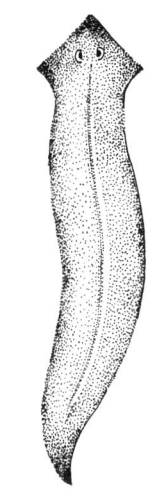

Planaria

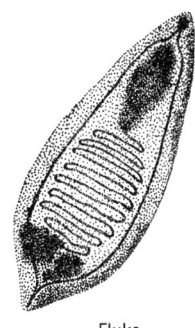

Fluke

proglottids. Like flukes, tapeworms are covered with a tough cuticle to resist the digestive enzymes of their host. They range in size from 1 millimeter (0.04 inches) to over 30 meters (100 feet) in length—the largest found in sperm whales. Some adult tapeworms live only a few days, and others may infest their human host for over 20 years.

Tapeworms are a serious health problem in parts of Asia, Africa, and South America, where sanitation is poor and meat is eaten raw or undercooked over open flames.

## The Importance of Flatworms

With their scavenging behavior, planarians play a positive ecological role in recycling dead material. In addition, they serve as both predator to small animals and prey to larger ones in aquatic food chains. Flukes and tapeworms, however, have a very negative and devastating effect on the people in parts of Asia, Africa, and South America, where they seriously affect the health, social structure, and economic development of those areas.

## COLLECTION OF SPECIMENS
### Flukes and Tapeworms

One can collect live flukes and tapeworms by cutting through slaughterhouse remains or even fresh road-killed animals. However, these worms produce prodigious amounts of eggs and can be highly infective. For your health and safety and that of your students, I recommend you do not collect live flukes and tapeworms. Instead, consider purchasing preserved specimens from the suppliers listed in Appendix B and use them for demonstration purposes.

### Planaria

Planaria can be found in most freshwater streams, ponds, and marshes, where they inhabit the undersides of rocks, logs, and plants. One might pick up or overturn rocks and logs to hunt for them, but I recommend a method of collecting planaria that is far less disruptive to the aquatic environment. Attach a piece of beef liver to a string and throw it out into shallow water. Within an hour or so, pull in the string and look for planaria feeding on the liver. Use forceful squirts of water from a dropper to rinse them off into a collecting container of pond water.

## MAINTENANCE OF SPECIMENS

Planaria are very hardy animals and are easily kept for extended periods in the classroom. Place clean pond water in a shallow glass dish, add the planaria, and cover the container loosely with cardboard or aluminum foil to retard evaporation and keep out foreign matter. You might want to put a few clean stones or shards from clay flower pots in the bottom of the dish for the planaria to hide under. I have had good results keeping planaria in the refrigerator at a temperature of 8 to 10°C (43 to 45°F). You can keep them for several weeks this way with no further care, but they will not grow at these low temperatures.

Healthy planaria can live three or four months without food. For maximum growth, however, keep them at room temperature and feed them every three or four days. A suitable food is beef liver (other types of liver do not work as well). Mince a piece of liver about the size of a quarter with a knife, add it to the planaria container, and leave it there for three to four hours. At the end of that time, gently shake or rinse the planaria from the liver. As you will note, the liver fouls the water so you must rinse the planaria container after each feeding. Carefully pour off the water. The planarians usually cooperate by attaching so you can pour off the water without loosing any worms. Rinse the container with clean pond water and pour it off again. Repeat this process several times to make sure the water in the container is clean.

Another food source that is not nearly as messy is live, rinsed brine shrimp. Hatch brine shrimp and rinse them according to the directions in Chapter 3 under activity F4 (Feeding) of the Teaching Activities. Some experts suggest feeding planaria mayfly nymphs, caddisfly larvae, or Tubifex worms.

If you purchase planaria from commercial suppliers, detailed instructions for their care and maintenance will accompany the culture.

Tapeworm

Live flukes and tapeworms pose the threat of possibly infecting you or your students. For the health and safety of everyone involved, stick to planaria and leave live flukes and tapeworms alone.

If you collect planaria from streams, ponds, or marshes, follow good safety procedures around water regardless of its apparent depth and be alert to possible contact with poisonous plants and biting or stinging animals.

Planaria pose no health or safety problems for students. However, it is a good precaution to have students thoroughly wash their hands before and after handling planaria containers and the pond water they contain.

Like hydra, if planaria dry, they die. Maintain adequate water around them at all times, especially when they are on microscope slides. Planaria are sensitive to water quality. Use only clean pond or spring water. Finally, planaria have very soft bodies and damage easily, so handle them carefully.

Planaria are so easy to collect and maintain and so interesting to watch that no study of the animal kingdom would be complete without some activities using live planaria.

To observe live planaria, pick them up with a small, soft paint brush (they are usually too large for a dropper or pipette) and transfer them to pond water in a depression slide or well slide. You may find that they crawl right off the slide. This often causes students to panic but is no cause for alarm as long as the worm does not dry out.

Planaria are considerably larger than the hydra studied in Chapter 3 so strong magnifiers or hand lenses will suffice for examining them, although dissecting microscopes will give the most detailed view,

**H1.** *Planaria Habitat.* Have students respond to the question, What is the natural habitat of your planaria? (Answer: Planaria are freshwater creatures found in ponds, streams, and marshes usually under rocks, sticks, and plant leaves.)

**H2.** *Flatworm Habitat Comparisons.* Have students respond to the question, Where might other types of flatworms be found? (Answer: Adult flukes and tapeworms are mainly internal parasites on all types of vertebrate animals.)

**H3.** *Planaria Defenses.* Planaria are soft, defenseless, and relatively slow moving. These characteristics make them tempting prey for animals in and around the water. Have students respond to the question, How do planaria avoid becoming lunch for larger animals? (Planaria are usually active at night. During the day they remain under rocks, sticks, and plant leaves. Some types are darker on the top, which makes them harder to see in the dim, murky areas where they live. Experts tell us that the incidence of predation on planaria is relatively low. Leeches, aquatic insects, and a few types of fish being are their only natural enemies.)

**H4.** *Not a Picky Eater.* Most animals are either plant-eating herbivores, flesh-eating carnivores, or decomposers and scavengers that eat dead remains. Pose this question to students: Why is it beneficial to the planaria to be both a carnivore and a scavenger? (The more food sources an animal can tap, the less competiton it has for food and the more likely it is to survive.)

**H5.** *Walk a Mile in My Shoes.* Have students try to put themselves in the flatworm's place by having them react orally or in written form to the following questions:
   a. Which flatworm—planaria, fluke, or tapeworm—has the easiest life, and why?
   b. Which type of flatworm would you rather be, and why?

**H6.** *Inhospitable Hosts.* Flukes and tapeworms are found in places where they are exposed to the strong digestive enzymes of their hosts. How are they able

HEALTH AND
SAFETY
Teachers

Students

Planaria

TEACHING
ACTIVITIES

Habitat

## Structure

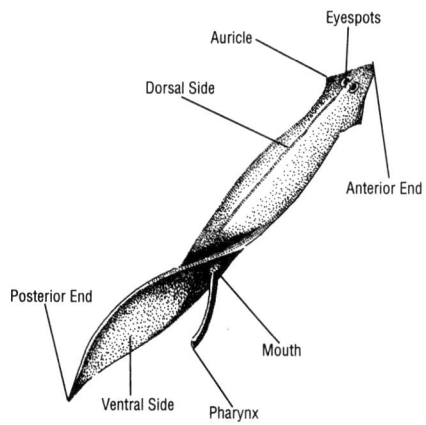

Planaria Structure — External

to withstand this? (Flukes and tapeworms are covered with a resistant layer of material called a cuticle.)

**S1.** *Planaria Structure.* Have students diagram and label the planaria and its parts: anterior (head), posterior (rear), dorsal (top), ventral (bottom), eyespots, auricles, mouth, and pharnyx.

**S2.** *Observe a Planaria.* Have students observe a live planaria and answer the following questions:

a. Does the planaria have a true head? (Answer: Yes, they always lead with the front end, which contains the greatest concentration of nerves and sense organs. Plus, as your students will tell you, it just looks like a head.)

b. What type of symmetry (proportions) does the planaria have? (Answer: Planaria exhibit bilateral symmetry: each side is more or less a mirror image of the other. All advanced animals possess this characteristic.)

c. Observe the dorsal (top) and ventral (bottom) surfaces. What differences do you see? (Students can carefully flip the worm over with a paint brush to observe the bottom. Usually the top is darker than the bottom. There are cilia on the bottom, but they are too small to see.)

d. Find and describe the eyespots. What is their function? (Students will observe that planaria appear to be looking up at them with tiny crossed eyes. However, they do not have true eyes and can see only light and dark. They use their eyespots to avoid bright light.)

e. Find and describe the auricles. What is their function? (The pointed protrusions sticking out from the head of the planaria are the auricles. The planaria uses them to detect chemicals in the water and thus locate food.)

f. Find and describe the pharynx (feeding tube). (The pharynx extends down out of the mouth on the underside of the body near the middle of the worm. It is not visible unless the worm is feeding. You may be able to get the worm to extend its pharynx by putting a small smear of blood and fluid from raw liver on the slide before you add pond water and planaria.)

**S3.** *Planaria Length.* Have students measure the length of the planaria when it is fully extended. (Students can use a small plastic ruler. This is not easy to do accurately as the gliding and squirming of the worms makes them very uncooperative.)

**S4.** *Flatworm Length Comparisons.* Have students compare and contrast the length of the planaria to the length of the fluke and tapeworm. (Planarias and flukes are about 1 to 2 centimeters [0.4 to 0.8 inches] long, while tapeworms range in size from 1 millimeter [0.04 inches] to over 30 meters [100 feet] long.)

**S5.** *Planaria Movement.* Have students observe and describe how a planaria moves. Encourage students to observe the planaria both from above and below by picking up the slide. (Planaria use muscular contractions and cilia on their underside and a mucal trail they secrete to produce a smooth, gliding movement.)

**S6.** *Planaria Graphs.* Famous planaria researcher Dr. I. M. Messy is working on the optimum conditions for best survival rate in regeneration experiments with planaria. However, she did not keep her data in a very organized fashion. Have students sort out the following hypothetical data (based on actual research) into data tables and then use these data tables to prepare graphs.

From the notebook of Dr. I. M. Messy:

*Survival rate at room temperature—around 21°C*
*(number of pieces of planaria still alive)*

| | | |
|---|---|---|
| Day #12 – 15 | Day #14 – 14 | Day #13–  14 |
| Day #2  – 22 | Day #5  – 19 | Day #16–  13 |
| Day #3  – 20 | Day #15 – 14 | Day #18–  12 |
| Day #10 – 16 | Day #6  – 19 | Day #19–  10 |
| Day #1  – 30 | Day #8  – 17 | Day #11–  15 |
| Day #7  – 19 | Day #20 – 9 | Day #17–  13 |
| Day #4  – 20 | Day #9  – 17 | |

*Survival rate in refrigerator—around 10°C*
*(number of pieces still alive)*

| | | |
|---|---|---|
| Day #11 – 28 | Day #5  – 29 | Day #4  –  30 |
| Day #14 – 26 | Day #19 – 24 | Day #6  –  29 |
| Day #15 – 26 | Day #12 – 27 | Day #2  –  30 |
| Day #10 – 28 | Day #1  – 30 | Day #20–  23 |
| Day #9  – 28 | Day #18 – 25 | Day #13–  26 |
| Day #16 – 26 | Day # 3 – 30 | Day #7  –  29 |
| Day #8  – 28 | Day #17 – 25 | |

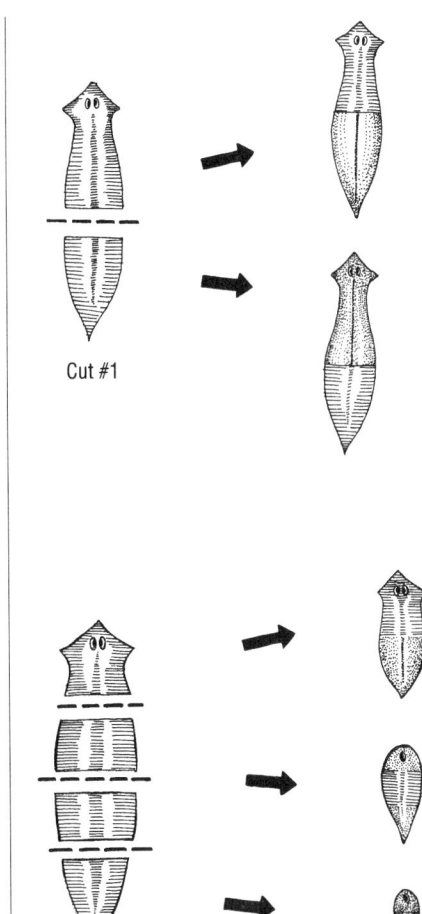

Cut #1

Cut #2

Once students have prepared their data tables and constructed their graphs, ask them to analyze the data by answering the following question: For best survival rate of planaria after regeneration experiments, should the pieces be kept at room temperature or in the refrigerator?

**S7.  Challenge:** *Planaria Regeneration.* Like sponges and cnidarians, planaria have tremendous powers of regeneration. Flukes do not possess this ability, but the scolex of the tapeworm can regenerate more proglottids.

To observe regeneration in planaria, have students place a microscope slide on an ice cube. Place a large drop of clean pond water on the slide and add a planaria. The cool temperatures will slow down the planaria and make the cutting easier. However, do not put the planaria directly on the ice or leave the slide on the ice too long as either can be fatal to the planaria. Make sure the slide is well lit.

Have students use a piece of broken microscope cover slip as a scalpel and make cuts in the planaria. Cuts should be made perpendicular to the slide by bringing the cover slip straight down, not sawing at an angle. I give my students the choice of making their cuts while looking through a dissecting microscope, looking through a magnifier, or just using their unaided eye. Most opt for just eyeballing it.

Suggest the following cuts to students:
Cut #1
This cut will demonstrate the fact that the ends retain polarity. That is, a new head will grow on the cut head end and a new tail will grow on the cut tail end.

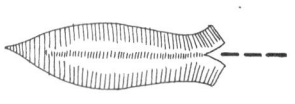

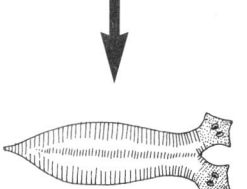

Two-Headed Worm

Cut #2

This cut will demonstrate the facts that the anterior (head) end retains the greatest capacity for regeneration and that this capacity decreases toward the posterior (rear) end.

Give the students some freedom to come up with their own possible cuts. Here are some possibilities you might suggest:

Two-headed worm

"Zorro" cut

Right angle head

Have students diagram the actual results of their "operations"—not what they planned to do, but the cuts they actually made. Then have students rinse the pieces of the cut worm into a shallow dish of pond water and cover it loosely. Petri dishes work well for this. Put the pieces from each worm in a separate dish.

These operations require considerable skill. The worms are not exactly cooperative and students often are not able to make the exact cuts they would like. Many of the pieces die and degenerate within 24 hours. Survival rate can be improved by keeping the dishes in the refrigerator at 8 to 10°C (43 to 45°F) (as students discovered by preparing data tables and graphs in activity S6), but regeneration will take longer. Discuss with your students whether they want high survival but slow regeneration or fast-track regeneration at the expense of planaria survival.

**S8.** *Flatworm Models.* Have students construct a model of a planaria, fluke, or tapeworm. Students might use colored modeling clay or colored bread dough. (See Chapter 3, activity S9, for a recipe for colored bread dough.)

## Behavior/Response

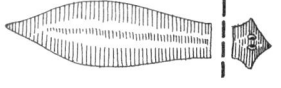

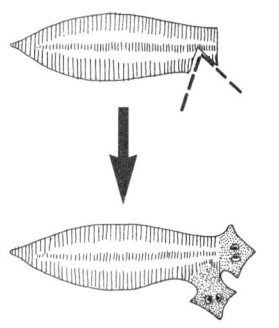

Right Angle Head

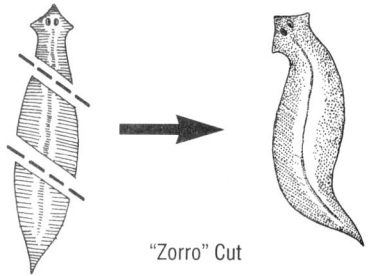

"Zorro" Cut

**B/R1.** *Gravity Response in Planaria.* Have students observe the response of the planaria to gravity (geotaxis) by carefully turning the worm over and seeing how it behaves. Have students drop planaria a short distance into water 6 to 10 centimeters (2.5 to 4 inches) deep and observe how they react. (Answer: Planaria will twist until their top side is up if flipped over. When dropped into water, they usually descend bottom side down with the head end touching down first.)

**B/R2.** *Touch Response in Planaria.* Have students observe the response of the planaria to touch (thigmotaxis) by carefully touching the head, middle, and tail of the planaria with a blunt glass probe made from a drawn piece of glass. (Answer: The head of the worm is more sensitive to touch than the other parts and will turn away from touch [negative reaction]. Interestingly, planaria are positive to touch on the bottom but negative on the top. This reaction helps them adhere to surfaces and to their food. Interested, older, or more advanced students may want to devise a method for testing this tidbit of taxis information.)

**B/R3.** *Light Response in Planaria.* Have students observe the response of the planaria to light (phototaxis). To devise a tiny spotlight, have students punch a hole with a compass point in a piece of cardboard or several sheets of black construction paper. Attach the cardboard or paper to a flashlight and shine the light on the worm.

Usually, if you shine the light on the tail, the worm crawls away. If you shine the light straight down on the head, the worm turns left or right. If you shine the light from the left or right, the worm turns in the opposite direction. Planaria are negative to light. In fact, planaria whose eyespots have been removed still react to light, but more slowly than normal. Evidently, they have light-sensitive cells over the rest of the body as well as in the eyespots.

I have also had success demonstrating the planaria's negative reaction to light by placing a shallow rectangular glass dish about half full of pond water so that half the dish rests over a black piece of paper and the other half over a white piece of paper. I also add dark-colored rocks and water-logged sticks to the dark half. I shine a bright light on the whole setup and add some planaria to the white half. Usually, the planaria make a beeline for the dark half as fast as their little cilia will carry them. This is not meant to be a controlled experiment with all variables regulated, but it makes a good demonstration. Verify the results by putting the same setup in the dark for a few hours. You will find planaria scattered randomly about on both halves of the dish.

**B/R4.** Challenge: *What Water Temperature Do Planaria Prefer?* Have students devise a way to test this problem. This activity will allow students to investigate thermotaxis, or response to temperature differences.

One design might be to get some clear plastic tubing 1 centimeter (0.4 inches) or larger from a hardware store. Put a stopper in one end of the tubing and fill it about three-fourths full of clean pond water. Add some planaria and stopper the other end. Allow the planaria time to randomly disperse through the tube. Now begin to run hot water on one end and cold water on the other end of the tube; this will create a temperature gradient between the two ends. Make sure all other variables such as light are equal everywhere in the tube. Have students predict what will happen before they begin. Have them keep data in appropriate tables, charts, or graphs and draw conclusions from their data.

**B/R5.** Challenge: *How Do Planaria Respond to Water Currents?* Have students devise a way to test this problem. This activity allows students to investigate rheotaxis, or response to currents.

One design is to direct jets of water from a fine pipette or dropper at planaria from different angles—head on, tail on, from the right side, and from the left side. Have students make predictions, collect data (data will be mainly observational), and draw conclusions from their data.

(Planaria tend to move against a current. When directed head on they move toward the current. When directed tail on, they turn around into the current, and when directed from either side, they turn into the current.)

**B/R6.** *Can Planaria Learn?* Planaria can be trained to run simple Y or T mazes. This training, however, takes a very long time. Several of the suppliers listed in Appendix B sell plastic trays rigged to batteries to train planaria to run a maze using negative reinforcement in the form of weak electrical currents (galvanotaxis).

Interestingly, studies have shown that when trained worms are cut into pieces, the regenerated pieces behave as if they had also been trained. Furthermore, when trained worms are eaten by untrained worms, the untrained worms seem to show signs that they have somehow developed training. Is memory stored throughout the body of a planaria? Not all biologists agree with the validity of these studies or what conclusions should be drawn from them, but this might be an interesting area of experiments for interested, older, or more advanced students.

**F1.** *Planaria Food.* Have students respond to the question, What do planaria eat? (Answer: Planaria eat live prey or scavenge the dead bodies of larger animals.)

**F2.** *Flatworm Feeding Comparisons.* Have students compare and contrast what planaria eat with what flukes and tapeworms eat. (Answer: Flukes eat the body tissues and/or blood of their host. The tapeworm directly absorbs the digested food of its host from the host's intestine.)

# Feeding

**F3.** *Observe Planaria Feeding.* Have students observe and describe the actual feeding behavior of planaria. Mince some beef liver (other types of liver do not work as well) and put a small portion of it in the center of a dish of clean pond water. Add planaria around the outer edge of the dish. Have students note how the planaria turn their head from side to side as they glide along. This allows them to "taste" the water with their auricles and crawl in the direction of the strongest chemical signal. This behavior often causes the planaria to circle around the food in an ever-tightening spiral. It may take a while for the planaria to locate the food, so be patient. When feeding begins, have the students try to locate the protruding pharynx if it is visible.

You can also feed planaria live prey such as brine shrimp, caddisfly larvae, or bloodworms. As they are digested they will color the planaria's intestine, making it easy to see. Caddisfly larvae are found in running streams and bloodworms in pond sediments. Brine shrimp can be raised from eggs (see Chapter 3, activity F4).

**Challenge:** How important are the auricles in finding food—very important, somewhat important, or not very important? Have students devise a way to test this problem. This activity allows students to investigate chemotaxis, or response to chemicals. However, do activity F3 before you have students attempt this challenge so they know what normal feeding responses are. You might also want students to do activity S7 in this chapter before attempting this challenge to give them some practice in making clean, precise cuts in planaria.

One design would be to carefully cut both auricles off some worms, cut only the right or left auricles off others, and keep an identical number of worms with the auricles left intact. Don't worry—you aren't harming the planaria. They have great powers of regeneration and will grow their auricles back quickly. Have students place equal numbers of worms from all four groups in the presence of food and time how long it takes the individuals of each group to find food. Have students watch for abnormal feeding responses. Have students predict what they think will happen before they begin; keep data in appropriate tables, charts, or graphs; and draw conclusions from their data.

**F4.** **Challenge:** *What Type of Food Is Best for Planaria?* Before students attempt to solve this problem, have them discuss the ambiguity of the word "best" in the question. What criteria can you use to determine the "best" food? Consider several possibilities:

a. Measure the length of individual worms over the period of time they are fed the different types of food. The best food would be the one that caused the greatest increase in the length of the worms.

b. Weigh the individual worms over a period of time as they are fed the different types of food. The best food would be the one that caused the greatest increase in weight of the worms.

c. Combine a & b.

d. It is no easy task to measure the length of a squirming planaria, and to weigh one would take a fairly sensitive scale or balance. Another possibility is to count how many new worms develop through spontaneous asexual fission, or "dropping tails." The more food worms receive, the higher the rate of asexual fission. The best food, therefore, would be the one that causes the highest rate of asexual fission.

Once you and your students decide how you will define the word "best" in the question, have the students reword the original question so that it more clearly states exactly what problem they will be attempting to solve.

Now decide what types of food to use. You might try beef liver, live prey, and moist cat food pellets, or you could test various types of liver (beef, pork, turkey, and so on) to see if one type really is superior to the others.

Divide your planaria into equal groups for as many food types as you will be using. Keep all other variables the same between the various dishes: amount of light, temperature, depth of water in the dish, and so on. The type of food must be the only difference between each group. Have students predict what they think will happen before they begin; keep data in appropriate tables, charts, or graphs; and draw conclusions from their data.

**R1.** *Planaria Reproduction.* Have students explain how planaria reproduce. (Answer: Planaria can reproduce asexually by fission or regeneration. They also reproduce sexually as hermaphroditic individuals cross-fertilize each other's eggs. The eggs pass out of the body in a cocoon. Each cocoon contains about 16 eggs, which hatch in several weeks.) The suppliers listed in Appendix B may be able to supply planaria egg cocoons in very early spring for demonstration purposes.

**R2.** *Flatworm Reproductive Comparisons.* Have students compare and contrast the reproduction of planaria with reproduction in flukes and tapeworms. (Answer: Flukes reproduce sexually in a manner similar to planaria but produce many more eggs. Tapeworms will cross-fertilize but can also self-fertilize their own eggs. Young planaria hatch from the egg looking like miniature adults and do not go through a larval stage. Flukes and tapeworms pass through several larval stages, with each stage requiring a different host animal.)

**R3.** *Enormous Numbers of Eggs.* Have students explain why flukes and tapeworms produce so many more eggs than the planaria. (Many eggs are necessary to ensure that at least a few worms make it to adulthood through all the steps in a very complicated life cycle.)

**R4.** *Tapeworm Calculations.* The most common type of human tapeworm is the beef tapeworm. These tapeworms produce about 100,000 slowly-maturing eggs per section (proglottid). Each day an average of 7 to 9 sections containing mature eggs detach from the end of the worm and pass out of the host's body along with the feces. Assuming that rate of egg production to be constant, have students calculate how many mature eggs from a single tapeworm could pass out of its host in one day, one week, one month, and one year.

**R5.** *Liver Fluke Life Cycle.* Scramble the information in the diagram about the life cycle of the liver fluke and have students put it into the proper sequence:

## Reproduction and Development

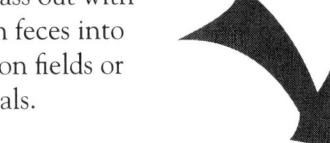
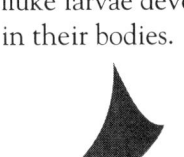
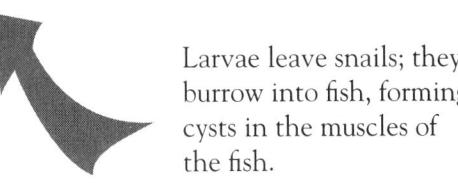

Eggs pass out with human feces into water on fields or in canals.

Snails in the water eat the eggs and fluke larvae develop in their bodies.

Humans eat raw or undercooked fish containing cysts.

Larvae leave snails; they burrow into fish, forming cysts in the muscles of the fish.

Now have students react orally or in written form to the following question: How would you break the fluke life cycle? Suggested answers:

1. Design better sewage treatment.
2. Drain swamps and marshy areas to reduce snail habitat.
3. Use poisons to kill snails.
4. Properly cook fish.
5. Develop drugs to kill the flukes inside a human.

Experts tell us a combination of these approaches holds the best hope for success.

## Integration with Other Subject Areas

**In1.** *Writing:*
  a. Ask students to imagine that they are displaced adult flukes or tapeworms. Have them write a newspaper ad seeking a suitable new host.
  b. Have students do a library report on a condition called schistosomiasis (also called bilharziasis) caused by blood flukes. This serious health problem is second only to malaria and may affect 200 to 300 million people.

**In2.** *Fine Arts:*
  a. Have students paint or draw a picture of a planaria, fluke, or tapeworm.
  b. Have students write a song or compose a poem entitled, "The Plight of the Planaria" in which a planaria longs for the easy life that its parasitic cousins enjoy.
  c. Have students diagram and explain their own design for the perfect parasitic worm.

**In3.** *Social Studies:*
  a. *History.* In 1970 the Aswan High Dam was completed across the Nile River in Egypt. This great achievement brought the promise of increased irrigation, flood control, and electric power. One unexpected result of the dam has been an increase of schistosomiasis. Have students explain the connection. (Answer: Irrigation canals and the lake behind the dam provide favorable habitat for snails, the host of the blood fluke larvae.)
  b. *Geography.* If possible, find references showing where flukes and tapeworms are a problem worldwide. Have students color in these areas on a blank world map. These maps could be included with the library report option in activity In1b.

**In4.** *Societal/Environmental Issues:*
  a. Have students react orally or in written form to the question: Why have so much time, effort, and money been spent investigating regeneration in sponges, cnidarians, and flatworms? (Answer: It would be an obvious human medical benefit if we could get our cells and bodies to perform the regeneration processes these animals are capable of. Imagine the possibilities: growing replacement organs for transplant, regenerating lost or damaged body parts, or even cloning entire new bodies from a small piece of tissue.)
  b. Have students imagine that they are the famous physician, Dr. I. Du Knot Know. One of their patients shows the following symptoms: tiredness, loss of weight, and low blood count. These symptoms could indicate any number of things, but Dr. Know suspects a tapeworm. Have students explain how they would determine if a tapeworm was indeed the culprit in this case. (Answer: Examine the patient's feces for shed proglottids and/or eggs.)
  c. Snail poisons are a convenient way of breaking the life cycle of blood flukes, but sometimes these poisons actually increase snail populations

and therefore the number of blood flukes. Have students explain why this happens. (Many snail poisons are not selective. If the poisons kill more of the snails' predators and competitors than they do snails, the snail population will increase.)

Planaria can be released safely back into unpolluted ponds, lakes, and marshes.

# RELEASE OF SPECIMENS

# SECTION TWO:
# UPPER INVERTEBRATES

## 5. SEGMENTED WORMS

**Kingdom:** Animalia
**Subkingdom:** Metazoa
**Phylum:** Annelida
**Classes:** Polychaeta (seaworms)
Oligochaeta (earthworms)
Hirundinea (leeches)

## DIVERSITY AND DISTRIBUTION

The worms we call annelids are round, legless animals with long, segmented bodies composed of muscular rings (Latin—*annelus*, little rings). The approximately 12,000 species of annelids are found in soil, fresh water, and salt water and live everywhere in the world except Antarctica and Madagascar (a large island off the southeastern coast of Africa).

Annelids range in size from tiny aquatic worms not even a millimeter (0.04 inch) long to giant earthworms over 3 meters (10 feet) long.

## General Phylum Characteristics

**Digestive System and Feeding.** Annelids may be thought of as a tube within a tube. Their digestive tract is a long continuous tube running through a hollow area (coelom) in the body with a mouth on one end and an anus on the other. Flatworms have neither the coelom body cavity nor an anus.

**Circulatory System.** Annelids have a closed circulatory system with two major blood vessels running the length of the body along the top (dorsal) and bottom (ventral). These main vessels are connected to smaller vessels known as ring vessels, which supply blood to the internal organs. Annelids lack a true heart. Blood is circulated through the body by the quivering action of blood vessels and by muscular contractions during movement.

**Respiratory System.** Aquatic annelids breathe through gills. These often feathery and brightly colored gills usually protrude from the worm's burrow or tube. Land annelids breathe through moist skin. To prevent drying, land annelids avoid dry areas and extreme heat and cover themselves with mucus.

**Muscle System.** Annelids have both longitudinal (lengthwise) and circular (round) muscles. By alternately contracting each type of muscle, annelids crawl, burrow, or swim. Hairlike bristles (called setae) provide an aid to movement.

**Excretory (Urinary) System.** Annelids eliminate liquid wastes through tube-shaped organs called nephridia. A pair of nephridia in each segment removes the liquid wastes through pores.

**Brain and Nervous System.** Annelids are active animals with a small brain and a relatively well developed nervous system.

**Reproduction and Development.** Most annelids reproduce sexually. Most seaworms have separate sexes, and eggs and sperm are released into the water where

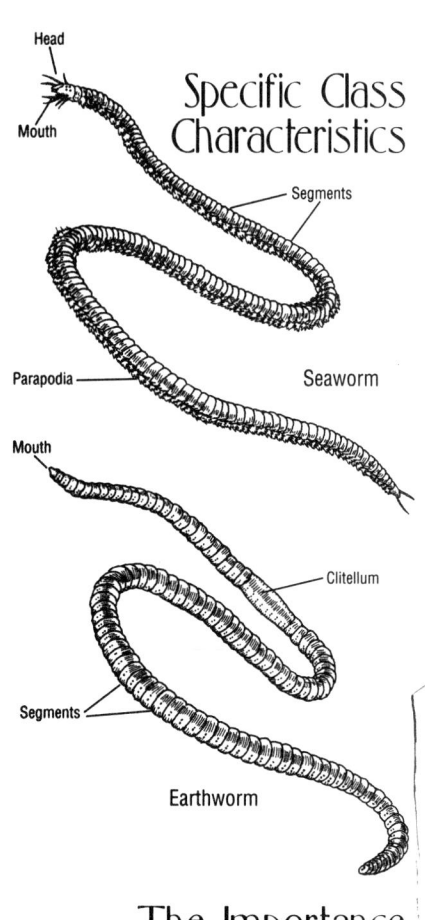

## Specific Class Characteristics

Head
Mouth
Segments
Parapodia
Seaworm
Mouth
Clitellum
Segments
Earthworm

## The Importance of Annelids

fertilization occurs. The earthworms and leeches are hermaphrodites (male and female in the same body) but usually do not self-fertilize. Instead they attach and exchange sperm. The fertilized eggs are deposited into a cocoon of mucous secreted by a band of specialized segments called the clitellum.

**Class Polychaeta (Seaworms).** This group has about 8,000 species, including clam worms, sand worms, plume worms, sea mice, fire worms, and palolo worms. Practically all of these worms live in or near the ocean. Some burrow in the sand and mud, some form tubes, and others swim freely about. Many are filter feeders that sift dead matter and plankton from the water with feathery gills or tentacles. Others eat their way through bottom sediments, and some carnivorous species use hooklike jaws to capture prey.

Seaworms differ from the other types of annelids in two ways:
1. They have a well-developed head and specialized sense organs.
2. They have paired, fleshy, paddle-shaped flaps (parapodia) tipped with bristles on most segments.

**Class Oligochaeta (Earthworms).** This group has about 3,100 species, including the earthworm and tubifex worms. Most of these worms burrow in soil, but some are found in fresh water and a few in the ocean. Nearly all are decomposers—they literally eat their way through the soil and digest the organic matter out of it.

Earthworms have no distinct head. They have fewer sense organs and bristly appendages than seaworms.

**Class Hirundinea (Leeches).** This group has about 500 species. Most leeches live in fresh water, but some are found on land in damp areas. Although most leeches are predators or scavengers, some have developed the ability to externally suck blood from vertebrates (including humans).

Leeches are not as distinctly segmented as seaworms and earthworms, and they have developed suckers at both ends of their bodies. Except for one species, leeches have no bristles (setae).

All annelids serve as important links in the food chain on land and in the water. As decomposers and scavengers, annelids help to recycle dead material. Earthworms are especially useful in this regard. The 50,000 or so worms per acre of fertile soil passing 9 to 16 metric tons (10 to 18 tons) of soil and organic matter through their intestines each year help aerate and enrich the soil.

Modern medicine has found an important role for the blood-sucking leeches. Although leeching and other forms of bloodletting were discredited long ago as medical practices, modern doctors have begun to use leeches to aid recovery after certain types of microsurgery such as the reattachment of fingers. The saliva of the feeding leeches contains an anesthetic and anticoagulant that promotes continued bleeding at the wound site. The continued oozing of blood after the application of leeches helps reduce swelling and allows fresh, oxygenated blood to enter the wound area until veins can regrow.

If you live close to the ocean you can gather specimens by overturning rocks and poking through tide pools. Concentrate on muddy areas rather than sandy areas. In addition, chipping the encrustments off pilings and sorting through them may yield specimens.

Tube worms usually are found in deeper water 4.5 to 6 meters (15 to 20 feet) deep and can be collected by pulling a small oyster dredge behind a boat.

Another opportunity for easy collection is made possible by the nighttime swarming reproductive behavior some of these worms exhibit from March to May. When conditions are right and the swarm is on, the writhing worms can be picked up or netted easily in the shallow waters of protected bays and coves. Collect some mud, a few rocks, and plenty of seawater to take along with the worms.

## COLLECTION OF SPECIMENS
## Seaworms

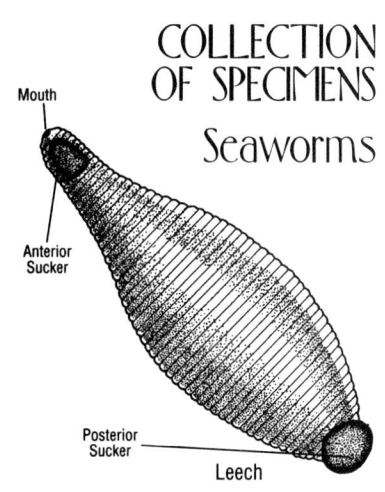

Mouth
Anterior Sucker
Posterior Sucker
Leech

Fish bait shops may be another source of live specimens.

The common earthworm is so widespread that digging into any moist, fertile soil usually yields some specimens. You can also pick them up off of lawns, sidewalks, and streets after a heavy rain. The best time for collection is at night on closely cut lawns where the soil is rich. Fish bait shops may also be a source of live specimens. The suppliers listed in Appendix B sell a robust variety whose large size makes observations and manipulations easier.

Aquatic earthworms such as tubifex worms can be collected from the bottom sediments of ponds or streams where considerable organic matter (such as sewage) is decaying. To collect the worms, drag a large tea strainer or fine mesh dip net along the bottom in shallow water. Collect some bottom mud and plenty of pond water to take along with the worms.

## Earthworms

Leeches are widespread in lakes and ponds (populations of 700 leeches per square meter have been recorded!). They lurk under rocks and logs and on plants or are attached to fish and especially turtles. You may have some luck in such ponds by dragging a fine mesh dip net through bottom muck or around vegetation beds in shallow water. If you can catch a turtle or two you may be able to do it and yourself a favor by removing the leeches from it. You might also construct a leech trap by placing raw liver in a basket made of light window screen or a can with small holes punched in it. Attach a plastic funnel pointing inward to the opening of the basket. Attach a line to the basket and sink it in shallow water. Leaving the trap undisturbed overnight may yield leeches (and some other interesting creatures). Collect some bottom mud and plenty of pond water along with the leeches.

## Leeches

Fish bait shops may also be a source of live specimens. Live earthworms and leeches can also be purchased from the suppliers listed in Appendix B.

Plan to keep seaworms for a very short time only. Place a few worms, some mud, and a few rocks in a shallow glass dish along with some of the seawater you collected. Aerate the water with an aquarium pump and keep the whole thing 20°C (65°F) or cooler. Replace seawater as necessary. Releasing the specimens as soon as possible does away with the need to feed them.

## MAINTENANCE OF SPECIMENS
## Seaworms
## Earthworms

Common earthworms can easily be kept by placing them in a plastic container (such as a cottage cheese container) in light, loamy soil. Avoid soils high in clay or sand. Spread a little cornmeal or some dried leaves on the top and add about one to two inches of soil. Cover the top of the soil with damp sphagnum moss and place the whole affair in a refrigerator at no lower than 15°C (60°F). This arrangement is sufficient to keep about a dozen earthworms nicely for several weeks.

Place aquatic earthworms such as tubifex worms in a shallow glass dish along with some of the bottom mud and pond water from the collection site. Keep the dish in a darkened area at room temperature. Replace the pond water as needed and aerate occasionally. If they are to be kept longer than a week, add a small amount of the yolk from a hard-boiled egg. Do not let a scum form on the surface of the water as it prevents air exchange.

Leeches are sensitive to trace metals in water (such as copper) so keep them only in the pond water from the collection site. Place a few leeches (avoid overcrowding) in a shallow glass dish along with some bottom

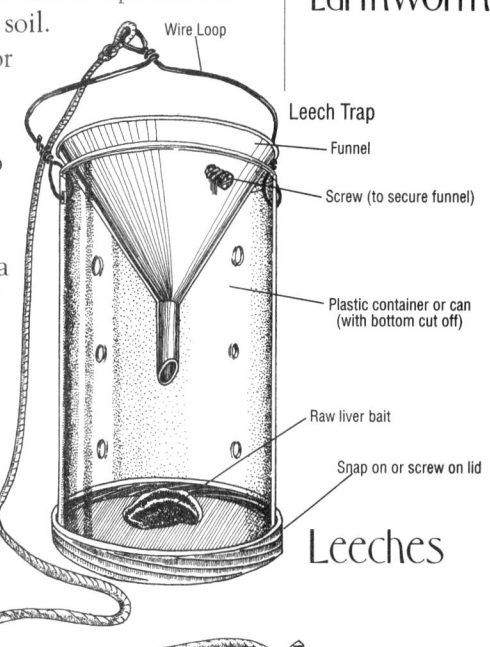

Wire Loop

Leech Trap

Funnel

Screw (to secure funnel)

Plastic container or can (with bottom cut off)

Raw liver bait

Snap on or screw on lid

## Leeches

mud and pond water. Keep the dish at room temperature and away from direct sunlight. Change the water every few days and aerate occasionally. Leeches like to wander, so cover the dish securely with a fine mesh screen. Leeches can go months between meals, but you might feed them raw liver once a week. To prevent fouling the water, place the leeches in a different container while feeding. Leave them on the food undisturbed for several hours. Again, securely cover the feeding container.

When collecting common earthworms, be considerate. Your neighbors won't appreciate your digging up their gardens or trampling down their flowers chasing nightcrawlers across their lawn. Get permission before digging on private or public land. Avoid areas where chemicals have been applied.

If you are collecting aquatic earthworms, be aware that areas where these worms are abundant are often polluted with sewage. Be extra attentive to personal cleanliness during and after collecting trips to such areas. Be alert and follow good safety procedures around water regardless of its apparent depth.

Collecting seaworms may bring you in contact with marine creatures that bite or sting. Wear shoes and possibly gloves and be cautious when turning over rocks or picking through tide pools.

If you chip encrustments off pilings to collect seaworms, wear safety glasses to prevent eye injury. If you are working from a small boat, follow all safe boating procedures and wear an approved life vest.

If you are after leeches, stay alert and practice good safety procedures around water regardless of its apparent depth. Be cautious about possible contact with poisonous plants and biting or stinging animals. Again, be attentive to personal cleanliness during and after such collecting trips.

Common earthworms pose no problems, but make sure students wash their hands thoroughly before and after contact.

If a culture of tubifex worms has been set up, make sure students keep their hands and equipment away from their faces and eyes and wash their hands thoroughly before and after contact. If the worms are collected from a heavily contaminated area, use them as a demonstration rather than allowing students to have direct contact.

Some seaworms have wicked hooklike jaws and can give a painful bite. Avoid letting students come in direct contact with such worms.

Leeches present very few problems. You may have a hard time getting some students to come near them, let alone make contact. Consider the quality of the water and mud and any possible contamination of the collection site. As usual, wash hands thoroughly before and after contact. I do not advise placing leeches on the body and letting them begin to feed. Probably no physical or medical problem could result from it, but such a scene reinforces the mistaken idea many students have of leeches as disgusting and repulsive creatures.

The main concern is that the specimens (especially seaworms) be returned to their natural habitat as soon as possible.

If earthworms are being studied, make sure they do not dry out. Students should moisten their hands before touching the worm and give it an occasional "bath" by dropping water on it. Active earthworms can crawl off the table or into inaccessible cracks and crevices if not closely watched. A fall from a table probably won't kill the worm, but it wouldn't be good for it. Be particularly attentive that some students don't try to frighten others by dangling worms in front of them or tossing the worms around.

Some laboratory manuals suggest testing chemotaxis, the reaction of the earthworm to various chemicals. Avoid substances such as soap, vinegar, ammonia, and salt as these could be deadly to the worm.

**HEALTH AND SAFETY**

*Teachers*

*Students*

*Worms*

Since earthworms are so easy to collect and maintain and are so familiar to students, most of the activities in this chapter deal with them.

To observe a live earthworm place it on damp paper towels in a clean pan (such as a dissecting pan or small cake pan). If available, hand lenses and/or dissecting microscopes can greatly aid observations.

**H1.** *Worm Habitat.* Have students respond to the question, What is the natural habitat of your earthworm? (Most students will be familiar enough with earthworms to answer this correctly).

**H2.** *Annelid Habitat Comparisons.* Have students respond to the question, Where might other types of annelids (segmented worms) be found? (Answer: Fresh water, salt water, and everywhere on land except Antarctica and Madagascar.)

**H3.** *Earthworm Life Span.* Have students estimate how long an earthworm lives. (Answer: The average life span is two years but may be as long as six years.)

**H4.** *Earthworms vs. Cold Temperatures.* Earthworms cannot tolerate very cold temperatures. Have students respond to the question, Where do earthworms go in the winter? (Earthworms live from 7.5 to 45 centimeters [3 to 18 inches] below the surface. In winter they burrow down below the frost line.)

**H5.** *Beneficial Annelids.* Have students explain how annelids (segmented worms) are beneficial to humans. (See "The Importance of Annelids" in this chapter.)

**H6.** *Where Did They Go?* How do earthworms get into the soil? Have students place an earthworm or several earthworms on top of damp soil in a container. Challenge students to observe and describe how the worms work their way back down into the soil.

**H7.** **Challenge:** *What Are the Effects of Earthworms on Soil?* Construct a viewing chamber with two glass or clear plastic plates about 1 centimeter (half an inch) apart over a wood frame. Add slightly moist soil with some dead leaves or grass on the top. Put a wire screen on top with weights on it to keep the worms from escaping. Place the apparatus in darkness for 24 hours. Have students observe
   a. any changes in the leaf/grass litter on the surface.
   b. any changes in the upper levels of the soil.
   c. the length of any tunnels formed. (You might have them calculate the length of tunneling that would occur after one week, one month, or one year based on the 24-hour tunneling rate.)

   You might also add different layers of moist materials like sand and clay and note the displacement of soil, sand, and clay from one layer to another. Have students predict differences in worm activity from one layer to another and then attempt to explain any differences observed.

**H8.** *Walk a Mile in My Shoes.* Have students try to put themselves in the worm's place by having them react orally or in writing to the question, What specific annelid would you be and why?

**S1.** *Earthworm Structure.* Have students diagram and label the worm and its parts: prostomium ("lips"), mouth, segments, clitellum, setae, anus, anterior (front) end, posterior (rear) end, dorsal (top) side, and ventral (bottom) side.

**S2.** *Segments.* Have students count the segments on their earthworm. How many are there? Compare worms for this characteristic. Does each worm have the same number of segments? How do leeches, seaworms, and earthworms differ in this regard? (Answer: Earthworms have 100-150 segments, and seaworms can have over 200 segments. All leeches have 32, 33, or 34 segments [depending on which reference you consult] regardless of length.)

# TEACHING ACTIVITIES

## Habitat

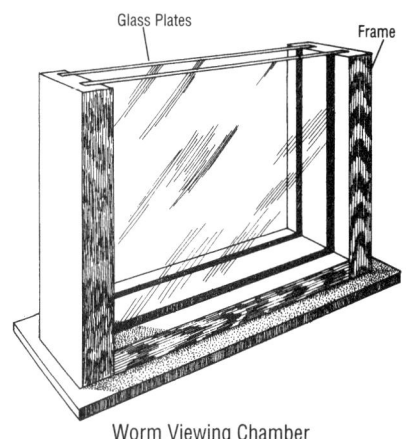

Glass Plates     Frame

Worm Viewing Chamber

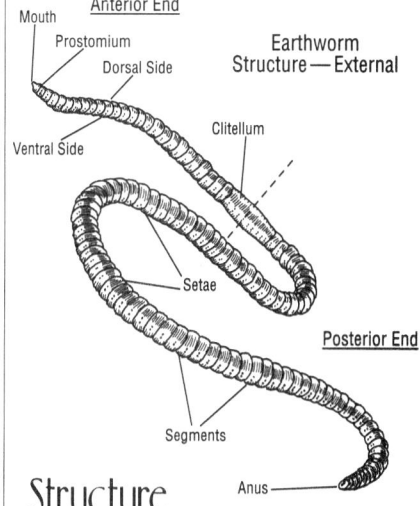

Anterior End

Mouth

Prostomium

Dorsal Side

Earthworm Structure — External

Clitellum

Ventral Side

Setae

Posterior End

Segments

Anus

## Structure

**S3.** *Measure a Worm.* Have students measure the length of their earthworm to the nearest millimeter. How long is it? How does the length of each worm compare to the others? (A measurement of 14 centimeters and 5 additional millimeters would be expressed as 14.5 cm. Lengths of worms will vary somewhat.)

**S4.** **Challenge:** *Was the Worm Difficult To Measure Because It Squirmed Around?* If so, have students devise a way to safely slow the worm or restrict its movements to make measuring easier. (Students may suggest cooling the worm, tying it down, or putting it in a thick, clear liquid. Accept any logical or innovative answer.) Note: If students actually attempt to test their restraining systems, do not let them put the worm directly on ice and be sure any system tested does not have the potential to harm the worm.

**S5.** *Weigh a Worm.* Have students weigh their earthworm to the nearest gram. What does it weigh? How does the weight of each worm compare to the others? (Scales or balances that weigh at least to grams, and even better to tenths of a gram, are necessary to be totally accurate. Student-constructed balances using weights such as coins can give some general comparisons. Weights will vary.)

**S6.** *Observe a Worm.* Have students observe the earthworm carefully and answer the following questions:

a. How can you tell the anterior (head) end from the posterior (rear) end? What are the differences between each end? (The anterior end is the shorter end from the clitellum. It is usually darker in color and the end that goes first as the worm crawls.)

b. The earthworm has an anterior (head) end, but does it have a head? (Seaworms do but earthworms and leeches do not.)

c. How are the ends of an earthworm and leech different? (Leeches have suckers on both ends; earthworms do not.)

d. Observe the dorsal (top) side and the ventral (bottom) side of the worm. What differences can you see? (The dorsal side is usually a darker color than the ventral side.)

e. Would you say the earthworm is protectively camouflaged (colored)? Does it need to be? (Not really—it spends daylight hours underground.)

f. Find and describe the clitellum. What is its function? (The clitellum is a band around the worm that secretes mucous. The mucous keeps the skin moist, lubricates the burrow, provides a passageway for sperm during reproduction, and forms a cocoon to protect the eggs after reproduction.)

g. What would happen if an earthworm's clitellum stopped functioning? (Reproduction would be impossible, and movement through burrows would be more difficult, but the greatest problem would be the threat of suffocation due to drying.)

h. Observe the thick dark line running the entire length of the worm on both the dorsal (top) and ventral (bottom) sides. These are the dorsal and ventral blood vessels. Watch carefully and you can see ripples of blood flowing through these vessels. Each ripple represents a pulse of blood, or the "heartbeat" of your worm. What is the "pulse rate" of your worm per minute?

Hand lenses will suffice for this activity but dissecting microscopes will give a much better view. Note: If worms are placed on a microscope, added attention is needed to keep them moist.

**Challenge:** Can you change the "pulse rate" of an earthworm? Have students devise a way to test this problem.

One possible design would be to put an earthworm in a shallow dish, put the dish into warm or cold water, and count the "pulse rate." Have students predict what will happen before they begin and then get the "pulse rate" of a worm at room temperature to serve as a control. Have students collect data by recording water temperature and "pulse rate" for both the control and the experimental worms. Have students graph the data and draw conclusions.

Note: Do not let students touch the worm directly to ice. Use only warm tap water; avoid very hot water.

**S7.** *Observe Worm Movement.* Have students place the worm on a piece of glass and view it from above and below as it crawls. Have students diagram and describe how the worm moves.

**S8.** *Faster than a Speeding Earthworm?* Have students measure to the nearest centimeter how far their worm crawls in one minute. Compare each worm's speed with the others. Have students calculate how long would it take their worm to crawl around a running track (400 meters).

Speeds will vary. A typical calculation might look like this:

a. Distance crawled in one minute to the nearest centimeter = 70 cm.
b. To convert centimeters to meters, divide by 100. 70 divided by 100 = 0.7.
c. Now solve the initial problem:

$$\frac{1 \text{ minute}}{0.70 \text{ m}} = \frac{x \text{ minutes}}{400 \text{ m}}$$

Cross multiply: $0.70x = 1 \times 400 = 400$
To solve for $x$, divide both sides by 0.70:

$$\frac{0.70x}{0.70} = \frac{400}{0.70} = 571.4 \text{ minutes}$$

To convert the answer to hours, divide 571.4 by 60 = 9.52 hours. (Answer: Assuming a constant rate of crawl, it would take this worm 571.4 minutes, or 9.52 hours, to crawl around a 400-meter running track.)

**S9.** *Touch a Worm.* Have *willing* students run their finger down the ventral (bottom) side of the worm. Ask them what structures they feel and how these sturctures help the worm move. (Setae—these bristles give the worm traction and leverage for movement.)

**S10.** *Come Out!* Have students respond to the question, Why do birds and people often have such a hard time pulling earthworms from their burrows? (The worms can flatten out their posterior end, wedging them into the burrow. They further anchor themselves by digging in with their setae.)

**S11.** *Surface or Die.* After a heavy rain large numbers of earthworms appear on lawns and sidewalks. Ask students why this happens. (Earthworms cannot absorb oxygen from water so, as their burrows flood, they must come up or suffocate.)

**S12.** *Leech Saliva.* Have your students visualize the following scenario: You are attending a lecture by the famous leech expert, Dr. I. M. Brilliant. Dr. Brilliant tells the audience that leech saliva contains an anesthetic. He then catches you completely off guard by asking you to explain to the audience why having an anesthetic in its saliva is beneficial to a leech. What would you say? (The anesthetic deadens the area where the leech is feeding and allows it to feed undetected).

**S13.** *Can Earthworms Regenerate?* Sponges, cnidarians, and flatworms have tremendous powers of regeneration and/or reassociation. Ask students if earthworms possess such powers. (Earthworms are more limited in their powers of regeneration than previous animals we have discussed so far in this book. At the anterior (head) end, they may lose six to nine segments and be able to regenerate them. More segments can be removed from the posterior (rear) end, and the worm can still survive. Experiments in grafting have produced worms with two tails or extra-long worms formed by joining parts of three worms.

**S14.** *Anneild Models.* Have students construct a model of an earthworm, seaworm, or leech. (Students might use colored modeling clay or colored bread dough (use the recipe listed in Chapter 3 under activity S9.)

## Behavior/Response

**B/R1.** *Who Gets the Worm?* Ask students if they think there is any truth to the old saying that "the early bird gets the worm." (Answer: Since earthworms are active on the surface at night, an early bird might catch them in the morning before they can burrow down.)

**B/R2.** *Gravity Repsonse in Earthworms.* Have students roll the earthworm over so that the ventral (bottom) side is up. How does the earthworm react? Ask students if they think earthworms can sense when they are not in their normal posture. Do they think an earthworm would behave the same way if it were weightless in an orbiting science classroom? This activity allows students to investigate geotaxis, or the response to gravity. (Answer: The worm will usually roll itself over so that the dorsal side is up. They can sense when they are not in a normal orientation.)

**B/R3.** *Danger Ahead.* Have students place an earthworm several inches away from the edge of a table and describe what happens when the worm gets to the edge. Do not let the worm fall to the floor—catch it a few inches below the edge of the table. Ask students if they think the worm could sense danger based on their observations. (Depending on the condition of the worm, most will crawl blindly off the table, but some may be more cautious that others.)

**B/R4.** *Will the Worm Learn?* Have students predict whether the worm will learn to avoid falling off the table if they let it repeat the experience over and over. Now let the worm repeat the experience several times. Was the prediction correct? Does the worm become more cautious after falling several times?

**B/R5.** *Touch Response in Earthworms.* Have students lightly touch the anterior (head) end of their earthworm with a blunt probe or the eraser of a pencil. Do this several times. Have students explain how the worm responds. This activity allows students to investigate thigmotaxis, or the response to touch. (The worm will usually react negatively by pulling back.)

**B/R6.** *Sensitive Ends.* Have students predict whether the worm's posterior (rear) end will react the same way as the anterior (head) end when touched. Have them touch both ends of the worm with a blunt probe. Was the prediction correct? Have students explain the reasons for any differences in response they observe. (The posterior end is usually not as reactive when touched. One explanation may be that the worm sticks its anterior end out of the burrow, so that end would need to be more responsive to danger.)

**B/R7.** Challenge: *Do Earthworms Prefer a Dry or a Damp Surface?* Have students devise a way to test this problem. This activity allows students to investigate hydrotaxis, or the response to water (or the lack of it).

One design might be to put half the earthworm on a dry paper towel and the other half on a damp towel. Have students predict what they think will happen before they begin. Ask them to record their data, which will be mainly observational, and draw conclusions from their observations. Ask students if it would be sound science to switch the ends of the worms. (The worms usually prefer the damp towel. It is sound science to switch each half of the worm because this verifies the previous results. If it doesn't, then you have a different problem to solve—such is the nature of science.)

**B/R8.** Challenge: *Are Earthworms Sensitive to Light?* Have students devise a way to test this problem. This activity allows students to investigate phototaxis, or the response to light.

One design would be to have students punch a small hole with a compass point in a piece of cardboard or several pieces of black construction paper and attach the cardboard or paper to a flashlight. Darken the room and have students shine the light on various parts of the worm's body to see how it reacts. Have students predict what will happen before they begin, record their data, which will be mainly observational, and draw conclusions from their observations. Have them explain possible reasons for any differences in response that they observe. (The anterior end is usually more sensitive to light than the posterior. Again, since this end is most often out of the burrow, it needs to be more attuned to possible danger.) By placing colored cellophane over the pinhole "spotlight," students could investigate whether the worm is sensitive to various colors.

**B/R9.** Challenge: *Can Earthworms Learn?* Have students devise a method to test this problem. One possible design would be to construct a T-maze (a maze in the shape of a T) from cardboard, wood, or plastic tubing. On one side put a pile of moist, loose soil and on the other side put bright lights and dry sand—something irritating but safe to the worm. Let worms crawl the maze and observe if they learn which way to turn to avoid the irritations your students have concocted for them. Have students make predictions; keep data in appropriate tables, charts, and graphs; and draw conclusions from their data. Note: Do not use negative reinforcement such as electrical shock or harsh chemicals.

**F1.** *Earthworm Food.* Have students respond to the question, What do earthworms eat? (Answer: Any organic matter encountered while burrowing. They literally eat their way through the soil and digest the organic matter from it.)

## Feeding

**F2.** *Getting Earthworm Food.* Have students respond to the question, How do earthworms eat? (Use appropriate reference materials that show the internal structures of the earthworm and describe its digestive process. Ask students to explain the digestive process of the earthworm in their own words, or scramble the following steps and have students put them into the proper sequence.

Step 1. Soil containing organic matter is drawn in by the muscular action of the prostomium ("lips") and pharynx.

Step 2. Calcium carbonate is secreted by the calciferous glands of the esophagus to neutralize any organic acids present in the food/soil.

Step 3. Food/soil is temporarily stored in the crop and later ground up in the muscular gizzard.

Step 4. Food/soil passes down the intestine where digestive enzymes break it down. Digested material is absorbed from the intestines into the blood, where it is carried to all parts of the body by the circulatory system.

Step 5. Food residue/soil passes out of the worm's anus.

**F3.** *What Are Those Little Piles?.* Ask students if they have ever seen earthworm castings. If so, ask them to explain what earthworm castings are. (Answer: Mounds of soil and food residue that earthworms deposit on top the soil.)

**F4.** *Feeding Comparisons.* Have students compare and contrast the feeding of an earthworm to the feeding of a leech. (Earthworms are decomposers that digest organic matter out of the soil. Some leeches eat dead material, but most are carnivores or external parasites that feed off the blood and body fluids of vertebrates.)

## Reproduction and Development

**R1.** *Earthworm Sex Organs.* Have students turn a live earthworm ventral (bottom) side up. Between segments 9 and 10 and 10 and 11 on the anterior (head) end, have them find the openings to the seminal receptacles (sperm storage sacs). A pair of female openings that lead to the ovaries (which produce eggs) are found on segment 14, and a pair of male openings leading to the seminal vesicles (which produce sperm) are found on segment 15. A powerful hand lens or dissecting microscope may be necessary to see these structures.

**R2.** *Earthworm Reproduction.* Have students explain how earthworms reproduce. Direct them to appropriate references and let them describe the reproductive process in their own words, or scramble the following steps and have the students put them in the proper order.

Step 1.  On a warm, moist night two worms stretch out of their burrows (earthworms reproduce all year but are most active in warm weather).

Step 2.  The worms join their ventral sides together with the anterior end of each worm pointing in the opposite direction.

Step 3.  Each worm covers itself with mucus from the clitellum. Grooves develop along which sperm from one worm travels to and enters the seminal receptacles of the other.

Step 4.  After several hours the worms separate.

Step 5.  Sometime later each worm forms a mucal ring that moves forward (toward the anterior end) from the clitellum.

Step 6.  As the ring passes the female openings (segment 14), eggs are deposited into the ring. As the ring passes the openings to the seminal receptacles (segments 9-10 and 10-11), sperm from the other worm is deposited into the ring and fertilizes the eggs.

Step 7.  The ring passes off the worm's body and forms a cocoon that protects the eggs until they hatch.

Note: As a demonstration you might wish to purchase earthworm cocoons from the suppliers listed in Appendix B and observe the hatching of young earthworms.

**R3.** *Annelid Reproductive Comparisons.* Have students compare and contrast the reproductive process of earthworms, leeches, and seaworms. (Seaworms are separate sexes. Their sperm and eggs are shed into the water, where fertilization occurs. Earthworms and leeches are hermaphrodites. That is, they have both male and female sex organs in the same body. The earthworms and leeches attach and cross-fertilize [exchange sperm]).

## Integration with Other Subject Areas

**In1.** *Writing:*

a.  Have students imagine that they are unemployed earthworms. They are to write a "work wanted" ad in which they list the qualifications they have to be employed by a tunneling or ditch-digging firm.

b.  Have students write a short report on how leeches were used by physicians in ancient times and how they are being used by modern doctors today.

**In2.** *Fine Arts:*

a.  Have students draw or paint a picture of an earthworm, seaworm, or leech.

b.  Have students write a song or compose a poem entitled, "The Woes of a Worm."

c. Have students draw a cartoon about an earthworm that is tired of eating just soil.

**In3.** *Social Studies:*

a. *History.* Charles Darwin, who studied earthworms for many years, wrote, "It may be doubted whether there are many other animals which have played so important a part in the history of the world as have these lowly organized creatures." Have students react to Darwin's idea that earthworms actually have played a role in human history. One approach might be to have students imagine they are Charles Darwin defending his comment in a letter to an imaginary colleague. Suggest that students gather background information on Charles Darwin from appropriate resources.

b. *Geography.* Have students write a library report in which they describe the giant earthworms of Ecuador and/or Australia. Have them include maps with their report that show the location of Ecuador and/or Australia and, if possible, maps that show where in Ecuador and/or Australia these giant worms are found.

**In4.** *Societal/Environmental Issues:* A farmer wished to use pesticides on his fields to kill harmful insects. However, he did not wish to harm the creatures in the soil any more than necessary. Chemical companies sent him the following information about three different pesticides:

| Pesticide X | number of worms per square meter (experimental) | number of worms per square meter (control) |
|---|---|---|
| Before Pesticide | 75 | 75 |
| After Pesticide Application | | |
| 1 week | 21 | 92 |
| 2 weeks | 12 | 118 |
| 3 weeks | 11 | 127 |
| 4 weeks | 18 | 136 |
| 5 weeks | 39 | 151 |
| Pesticide Y | | |
| Before Pesticide | 75 | 75 |
| After Pesticide Application | | |
| 1 week | 76 | 90 |
| 2 weeks | 74 | 112 |
| 3 weeks | 75 | 130 |
| 4 weeks | 76 | 141 |
| 5 weeks | 75 | 147 |
| Pesticide Z | | |
| Before Pesticide | 75 | 75 |
| After Pesticide Application | | |
| 1 week | 87 | 91 |
| 2 weeks | 117 | 117 |
| 3 weeks | 131 | 133 |
| 4 weeks | 142 | 141 |
| 5 weeks | 153 | 155 |

Have students construct a line graph for the data on each pesticide and answer the following questions about the information and graphs:

1. What are we graphing? (The effect of three different pesticides on a population of earthworms.)
2. Why was one group of worms labeled experimental and the other group control? (The experimental group received pesticide while the control group did not.)
3. Which pesticide
   a. had no effect on the number of worms? (Z)
   b. reduced the number of worms? (X)
   c. did not reduce the number of worms but apparently kept them from reproducing? (Y)
4. In your opinion, which pesticide should the farmer use?
5. **Challenge:** Suppose the pesticide that harmed the worms the most was the cheapest or the most effective. Would this change your opinion about which pesticide to use? Write a short defense of your opinion.

## RELEASE OF SPECIMENS

Common earthworms can be dug back into the soil in the area from where they were collected. Aquatic worms such as seaworms and leeches can be returned back to their liquid homes.

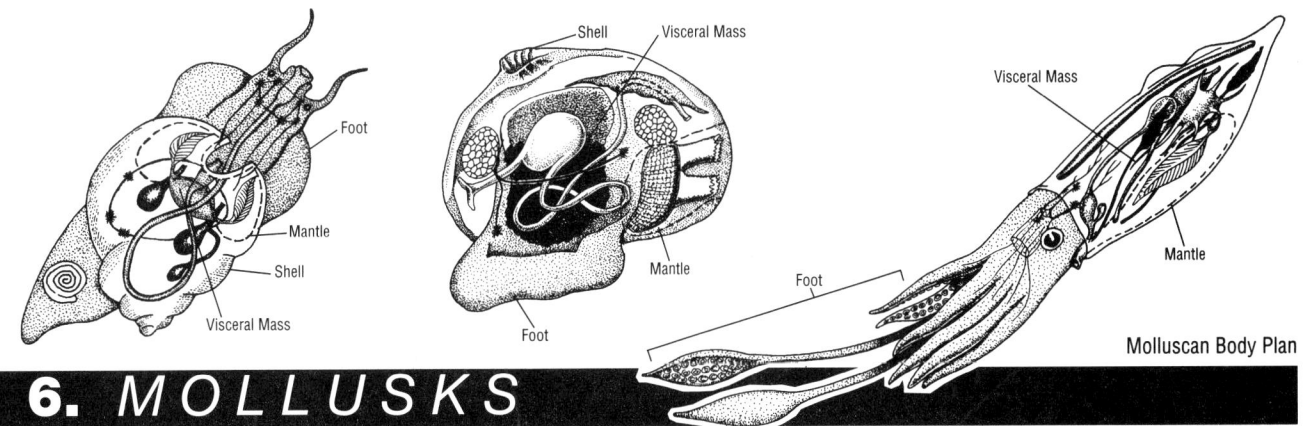

Molluscan Body Plan

# 6. MOLLUSKS

| | |
|---|---|
| **Kingdom:** | Animalia |
| **Subkingdom:** | Metazoa |
| **Phylum:** | Mollusca |
| **Classes:** | Gastropoda (snails and slugs) |
| | Bivalvia (clams, mussels, oysters, and scallops) |
| | Cephalopoda (squid, octopus, and nautilus) |

Mollusks have soft, fleshy unsegmented bodies (Latin—*mollis*, soft). Many types of mollusks protect their soft bodies by encasing themselves in hard, external shells of lime (calcium carbonate), which they secrete. There are at least 110,000 species of living mollusks, all adapted to many types of existence. Some creep about on land, some burrow into the bottom sediments of fresh and salt water, and others swim freely about the ocean actively pursuing prey.

Mollusks range in size from minute snails and clams, less than a millimeter (0.04 inch) in length, to the giant squid, which can reach 30 meters (100 feet) in length and is exceeded in size only by some of the larger whales.

Students are often confused when first encountering this group. They frequently ask how snails and clams—animals with external shells—can be classified in the same phylum with the squid and octopus—animals with no external shells but with arms and well-developed eyes. Actually, these creatures have many similarities that are not readily apparent. They all develop along similar lines, and their bodies consist of the same basic parts: foot, mantle, and visceral mass. In each mollusk group, however, the muscular foot takes on a different appearance and function: flat for crawling, spade-shaped for burrowing, and armlike for capturing prey. The mantle is a thin layer of delicate tissue that secretes the shell found around most mollusks or forms the muscular body of the squid and octopus. Beneath the mantle is the visceral mass of internal organs.

**Digestive System and Feeding.** All mollusks have a complete digestive system—mouth, stomach, intestine, digestive gland, and anus. However, there is considerable variety in the methods by which mollusks feed and the types of food they consume.

**Circulatory System.** Mollusks possess a simple but true heart that pumps blood throughout their body. Slow-moving or nonmoving mollusks are equipped with an open circulatory system in which the blood does not travel inside blood vessels at all times. The larger and faster-moving mollusks require a closed circulatory system in which the blood never leaves the blood vessels. The blood of some mollusks is clear; in others the presence of hemoglobin gives the blood a reddish appearance.

**Respiratory System.** Aquatic mollusks take oxygen from the water through well-developed gills. In land snails and slugs, the mantle cavity acts as a modified lung and allows them to extract oxygen from the air. The wrinkled lining of the mantle cavity must be kept moist in order to function properly. Consequently, most land snails and slugs live in damp places and are most active at night or during rainstorms.

**Muscle System.** Mollusks have well-developed muscle systems and are capable of very powerful yet finely coordinated movements.

**Excretory (Urinary) System.** Mollusks filter out liquid wastes with a simple kidney. Liquid wastes are released into the surrounding water in aquatic mollusks and into the mantle cavity of land mollusks.

**Brain and Nervous System.** The inactive, burrowing bivalves that lead sedentary lives have simple nervous systems with no true head and few sense organs. The crawling, gliding gastropods are only somewhat more advanced than the burrowers. The cephalopods are intelligent creatures with a large brain and well-developed sense organs. Extensive research on learning and visual perception in the octopus has shown it to be possibly the most intelligent of all the invertebrates.

**Reproduction and Development.** Except for the hermaphroditic land snails, mollusks are separate sexes. Male and female bivalves release great quantities of sperm and eggs into the water in hopes of accomplishing fertilization. The male gastropods internally fertilize the females, and the land snails pair up and fertilize each other's eggs. The cephalopods accomplish fertilization by means of a specialized arm on the male, which he uses to transfer sperm packets into the body of the female.

Taxonomists recognize seven classes of mollusks, but we will limit our discussion to the three most familiar and largest classes.

**Class Gastropoda.** This group has about 80,000 species, including snails, slugs, abalones, and conchs. Most gastropods are characterized by a thin, one-piece spiral shell. The slugs, however, have no shell or only the internal rudiments of a shell. Because the gastropods have a one-piece shell, they are sometimes referred to as univalves (*uni* = one and *valve* = shell).

The thin, membranous mantle secretes the gastropod's lime shell as well as a slime trail that smooths the way as the gastropod glides on ripples traveling the length of the muscular foot. The class name for this group literally means "stomach foot" and refers to the fact that the foot protrudes from the ventral (belly) side of the shell.

Gastropods are found on land in damp areas, in fresh water, and in the ocean. Most gastropods are rasping feeders that use a filelike "tongue" called a radula to scrape algae off rocks in the water or grind off tiny pieces of soft land plants. Some gastropods are predatory.

**Class Bivalvia.** This group has about 10,000 species including clams, mussels, oysters, and scallops. Like the gastropods, the bivalves possess a lime shell secreted by the mantle. As their class name suggests, they have two shells rather than one, and their shells tend to be thicker and heavier than those of the gastropods. Bivalve shells are hinged and are held together by large bands of muscle. The cup-shaped shells provide a perfect chamber of protection for the creature. Bivalves are soft and quite sensitive to irritation so to guarantee their comfort, they secrete a mucous material called mother-of-pearl that hardens and lines the inside of the shell. This material is hard and slick and has a beautiful luster. When a foreign particle or parasitic worm lodges inside the shell, the bivalve, to protect itself, covers the offender with layer after layer of the mother-of-pearl

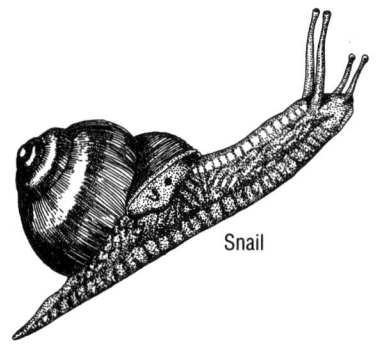

Snail

## Specific Class Characteristics

Clam

mucous. By this process a pearl is formed. Many kinds of bivalves produce pearls, but the most commercially desirable come from the marine "pearl oysters." Divers must collect about 1,000 oysters to find one valuable pearl.

Being encased in a rigid, heavy shell provides a great defense but severely restricts movement in bivalves. The clams move along slowly by contracting the large muscular foot extending out between the shells. Mussels seldom move, and oysters are permanently attached. Some scallops swim for short distances by rapidly clapping their shells together.

The arrangement of shells and lack of mobility also make food-getting a challenge for mollusks. Most solve this problem by being filter feeders. Burrowed into sediments or anchored to objects, they create a current with hairlike cilia on their gills. This current draws water into the mantle cavity through a specialized tube, the incurrent siphon. Food such as bacteria, algae, and organic particles are strained out on the gills and shuttled to the mouth. Oxygen is also removed by the gills. Wastes—carbon dioxide, feces, and urine—are dumped into the current as it exits through another tube called the excurrent siphon.

**Class Cephalopoda.** This group has about 600 species, including the octopus, squid, nautilus, cuttlefish, and giant squid. All cephalopods possess the molluscan characteristics of foot, mantle, and visceral mass, but only the nautilus maintains that most obvious of molluscan features, an external shell. Squid possess a thin, chitinous internal shell called a pen, and octopi have only the slightest trace of an internal shell.

The foot of the squid is formed into ten arms, or tentacles, with suckers. Two of the squid's arms are longer than the others and can shoot forward to grasp prey. The octopus has eight arms of equal length. The arms of both the squid and the octopus project from a well-defined head equipped with a large brain and elaborate eyes. In fact, the class name of this group literally means "head foot."

The mantle in the squid takes on the form of a conical muscular tube with two fins at one end and the head and arms at the other. The mantle of the octopus is round and baglike and lacks fins. Squid are able to swim like fish with their fins; the octopus seems to flow as it gracefully crawls along the bottom. Both the squid and the octopus can forcefully expel water from the mantle through a tubelike siphon beneath the head. This form of jet propulsion allows them to move quite rapidly to avoid predators or to pursue prey.

All cephalopods are agile, aggressive predators. The squid eats crustaceans and other mollusks by settling quietly to the bottom and covering them with its arms. It will also feed on fish that it seizes as they swim by. The octopus eats crustaceans, other mollusks, worms, and fish. In both the squid and the octopus, the prey is torn into pieces by the action of beaklike jaws at the base of the arms.

Although they lack shells, squid and octopi are far from defenseless. They can use the jet propulsion action of the siphon to rapidly flee, and both can release a cloud of inky material that may confuse a predator and hide their escape. Most cephalopods can change color to confuse a predator or camouflage themselves. The octopus can change color as well as surface texture to match its surroundings so completely that it becomes nearly invisible.

Since humans first ventured near the sea, mollusks of all types have been important food sources to us. An Indian shell mound at San Francisco Bay contained over one million cubic feet of shells and may have taken 3,500 years of eating to accumulate. The danger is that bivalves, due to their filter feeding, can accumulate high concentrations of disease-causing bacteria and viruses as well as pollutants and toxins. Eating contaminated mollusks can result in illness and possible death. Fish, birds, and mammals also depend on mollusks as an important part of their diet.

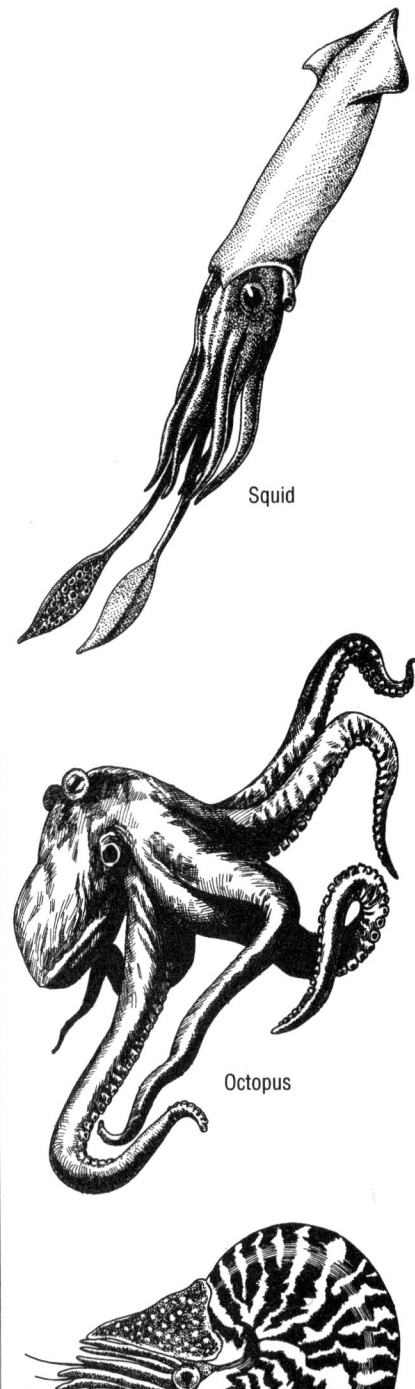

Squid

Octopus

Nautilus

The Importance of Mollusks

Some mollusks are quite destructive. The plant-eating land snails and slugs can cause great destruction in certain agricultural areas. A bivalve called the shipworm (often described as the "termite of the sea") burrows into wooden ships, docks, and pilings and costs millions of dollars in damage yearly.

The shells of mollusks are useful in a variety of ways. They can be ground and used to surface roads, and durable "pearl" buttons can be cut from them. The shell of the cuttlefish is used as a beak conditioner for caged birds. Since antiquity, some societies have used shells as money and decorations. The beautiful lumps called pearls formed by oysters are highly prized for their rarity and are displayed in jewelry.

Medical research into why snails and other mollusks never develop cancer may result in valuable insight into ways to battle this disease in humans.

## COLLECTION OF SPECIMENS

For practical reasons, I recommend that you collect land snails and/or aquatic snails for live mollusk activities. Collecting freshwater and saltwater bivalves such as clams and mussels is relatively easy, but long-term maintenance is difficult as they require large volumes of water with high plankton content. Furthermore, bivalves, being sedentary and encased totally in shells, do not lend themselves well to hands-on types of activities. Collecting cephalopods such as the squid and octopus is not practical, and maintaining them properly in the typical classroom setting would be extremely difficult, at best.

Aquatic snails are some of the easiest animals to collect and keep in captivity. Practically any permanent body of water or flowing stream will have an aquatic snail population. Aquatic snails can be collected by carefully sliding (not yanking) them off submerged vegetation or submerged objects. They often can be plucked directly from the shallow water along the margins of ponds. Place aquatic snails in a large container filled with water taken from the collection site, put a lid loosely on the container to prevent the snails from crawling out, and transport them to the classroom as soon as possible. Gather some mud/sand/sediment, small rocks, and waterlogged sticks from the collecting site in a separate container and bring them back to the classroom as well.

Various types of aquatic snails can be purchased at local pet shops or aquarium stores.

Land snails are not as widely distributed as aquatic snails. They are found primarily in forests and woodlands where moisture and humidity levels are high (although the desert snail survives even in the hostile environment of the Sahara Desert). Land snails are bagged easily on a rainy evening or early in the morning after a rain by searching under leaves, stones, or logs. As with aquatic snails, carefully slide the snail off whatever it is attached to. Place the snails in a container with damp soil and a few leaves taken from the collection site, loosely affix a lid to the container to prevent them from wandering out, and transport them to the classroom as soon as possible.

Aquatic snails and land snails can be purchased from the suppliers listed in Appendix B.

## MAINTENANCE OF SPECIMENS
### Aquatic Snails

Maintenance of aquatic snails is relatively simple. Place 8 to 10 centimeters (3 to 4 inches) of pond mud/sand/sediment in a glass or transparent plastic container. Add a few small rocks and several small waterlogged sticks. Fill the container about three-fourths full of pond water from the collecting site. Let the container stand for 24 to 48 hours to allow the water to clear. Pond snails are adapted to lower oxygen levels than stream snails, but if the water in your container is over 6 inches deep you may need to provide aeration regardless of which type of snail you collect. Now add the snails. Aquatic snails have gills inside their mantle cavity but may occasionally attempt to crawl out, so loosely cover the container—enough to prevent their escape but not so tightly as to restrict air exchange with the water.

Feed the snails small bits of lettuce or flakes of dried fish food periodically. Placing the container in a well-lit area will encourage the growth of algae, which the snails can eat.

Be careful about adding field-collected aquatic snails to established aquariums. The snails may harbor parasites or diseases that could be harmful to fish, and they will sometimes eat aquarium plants if they are hungry.

Although land snails are terrestrial and possess a modified lung inside their mantle cavity, they are susceptible to dessication (drying out). Consequently, high humidity and adequate moisture must be provided in order to maintain them. A properly designed terrarium will provide suitable quarters for land snails.

A terrarium can be set up in nearly any container, but an unused aquarium will give the best results. Cover the bottom of the container with an inch or so of gravel or pebbles. Add 2.5 to 5 centimeters (1 to 2 inches) of soil. Moisten both layers with clean pond water (tap water may contain chlorine and traces of metals) until they are thoroughly damp but not to the point where water stands in puddles on the surface. On the surface place a few stones, some dried leaves, and several dry sticks. Cover the terrarium with a glass or plastic plate. The plate helps maintain high humidity in the terrarium and prevents the snails from crawling out.

Keep the soil evenly moist by misting with water as needed. Feed the snails several times a week by adding lettuce leaves. They also will eat moistened, uncooked oatmeal from a shallow container. (Oatmeal molds easily, and having it in a dish allows easy removal of uneaten portions.)

Land snails need a source of calcium for healthy shell growth. Provide calcium by lightly sprinkling calcium carbonate powder periodically on their food.

Land snails may undergo periods of estivation (dormancy) when they crawl up the container, withdraw into their shells, and seal down with mucous that dries hard. They may appear dead, but they are not. To revive them, gently twist their shell back and forth until the hard seal breaks, mist or dampen them, and place them on the damp surface of the terrarium soil or directly on their food.

If you are collecting aquatic snails from ponds or streams, follow good safety procedures around water regardless of its apparent depth. When collecting either land snails or aquatic snails, be alert to possible contact with poisonous plants and biting or stinging animals.

Snails pose no health or safety problems for students. However, it is a good precaution to have students thoroughly wash their hands before and after handling snail containers, pond water, and/or snails.

Unlike some of their marine cousins, land snails and freshwater aquatic snails do not have thick, heavy shells. Their shells, being relatively thin and brittle, can be cracked and broken if the snails are dropped or squeezed too hard. Caution students to avoid handling the snails roughly. Instruct students to remove an attached snail by grasping the snail's shell and gently sliding the snail off the object.

All snails require moisture. Maintain aquatic snails in adequate amounts of clean pond water (preferably from the collection site) and land snails at the same level of dampness and humidity found in their natural habitat. Have students moisten their hands before handling a land snail. They can give the snail an occasional "bath" by dropping water on it.

Since snails are so familiar to students and so easy to collect and maintain, most of the hands-on activities in this chapter will deal with them.

Land snails are large enough that students should be able to see all their major structures with the unaided eye. Some pond snails, however, are small and students may need a magnifier to adequately view them.

## Land Snails

## HEALTH AND SAFETY
### Teachers
### Students

### Snails

## TEACHING ACTIVITIES

Some students like to observe land snails by letting the snails crawl on their hands. Other students may feel more comfortable observing land snails as they crawl around in a beaker. Students may view aquatic snails by placing several snails in a beaker of pond water and then observing them through the beaker.

## Habitat

**H1.** *Snail Habitat.* Have students respond to the question, What is the natural habitat of the snail? (Answer: Aquatic snails are found in practically any permanent body of water—ponds, lakes, and streams. Land snails are found primarily in forests and woodlands where moisture and humidity levels are high.)

**H2.** *Mollusk Habitat Comparisons.* Have students respond to the question, Where are other types of mollusks found? (Answer: Gastropod relatives of the land snail and freshwater aquatic snail such as sea snails, whelks, conchs, and slugs abound in the ocean. Bivalves inhabit both fresh and salt water, where they creep over the bottom, burrow into the bottom, or attach to solid objects. The cephalopods are found only in the ocean. The squid, cuttlefish, and nautilus are free swimming, and the octopus mainly creeps along the bottom.)

**H3.** *Mollusk Adaptations.* Each type of mollusk is uniquely adapted to survive in its natural habitat. Have students explain the survival benefits of each of the following molluscan adaptations:

a. Snails can withdraw completely into their shells. Many snails have a hard, permanent plate, called an operculum, used to cover the shell opening. Other types, lacking an operculum, seal the shell opening by secreting mucus, which dries and hardens. (Drying is a constant threat to snails, and these are adaptations to prevent it.)

b. Most bivalves burrow into bottom sediments or attach to submerged solid objects. From this stationary location, they quietly filter feed by flushing great quantities of water in and out of the body cavity. The scallop, however, can "swim" for short distances by rapidly clapping its shells together. (Scallops often move fast enough to avoid predators such as the slow-moving sea star.)

c. Squid travel forward by beating their fins and backward by jet propulsion. This forceful expulsion of water allows some squid to move through the water at speeds of 32 kilometers (20 miles) per hour and even to shoot 5.5 meters (18 feet) out of the water. (Such rapid movements and explosive speed would be a definite aid in escaping predators or capturing food.)

d. The octopus has the amazing ability to change not only its color but also the texture of its body. (By assuming the color and texture of the object it is resting on, the octopus totally camouflages itself from both its predators and its prey.)

e. Many slow-moving nudibranchs, or sea slugs, do not attempt to camouflage as the octopus does; rather, they display bright colors when threatened. (These nudibranchs contain chemicals in their body that taste bad or may be poisonous to predators. Some nudibranchs also use the nematocysts, or stinging cells, from the cnidarians they eat to sting intruders. The bright colors warn predators to stay away.)

**H4.** *Clam Calculations.* Some bivalves exist in tremendous numbers. At one time it was estimated that 4.5 million clams occupied 700 square miles of the Dogger Bank in the Atlantic Ocean east of England. Have students imagine they are individual clams on the Dogger Bank. Ask them to calculate how much space each can call his or her own.

a. 1 mile = 5,280 feet.

b. Square both sides of the equation: 1 square mile = 5,280$^2$.

c. 1 square mile = 27,878,400 square feet.

d. 700 square miles = 27,878,400 × 700.

e. 700 square miles = 19,514,880,000 square feet.

f. Divide the area—19,514,880,000—by the number of clams—4,500,000,000—to calculate how much space each individual clam would have.

g. Each clam has 4.34 square feet of territory.

**H5.** *Walk a Mile in My Shoes.* Have students try to put themselves in the mollusk's place by having them react orally or in written form to the following questions:

a. Would you rather be a land snail, freshwater clam, squid, or octopus, and why?

b. You are a camouflaged octopus resting on a pile of rocks minding your own business. Suddenly you are threatened by a very large predator. What would you do? (Students should suggest a variety of survival strategies such as squeezing down into cracks in the rock, rapidly fleeing by shooting water through the siphon, and/or releasing "ink" to confuse the predator and hide the octopus's escape.)

c. You are a type of bivalve called a pearl oyster. Your soft body is encased in two hard shells that are lined with a hard, smooth material you secreted from your mantle. However, a tiny grain of sand has gotten into your shell and has been "rubbing you the wrong way." What are you going to do about it? (Students will most likely suggest covering the sand grain with the mother-of-pearl mucous that lines the shell. In time the irritation would become a hard, round object we call a pearl and far less irritating to the oyster.)

   Cultured pearls are produced by forcing objects into oysters, placing the oysters on racks in protected areas, and then harvesting the oysters several years later to remove the pearl.

   The iridescence of pearls arises from the alternation of very thin layers of calcium carbonate and films of moisture. The owners of very valuable pearls are advised to wear them regularly so that the moisture of the wearer's skin will keep them hydrated. Otherwise they will gradually lose their luster.

d. You are a nautilus with a heavy coiled shell and many (80 to 90) sticky arms. Yet you are an active, swimming predator. How is this possible? (The nautilus carefully regulates the amounts of gas and liquid within chambers in its shell. By increasing or decreasing buoyancy, the nautilus can move freely despite the heavy shell.)

**H6.** *Mollusk Life Spans.* Have students predict which mollusks live the longest and have them estimate the life span of their selection. (The squid and octopus mature sexually within one to several years and then reproduce and die shortly after. The common garden snail can live up to 5 years. The nautilus reaches sexual maturity in 10 to 15 years and can live a considerable time after mating. However, the longest life span is enjoyed by the freshwater mussel, which can live to be over 30 years old.)

**S1.** *Snail Structure.* Have students diagram and label a land snail and its parts: shell, tentacles, eyespots, mouth, foot, mantle, anus, and respiratory pore (an opening to the modified lung).

**S2.** *Observe a Snail.* Have students observe a live snail as they answer the following questions and do the following activities:

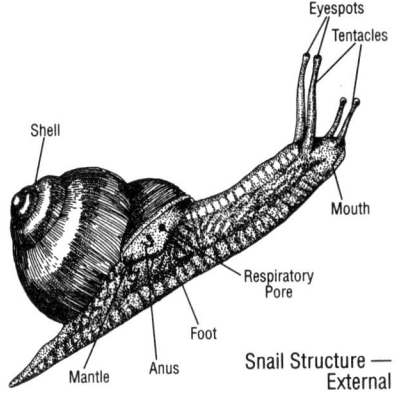

Snail Structure — External

Structure

a. Describe the shell of the snail and explain its origin. (Answer: A snail's shell is a hard, spiral structure composed of calcium carbonate, or lime, secreted by a fleshy band of tissue called the mantle.)

b. Are all of the snails' shells alike? Account for any differences. (Answer: The shells of the snails will differ by size, color pattern and subtle differences in shape. Students may speculate that these differences are caused by age, amount of moisture, temperature, mineral content of food, or other factors.)

c. Does the snail have a head? Do all mollusks have a head? (Snails and cephalopods such as the squid and octopus have heads but bivalves such as the clam and oyster do not.)

d. How long is the foot of the snail when it is fully extended? Have students use a ruler to measure the length of the foot as the snail crawls along.

e. How much does a snail weigh? Use appropriate weighing devices to determine the snail's weight.

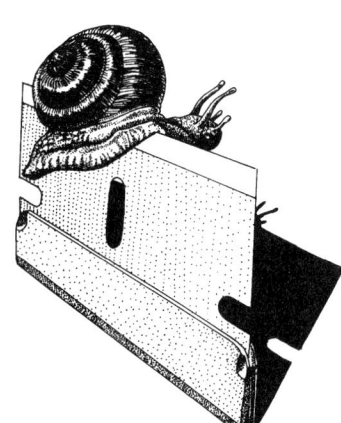

f. View the snail from the bottom as it crawls along a piece of glass or clear plastic and describe how the snail moves. (The snail glides along on a layer of mucous propelled by muscular ripples traveling the length of the foot.)

g. **Challenge:** Devise a test to determine if snails can crawl backward. (Snails cannot crawl backward. The ripples in the foot move in one direction only. To reverse directions, the snail must turn completely around.)

h. How can snails crawl uninjured over jagged and sharp surfaces? (The skin of the snail's foot is thick and tough. That feature and the mucous secreted by the snail make it possible for the snail to crawl uninjured on very jagged and sharp surfaces.)

    I demonstrate this for my students by taping single-edged razor blades with the sharp edge up all the way around a small block of wood. I then place a land snail inside this "Dungeon of Doom" and ask the students to predict what will happen. They are usually amazed as the snail crawls nonchalantly up, over, and even along the sharp edge of the razor blade without being harmed.

i. **Challenge:** Snails are reputed to be able to pull 200 times their own weight—the equivalent of a human pulling eight full-sized automobiles. Devise a method to determine how much weight a snail can pull.

    One method students may come up with is to tape a string around the snail's shell and then attach the string to a piece of paper. Weights may then be added to the paper to determine the snail's pulling ability.

    Have students compute a Pull Power Index by setting up a ratio comparing snail weight to weight pulled by the snail:

$$\frac{\text{weight pulled}}{\text{weight of snail}}$$

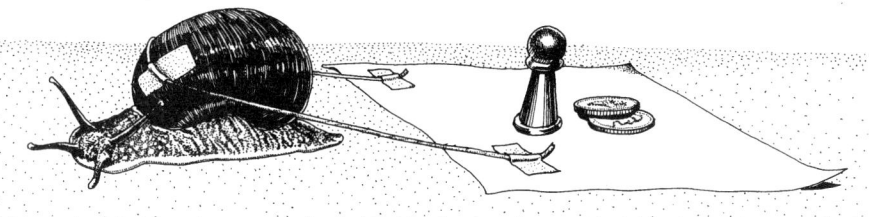

For example, a snail weighing 8.3 grams and pulling 330 grams would have a Pull Power Index of 39.76:

$$\frac{330}{8.3} = 39.76$$

Students will enjoy a class competition to determine whose snail has the highest Pull Power Index.

j. Someone moving slowly is said to be going "at a snail's pace." Determine what a snail's pace is.

Have students make a mark on any smooth, clean surface; time the snail for one minute; and then measure how far the snail traveled. Repeat three or four times, recording each distance in a data table, and then determine the average speed of the snail. The snail with the fastest average speed could win the "Speedy Snail" award.

In conjunction with this activity, we hold annual snail races at Mid-Mollusk Raceways. We use the average speed of each snail to set up tournament brackets. The fastest snail races the slowest snail, the next fastest races the next slowest, and so on. If you are not familiar with tournament bracketing, perhaps a coach at your school could help you. You can increase the interest level by asking students to give their snails imaginative names.

Our racetrack is a rectangular piece of glass 21.5 centimeters (8.5 inches) wide and 44 centimeters (17.75 inches) long marked with a starting line drawn about 7.5 centimeters (3 inches) from one end. Two competing snails are placed at the starting line, the glass is picked up and held in a near vertical position (snails love to crawl up), and the clock starts. Preliminary races last one minute, semifinal races last two minutes, and final races last three minutes. This activity is great fun; the other students in our school are interested each year to see who wins the snail races.

**S3.** *Clam Growth Graphs.* The famous freshwater mollusk expert, Dr. I. M. Clammy, has organized her data on freshwater clam growth into the following graphs. Analyze the graphs and answer the questions that follow:

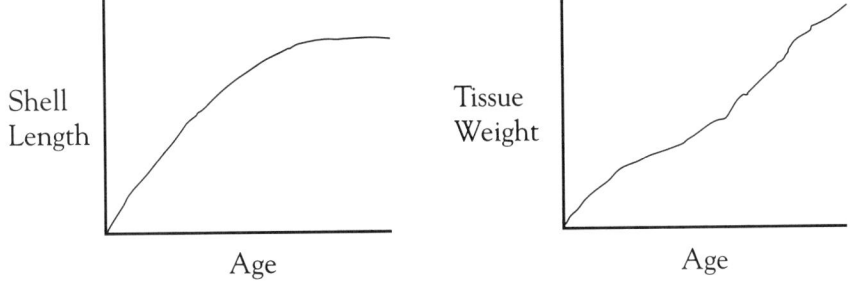

a. Does the shell of this particular type of freshwater clam continue to grow throughout its life?
b. Does the tissue (body) of this particular type of freshwater clam continue to grow throughout its life? (In some freshwater bivalves called unionids, shell length declines with increasing age while tissue weight continues to increase.)

**S4.** *Elusive Octopi.* The octopi are among the most elusive of animals. Lacking a shell, they can squeeze their bodies into and through remarkably small openings by lengthening the arms, flattening the body, and changing the shape of the head and the location of the eyes. Stories of this ability abound. For example, observers watched one octopus escape from a box with an opening no bigger than one of its arms. Ask your students to visualize humans trying to do that. Have them explain how this ability benefits the octopus. (The octopus can crawl into small cracks and openings in the rocks to search for food or avoid predators.)

**S5.** *Mollusk Models.* Have students construct a model of a snail, clam, octopus, and/or squid. Students might used colored modeling clay or colored bread dough (see the recipe in Chapter 3, activity S9).

## Behavior/Response

**B/R1.** *Gravity Response in the Snail.* Have students observe the response of the snail to gravity (geotaxis) by rolling the snail over so that its foot is on top. Have students describe how the snail responds. (Answer: The snail will twist and turn and eventually right itself.)

**B/R2.** *Touch Response in the Snail.* Are snails sensitive to touch (thigmotaxis)? If so, are all areas equally sensitive? Which areas seem negative or positive to touch? To find the answer, have students carefully touch various parts of the snail's body with a blunt probe. Ask them to describe how the snail responds and then draw appropriate conclusions.

**B/R3.** **Challenge:** *Do Snails Show Any Preference for Rough or Smooth Surfaces?* Have students devise a way to test this problem. This activity will allow students to further investigate thigmotaxis.

One design might be to measure how far snails travel over different textured surfaces in a fixed amount of time. Suggest that students place snails on dry glass or plastic, dry wood, dry sand, and dry soil. The students also could make note of any negative reactions by the snails to any of the textures. Avoid using materials caustic or possibly toxic to the snail. Before they begin, students should predict what they think will happen. Have students keep data in appropriate tables, charts, and graphs and draw conclusions from their data.

Once students have solved this problem, ask them to investigate the question, Will the snail show the same reactions to the various surfaces if the surfaces are damp? Follow the same procedure using damp glass or plastic, damp wood, damp sand, and damp soil. This variation would allow students to investigate hydrotaxis and perhaps chemotaxis.

**B/R4.** *Sense of Depth in Snails.* Do snails have a sense of depth? After students predict an answer to that question, have them place a snail several inches from the edge of a table and describe how the snail reacts when it approaches the edge. Have the students draw appropriate conclusions from their observations. (Snails usually will not crawl blindly off the table as the earthworm probably did in Chapter 5. The snails are much more aware and cautious. Even so, take precautions to prevent snails from falling to the floor. Such an accident could prove fatal to them.)

A logical progression of this activity is to have students predict whether the snails become even more cautious and hesitant at the edge of the table if they are forced to repeat the experience a number of times.

**B/R5.** **Challenge:** *How Do Snails Respond to Light?* Have students devise a way to test this problem. This activity allows students to investigate phototaxis, or response to light.

One design for aquatic snails is to purchase from a hardware store some clear plastic tubing of an appropriate size to hold pond snails. Put a stopper in one end and fill the tube about three-fourths full of clean pond water. Position the tube horizontally, and set up an appropriate light source (but not too close—we want to test response to light, not response to temperature). Allow the snails time to randomly disperse and then totally darken one-third of the tube, partially darken one-third of the tube, and leave the remaining one-third of the tube fully exposed to the light.

With land snails students could test phototaxis in at least two ways:

1. Construct a "spotlight" (see Chapter 5, activity B/R8) and shine the narrow beam of light on various parts of the snail's body while observing how the snail reacts.

2. Place the snails in a large glass or plastic tube or in a jar. Position the tube or jar horizontally and shade parts of it totally, partially, or not at all.

For all approaches, have students predict what will happen before they begin. Instruct them to keep data in appropriate tables, charts, or graphs and to draw conclusions from their data.

By using assorted colors of cellophane over the light, interested, older, or more advanced students could investigate the snail's response to various colors.

**F1.** *Snail Food.* Have students respond to the question, What do snails eat? (Answer: Snails eat tiny bits of algae or soft plant material. A few types of snails are carnivorous.)

**F2.** *Getting Snail Food.* Have students respond to the question, How do snails eat? (Answer: The common land and aquatic snails are rasping feeders. They use their filelike tongue, called a radula, to scrape off algae or tiny bits of soft plant material, which they then eat.)

**F3.** *Observe a Snail Feeding.* Have students observe and describe the actual feeding behavior of the snail. (To demonstrate feeding land snails, place the snails on a lettuce leaf. Students will be able to see and hear the snails feeding. Careful observation will show the action of the radula. If you set up your container for aquatic snails according to the directions given in "Maintenance of Specimens" in this chapter, algae will begin to grow on the sides of the container. Students should be able to see the feeding behavior of the snails as they rasp algae off the sides of the container.)

**F4.** **Challenge:** *Do Land Snails Show a Food Preference?* Have students devise a method to test this problem. Students might design a habitat in which land snails have equal access to a variety of food such as lettuce leaves, pieces of fruit, pieces of vegetables, and moistened rolled oats. Have students predict what they think will happen before they begin. They should keep data in appropriate tables, charts, and graphs and then draw conclusions from their data.

**F5.** *Mollusk Feeding Comparisons.* Have students compare and contrast the feeding of snails to the feeding of other mollusks. (The bivalves, such as the clam, oyster, and mussel, are filter feeders. They burrow in or attach and create currents using cilia. The currents carry water into a tube called the incurrent siphon and across the gills where algae, bacteria, and organic particles are strained out and moved to the mouth. The cephalopods such as the squid and octopus are active, aggressive predators that eat crustaceans, bivalves, fish, and worms. The prey is captured with the arms and crunched into bite-sized bits by the beaklike jaws at the base of the arms.)

**F6.** *The Deadly Cone Snail.* The cone snail is a burrowing carnivorous mollusk of the Indian and Pacific oceans. The sting of some species can be fatal to humans. Scramble the following information about the feeding behavior of the cone snail and have students put it into the proper sequence:

Step 1. The cone emerges in seconds from its burrow when it detects chemical signals from a fish.

## Feeding

## Reproduction and Development

Step 2. The fish touches the tip of a tube on the cone shell called the proboscis.

Step 3. The single hollow tooth on the proboscis is driven into the fish while injecting a paralyzing venom.

Step 4. The proboscis contracts, drawing the fish into the mouth.

**R1.** *Snail Reproduction.* Have students explain how snails reproduce. (Answer: Some snails are separate sexes, but land snails and a few freshwater aquatic snails are hermaphroditic; that is, they possess both male and female sex organs in the same body. Among the separate-sex snails, the male transfers sperm directly into the body of the female and fertilizes her eggs. In the hermaphroditic types, two snails transfer sperm to the body of the other so that they fertilize each other's eggs. The eggs are laid in gelatinous clumps on objects in the water or hidden in damp places on land.)

**R2.** *Mollusk Reproductive Comparisons.* Have students compare and contrast the reproduction of snails with other mollusks. (Answer: In bivalves the sexes are separate. The sperm of freshwater bivales are shed into the water by the male. They enter the shell of the female through her siphon and fertilize her eggs. The eggs develop into larvae inside the female and are then expelled. In marine bivalves both the sperm and the eggs are usually shed into the water, where fertilization takes place. This is a haphazard method of fertilization so, to ensure success, vast numbers of eggs are released—up to 60 million from one female.

The cephalopods are also separate sexes. The male squid and octopus transfer packets of sperm directly into the body of the female using one of their arms specialized for this purpose. Female squid deposit the gelatinous egg capsule on the ocean bottom, often anchoring it into the sand. Squids mate by the thousands in a frenzied reproductive free-for-all [males may be so intent that they will not release females being eaten by sharks and are themselves devoured], and in a short time large areas of the ocean floor are covered with squid eggs. Soon after both the male and female squid die, their bodies littering the ocean floor three to four feet thick. The female octopus hides her eggs in hollows in the rocks and guards them. The female octopus dies about ten days after the eggs hatch, and the male octopus dies about seven months after reaching sexual maturity.)

**R3.** *Reproduce and Die.* Until recently no one knew why the female octopus dies so soon after mating. A researcher has discovered a likely explanation. The octopus literally self-destructs. When triggered by the reproductive cycle, a pair of glands begins to secrete a hormone that speeds up the aging process and inhibits feeding in both male and female octopi.

Have students suggest a method to test this researcher's theory and speculate about why the octopus carries the seeds of its own destruction. (When the self-destruct glands are surgically removed, the octopus lives longer than usual. Biologists speculate that the glands serve as a method of population control.)

**R4.** *Observe Snail Eggs.* Have students observe the development of snail eggs. Aquatic snails will lay egg masses on the side of the container you are keeping them in. Students can view the developing eggs through the container using a hand magnifier. For a closer view, suspend small glass plates or microscope slides in the water. If the snails cooperate and lay eggs on the glass plates or slides, they can be removed and viewed through a microscope. Remember to keep the egg mass constantly damp while viewing.

Land snails will occasionally lay eggs in the damp soil of a terrarium. The eggs usually are hidden under leaf litter or in a burrow. Carefully overturning leaves and litter may reveal eggs that students can observe.

**In1.** *Writing:*

a. Destroy the devilfish! Kill the kraken! The scene is sometime in the future. A loud and powerful group is trying to convince the Oceanic Control Council to hunt down and totally destroy the deadly and monstrous devilfish and kraken. Have students imagine that they are the famous animal defense attorney, I.M.A. Legaleagle, and have them prepare a defense of these creatures. (The cephalopods have been one of the most maligned and misunderstood groups of animals that have ever existed. Mainly because of their appearance and the highly active imagination of humans, the octopus was often referred to as the devilfish and the giant squid as the kraken. This misrepresentation of the true nature of these animals continues today. Contrary to legend, the giant squid does not drag entire ships and their crews to a watery doom, and bikini-clad beauties are not plucked off surfboards by the octopus except in the minds of movie script writers.)

b. Have students write a short story or play entitled, "A Day in the Life of a Mollusk." Have them choose which mollusk they wish to write about.

c. Have students write a research report on the mollusk of their choice.

**In2.** *Fine Arts:*

a. Have students paint or draw a picture of any mollusk and its habitat.

b. Honk your conch! If large mollusk shells are available, saw or file off the tip of the spiral, make a trumpeter's lip, and blow away! With practice you and your students should be able to produce as sonorous and mournful a sound as any Polynesian, famed for playing the conch trumpet. By varying the size of the shells (and with a little help from the music teacher), you may be able to hold a conch concert.

c. The octopus can regenerate lost arms. Have students draw a cartoon depicting the temporary difficulties an octopus would face after its arms were eaten off by a moray eel.

**In3.** *Social Studies:*

a. *History.* Our relationship with mollusks has been a long one. Have students prepare a chart with two columns. In one column list all the positive aspects of the human-mollusk relationship. In the other column list the negative aspects of this relationship. (For positive aspects, see "The Importance of Mollusks" section in this chapter. On the negative side, the bite of the blue-ringed octopus and the sting of the cone snail both can be potentially fatal. Bivalves contaminated with bacteria, viruses, toxins, or pollutants can cause illness or possibly death if eaten by humans. Some types of snails serve as a major vector of parasitic worms that cause severe and possibly fatal infections in humans. The shipworm destroys millions of dollars' worth of wooden ships, docks, and pilings yearly. Land snails and slugs destroy great amounts of crops and produce annually. On the human side of the ledger, development of coastal areas, dumping of chemicals and wastes into the water, and overfishing has decimated the population of many mollusks [especially bivalves] worldwide.)

b. *Geography.* Little is known about the giant squid. They are often called kraken after a legendary Norse monster. Where does this strange creature roam? During the late 1800s Newfoundland was a hotbed of giant squid sightings; today there are still twenty times more sightings there than anywhere else. Over the years dozens of giant squid have been sighted in the Florida Strait and in Bahamian waters. An 18-meter (57-foot) specimen once washed up on the beaches of New Zealand. Expeditions are being planned to capture or film live giant squid. A likely place to look, some squid experts believe, is off the Azores (off the coast of Portugal) when sperm whales are migrating past the islands. Deep-diving sperm whales feed on the giant squid. The largest giant squid ever reliably recorded was a 20-meter (65-foot) monster taken from the stomach of a sperm whale. Experts speculate that giant squid 22 meters (73 feet) or more in length and weighing more than 1800 kilograms (two tons) may exist.

Have students use an atlas or globe to locate the areas of giant squid activity and then mark the areas on a blank world map. Ask them to determine if any patterns seem to appear in the locations of giant squid sightings or activity.

**In4.** *Societal/Environmental Issues:*

a. A great deal of research has been done on the intelligence of the octopus and the workings of its well-developed eyes. Have students speculate orally or in writing about the purpose of such research and the benefits humans may derive from it. (The more we learn about the workings of the brains and eyes of the octopus, the better we understand the workings of our own brain and eyes.)

b. The European garden snail (Helix aspersa) has been introduced onto the North American continent and has come to be known as "the curse of California." Have students speculate about why this snail is considered a curse. (Freed of its natural predators and parasites, the snail has had a population explosion. In addition, it feeds on great quantities of soft plant material. In short, this snail is a destructive agricultural pest in farms and gardens.

This may be an appropriate time to discuss the environmental devastation caused around the world by introduced plants and animals.

## RELEASE OF SPECIMENS

Aquatic and land snails collected locally may be released back into the pond or woodlands where they were collected. If you purchased snails, do not release them unless the supplier can guarantee the snails shipped are native to your area. Remember: *Any* organism not native to an area has the potential to severely disrupt the environmental balance of that area.

The safest method of releasing purchased snails is to give them to the students. I usually have more students who want a land snail than I have snails, so we have a drawing. Students who win snails must bring a parent permission slip and a suitable container from home (a gallon jar with a lid works best). We set up a small terrarium by placing about one inch of gravel in the bottom of the jar and then covering that with about two inches of moist soil. We add a few dried leaves, a dried stick or two, and the snail(s). After poking a few small holes in the lid and giving the student a sheet of care instructions, I release the snail. Students have reported that their snails lived for several years in such containers.

Students can take aquatic snails home by placing some pond mud/sand in the bottom of a container and filling it about three-fourths full of pond water. Affix a lid tightly to the container so no water spills on the way home. Send with the student a sheet of instructions on how to care for aquatic snails. Instruct the student to remove the lid on arriving home and to put the container in a well-lit area.

I have found this snail adoption plan to be an excellent way of extending classroom knowledge and activities into the home.

# 7. ARTHROPODS

**Kingdom:** Animalia
**Subkingdom:** Metazoa
**Phylum:** Arthropoda
**Classes:** Arachnida (spiders, scorpions, and mites)
Chilopoda (centipedes)
Diplopoda (millipedes)
Crustacea (crabs, crayfish, lobster, shrimp, and pill bug)
Insecta (insects)

## DIVERSITY AND DISTRIBUTION

In terms of sheer numbers and mass, arthropods are the most biologically successful animals on the earth. Of the 1 to 2 million known species of animals, at least three out of four are arthropods. More than 900,000 species of arthropods have been described, but taxonomists estimate there may be millions more awaiting discovery. On one tree in the Amazon rain forest biologists identified over 2,000 different species of insects. Their numbers stagger the imagination.

Arthropods occur at altitudes of over 6,000 meters (20,000 feet) on mountainsides and at depths of over 9,000 meters (30,000 feet) in the ocean. They are adapted for life in the air; on land; in soil; and in fresh, brackish, or salt water. Some are adapted to a parasitic existence on plants or on and in the bodies of other animals. Most are solitary creatures, but some insects have developed complex social organizations.

## General Phylum Characteristics

Arthropods display a wide range of forms, but they all exhibit several key features: a tough, plasticlike exoskeleton; a segmented body; and jointed appendages (Greek—*arthros*, joint + *podos*, foot).

**Digestive System and Feeding.** Arthropods have well-developed feeding appendages that allow them to eat almost any food. Depending on the species, they are herbivores, carnivores, external and internal parasites, filter feeders, and scavengers.

**Circulatory System.** A well-developed heart pumps blood through an open circulatory system. As the blood enters the tissues in small vessels, it leaves the vessels and bathes the tissues. Eventually, the blood collects in large cavities surrounding the heart, from which it reenters the heart through small openings. The blood of many arthropods is clear and in others is faintly tinted various colors by certain respiratory pigments.

**Respiratory System.** Depending on the species, arthropods exhibit three basic types of respiratory structures: gills, book lungs, and tracheal tubes.

Aquatic arthropods such as the crab and crayfish have feathery gills under the cover of their exoskeleton. By moving their mouthparts and other appendages, they keep a steady flow of water moving over the gills.

Many spiders have a unique system of leaflike plates called book lungs within a chamber. Air is drawn into and out of the chamber.

Most terrestrial arthropods such as insects and millipedes have a system of air tubes called tracheae throughout the body. The air enters through openings along the side of the animal and, as the arthropod moves, body muscles expand and shrink the tracheal tubes, moving air around the body.

The inefficiency of their respiratory system tends to limit the size of arthropods compared to vertebrates.

**Muscle System.** Arthropod muscles are both varied and versatile. The muscles are attached to the exoskeleton and pull against it. At each body joint, muscles are positioned to flex the joint back and forth, allowing arthropods to fly, swim, and walk.

**Skeletal System.** All arthropods are covered by a hardened exoskeleton that is secreted from within by an inner layer called the epidermis. The exoskeleton is composed primarily of a protein called chitin and is both tough and flexible. It provides support and protection without sacrificing mobility.

One drawback of the exoskeleton is that it is not living material and consequently does not grow as the animal inside does. The exoskeleton must be periodically cast off and a new one formed through a process called molting. Molting is controlled by hormones in the arthropod.

**Excretory System.** The terrestrial arthropods, such as spiders and insects, collect waste fluids in projections called Malpighian tubules along the digestive tract.

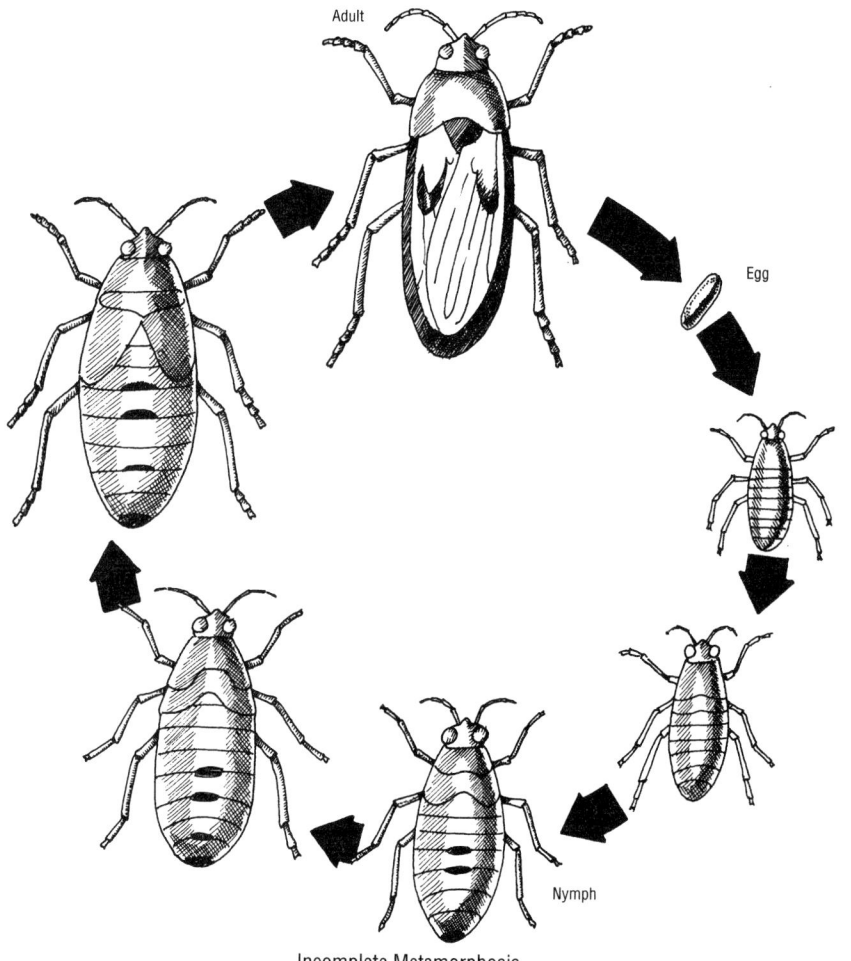

Incomplete Metamorphosis

These waste fluids are dumped into the digestive tract and eliminated through the anus. In aquatic arthropods, wastes diffuse out into the surrounding water from the body through uncovered areas such as the gills. Some aquatic arthropods, such as the lobster and crayfish, also eliminate waste fluid through a pair of green glands located at the base of their antennae.

**Brain and Nervous System.** Arthropods have complex nervous systems with well-developed brains located in a definite head. Strangely, a great deal of nervous control in arthropods lies in large nerve cords outside the brain and within the body so that many functions such as eating and moving can be carried out even after the brain has been removed.

All arthropods have at least some sense organs such as chemical and balance receptors. Crustaceans, insects, and some others have highly developed senses of sight, taste, touch, and sensitivity to air and water movement. The large compound eyes of insects may contain thousands of individual optical units and can detect color and motion extremely well. Insects can detect things such as ultraviolet light and other stimuli that human senses cannot perceive at all.

**Reproduction and Development.** Arthropods are separate sexes. In most species fertilization of the eggs is accomplished by the male transferring sperm directly into the body of the female. In spiders and some crustaceans, however, the male deposits a small packet of sperm that the female picks up.

The eggs of some freshwater crustaceans, arachnids, centipedes, millipedes, and some insects undergo direct development through incomplete metamorphosis. That is, the young hatch out looking like miniature adults.

The eggs of many insects such as bees, butterflies, moths, and beetles develop indirectly; that is, the hatched young bear no resemblance to the adults. The young pass through several stages of change called complete metamorphosis on their way to adulthood. Each stage may be marked by startling and dramatic changes in structure and appearance.

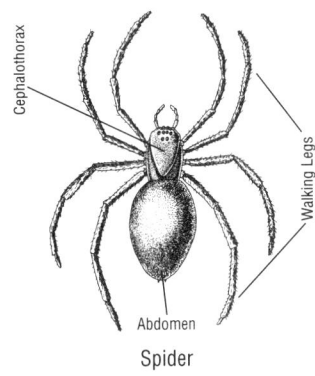

Spider

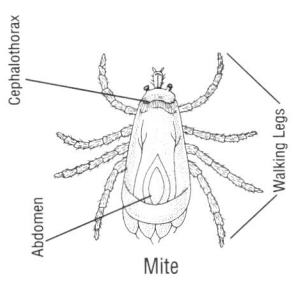

Mite

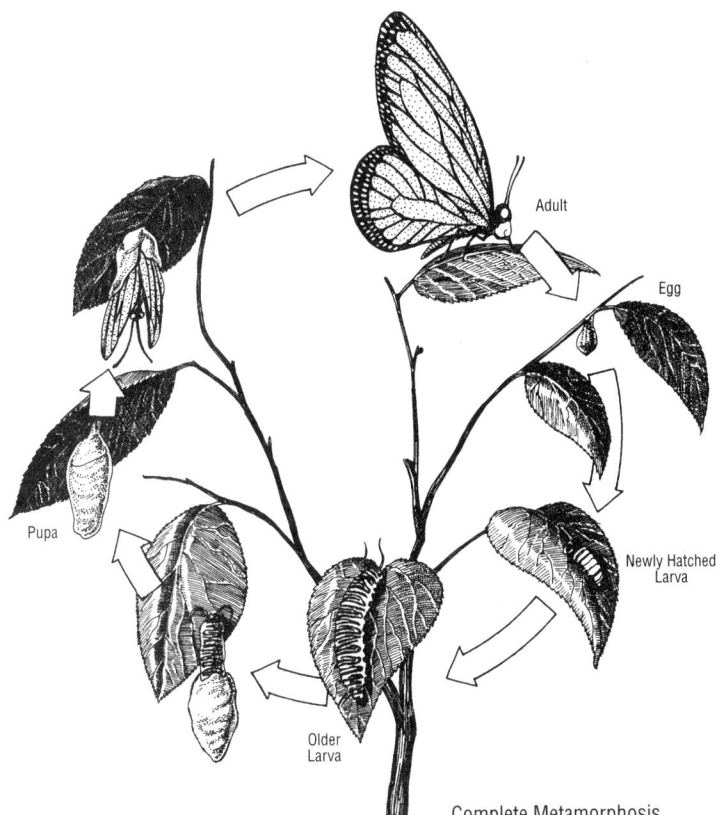

Complete Metamorphosis

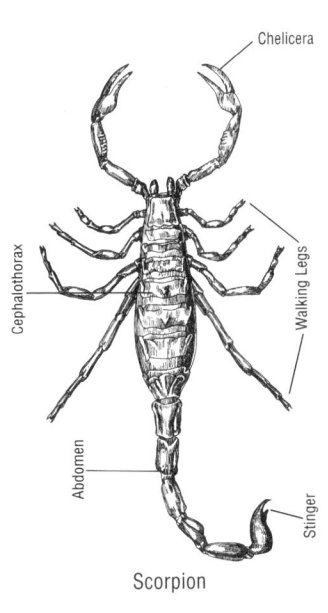

Scorpion

# Specific Class Characteristics

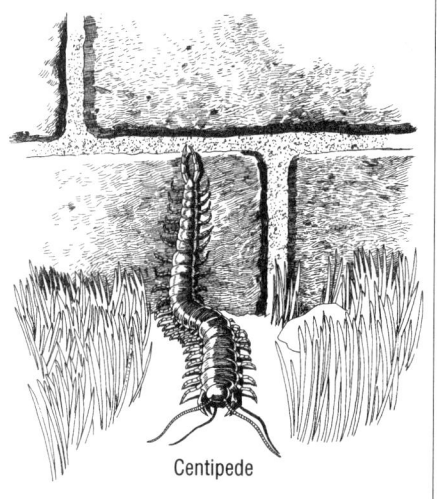

Centipede

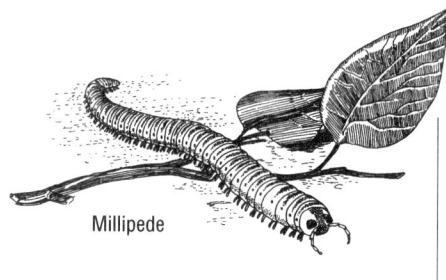

Millipede

Lobster

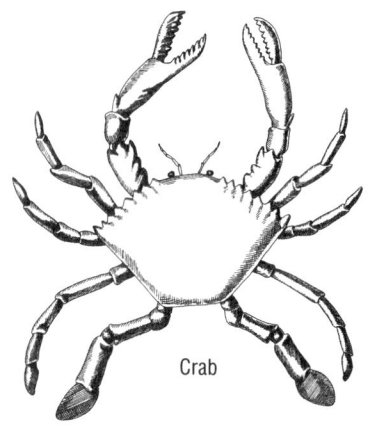

Crab

**Class Arachnida.** This group has about 70,000 species, including spiders, scorpions, and mites. The arachnid body is divided into two segments: chephalothorax and abdomen. The cephalothorax represents a fusion of the head and thorax (trunk). Attached to the cephalothorax are four pairs of legs, a pair of appendages called cheliceras in the form of pinchers or fangs, and a pair of leg-like pedipalps around the mouth.

Spiders range in size from less than 0.5 millimeters (0.02 inches) to 9 centimeters (3.6 inches) in the case of some tarantulas. Spiders are predators, mainly of insects. Depending on the species, some spiders chase their prey, some snare their prey in webs, and others capture their prey by leaping out from burrows in the ground equipped with a trap door. Most spiders are found on land, but one species makes it home in fresh water.

Scorpions are widespread in tropical and semitropical areas, dry temperate areas, and desert regions. Scorpions have a more elongated body than spiders and mites, and their pedipalps are enlarged into pinchers. All scorpions are predators. They grab their prey with their pinchers and inject a paralyzing or lethal poison with an arching thrust of their abdomen. Adult scorpions range in size from 1 to 18 centimeters (0.4 to 7 inches).

Mites range in size from 1 millimeter (0.04 inch) to as large as 3 centimeters (1.2 inches). Ticks are considered to be large parasitic mites. All mites are fluid feeders and use a sucking pharynx to injest animal or plant tissue fluids. Most mites are terrestrial, but 4,000 or so species live in fresh water and a few species live in the ocean.

**Class Chilopoda.** This group has about 2,800 species known as centipedes. Centipedes have long bodies with many segments. On the first segment is a pair of hooked fangs for injecting poison into prey. Centipedes are predators that feed mainly on earthworms and insects. The name *centipede* suggests an animal with a hundred legs, but centipede may have anywhere from 15 to 175 pairs of legs, with one pair per body segment. Centipedes are land dwellers and take shelter beneath rocks, logs, and leaves.

**Class Diplopoda.** This group has about 8,000 species known as millipedes. Although the word *millipede* literally means "thousand legs," most have around 50 pairs of legs, with the record being 376 pairs of legs. Like centipedes, millipedes have long, segmented bodies. Unlike centipedes, they have two pairs of legs attached to each segment. Most millipedes are herbivores, but a few types are predatory. For convenience rather than taxonomic purposes, the centipedes and millipedes are often referred to as the myriapods ("many legs").

**Class Crustacea.** This group has about 35,000 species, including the crayfish, lobster, shrimp, crab, and isopods. The crustacean body is divided into two main areas: cephalothorax and abdomen. Crustaceans differ on the proportions of the two areas. The lobster, crayfish, and shrimp have an elongated cephalothorax and abdomen, and the crab has a rounded cephalothorax with the abdomen tucked up underneath it.

Most crustaceans have two pairs of antennae and three pairs of chewing appendages. There are various numbers of pairs of legs in the crustacean group, but the most familiar crustaceans (crayfish, lobster, shrimp, and crab) have five pairs of legs, including the pincherlike chelipeds.

Crustaceans are so abundant in freshwater and marine environments that they are often called "the insects of the water." Some lakes and areas of the ocean may contain so many thousand per cubic meter that they tint the water with the collective coloration of their bodies. Some types of crustaceans, such as certain crabs and isopods, are terrestrial.

Crustaceans range in size from microscopic water fleas about 0.25 millimeters (0.01 inches) long to the Japanese spider crabs that may grow up to 6 meters (20 feet) across and lobsters that may have a mass of 20 kilograms (45 pounds).

**Class Insecta.** This group has about 800,000 identified species, and the number continues to increase as thousands more are identified each year. In fact, some entomologists believe there may be as many as 10 million insect species. There are approximately 25 orders of insects (depending on which expert you consult), including such examples as termites, ants, bees, beetles, dragonflies, butterflies, moths, flies, grasshoppers, and crickets.

Even though insects vary widely in color, shape, and appearance, they all have certain body characteristics in common: a three-part body consisting of a head, thorax, and abdomen; three pairs of legs attached to the thorax; and one pair of antennae and compound eyes on the head. Some insects have developed into the only aerial arthropods and possess the ability to fly. Flies and some other insects have only one pair of wings, and the butterflies, bees, wasps, and dragonflies have two pairs of wings. Moths have large, easily seen wings, but in beetles hard, outer forewings called elytra cover the thin, nearly transparent inner flight wings. You can demonstrate this by separating the wings of a dead adult beetle.

The wings of insects are flattened extensions of the body wall and are far superior to human-made machines in many respects. An insect can hover like a helicopter, then suddenly start away in any direction, stop equally fast, catch other insects in flight, mate in the air, and maintain a steady relationship to another moving object. The flight muscles of an insect are attached not to the wings but to the inside of the exoskeleton. As opposing muscles contract, changes in the shape of the thorax flip the wings up and down with impressive speed. Bees and wasps fly at 200 beats per second, mosquitoes top 600 beats per second, and midges reach 1,000 beats per second.

Insects are inconceivably abundant (about 200 million living insects are alive at any one time for each human), and they have adapted to every possible habitat on land and in fresh water. Only a few have invaded the ocean, and none are found at the greatest depths of the ocean.

The smallest insect is the "fairyfly," about 0.21 millimeters (0.008 inches) long. The largest insects tend to be found in tropical areas and include some moths with wingspans of 28 centimeters (11 inches), walking sticks nearly 30 centimeters (12 inches) long, and massive beetles nearly as large as a person's hand.

**Arachnids.** The bite of most spiders is harmless to humans, although the brown recluse and black widow spiders do possess potentially serious poisons. In general, spiders are beneficial predators of many insect pests.

Only spiders can produce the lightweight but tough material called spider's silk from special glands in their bodies called spinnerets. Biologists are attempting to genetically engineer bacteria to produce this remarkable material for potential use in bulletproof vests, tents, sleeping bags, and clothing.

Like spiders, some scorpions have powerful poisons in their sting; the Mexican scorpions are more dangerous than those of the southwestern United States. Scorpions are beneficial predators of insects and small rodents.

Mites can cause serious damage to agricultural crops. They also infest domestic livestock with problems such as mange and scabies and poultry with skin and feather diseases. They infect humans with Rocky Mountain spotted fever, Lyme disease, encephalitis, tularemia, and dust allergies. Mites can be beneficial in controlling mold or grain-eating insects on stored grain, and they help break down organic material on the forest floor.

Viceroy Butterfly

Bumblebee

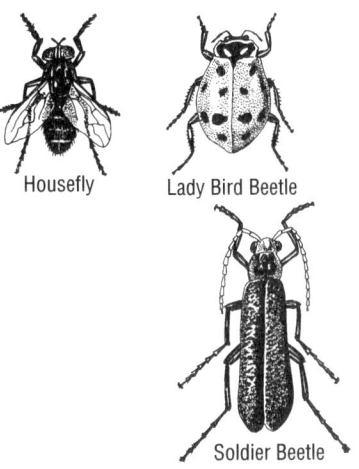
Housefly Lady Bird Beetle
Soldier Beetle

## The Importance of Arthropods

Grasshopper

**Crustaceans.** The aquatic crustaceans such as the crayfish, lobster, crab, and shrimp are highly prized for food. Great quantities of them are eaten every year by humans, fish, octopi, birds, and mammals. Chitin extracted from crustacean exoskeletons is used for contact lenses, fertilizer, poultry food, artificial skin, and wound dressings.

**Insects.** Every human on this planet is affected in some way by insects. Agriculture would be impossible without bees, butterflies, wasps, moths, and flies that pollinate crops, and insects serve as major food sources for fish, amphibians, reptiles, birds, and mammals including humans—yet insects eat or otherwise ruin billions of dollars worth of crops and foodstuffs every year. Scavenger beetles and some other insects decompose organic matter into the soil—yet termites eat away our homes and buildings. Live maggots are used on wounds to clean out dead tissue and promote healing—yet insects serve as vectors (carriers) of numerous human diseases such as malaria, sleeping sickness, filariasis, typhus, yellow fever, and plague.

## COLLECTION OF SPECIMENS

### Arachnids

Spiders are relatively easy to collect. Catch them in open fields in the fall or spring or from your own home or classroom any time of year by gently coaxing them into a jar with holes punched in the lid.

Live arachnids, including tarantula spiders and scorpions, can be purchased from some of the suppliers listed in Appendix B. Give careful consideration to possible health and safety problems when collecting or purchasing potentially poisonous arachnids.

### Myriapods

Centipedes and millipedes can be collected in their natural habitat by gently lifting or rolling logs or rocks. Scoop them up with a plastic spoon and place them in a jar containing some soil and leaf litter and with holes punched in the lid. Collect additional soil and leaf litter as well as some pieces of bark and small rocks from the site. These can be used to establish a myriapod habitat when you get the centipedes and millipedes back to the classroom. Live centipedes and millipedes can be purchased from the suppliers listed in Appendix B.

### Crustaceans

Crayfish, also known as crawfish, crawdads, or mudbugs, are found in almost every imaginable aquatic environment throughout the United States and in southern Canada. Crayfish hide under objects, especially rocks. Collect them by slowly overturning rocks and netting the crayfish as they attempt to escape. Another way to collect them is to draw a net through the muddy bottom and among the plants in shallow water.

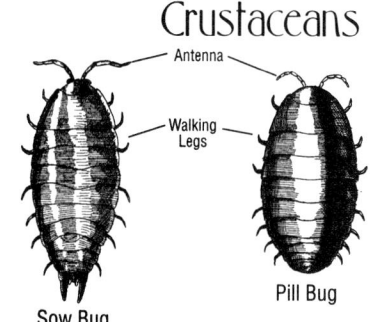

Sow Bug          Pill Bug

Another fun way of collecting crayfish is to try fishing for them. Dangle a piece of meat or liver on a string into suitable crayfish habitat. No hook is needed as the crayfish will grasp the bait and hold on. Lift them from the water and transfer them to a collecting pail with 15-20 centimeters (6-8 inches) of clean pond water in it. Note: Crayfish are protected in some areas, so check with the proper wildlife authorities in your area (listed in Appendix C) before collecting.

Terrestrial crustaceans, called isopods, or more commonly pillbugs, sowbugs, or wood lice, can be collected from under rocks, logs, boards, or bricks. Scoop up the isopods with a plastic spoon and place them in a jar containing some soil and leaves for them to hide under. Punch holes in the jar's lid. Isopods also can be collected in a potato trap like the one shown here.

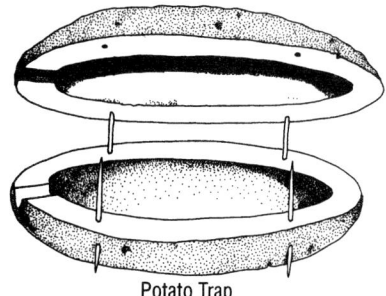

Potato Trap

### Insects

Live crayfish and isopods can be purchased from the suppliers listed in Appendix B.

Insects are so numerous that you will have no problem finding some types to collect. For health and safety reasons, do not collect stinging or bloodsucking insects such as wasps, bees, and mosquitoes. Avoid insects such as roaches and termites that can become serious pests if they escape in the classroom as well as insects that have space and/or food requirements that make them difficult to maintain in the classroom.

The insects recommended in this book for collection and maintenance are easily collected or obtained, easily maintained, and suitable for observation and hands-on activities.

**Ants.** Ants are quite common and easy to collect. Try one of these methods: (1) Bait a glass jar with paper soaked in syrup or spread with fruit jam. Lay the jar on its side near an ant mound and darken the jar by draping a cloth over it. (2) Place a rag on top the mound and, when the ants have crawled onto the rag, shake them off into a container. (3) Use an aspirator (see the illustration).

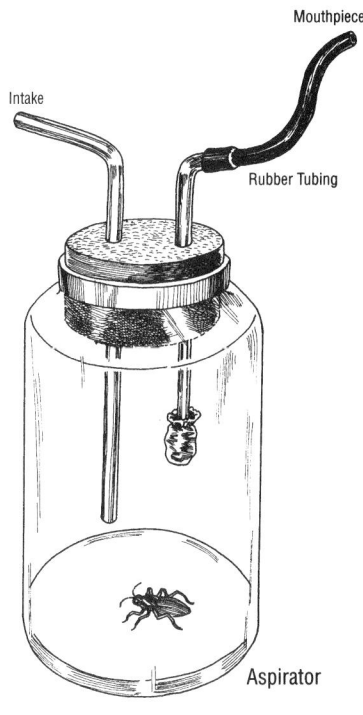

Aspirator

Worker ants without a queen will establish a short-term colony and even lay eggs (but all the offspring will be males). To establish a more permanent colony a queen must be captured. You may be able to find young queens under stones or logs in the spring or fall after they swarm from the nest. Most likely you will have to dig up an ant mound to get them. If you dig, carefully collect some workers beforehand using a baited trap, rag, or aspirator. As you dig, carefully collect some larvae and eggs by scooping them up with a plastic spoon. The queen will resemble the workers but will be considerably larger. Place workers, larvae, eggs, and queen along with some soil from the mound in a large container with a secure lid. Replace earth back on the mound carefully. Other queens may be in the nest and the colony may be able to reorganize.

Before transferring the ants to their classroom nest, place them in the refrigerator for a short time. The cooler temperature will quiet them and make them easy to handle.

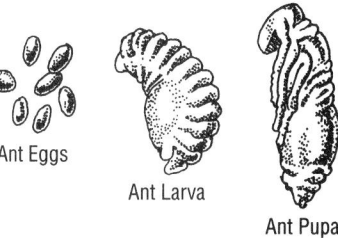

Ant Eggs      Ant Larva      Ant Pupa

Worker ants only may be purchased from the suppliers listed in Appendix B. Shipment of ants to some states may require a Department of Agriculture permit. Contact suppliers for details.

**Butterflies and Moths (Lepidopterans).** Having bizarre-looking caterpillars and brightly colored adult butterflies and moths in the classroom will certainly grab students' attention. However, properly maintaining these creatures presents some challenges, which will be discussed in the "Maintenance of Specimens" section of this chapter.

If you wish to observe the development of beautiful butterflies or moths as they change from caterpillar to adult, the easiest and most reliable method is to order one of the numerous butterfly/moth rearing kits sold by the suppliers listed in Appendix B. These kits provide containers, food, caterpillars, and complete instructions for rearing the insects.

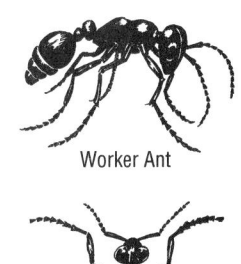

Worker Ant

If you wish to maintain an ongoing culture of some type of lepidopteran in the classroom, I recommend the greater wax moth. You may be able to obtain the larvae from fish bait shops, where they are called wax worms. These moths are also known as bee moths because they are pests on honey bee combs. Beekeepers may be able to supply you with some specimens. Wax moths and their food may be ordered from the suppliers listed in Appendix B.

You can also collect insects for observation without having to actually bring them into the classroom. Find a branch containing some feeding caterpillars. Wrap a muslin bag or other suitable covering around the branch and securely fasten each end of the bag. When the leaves are eaten, move the insects and bag to a fresh branch. With this method, students can watch the feeding and development of the insects without the problems of housing and maintaining them in the classroom.

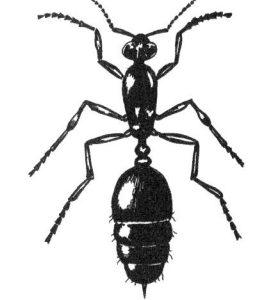

Wingless Queen Ant

**Cockroaches.** Do not collect common roaches as they can get loose and become serious pests in the classroom. Instead, I recommend the Madagascar hissing roach. These large but docile insects are ideal for rearing in the classroom and for hands-on activities. As their name indicates, they are not native to North America so you cannot collect them in the wild. Instead, consult the entomology departments of colleges, state extension services, museums, or zoos. I some-

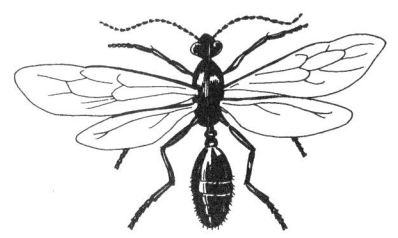

Winged Male Ant

Waxworm Cocoon

Waxworm Larva

Male Waxworm

## MAINTENANCE OF SPECIMENS

### Arachnids

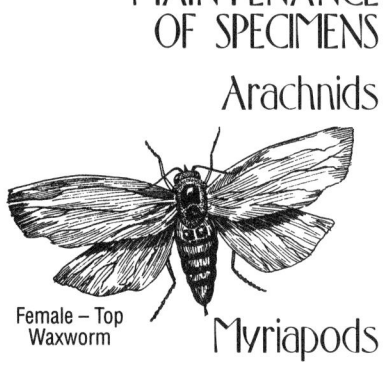

Female – Top Waxworm

### Myriapods

Female – Side Waxworm

Hissing Cockroach

### Crustaceans

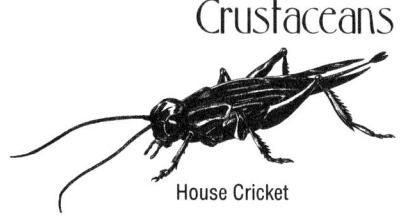

House Cricket

times see them changing hands at science educator meetings, which suggests that other life science educators in your area may have colonies. Some suppliers listed in Appendix B sell giant roaches, but they are in the genus Blaberus; the Madagascar hissing roach is in the genus Gromphadorhina. I have maintained colonies of both types, and I believe the Madagascar hissing roach is better for hands-on student activities.

**Crickets.** The two main types of crickets you will encounter are the black field cricket and the brownish-gray house cricket. If you intend to establish a breeding colony, the house cricket is superior for rearing and breeding. Crickets can be found under rocks and logs or perhaps in your basement. Pet shops or fish bait shops may be the easiest way to obtain them. Live crickets are sold by the suppliers listed in Appendix B. A note of caution: Do not establish a cricket colony unless you enjoy their melodious chirps.

**Mealworm Beetles (Tenebrio).** If you have the space and time to keep only one type of insect, this would be the best choice. They are easy to maintain, require very little attention, make good subjects for student activities, show the dramatic changes of complete metamorphosis, and make an excellent food source for other animals such as fish, amphibians, and reptiles that you may have in the classroom. The larvae may be collected from flour mills or livestock feed stores, where they are referred to as mealworms. They also can be obtained from pet stores or fish bait shops, and the suppliers listed in Appendix B sell live adults, pupae, larvae, and food.

The hunting spiders, which do not spin webs, need only a little space and shelter. You can maintain them in a large jar with holes punched in the lid. Put some soil in the bottom of the jar and place some leaves and twigs on the soil. The web-spinning spiders need enough space in which to spin their web. Spiders will eat each other, so keep only one per container.

Feed spiders live food such as crickets, small mealworms, or flies about every two weeks. Temperature is not critical. Lightly mist the soil occasionally to maintain high humidity.

Due to their limited distribution and stinging behavior, I recommend that you do not maintain scorpions in the classroom.

Make a terrarium by placing soil to a depth of about 5 centimeters (2 inches) in an aquarium, large glass jar, or plastic storage box. Put leaf litter on the soil and add pieces of bark, twigs, and small stones. Millipedes are herbivores (plant eaters) and can be kept together in peace. Millipedes and centipedes, which are carnivores (flesh eaters), can be kept together because irritating secretions given off by the millipedes will prevent the centipedes from bothering them. However, centipedes will prey on each other if crowded together.

Keep a tight-fitting cover on the container. Put a screen on aquariums or punch holes in the lids of jars or plastic storage boxes. Plastic storage boxes come in various sizes and make excellent containers for keeping a variety of creatures.

Myriapods do not require free water; instead they absorb water from their surroundings. Periodically mist the soil in the terrarium. Millipedes feed on decaying leaf litter, but you can supplement this diet with an occasional slice of raw potato or carrot. Place some isopods in the terrarium as food for the centipedes. The isopods will feed on the decaying leaf litter, reproduce, and provide a continuous food supply for the centipedes.

**Crayfish.** Crayfish can be kept in aquariums, plastic storage boxes, or a child's plastic wading pool. Lids are not necessary except to reduce evaporation. Place about 4 to 5 centimeters (1.5 to 2 inches) of gravel and sand and several large stones in the bottom of the container. Add clean pond water to a depth of 8 to 10 centimeters (3 to 4 inches) above the gravel.

Crayfish burrow and plow the gravel into their own area and then defend their niche fiercely. Therefore, only two or three crayfish can be kept in a 40-liter (10-gallon) aquarium. More can be kept in a larger container such as a wading pool.

Crayfish eat pieces of lettuce, raw liver or beef, and canned or frozen fish. They are messy eaters so it is best to feed them in a different container than the one you are housing them in.

Crayfish do not bite, but they can give a painful pinch with their powerful chelipeds. Pick them up by approaching them from behind and grasping them on either side of their cephalothorax with thumb and forefinger.

**Isopods.** Sowbugs and pillbugs live under undisturbed objects on the ground—logs, rocks, boards, or bricks. Duplicate their environment by placing 4 to 5 centimeters (1.5 to 2 inches) of soil and leaf litter in an aquarium or plastic storage box. Place large twigs or pieces of bark and small stones on the soil for the isopods to hide under. Cover an aquarium with a screen or poke holes in the lid of a plastic storage box.

Mist the soil occasionally so that it remains damp but not saturated. Isopods eat decaying leaf litter, but this diet can be supplemented occasionally with a slice of raw potato or carrot. Remove any food that molds.

Isopods are quite prolific and will produce many offspring in three or four weeks.

**Ants.** Ant houses are available from the suppliers listed in Appendix B, but handmade houses are cheaper and easy to construct. A simple nest can be made of two 30-centimeter (12-inch) panes of glass or clear plastic set in a frame so that they are about 2.5 centimeters (1 inch) apart. Drill holes in the top frame for a water tube and feeding opening. Place wood blocks at right angles to the frame for support.

Fill the nest with soil (preferably from the collection site), leaving several centimeters (inches) of space at the top. Cover the soil surface with some leaf litter or sphagnum moss. Ants shun light so to encourage them to work next to the glass where you can see them, temporarily cover the sides of the nest with black paper or black construction board. Ants cannot perceive red light so you might try covering the sides of the nest with red cellophane. This would allow you to watch the ants at work without having to remove the cover and disturb them.

A simpler nest can be made from two glass jars or containers of different sizes. Place the smaller container inside the larger, hold a water tube in place, and fill the space between the containers with soil. Anchor a heavy string or cord into the soil for the ants to use as a ladder to reach food placed inside the bottom of the small container.

Put a fine mesh screen on top of the nest. Keep the soil moist but not saturated by dropping water down the water tube. Feed ants very small pieces of lettuce, raw potato, raw carrots, bread crumbs, sugar cubes, hard-boiled eggs, or raw ground meat. Remove leftovers before they mold. Temperature is not critical; ants can be maintained successfully at room temperature.

Ants move rapidly and can escape the nest quickly. To perform necessary housekeeping chores in the nest or to transfer ants, place the nest in the refrigerator for a short time. The ants will slow down and often clump together, which will make them easier to work with.

**Butterflies and Moths (Lepidopterans).** Large caterpillars are somewhat difficult to rear because they are voracious eaters and must be supplied with a continuous stock of fresh leaves for several weeks to several months. Large adult butterflies and moths can be kept for short periods in easily constructed viewing cages. Feed them by placing sugar water on cotton balls in a shallow dish. Always release adult Lepidopterans after several days of observation.

Mealworm Larva

Mealworm Pupa

Adult Mealworm

## Insects

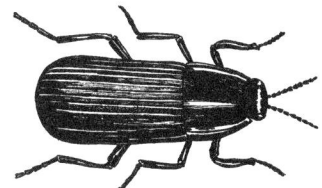

Framed Ant Nest

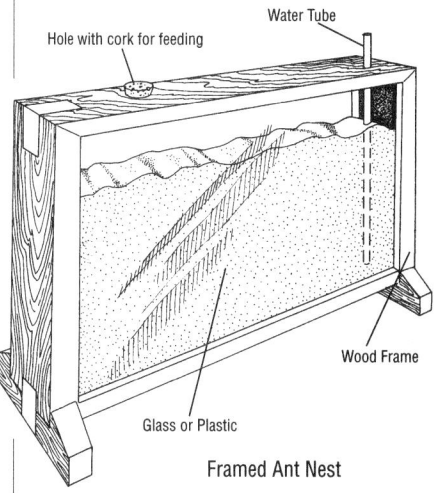

Jar Ant Nest

Butterfly/Moth
Viewing Chamber

One Lepidopteran that is easily maintained throughout its life cycle is the wax moth. Keep specimens in a glass or heavy plastic container as the larvae can eat through wood or cardboard. Nothing is needed in the container except food, but, if you like, you could put a thin layer of coarse wood shavings in the bottom of the container. A gallon jar can yield 50 or more insects for class use. Newly hatched larvae are quite small and can crawl out so place a very fine mesh screen or lid with very small holes punched in it on the jar. Although escape presents no pest potential for the classroom, wax moths should never be knowingly released because the larva is a major pest of the beekeeping industry. Food for the larvae may be purchased from the suppliers listed in Appendix B. If you wish, you can make your own food from the following recipe:

1 lb. box of dry mixed baby cereal
3/4 cup of glycerine (available at drugstores)
1/2 cup sugar
1/2 cup water
0.6 ml. baby vitamins (available at drugstores)

In a saucepan, mix glycerine, sugar, and water. Heat, stirring occasionally, until sugar dissolves and liquid is clear. Allow to cool and add the baby vitamins. Pour cereal into a large mixing bowl. Add liquid and stir until all cereal is coated. Food can be stored for months in the refrigerator in a plastic sack. Adult moths will eat diluted sugar water from a vial and wick.

Wax moths require no free water as long as their food remains moist. To maintain a permanent culture of wax moths, you must have warm temperatures, with the optimal being 32° to 35°C (90° to 95°F). Keep the culture near a desk lamp so that the jar is warm to the touch. Do not place the container over a direct source of heat. Wax moths like darkness so place the container in a paper sack (but be aware of a possible fire hazard and do not put the lamp too close to the paper sack). Wax moths also like a high humidity level—about 75 to 80 percent. Development from egg to adult in these conditions will take four to six weeks. The larvae will pupate and spin white cocoons toward the top of the jar. The side of the cocoon next to the jar is often thin enough that students will be able to observe the development of the moth inside through the glass.

Collect eggs to set up new cultures by placing in the jar a piece of wax paper accordion-folded and held together with a paper clip. Egg masses will be laid between the folds and can be removed by flicking them off with a fingernail or sharp blade or cutting out a piece of waxed paper with the eggs on it. Place the eggs or small larvae directly on a fresh lump of food and the cycle will continue.

Wax moths are good insects to rear in the classroom because they require no daily care, the sexes can be readily distinguished from each other, they are large enough for students to manipulate and easily observe, and they make a good food source for other animals you may have in the classroom such as fish, amphibians, or reptiles. However, their temperature and humidity requirements can be difficult to maintain.

**Madagascar Hissing Roaches.** An active colony of these unique insects can be easily maintained in a standard 40-liter (10-gallon) aquarium or a large plastic storage box.

Place about 5 centimeters (2 inches) of dry hardwood shavings in the bottom of the container. Do not use pine or cedar shavings as chemicals in these woods suppress the reproduction of the roaches. These roaches do not like light, so place some shelter such as inverted plastic plates or large pieces of bark on top the wood shavings.

Feed the roaches by placing dry dog food or cat food pellets in a shallow dish in their container. Supplement this diet with occasional pieces of raw apple, carrot, or potato. Provide water from a vial-and-wick device (see the illustration). Do not place an open dish of water in the container as the insects, especially the young, may drown.

The container should have a tight-fitting lid as the young can and will crawl glass and escape. A ring of petroleum jelly around the top of the container will assure that the young do not get out. Escape presents no pest potential, however.

Temperature is not critical; you can maintain the colony at room temperature. If you have a population explosion, practice cockroach contraception by throwing a few pine cones into the container. As long as the roaches are nibbling on the pine cones, they will not reproduce. Removal of the pine cones should result in a return to normal breeding.

About every three to four months discard the wood shavings and put fresh ones in the container. Carefully search through the old shavings and remove young roaches so they are not inadvertently discarded.

**Crickets.** To keep crickets only for a few days, place 2 to 4 centimeters (1 to 1.5 inches) of sand or soil in a jar with small holes punched in the lid. Add some leaves or crumpled paper towels for shelter.

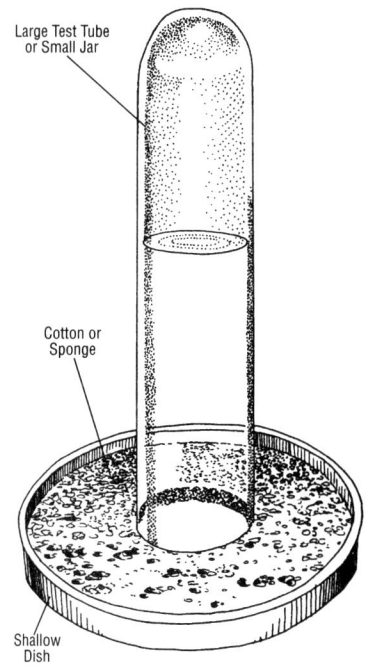

Vial-and-Wick Waterer

A breeding colony of crickets can be kept in much the same way but in larger quarters. A standard 40-liter (10-gallon) aquarium works well. Provide a screen cover for the container as crickets are good jumpers and can escape. Escape presents no serious pest problems, however.

Place about 8 to 10 centimeters (3 to 4 inches) of dry sand in the container. At one end provide plenty of shelter in the form of dry grass, leaves, small pieces of bark, and/or pieces of egg cartons stacked to form a castle. In the middle of the container bury a small dish or can (such as a tuna fish can) to ground level to provide a place for the crickets to lay their eggs. The crickets are attracted to damp sand for egg laying, and the developing eggs require moisture, so this area should remain constantly damp. Cover the moist sand area with window screen and cover the edges of the screen with sand so the adults cannot get under the screen. Adult crickets will eat their eggs; the screen permits egg laying into the sand but prevents egg eating. Covering the can with dry pine needles also works.

On the other end of the container provide water in a vial and wick. Do not put dishes of open water in the container as the crickets will fall in and drown. An important requirement in raising crickets is to keep the environment dry. They do require lots of water to drink, and the egg-laying area must be kept moist, but the rest of the habitat must be dry or the colony will not thrive.

Feed the crickets by placing in the cage a shallow dish containing a mixture of dry dog food pellets or crumbled dog biscuits, dry rolled oats, and a "frosting" of yellow corn meal. Supplement this diet with slices of raw potato and apple and pieces of lettuce. Place close attention and immediately remove any food that begins to mold.

Crickets will survive room temperature but will be more active, sing louder, and reproduce faster at 27° to 32°C (80° to 85°F).

**Mealworm (Tenebrio) Beetles.** Mealworms can be housed in almost any type of container except paper and cardboard. A 20-liter (5-gallon) aquarium will house hundreds of mealworms, but large plastic ice cream containers, glass jars, and plastic storage boxes work equally well. The adult beetles cannot fly but you should cover the container to prevent them from crawling out. The colony will not do well if conditions are too humid, so provide plenty of ventilation into the container. Poke holes in the lids of ice cream containers or jars and cover aquaria with screens. If using plastic storage boxes, cut a piece out of the lid and affix a piece of window screen to the inside of the lid with hot glue. Use sufficient glue to prevent the beetles from getting underneath the edges of the screen and escaping. Escape presents no serious pest problems, however.

The mealworms live in their food supply. Set up your culture by placing 5 to 8 centimeters (2 to 3 inches) of wheat bran or chick starter mash in the container. Wheat bran and chick mash are available from stores that sell pet and/or livestock feed and are also handled by the suppliers listed in Appendix B. Mix in a small amount of dry dog food pellets, dry rolled oats, and yellow corn meal. Cover the surface with several pieces of paper towel folded accordion style to provide shelter. Free water is not necessary, but the culture will prosper if you periodically add a small amount of moisture in the form of a piece of raw potato.

Although temperature is not critical, mealworms do best at around 32° C (85°F). Mealworms show complete metamorphosis, and the larvae, pupae, and adults are easy for students to find and identify. However, they are rather slow growing and take around three months to mature from egg to adult.

## HEALTH AND SAFETY
### Teachers

Collecting arthropods may put you in areas where you could come in contact with biting, stinging, or parasitic animals and poisonous plants. Dress accordingly and be alert to contact with such creatures. If collecting aquatic arthropods, follow good safety procedures around water regardless of its apparent depth.

If setting up observation tubes with biting, stinging, or parasitic arthropods, use extreme caution when handling such creatures. Wear appropriate protective gear such as gloves and safety glasses.

### Students

Do not conduct hands-on activities that expose students to arthropods that can bite or sting or to those that are parasitic. Students can safely and closely observe living arthropods such as spiders (biting), scorpions (stinging), centipedes (biting), and the numerous stinging or biting insects if such creatures are in securely sealed glass tubes. Maintain tight control in such situations and be alert to the possibility of a student tampering with the observation container and trying to release the specimen inside.

Remind students to keep their hands away from their eyes, nose, and mouth while working with even harmless arthropods. As usual, have students thoroughly wash their hands before and after contact with arthropods or the containers housing the arthropods.

### Arthropods

When considering rearing and maintaining arthropods in the classroom for the long term, take their food and space requirements and life cycles into account. Do not attempt to raise large caterpillars and let them starve to death for lack of fresh food or hatch out a beautiful butterfly in the middle of winter when it cannot be shortly and safely released. Learn and respect the needs of the arthropods.

Many students (and adults) have very strong negative feelings or outright fear toward many types of arthropods. Take precautions that fearful students in a panic do not drop, throw, or smash any arthropod they may be working with. Through your patience, understanding, and example you may be able to correct some of the misconceptions and unrealistic fears students have about these amazing creatures.

## TEACHING ACTIVITIES
### Habitat

The activities in this chapter use arthropods that pose no health or safety problems, are large enough for students to manipulate and easily observe, and are relatively easy to collect and maintain in the classroom.

**H1.** *Centipede Habitat.* A creature's habitat is the result of a complex interplay of various factors. To show this, have students respond to the question, What is the natural habitat of the centipede? (Answer: Centipedes are found during the day under rocks and logs and are active at night.) Continue with this line of questioning by asking students to respond to the question, Why are centipedes found under rocks and logs during the day? (Students may theorize that the centipedes are showing a negative response to light, which is partially true.) Continue questioning students about what other factors may be involved in the centipede's choice of habitat. (Students may suggest that other factors such as a positive reaction to moisture and a positive reaction to physical contact may play a role in the hiding behavior of centipedes. Centipedes have little capacity for water regulation. Biologist believe that they seek habitats during the day where moisture levels are high. They find such habitats by being negative to light and positive to moisture and physical contact. They are active at night when water loss is much less of a problem.)

**Challenge:** What role do light and physical contact play in the choice of a habitat by a centipede? Have students devise ways to test this problem.

a. One design would be to put a centipede in a dry, well-lit glass dish and observe its behavior. (The centipede will usually run about ceaselessly.)

b. Put a centipede in a dry dish covered with a piece of black paper to shade the bottom of the dish. Do not put anything into the dish that the centipede can crawl under. Observe the behavior of the centipede. (The centipede will usually show much the same behavior as in the lighted dish.)

c. In the dry, well-lit glass dish put a centipede and a piece of clear glass or plastic tubing just large enough in diameter for the centipede to crawl into. Observe the behavior of the centipede. (The centipede will soon crawl into the tubing and come to rest.)

d. Put a centipede in a dry, well-lit glass dish with both clear glass or plastic tubing and glass or plastic tubing of the same size that has been painted black. Observe the behavior of the centipede. Make several trial runs or use a large dish with numerous tubes and several centipedes. Have more tubes of each type than you have centipedes so the centipedes have a choice of habitat. (Ideally, the centipedes will choose the dark tube as they are supposed to be positive to contact and negative to light.)

For each step, have students predict what will happen before they begin. They should keep appropriate data, which will be mainly observational. Have students draw conclusions from their data.

**H2.** *Collect Imaginary Arthropods.* Have students imagine they are the head collector for Arthropod Acquisitions, a company that specializes in collecting arthropods for supply houses and research laboratories. Where would they go to collect the following specimens?

a. hunting spiders that do not build webs
b. web-spinning spiders
c. scorpions
d. centipedes
e. millipedes
f. crayfish
g. isopods
h. any four types of insects

This activity will not only give students a better understanding of the wide variety of arthropod habitats but also allow them to compare and contrast the various arthropod habitats.

**H3.** *Walk a Mile in My Shoes.* Have students try to put themselves in the arthropod's place by asking them to react orally or in written form to the question, What specific arthropod would you be and why?

**H4.** *Spin-a-Web.* An acre of undisturbed meadow may harbor 2 million spiders with their webs snaring up to 500 small insects per web per day. Clearly,

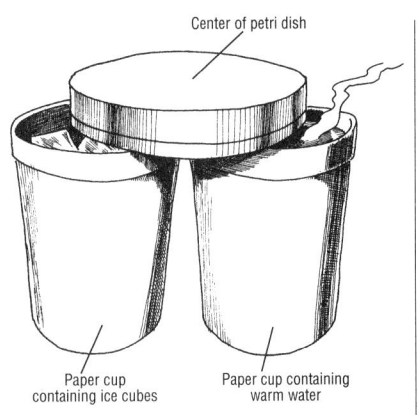

Center of petri dish

Paper cup containing ice cubes

Paper cup containing warm water

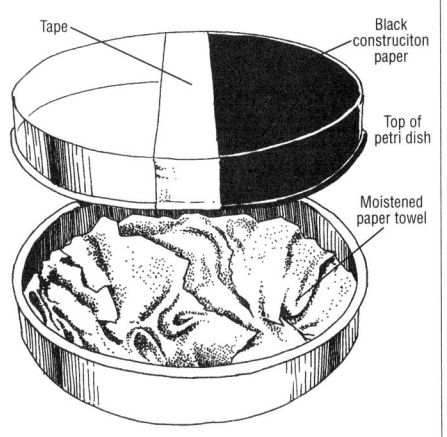

Tape

Black construciton paper

Top of petri dish

Moistened paper towel

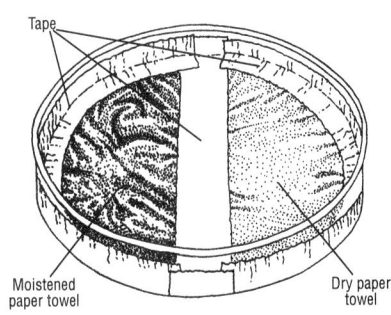

Tape

Moistened paper towel

Dry paper towel

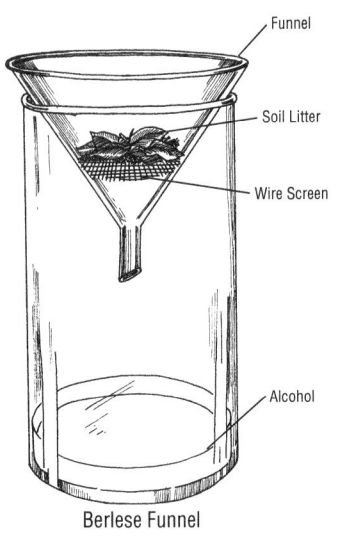

Funnel

Soil Litter

Wire Screen

Alcohol

Berlese Funnel

spiders are an important part of their habitats. Have students explain how and why spiders spin webs. Give students fine thread and have them attempt to spin their own web in some area of the classroom. (Spider silk is a fluid that issues from glands called spinnerets and hardens as it is stretched into a thread. All spiders produce this amazingly strong fiber for a variety of purposes—safety draglines, a chamber in which to hide, the egg sack during reproduction, and many others. Spiders can produce six different kinds of silk. Only about 10 percent of the spiders weave the geometrically precise webs we usually think of as common.)

Have students research appropriate references if they are available to learn more about spider silk and the many things spiders do with it. If students weave their own webs, have them test their work by throwing a tennis ball at their net. If their net holds, symbolically they have eaten for the day but if their net breaks, they go hungry. (A spider web absorbs the proportionally equal impact of a jet fighter plane slamming in for a landing on an aircraft carrier every time a small insect flies full speed into it.)

**H5.** *Escaping from Insects.* Have students react to the following imaginary situation: Your next door neighbor, Cornelius P. Numbmind, absolutely hates any and all insects. He wants to go where there are as few insects as possible—none would be preferable. He asks for your advice. What would you say? (Tell him to dive into the ocean, especially the benthic [deep sea] regions. Insects are not adapted to salt water.)

**H6.** Challenge: *What Type of Habitat Do Isopods Prefer?* As it stands this is a vague, poorly worded problem. Have students discuss how to focus the problem so they know exactly what factors they are investigating. Students may suggest specifically testing the isopods' preferences regarding temperature, light conditions, or moisture levels. Have students brainstorm ways to test these problems (the illustrations offer possiblities of experimental design for each investigation):

a. What temperature—warm or cool—do isopods prefer?
b. What light level—bright or dark—do isopods prefer?
c. What moisture level—dry or damp—do isopods prefer?

When testing any or all of the isopod habitat preference problems, have students predict what they think will happen before they begin. Make sure they keep data in appropriate tables, charts, and graphs and draw conclusions from their data.

You could substitute any type of small insect for the isopods in these habitat preference problems or compare the habitat preference of the isopods with several types of small insects under the same test conditions.

**H7.** *Soil Arthropods.* Many arthropods are small, unseen creatures that spend their lives in total anonymity. Have students attempt to trap and collect some of these tiny arthropods. A good place to look is on and in the soil. There are several ways to trap soil arthropods:

a. Paint glass plates with resin or a similar sticky substance. Leave the plates sticky side up in various types of habitats such as woods, grassy areas, and so on. After several days, collect the plates and see what organisms have stuck to them.
b. Place several unpainted boards on the ground for several days. Then carefully turn the boards over to see what organisms are under them.
c. Place soil litter—dead grass and leaves from the surface of the soil—in a Berlese funnel. Place a light source close to the funnel and leave it on for several days. Tiny creatures in the litter will be driven downward and fall into the liquid in the bottom of the jar. Filter the liquid in the

bottom of the jar and examine the organisms collected on the filter paper, preferably with a dissecting microscope.

This activity is a good opportunity for your students to do some field work. Be aware that you will capture more kinds of creatures than arthropods using any of the traps described. Take caution when overturning board traps: Larger animals such as salamanders, lizards, snakes, and mice often will be found under the board. To prevent being startled or even bitten, fashion a hook on one end of a straightened coat hanger, step down on the edge of the board closest to you and lift the board up toward you with your hook. That way the board is between you and whatever may be underneath.

Space limitations in this book do not provide room for identification of the possible soil arthropods (or other creatures) you may trap. Consult other appropriate references for such information.

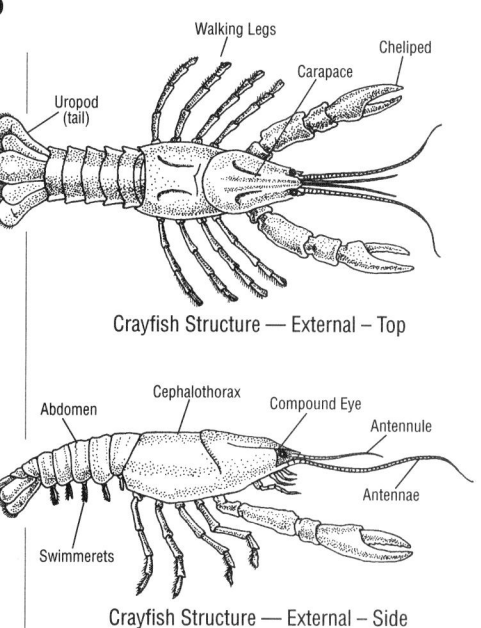

Crayfish Structure — External – Top

Crayfish Structure — External – Side

**H8.** *Temperature and Cricket Chirps.* Crickets are especially melodious creatures. A formula has been developed for determining the temperature by the number of cricket chirps per minute. The formula for the house cricket (where T equals temperature in Farenheit and N equals the number of chirps per minute) is

$$T = 50 + \frac{N - 40}{4}$$

Give students several values for N and have them calculate the temperature in each case. **Challenge:** How accurate is the formula? Students could put crickets in various temperature conditions, use the formula to predict how many chirps a minute the crickets should make, and then count the chirps per minute the crickets actually do make.

**S1.** *Arthropod Stucture Comparisons.* Have students compare and contrast living or preserved specimens from each class of arthropods. Have students observe and discuss what features the arthropods have in common and then prepare a chart listing the differences between arthropods for categories such as number and name of segments, number of legs, number of antennae, and presence or absence of wings.

**S2.** *Crayfish and Insect Structure.* To observe the structure of an arthropod, let students work with a crayfish and/or a large insect such as a hissing roach, a mealworm, or a wax moth. To facilitate observation or manipulation of small insects, place them in the refrigerator for a short time to slow them down and make them easier to work with. This is usually not necessary for large insects such as hissing roaches.

Have students diagram and label the crayfish and its parts: cephalothorax, abdomen, walking legs, chelipeds (pinchers), swimmerets, antennae, antennules, mouthparts, compound eyes, carapace, and uropod (tail).

Have students diagram and label an insect and its parts: head, abdomen, thorax, walking legs, compound eyes, antennae, and mouthparts. Add wings to this list if students are observing beetles or moths (hissing roaches do not have wings).

**S3.** *Observe an Arthropod.* Have students observe a live crayfish and/or insect carefully and do the following activities:

a. Weigh and measure the length of your specimen. **Challenge**: Devise a way to measure the diameter of your specimen. (Answer: Diameter might be measured by wrapping a piece of string around the widest part of the specimen and then measuring the length of the string with a ruler.)

## Structure

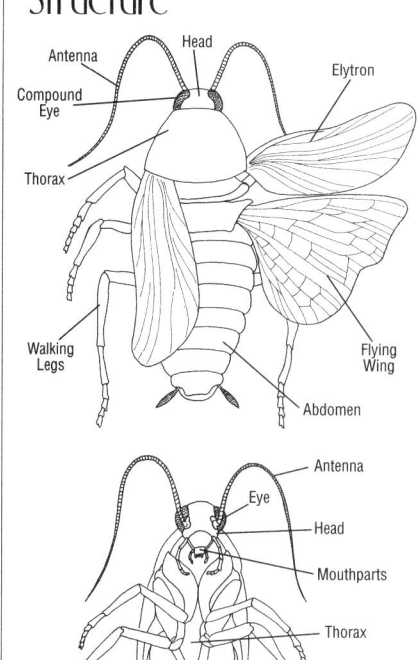

Insect Structure – Top and Bottom

b. Describe the exoskeleton of your specimen. (Answer: The exoskeleton is a hard, plasticlike covering found on all arthropods.)

c. Explain where the exoskeleton comes from. (The exoskeleton is secreted from the inside by the underlying epidermis layer.)

d. Prepare a chart listing the advantages and disadvantages of an exoskeleton. (Some advantages: offers protection and support and prevents dehydration. Some disadvantages: heavy and cumbersome and must be shed periodically to allow for growth.)

e. Have students explain the following story (or create your own scenario): When my son was a small boy he had an aquarium in his room. His favorite creature was a small red crab he named Freddie. One evening he led me to the aquarium to show me Freddie's limp and lifeless remains. With tears in his eyes, he flushed Freddie down the toilet. Several days later he came racing downstairs to loudly proclaim, "Freddie's back!" (All growing arthropods periodically shed their exoskeleton in a process called molting. Freddie molted his exoskeleton and the exoskeleton is what my son thought was dead Freddie. Freddie was soft as all arthropods are after molting and hid under the rocks in the aquarium until its new exoskeleton hardened.)

   If you keep crayfish, they may molt, especially in the spring. Collect such molts promptly, as the crayfish will eat them. Show them to your students and have them compare the size of the molt to the new size of the crayfish.

f. **Challenge:** Have students put themselves in an arthropod's place by actually constructing and wearing an exoskeleton made of cardboard and/or plastic parts. Have students orally or in written form describe the experience and explain why an exoskeleton must be jointed.

g. In spite of their cumbersome exoskeleton, most arthropods are surprisingly agile and capable of rapid movements. Have students predict the sequence of walking leg action in crayfish or insects and then observe the actual walking action. Have students prepare a leg sequence diagram such as the one illustrated to describe the walking leg sequence of their specimen.

   Students can observe the action of insect wings by anesthetizing a large fly or bee in the refrigerator and then attaching a glass rod, paper clip, or matchstick to the thorax of the insect by means of melted paraffin wax. Make sure the insect's wings are free to function normally. As the insect warms, it will begin to beat its wings.

   Wing action normally happens so fast that it is difficult to observe. Try painting the wingtips of the insect with bright paint and observing the wing action in bright sunlight or in bright light against a dark background. Does the physics department of your school have a strobe light? If so, you might have students try to regulate the frequency of the strobe to nearly match the frequency of the insect's wingbeats. Wing speed will seem to slow to the point where observations are much easier to make.

h. **Challenge:** Can arthropods regenerate lost appendages? The regenerative powers of crustaceans such as the crayfish and lobster allow them to replace or repair almost any lost or injured appendage. Insects vary. Some can regenerate lost legs only after a molt, and a limb lost or injured in the mature stage is not regenerated. Others that go on growing and molting even after reaching sexual maturity can regenerate lost or injured legs in the adult stage.

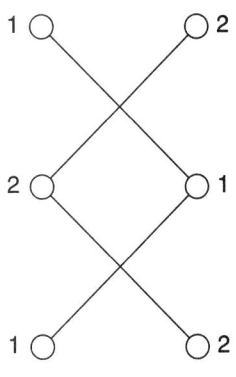

Leg Sequence Diagram

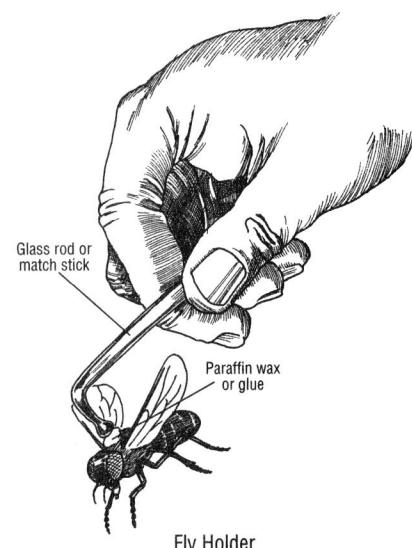

Glass rod or match stick

Paraffin wax or glue

Fly Holder

Students can investigate what appendages, if any, crayfish can regenerate. Test for regeneration of antennae and antennules, walking legs, chelipeds (pinchers), and swimmerets by having students snip off portions or entire appendages with small, sharp scissors. Cut only at a joint, which causes minimum damage and allows faster healing. Use young crayfish if possible as they grow and molt more rapidly and results will be visible sooner. Basic appendage regeneration experiments with crayfish could lead to more refined and specific investigations. For example, do male and female crayfish possess the same powers of regeneration? What role do environmental factors such as temperature, light, and amount of food have in regeneration?

With insects you might compare and contrast the regeneration powers of larvae, pupae, and adults. Have student carefully snip off portions or entire legs of larvae, pupae, and adult mealworms. The legs of the larvae are small, so hand magnifiers or dissecting scopes would allow for more precise cuts. Isolate the larvae, pupae, and adults in small, closed containers with some food inside and observe development. As with crayfish, this basic experiment could lead to investigations regarding the influence of environmental factors such as temperature and light on insect regeneration.

With each experiment have students predict what will happen before they begin; keep data in appropriate tables, charts, and graphs; and draw conclusions from their data.

i.  Locate and describe the eyes of an arthropod. (Insects have large compound eyes that may be composed of thousands of closely packed individual visual units. Insects also have simple eyes that can detect changes in light intensity. Crustaceans have compound eyes, often on stalks. Most other arthropods have a single-lens eye.)

j.  Locate and describe the antennae of an arthropod and explain the role the antennae play in the life of the arthropod. (Antennae protrude from the head of the arthropod. Arachnids have no antennae, myriapods and insects have two antennae, and some crustaceans have four antennae. Antennae are the chief site of the sense of touch, but they may also bear receptors for the senses of smell and taste and for humidity and temperature.

k.  Stimulate the antennae of an arthropod and observe how the arthropod responds. Students could touch the antennae using a blunt probe. To test for chemotaxis, touch cotton swabs soaked in sugar, salt, and vinegar to the antennae of an arthropod and note the reaction. Do not use any chemical that could be dangerous to the arthropod. (Try touching the mouthparts and even the tips of the legs; some arthropods have taste receptors located in those sites.)

l.  Observe the sensory bristles scattered over the body of an arthropod. Using a hand magnifier or dissecting scope and illuminating the specimen from the side will give the best view of these bristles. In crayfish and lobsters, the eyes may be secondary sense organs to the sensory bristles scattered over the antennae, legs, and body. Insects also have such bristles on their bodies.

m. Respiration in arthropods is by means of gills, book lungs, or tracheal tubes. Have students observe the flow of water through the body of a crayfish and over the gills by dropping food coloring along the sides of the crayfish and watching current flow.

Insects take air into their branched tracheal tubes through openings called spiracles. Using hand magnifiers or dissecting scopes, have students find, observe, and describe the spriracles on the abdomen of an insect.

Have students react to the following imaginary situation: Your neighbor, Cornelius P. Numbmind, is at it again. Mr. Numbmind has a large garden and does not like the insects eating up a great portion of his vegetables. However, he refuses to spray environmentally harmful pesticides. He comes to you with a scheme to drown all the insects by catching them and holding their heads underwater. What would you say to him? (No one could catch all the insects in even a small garden, and who would have the time to try to drown each insect individually? More important, the insects wouldn't drown because they take air in through spriracles on their abdomen. Insects do not breath through their mouths.)

n. All arthropods are highly prized for food by many of the other animals of this planet, and great quantities are eaten every day. To counteract this assault, arthropods have developed a wide array of strategies to defend themselves. Have students investigate the following defense mechanisms and guess which types of arthropods might employ them: running, flying, jumping, swimming, biting, stinging, pinching, hiding, camouflaging, mimicking, emitting caustic chemicals, and making warning sounds.

| | |
|---|---|
| Running: | Some spiders, myriapods, crabs, and many insects |
| Flying: | Some insects such as flies, bees, and wasps |
| Jumping: | Some spiders and insects such as crickets, grasshoppers, and fleas |
| Swimming: | Lobster and crayfish. Demonstrate by agitating a crayfish in a small container and observe the rapid backward motion caused by the rapid flexing of the abdomen and uropod. You can also cause this motion by picking up a crayfish and touching it under the abdomen. |
| Hiding: | Most arthropods will try to get into crevices or under objects to hide from predators. |
| Camouflaging: | Many arthropods are colored to blend into their environment. Some insects, such as the walking stick and certain tropical mantids, are structured to be nearly invisible against objects in their natural environment. |
| Mimicking: | Some insects appear or behave like stinging or foul-tasting insects. For example, the harmless syrphid fly mimics the stinging honeybee, and the good-tasting (to a bird) viceroy mimics the foul-tasting monarch butterfly. |
| Emitting chemicals: | Millipedes and some insects such as stink bugs and the bombardier beetle. Some tropical species of millipedes can spray strong defensive chemicals up to 30 centimeters (12 inches). Never hold or allow students to hold any millipede close to the eyes. |
| Making sounds: | Many insects buzz, click, and whir when disturbed. The loud hiss of the hissing cockroach is a good example. If you are working with these roaches, forewarn students so they are not startled and drop the insect. |

## Behavior/Response

**B/R1.** *Dance of the Bees.* Social ants and bees have been the subject of most learning experiments with insects. Bees remember not only the scent of the flowers from which they have collected nectar and pollen but the location as well. Amazingly, they can transfer this knowledge to other bees through a communicative dance "language" and odor and visual cues. The waggle dance of the bee makes use of sound pulses to convey information. Have students analyze the graph and answer the questions.

a. What information does this graph show? (The average number of waggles [sound pulses] and the distance of food from the hive.)
b. What conclusions can be drawn from the graph? (The more waggles, the farther food is from the hive.)

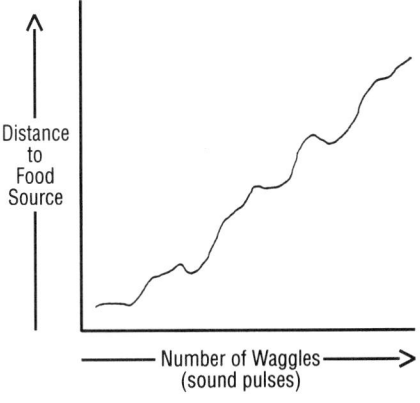

Distance to Food Source

Number of Waggles (sound pulses)

**B/R2.** Challenge: *Can Insects Learn?* Have students devise a way to test this problem.

Ants, mealworms, and other species can learn simple mazes. Have students construct simple mazes, develop experiments, and use rewards such as darkness or food to induce learned behavior. For active crawling or flying insects, a network of clear plastic tubing of various sizes can serve as a maze and prevent the insects from escaping. Mark individual insects by placing a small dot of brightly colored fingernail polish on their backs. If working with many insects, you may need to develop a pattern of dots.

Through such experiments students might investigate a number of problems. For example: Can insects learn? How long do insects retain information they have learned? Do larvae and adults learn (or retain) information equally well? What role do environmental factors such as temperature play in learning and retention of knowledge in insects?

Have students predict what they think will happen before they begin each experiment. Instruct them to keep data in appropriate tables, charts, and graphs and to draw conclusions from their data.

**B/R3.** *Arthropod Responses.* Have students investigate a variety of arthropod responses:

a. Response to touch (thigmotaxis). Use a blunt probe to touch different areas of an arthropod's body to see how it responds.
b. Response to gravity (geotaxis). Observe the righting response in crayfish and large insects by turning the crayfish or insect over and observing its reaction.

   Place a smooth board at a 45-degree angle. Place 5 to 10 insects or larvae in the center of the board. Make sure the board is evenly lit along its entire surface. Have students observe and collect data. Some insects move slowly, so allow adequate time. Verify the data by repeating this experiment in the dark.
c. Response to light (phototaxis). Shine a light on various parts of an arthropod to see how it behaves. See Chapter 3, activity B/R2 for directions on making a spotlight.

   Develop a light gradient along a shallow container or length of plastic tubing by brightly lighting one end and then covering the container or tubing with materials that are more and more opaque until total darkness is achieved at the other end. Place appropriate arthropods in the container or tube and observe how they react.

   When doing any or all of the response activities, have students predict what will happen before they begin; keep data in appropriate tables, charts, and graphs; and draw conclusions from their data.
d. **Challenge:** Do mealworm larvae respond to magnetic fields? Have students devise a way to test this problem. This activity will allow students to investigate magnetotaxis, or response to magnetic fields.

   One design would be to have students make an orientation chart (similar to the one illustrated) on a piece of paper approximately 100 centimeters (39 inches) square. Use a compass to align the chart so that

**Orientation Chart**

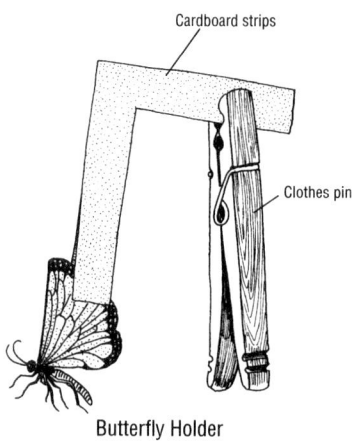

N on the chart points north. Darken the room as completely as possible and light the chart as evenly as possible directly from above. Release the larvae in the center of the circle. Have students mark where each larva crosses the inner circle. After a fixed amount of time record how many larvae are in each section of the chart. As usual, have students make predictions, keep data, and draw conclusions.

**B/R4.** *Social Activity in Arthropods.* The social behavior of some arthropods can be the basis for a fascinating study. Have students investigate the behavior of ants in an active ant colony. If this is not possible, have students consult appropriate references and view audiovisual materials on social behavior in ants, bees, and/or termites. Ask them to explain how the colony is organized, define the various social levels within the colony, and explain the role of each social caste in the survival of the colony.

Have students observe the social order that develops when four or five crayfish share a small territory such as a plastic wading pool. Use crayfish of the same sex (see activity R4 in this chapter for how to sex crayfish) that have been marked with colored nail polish for identification. Students can investigate the following problems: Does a social hierarchy develop among the crayfish? Does one or several crayfish become dominant over the others? If so, do dominant crayfish claim more territory? What happens when the dominant crayfish is removed? What happens when a crayfish of another sex is added to the pool?

## Feeding

**F1.** *Athropod Feeding Comparisons.* Have students imagine the following scenario: At some time in the future they are feeding technicians in the Arthropod Array section of a gigantic space station. What would they feed the following arthropods: web-spinning spiders, scorpions, centipedes, millipedes, crayfish, isopods, butterflies, bees, grasshoppers, and ladybugs? (Use appropriate references and see the "Maintenance of Specimens" section in this chapter to determine what these arthropods would eat. This activity allows students to learn what various arthropods eat and to compare and contrast what is eaten.)

**F2.** *Feeding an Arthropod.* Have students view the actual feeding behavior of an arthropod. There are a number of possible ways to demonstrate this:
a. Feed a hunting spider (non-web spinner) a cricket or other small insect.
b. Feed a centipede an isopod.
c. Feed a crayfish a small piece of raw fish. Do this in a small jar so that students can pick it up and view the action of the mouthparts of the crayfish.

    **Challenge:** What food do crayfish prefer? Have students devise a method for testing this problem. They might feed crayfish various foods such as fresh, frozen, or canned fish; raw liver; chopped earthworms; insects; raw carrots; raw potato; apples; and celery. Food preference can be determined by observing whether the crayfish eats the food at all. If the food is eaten, students need to quantify how much food was eaten in a certain time period. Have students predict what will happen before they begin. Make sure they keep appropriate data in tables, charts, and graphs. Have students draw conclusions from their data.
d. Feed a hungry butterfly, housefly, or bee sugar water. Safely restrain the insect (see the illustration). Touch the front legs, antennae, and mouthparts of the insect with the tip of a paint brush that has been dipped in sugar water solution and observe the action of the mouthparts. **Challenge:** What is the lowest concentration of sugar water that a butterfly or fly can detect? Mix up various concentrations of sugar water and

Cardboard strips

Clothes pin

Butterfly Holder

repeat the touching process above. Another feeding response problem to investigate is whether a butterfly, fly, or bee can distinguish between natural sugar and artificial sweeteners.

**F3.** *The Sweet Life.* Professor Buzz Drosophila has been researching the relationship between length of life in fruit flies and the amount of sugar they receive in their diet. His data is listed in the following table:

| Percentage of sugar | Time of survival (hours) |
| --- | --- |
| 0 | 50 |
| 0.125 | 75 |
| 0.500 | 100 |
| 0.750 | 150 |
| 1.000 | 225 |
| 2.500 | 200 |
| 5.000 | 475 |
| 10.00 | 480 |
| 20.00 | 600 |
| 30.00 | 580 |
| 50.00 | 500 |
| 80.00 | 400 |
| 90.00 | 225 |
| 95.00 | 195 |
| 100 | 100 |

Have students graph the data from the table and answer the following questions about their graph:

a. What information does this graph show? (Answer: The survival time in hours against the concentration of sugar in the diet.)

b. What percentage of sugar provides for the longest life in fruit flies? (Around 20 percent.)

c. Why did the survival rate go down as the percentage of sugar went up? (Students may theorize that the increased concentration of sugar was detrimental to the flies. Another possibility students may raise, and the actual answer to the problem, is that the flies were receiving less and less moisture as the sugar concentration went up.)

**F4.** *Predatory Searching Behavior.* Have students investigate the predatory search behavior of an insect. Place a piece of graph paper beneath a petri dish, scatter five or six aphids or other small, soft-bodied insect prey in the dish and add one lady beetle. On another piece of graph paper have students trace the path of the beetle as it searches for food. From their observations have students answer the following questions:

a. Does the search pattern of the beetle appear random or nonrandom?

b. Does the beetle appear to detect the aphids by sight? by smell? by touch? by sound?

c. Which organs of the beetle seem to be sensitive to the aphids?

Some of suppliers listed in Appendix B sell lady beetles and/or aphids. Very tiny caterpillars will work in place of aphids for this activity. If no prey animals are available you might alter the activity by substituting small drops of sugar water for prey animals.

**R1.** *Reproductive Comparisons.* Have students prepare a chart listing the various methods of reproduction and parental care given to the eggs or young in the various classes of arthropods. (All arthropods are separate sexes and at least technically all have internal fertilization.)

a. *Arachnids.* A male spider deposits a drop of sperm and then picks it up in bulbous organs on his pedipalps. The tip of the pedipalp is inserted

## Reproduction and Development

into the female and the sperm are transferred. Female spiders spin egg sacks which they guard fiercely and may carry with them. Some spiders also carry the young on their back for a time after hatching. In scorpions, the male deposits a packet of sperm on a stalk. He drags the female over the stalk in the proper position and sperm are transferred into the female. The female does not lay eggs but gives birth to young. The young cling to the mother and stay with her for up to two months before venturing out on their own.

b. *Crustaceans*. In lobsters and crayfish, the male grasps the female and inserts sperm into her body with specialized swimmerets. Days, weeks, or even months later, the female releases the eggs and fertilizes them with the stored sperm. The eggs stick to her swimmerets and remain attached until they hatch. The young may cling to the female's swimmerets through several molts before leaving her. Crabs reproduce in similar fashion.

c. *Myriapods*. Centipedes accomplish fertilization in a fashion similar to some arachnids, with the female introducing a sperm packet into her body. In some centipedes the female lays the eggs and then coils tightly around them. In others the eggs are laid and buried and the mother leaves. Millipedes reproduce in similar fashion.

d. *Insects*. In most insects separate male and female individuals mate and the females lay the eggs and depart. There is very little parental care in most insects other than to perhaps hide the eggs or lay them on a suitable food source. This lack of care means that insects must lay tremendous numbers of eggs to ensure the survival of the species. Even in termites, which do care for their eggs, the queen termite lays as many as 30,000 eggs per day.

**R2.** *Observing Arthropod Reproduction*. Have students observe the reproduction and development of arthropods. I suggest you use insects for this activity. Many types have a short life cycle and will churn out a good many offspring without any special accommodations or work on your part. Students can investigate incomplete metamorphosis by observing a colony of crickets or hissing roaches and complete metamorphosis by observing a culture of wax moths or mealworms. Have students compare and contrast each type of metamorphosis through diagrams of the various stages of development.

**R3.** **Challenge:** *What Is the Effect of Temperature on the Rate of Development of Arthropods?* Have students devise a method to test this problem. Mealworms make a convenient subject for this investigation. Place the same number of mealworm adults in two identical rearing containers with plenty of food in each container. Maintain the cages at different temperatures. Remove the parent generation of adults once the first larvae appear. Have students keep careful records on the appearance of the first larvae, first pupae, and first appearance of second-generation adults. Have students predict what will happen before they begin; keep appropriate data in tables, charts, and graphs; and draw conclusions from their data.

**R4.** *Sexing an Arthropod*. Have students identify the different sexes in several types of arthropods. In male crayfish the first two swimmerets are long and leglike and in female crayfish all swimmerets are small and threadlike. Male wax moths are usually lighter in color and have shorter antennae than the females. The male's forewings are notched and the female's are straight. Male hissing roaches have large bumps ("horns") on the top of the thorax; females do not.

**R5.** *Metamorphosis Mix-up.* Mix up pictures of the various stages of incomplete and complete metamorphosis and have students sequence them into their proper cyclic order.

**In1.** *Writing:*

a. Read students the opening sentences of Franz Kafka's story "The Metamorphosis": "As Gregor Samsa awoke one morning from a troubled dream, he found himself changed in his bed to some monstrous kind of vermin.

   He lay on his back, which was as hard as armour-plate, and, raising his head a little, he could see the arch of his great brown belly, divided by bowed corrugations. Gregor's legs, pitiably thin compared to their former size, fluttered helplessly before his eyes."

   Have students write a story in which they awake one morning to find they have become an arthropod. Have them describe what specific arthropod they have become, how they move, how they feed, and how they feel and see the world around them.

b. Have students do a library report entitled "Bizarre Beasts" in which they write about the most unusual or bizarre arthropods they can find information about.

c. A heated debate is raging in the Great Hall of Biology. The arthropods are on trial. The prosecutor declares that arthropods are humans' worst foe while the defense maintains that arthropods are humans' greatest ally. Have students take either role or both and prosecute and/or defend the relationship between arthropods and humans. (See "The Importance of Arthropods" section in this chapter and other appropriate references.)

d. Have students write an essay comparing the hardened material of an arthropod's exoskeleton to human-made plastics and metals.

**In2.** *Fine Arts:*

a. Have students paint or draw a picture of any arthropod and its natural environment.

b. Have students compose a song or poem entitled "Almighty Arthropod Armada" in which they touch on the great diversity of arthropods and their tremendous biological success at filling nearly every conceivable niche on this planet.

c. Use the round and waggle dance of bees to indicate where some object like a jar of honey is hidden in the classroom. Reference appropriate sources on the dance "language" of the bees.

d. Write-a-Riddle. What goes pitter-patter 99 times and thump once? A centipede with a wooden leg. Have students write riddles about arthropods. Then have students evaluate their riddles for biological accuracy.

**In3.** *Social Studies:*

a. *History.* Throughout history arthropods have been both feared and revered. For example, the ancient Egyptians regarded the scarab beetle (also known as the dung beetle) as sacred. Share some famous fables with students and then ask students to write fables to explain

   1. why centipedes and millipedes have so many legs.
   2. how the scorpion got its sting.
   3. why the spider weaves a web.
   4. why ants, bees, or termites live in groups and have different social classes.

b. *Geography.* Have students compare and contrast the types of insects found in their general area with those found in other states or other

Integration with Other Subject Areas

countries. Groups of students might investigate different categories of insects. For example, one group might study agriculturally beneficial insects and another agriculturally damaging insects. Students could contact the wildlife and natural resource authorities listed in Appendix C for help in compiling lists of insects in various states and Canadian provinces. For other countries contact the United Nations or various national embassies. Also, some of your students might have foreign pen pals whom they could enlist to help in such an activity. Have students keep their findings on appropriate maps.

**In4.** *Societal/Environmental Issues:*

a. Have students write an essay in which they react to the following statement by Edward O. Wilson in his book *The Diversity of Life*: "Humans dwell among the six-legged masses with a tenuous grip on the planet. Insects can thrive without us but we would perish without them." (See "The Importance of Arthropods" in this chapter. Older or more advanced students could be assigned Wilson's exact quote. Younger or lower-ability students could still benefit from contemplating this idea if it were paraphrased.)

b. Have students do some background research on biological control methods and then write a newspaper advertisement for a fictional biological control company. Their advertisement should list the company name, the products sold by the company, and why biological controls would be preferable to chemical controls.

c. Every year insects destroy about 10 percent of the crops in the United States alone. It is most often the larvae stage that is the most damaging because in this stage the insects are growing rapidly and feeding voraciously. Have students imagine the following scenario based on actual field studies: The Organic Gardening Organization has been studying insect pests in gardens and has found that a certain kind of caterpillar feeds on the leaves of several different kinds of plants. The table shows the number of caterpillars found on each type of plant. Have students study the table and answer the questions and do the activity that follow.

| Number of Caterpillars | Plant |
|---|---|
| 105 | green bean |
| 62 | pea |
| 47 | tomato |
| 4 | onion |

1. Which kind of plant does this type of caterpillar seem to prefer? (Green bean.)
2. Which kind of plant does this type of caterpillar seem to like the least? (Onion.)
3. The organic gardeners noticed that plants growing near the onions were eaten by fewer caterpillars than other plants of the same type farther from the onions were. Have students theorize why. (Perhaps the chemicals that repelled the insects in the onion were also protecting nearby plants.)
4. Have students draw a plan on a piece of graph paper for planting a garden that makes use of the information in the table.

## RELEASE OF SPECIMENS

Arthropods collected locally may be released back into their natural habitats once you have finished with them. Be sure that the timing of the release does not subject the arthropod to inclement weather or food shortage difficulties. Do not release commercially purchased arthropods in your area unless you can absolutely verify that they are native to your area.

# SECTION THREE:
# LOWER VERTEBRATES

## 8. FISH

| | |
|---|---|
| **Kingdom:** | Animalia |
| **Subkingdom:** | Metazoa |
| **Phylum:** | Chordata |
| **Subphylum:** | Vertebrata (possessing a backbone) |
| **Classes:** | Agnatha (lampreys and hagfishes) |
| | Chondrichthyes (sharks, skates, and rays) |
| | Osteichthyes (bony fish) |

## CLASSIFICATION

Fish populate the waters of our planet in numbers we can scarcely imagine. Not even insects, with many more species, can compare to the diversity of size, shape, and structure of fish. There are at least 20,000 known species of fish and certainly more awaiting discovery.

Fish exploit every imaginable nook and cranny of their watery domain, from the tops of mountains to the bottom of the ocean and even in underground rivers. They live in habitats hot enough to cook most other animals and in waters so cold that the fish need natural antifreeze in their blood. Some can survive even when their pools dry and harden. Some migrate thousands of miles; others spend their entire life in the same hole. Their liquid existence has imposed on fish their shape; methods of breathing, eating, and movement; and mode of reproduction.

Some fish walk and glide as well as swim; some can breathe air as well as water. They range from tiny, barely visible creatures to monsters over 15 meters (50 feet) long. Some lay eggs, and others give birth to live young. There are round fish, flat fish, tube-shaped fish, and parasitic fish. Some graze, some eat other creatures, from urchins to insects, and some eat the parasites off other fish. Some fish are brightly colored and others are drab. Some can dramatically change color or glow with their own light.

In spite of their diversity, fish have certain common characteristics: they possess fins, they breathe mainly through gills, they spend most if not all their lives in water, and their eggs or young are born into water.

**Digestive System and Feeding.** Many feeding modes are seen in fish: They are herbivores, carnivores, scavengers, parasites, and filter feeders. The anglerfish even go fishing for smaller species.

Fish tear their food into bite-sized pieces or swallow it whole. Food passes from the mouth through the esophagus into the stomach, where it is partially digested. In many fish the food is further processed in fingerlike pouches called pyloric ceca between the stomach and the intestine. The intestine completes

## DIVERSITY AND DISTRIBUTION

## General Phylum Characteristics

digestion, and indigestible wastes eventually are eliminated out the anus.

**Circulatory System.** Fish have a closed circulatory system with a two-chambered heart pumping red blood through the body. Fish are ectothermic (cold-blooded), which means their body temperature is directly controlled by the environmental temperature. Their inability to regulate their body temperature is not as great a disadvantage for aquatic ectotherms such as fish as it is for terrestrial ectotherms such as amphibians and reptiles because the temperature of water does not change as quickly or as dramatically as air temperature.

**Respiratory System.** Fish breathe with gills located on either side of the head. In lampreys, hagfishes, sharks, skates, and rays, water enters the gills through the mouth or special openings on top of the body and passes out through numerous slits on the side of the body. The bony fish expel water through a single opening on each side of the head covered by a protective flap called the gill cover or operculum. Lungfish have modified swim bladders that act as simple lungs and allow the fish to gulp air at the surface and thus survive in the warm, oxygen-poor, stagnant pools where they are found.

**Muscle System and Movement.** Fish have very well developed muscles. The lampreys and hagfishes, species with practically no fins, clumsily wriggle through the water. The sharks, on the other hand, are very powerful swimmers capable of high speeds, but their stiff fins do not allow for graceful movements. The undulating winglike pectoral fins of the skates and rays give them the appearance of flying through the water. The many powerful and flexible fins of the bony fish give them the unbeatable combination of power, speed, and grace while swimming.

Bony fish also possess a gas-filled sac called a swim bladder, whose buoyancy makes the movements of these fish easy and more efficient. The other groups of fish lack a swim bladder and thus are forced to spend their lives struggling against the water.

**Skeletal System.** All fish have an endoskeleton (internal). The skeleton of the lampreys, hagfishes, sharks, skates, and rays is composed of hardened cartilage. The skeleton of bony fish is formed, as their group name implies, of bone.

**Excretory System.** Some wastes in fish diffuse out through their gills into the surrounding water. Other wastes are removed by the action of the kidney. Fish must carefully regulate the amount of water in their body through the action of the kidney. Fish in salt water tend to lose water as their body water constantly diffuses out in an effort to dilute the salt water around them. Their kidney concentrates liquid wastes and returns as much water back to the body as possible. Freshwater fish have the opposite problem: Water diffuses into their body and they expel quantities of very dilute urine.

**Brain and Nervous System.** Fish have a fairly well developed nervous system organized around a relatively small brain (compared to other vertebrates). They have excellent sense organs. Their large, well-developed eyes help them find their way in dark or murky water. Many possess extraordinary senses of taste and smell. Chemoreceptor cells are found mainly on the head and scattered over the entire body. Salmon migrating in from the ocean can smell/taste their birth stream and head toward it for spawning. Sharks can detect tiny amounts of blood in the water over great distances.

Fish have ears but don't hear well because the ears are inside the head. They can detect currents and vibrations in the water. Running the length of a fish is the lateral line, a series of pores connected to canals beneath the skin. This system is sensitive to vibrations and pressure waves and allows fish to detect prey, avoid unseen enemies or objects, and swim in large schools in murky water or total darkness.

**Reproduction and Development.** Fish are born as separate males and females, but some types change to the opposite sex as they grow older. Most female fish lay eggs that are externally fertilized by the male. Most fish of this type take no care of the young and must release thousands or even millions of eggs to ensure the development of a few. Some egg layers, however, are dedicated parents. The male betta, for example, builds a bubble nest on the water's surface, blows each fertilized egg into its own bubble, and fiercely stands guard until hatching. The sticklebacks build a nest of twigs, and some catfish brood their eggs in their mouth. In some species, the eggs are internally fertilized and held in the female's body as they develop; the young are born alive.

Many fish exhibit fascinating mating behaviors. Males flashing brilliant colors often perform intricate courtship routines to intice reluctant females. Building elaborate nests may also be part of the mating ritual in some fish.

**Class Agnatha.** This group, also known as the jawless fish, consists of about 32 species of lampreys and 31 species of hagfishes. The lampreys and hagfishes lack jaws and have only a hole for a mouth (Greek—*a*, not + *gnathos*, jaw). Both have long, slimy, tubular bodies lacking scales. They have a skeleton of cartilage and only one fleshy fin. They lack a swim bladder. Lampreys have large, well-developed eyes, but the eyes of the hagfishes are at best rudimentary.

Adult lampreys attach to fish and occasionally whales and porpoises by means of a suckerlike mouth. Once attached, they rasp a hole in their victim with their rough tongue and suck out blood and body tissues. Lampreys rarely kill their hosts, but they often leave them weak and wounded.

Hagfishes are scavengers. They have four to six sensory tentacles around the mouth and feed on dead fish, using a rough tongue to scrape off pieces of flesh. These peculiar creatures can produce incredible amounts of slime and sometimes tie themselves in knots!

Lampreys and hagfishes are found usually in salt or brackish water. Lampreys are free swimming, and hagfishes hide in the mud on the bottom of the ocean.

**Class Chondrichthyes.** This group, also known as the cartilaginous fish, has about 850 species, including sharks, skates, and rays. Unlike the agnathans, the sharks, skates, and rays possess well-developed fins and are covered with tiny, rough, toothlike scales. Like the agnathans, they have a skeleton of cartilage and lack a swim bladder (Greek—*chondros*, cartilage + *ichthys*, fish). Sharks, skates, and rays are found only in the ocean.

Sharks have torpedo-shaped bodies and swim powerfully through open waters. They are known as fierce predators that will eat practicallly anything. Cement blocks, beach balls, and license plates are a few of the strange (and often gruesome) things found in sharks' stomachs. One of the most noticeable characteristics of sharks is the enormous number of sharp teeth: A typical shark has about 3,000 teeth arranged in 6 to 20 rows. The teeth in front are constantly being lost and replaced from the rows behind; a shark may go through as many as 24,000 teeth in its lifetime. Some sharks are placid filter-feeders, and others have flat teeth for crushing the shells of mollusks and the exoskeletons of arthropods. Sharks can and do attack humans, but they have much more to fear from us than we do from them. Their numbers are dwindling rapidly as they are snagged for sport, slaughtered for their meat and fins, or trapped by accident in fish nets. It has been estimated that the bodies of all the sharks killed every year would weigh more than a billion pounds—more than seven aircraft carriers. Most sharks do not breed until they are 10 to 12 years old and may give birth only once every other year. Some countries are setting tighter quotas and restricting the types of sharks that can be taken; others are restricting shark fishing in cer-

## Specific Class Characteristics

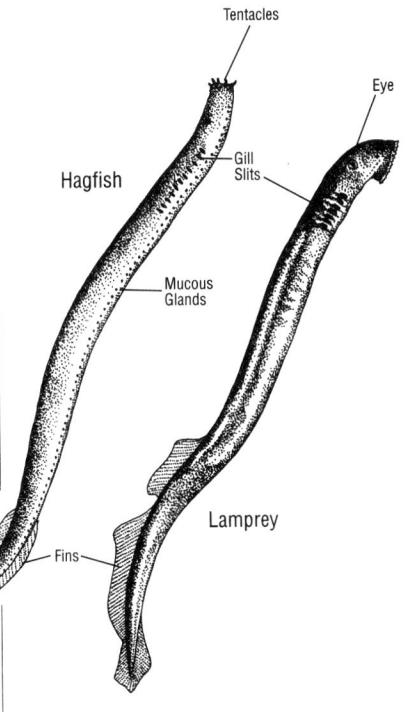

Tentacles

Eye

Hagfish

Gill Slits

Mucous Glands

Lamprey

Fins

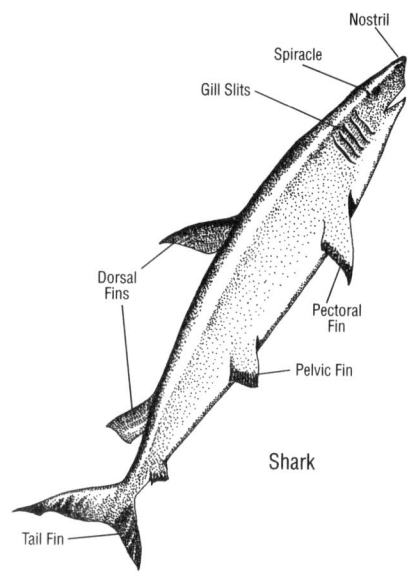

Shark

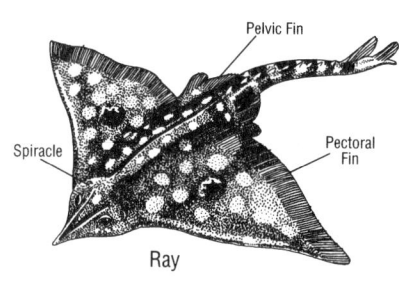

Ray

tain areas. Even with protective measures being taken, the vanishing stocks of sharks may take decades to recover from human exploitation, if ever.

Unlike sharks, skates and rays have a flattened body with the mouth on the underside of the body. They swim by flapping their winglike pectoral fins. Their tail is thin and whiplike and sometimes armed with a poisonous barb. Skates and rays possess flat crunching plates in their mouths. Most live on or near the bottom of the ocean and feed on mollusks and arthropods.

**Class Osteichthyes.** Scientists estimate the number of types in this group, also known as bony fish, to be somewhere between 15,000 and 40,000 species. The bony fish are characterized by an endoskeleton of bone (Greek—*osteon*, bone + *ichthys*, fish), a body covering of scales, a swim bladder, and gill covers. They are classified into three groups: lobe-finned fish, lung fish, and ray-finned fish.

The lobe-finned fish were thought to be extinct until 1938, when a living specimen called the coelacanth was netted off the coast of South Africa. Since then several more specimens have been taken from the same area. These fish have heavy jaws and limblike fins. Little is known about them except that they live near the bottom of the ocean between 70 meters (230 feet) and 600 meters (1,970 feet) and feed on fish and squid.

The six species of lungfish alive today are found in Africa, South America, and Australia. These fish use their gills when water is available, but, when the shallow pools they inhabit dry up, they gulp air into a modified lung. If their waters totally dry up, they can burrow down and wait until the next rain.

The rest of the bony fish belong to the ray-finned group. Their group name refers to the thin bony spines called rays that are connected together by thin skin to form their fins. The ray-finned fish show tremendous variety in size and form. Most ray-fins are under 3 feet long, but they range in length from the tiny Philippine goby at 1 centimeter (0.4 inches) to the Columbia River sturgeon at 3.7 meters (12.5 feet) and in weight from a few tenths of an ounce to 900 kilograms (2,000 pounds).

Ray-fins range from the polar seas to the equator, from temporary desert pools to streams at the tops of mountains 4,200 meters (14,000 feet) high, and from the ocean's surface to depths over 3,600 meters (12,000 feet). They live in open water or on sandy, rocky, or muddy bottoms; in reef crannies; in underground caverns; and in hot springs. Most are exclusive to fresh or salt water but some, such as sticklebacks and sculpins, are at home in either environment. Various species migrate from salt water to fresh water for spawning, and a few, such as eels, do the reverse.

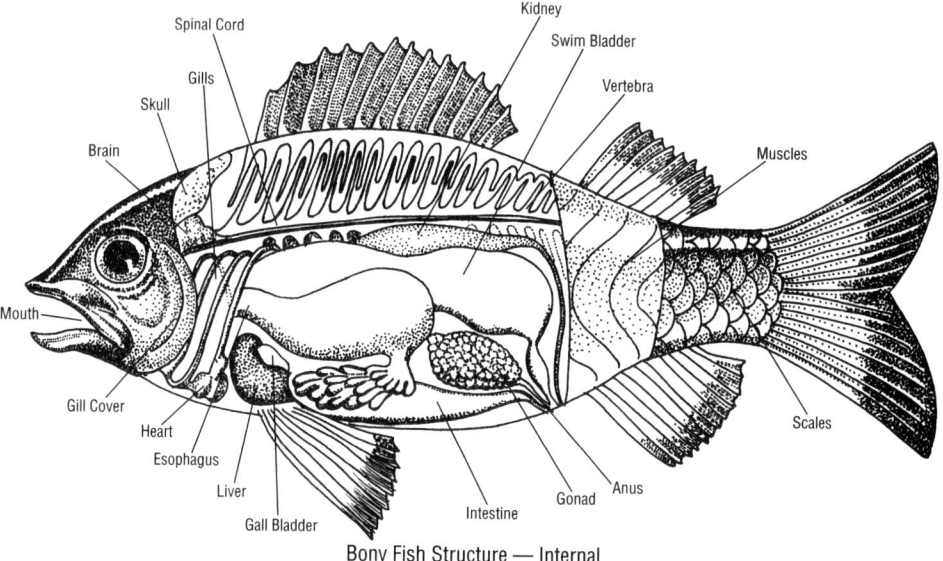

Bony Fish Structure — Internal

Fish are an immeasurably important source of food for many animals, including humans. World fisheries take billions of pounds of fish worth hundreds of millions of dollars annually. Fish products are also important. For example, fish oil is used in soap, paint, and glue.

As predators and herbivores, fish help control the populations of the things they eat. Humans take advantage of this characteristic by using the mosquito fish to consume insects and the grass carp to keep waterways clear of plant growth.

In the biomedical field, fish oil is a source of vitamin D and may protect humans from heart disease. Pufferfish poison may be useful as an anesthetic, and catfish slime could be used to treat wounds. Studies of why sharks never get cancer (or few other diseases) may give us a better understanding of ways to prevent this devastating disease in humans.

Fish provide both pleasure and profit in recreation. Sport fishing is an excellent source of relaxation for thousands of people. In addition, large amounts of money are spent each year by anglers matching wit and technology against their finny adversaries. People also take great pleasure in just watching fish. Studies have demonstrated that quietly sitting and watching a tank of fish can lower the blood pressure and heart rate. There is at least one tank of fish in every 11 American homes, and close to $4 billion a year is spent on the aquarium trade worldwide.

Live fish for classroom study can be obtained in a variety of ways. You may want to collect your own specimens of native fish from local streams or ponds as native fish are more desirable and less expensive than purchased specimens. However, every state has some laws protecting native fish, so consult with your state's wildlife authorities (listed in Appendix C) before collecting. When possible, collect small fish, as they adapt better than large fish to new surroundings. Fish collected from small, shallow ponds or slow-moving streams adapt more readily to classroom situations than do fish from deep or swift water.

Collect small native fish with a fine mesh net. Somewhat larger specimens can be taken carefully by hook and line without injury. Transport fish from the collecting site to the classroom in several plastic bags, one inside the other, placed in a pail or bucket for support and protection. Securely fasten the bags leaving an air space at the top. You could also use plastic cartons half-filled with water and covered with a secure lid. The area of water surface exposed to the air is more important for maintaining adequate aeration than is the depth of the water in the container.

Fish also may be obtained from aquarium shops, pet stores. or the pet centers of some discount and department stores. Buy only fish that appear active and healthy from these sources. The suppliers listed in Appendix B sell goldfish and several varieties of tropical fish. Carolina Biological Supply Company also offers several varities of native fish such as bass, bluegill, and catfish. If you must purchase fish, I recommend that you obtain goldfish or guppies. Both are hardy and especially tolerant of classroom conditions.

I recommend that you stick with freshwater specimens. Marine aquariums are expensive to set up and difficult to adequately maintain under classroom conditions. In addition, the collection of coral and exotic animals to supply the marine aquarium trade has damaged some marine ecosystems and put others in severe peril worldwide. Therefore, I strongly urge you not to collect, purchase, or attempt to maintain saltwater fish or other animals.

A class field trip to a commercial aquarium or to an aquarium store or pet shop will give you and your students an appreciation of the great variety of fish and an understanding of what is required to keep them healthy and happy in the classroom or at home.

# The Importance of Fish

# COLLECTION OF SPECIMENS

# MAINTENANCE OF SPECIMENS
## Preparation

Fish are the easiest and least expensive of all the vertebrates to keep in the classroom. Once an aquarium is properly established, little further work is required.

The first step in keeping fish in the classroom is to determine the function of your aquarium. Will it house only a few hardy fish for a short time? If so, a minimum aquarium will suffice. This setup requires an aquarium filled with clean water, appropriate bottom material, adequate plants for oxygen, and a cover to reduce evaporation and prevent the fish from jumping out. Nothing else is needed providing adequate light and temperature requirements can be maintained.

If you intend to keep fish for an extended period or wish to keep exotic tropical fish, a maximum aquarium should be established. This more sophisticated setup requires an aquarium filled with clean water, appropriate bottom material, adequate plants for oxygen, a filtration system, a heater, and a cover with lights.

Minimum Aquarium

The next step is to determine the best location for the aquarium. The aquarium should be placed on a sturdy, flat surface where it can remain undisturbed. Moving a tank filled with water distorts the seams and can cause leaks. If an aquarium must be relocated, remove most of the water before attempting to move it. The aquarium should not be placed in a location where it receives more than two hours of direct sunlight each day. Too much light will encourage the unsightly growth of algae on the sides of the tank and may cause the water temperature to fluctuate dangerously. Select a well-lit place with a north or east exposure if possible. If necessary, shade the window side of the tank with a green cloth or decorative backing available at aquarium stores, pet shops, or pet centers. Avoid placing the aquarium directly on a window sill or over heat ducts or radiators, as such locations are subject to wide temperature fluctuations that could be harmful to the fish.

Maximum Aquarium

Once the type of aquarium to be established and the proper location for it have been decided, you are ready to obtain the aquarium. The most common and convenient size is a 40-liter (10-gallon) aquarium. The 60-liter (15-gallon) and 80-liter (20-gallon) sizes allow for more flexibility and diversity but are somewhat more expensive to obtain and establish. You can purchase a new aquarium from an aquarium store, pet shop, pet center, or the suppliers listed in Appendix B. You may be able to get free aquariums by requesting donations to your school through newspaper advertisements. You might also survey your students and contact the parents of those who say they have unused aquariums at home. In addition, check out the ads in the newspaper and scout garage sales for aquariums at very reduced prices (even aquariums that leak make excellent terrariums or cages for small mammals). To determine the volume in gallons of a donated or cheaply purchased used aquarium, take length × height × width and divide by 231. Avoid using jars (except temporarily for activities) and especially round fish bowls with small openings. Their shape does not provide sufficient air-to-water exposure to ensure an adequate supply of oxygen.

## Setting Up the Aquarium

You are now ready to set up your aquarium. Follow the steps here, consult your local aquarium store or pet shop, or obtain one of the appropriate references listed in Appendix F.

**Step 1: Clean the Aquarium.** If the aquarium is new, rinse it well with water. If the aquarium has been used previously, wash it thoroughly with warm water to which some mild detergent and a little household ammonia has been added. To remove light lime deposits, fill the aquarium with water and add about 100 milliliters (3.4 ounces) of hydrochloric acid or commercial lime solvent to the water.

Let this mixture soak until the deposits dissolve. Heavy deposits may require a stronger concentration of acid and extended soaking time. If working with acids, always wear protective clothing, gloves, and eyewear and always carefully add the acid into the water, not vice versa. Once the aquarium is thoroughly cleaned, rinse at least three times with clear water inside and out.

**Step 2: Add Bottom Material.** Coarse gravel is the substrate of choice. You can collect your own from gravel roads or purchase it from gravel pits or cement companies. You also can buy this material in a variety of colors from aquarium stores, pet shops, or pet centers. Avoid using soil or very fine sand, as murky water will result.

Thoroughly wash the gravel in a large pan or bucket by running hot water over it and stirring vigorously. Let the gravel stand a few minutes and pour off the water. Repeat this process until the water pours off clear.

Place about 3 to 5 centimeters (1 to 2 inches) of gravel in the bottom of the aquarium. Landscape the bottom material so that it is higher in the back and slopes to the front. This arrangement allows for easy removal of dead matter and uneaten food. If you are setting up a maximum aquarium and wish to use an undergravel filtration system, this system goes in before the bottom material is added.

**Step 3: Begin To Fill.** To avoid disturbing the bottom material, place a piece of cardboard over it and pour water onto the cardboard. Fill the aquarium about one-third full of spring water, clear pond water, or tap water that has been aged. (Allow tap water to stand in uncovered containers at least three days before use so that chlorine gas, which is deadly to fish, can escape.) Aquarium stores, pet shops, pet centers, and the suppliers listed in Appendix B sell water conditioning kits for this purpose. After filling, let the aquarium stand for a time and then check for leaks.

**Step 4: Add Plants and Other Items.** Live plants play many roles in an aquarium. They remove carbon dioxide and add oxygen to the water, they remove nitrogenous waste products released by the fish, they provide cover for the fish, and they make the aquarium look natural and attractive. Live plants are a necessity in establishing a minimum aquarium. The water in a maximum aquarium is filtered and aerated, so you may be able to get by with no plants or artificial decorative plants. A wide variety of artificial plants are sold by aquarium stores, pet shops, and pet centers.

Some living plants recommended for aquariums are Vallisneria (eel grass), Cabomba (fanwort), Elodea (anacharis), Sagittaria (grassleaf), Ludwigia (false loosestrife), Ceratophyllium (hornwort), and Echinodorus (sword plant). These plants may be purchased from aquarium stores, pet shops, or the suppliers listed in Appendix B.

Place tall plants at the rear of the aquarium and shorter plants at the front and sides. Consult your supplier about the mature height of the plants you have selected. Leave the middle of the aquarium open for viewing the fish. Space the plants about 8 to 10 centimeters (3 to 4 inches) apart and cover the roots with gravel.

Use large, straegically placed rocks to provide a hiding place for the fish and to add to the scenic effect. Add other items for decoration or to enchance the natural setting as you desire.

**Step 5: Finish Filling.** Continue pouring water slowly onto a piece of floating cardboard to within 2.5 centimeters (1 inch) of the top of the aquarium. Again, let it stand for a time and check for leaks.

**Step 6: Add a Suitable Cover.** A cover is necessary to reduce evaporation, keep dust out, and keep active, jumping fish in. An adequately lit minimum aquarium will require only a piece of glass or clear plastic large enough to cover the aquarium. Glue small pieces of cork to each corner of the cover to leave space for adequate ventilation. If your minimum aquarium will not receive adequate light or if you are establishing a maximum aquarium, a full aquarium hood with fluorescent tubes will be necessary. These hoods can be purchased from aquarium stores, pet shops, or the suppliers listed in Appendix B. You may find someone to donate one or you may find one at bargain prices at a garage sale.

If you are establishing a minimum aquarium your setup is complete. However, if you are establishing a maximum aquarium, you must consider temperature regulation and filtration and aeration.

1. *Temperature regulation.* Goldfish and native fish can be maintained at room temperature of 20° to 24°C (68° to 75°F) in unheated tanks. Tropical fish require water temperatures of 24° to 27°C (75° to 80°F). Guppies will tolerate unheated tanks, but they thrive in a heated aquarium. Aquarium heaters with thermostatic controls can be purchased from aquarium stores, pet shops, or the suppliers listed in Appendix B. You may get one as part of a donated set or cheaply purchased garage sale set of aquarium and related supplies. Make sure you have a heater large enough for your aquarium. Allow 5 watts per gallon; if room temperature fluctuates greatly, allow 10 watts per gallon.

2. *Filtration and aeration.* Two basic types of filtration units are bottom filters placed under the bottom material and basket filters that sit inside the aquarium on the bottom material or hang outside the tank. Some systems have an enclosed pump, but others depend on an air pump that must be purchased or obtained separately. Some provide aeration as well as filtration; with others, a separate air pump, tubing, and air stones would be needed to provide aeration. Depending on the type, basket filters require filter carbon, filter fiber, or diatomaceous earth. If you have no experience in this area, consult with an aquarium store or pet shop and see the various systems in action before purchasing such equipment. Filtration and aeration equipment can be obtained from aquarium stores, pet shops, pet centers, and the suppliers listed in Appendix B, or you may acquire this equipment as part of a donated set or a cheaply purchased garage sale set.

**Step 7: Add Fish.** First determine the number of fish your tank can safely hold:

| Capacity of tank | Number of 1" fish |
|---|---|
| 10 gallons | 8 |
| 15 gallons | 12 |
| 20 gallons | 17 |
| 25 gallons | 24 |
| 50 gallons | 46 |

Reduce the number of fish for larger fish. For example, a 10-gallon aquarium could hold only 4 two-inch fish safely. In their enthusiasm, many people seriously overcrowd their fish and then wonder why the fish suffer, decline, and die.

Introduce fish into the aquarium by floating the plastic sac containing them in the aquarium for about half an hour to allow them time to adjust to the temperature of the aquarium water. Then gently tip the bag and allow the fish to swim out into their new home. Be careful that none become entrapped in the folds of the plastic bag.

Once your aquarium is established, you may have questions about care and maintenance:

1. How often should the water be changed and the aquarium cleaned? A properly established aquarium does not require much cleaning. Use an oven baster to remove uneaten food or other debris from the bottom and promptly remove dead fish or dead plants. Under normal conditions replacing all the

water in your aquarium in not advisable. However, it is a good idea to siphon out (do not dip water out, as this disturbs the fish and plants) about one-fourth to one-third of the water each month or so and replace it with spring water, clean pond water, or aged tap water. If the water turns cloudy and/or smells foul, change all of it immediately. These conditions are the result of explosive bacterial growth due to overfeeding or accumulation of dead material (fish or plants). Such runaway bacterial growth removes oxygen from the water and may cause fish to die. Replace water lost through evaporation with distilled water if possible or aged tap water if necessary.

2. How much and how often should fish be fed? The amount of food and frequency of feeding depend on the type, maturity, and number of fish being kept. Some fish such as guppies, goldfish, and many small native fish are omnivores that eat both plant material and small live animals, so a variety of food will produce healthier fish. To avert nutritional deficiencies, purchase three or four brands of prepared food from an aquarium store, pet shop, or pet center and mix them together or feed a different brand each day.

As a general rule, feed your fish daily with as much food as they will consume in five to ten minutes. Fish will not overeat to the point of harming themselves, but don't be too generous as uneaten food will quickly foul the water. Fish in a well-established aquarium containing some healthy plants will survive weekends without feeding, but they should never be left unattended for more than two days.

3. What if some of my fish become sick? Occasionally fish become ill even under the best of conditions. Symptoms of poor health to watch for are sluggishness or inactivity, drooping fins, and white patches on fins and body. Unless a fish is costly or an unusual type, the most realistic thing to do is dispose of the sick fish immediately. Treatment of individual fish is usually expensive, time-consuming, and mostly unsuccessful. Humanely dispose of sick fish by placing them in a small container of aquarium water. Place the container in the refrigerator for several hours and then transfer it to the freezer section overnight. Dead fish should be incinerated.

Follow good safety procedures around water. Dress appropriately and be alert to contact with poisonous plants or stinging, biting, or parasitic animals. Do not handle fish with your bare hands if your hands have cuts or scrapes on them. A disease similar to tuberculosis has been spread to humans in this manner. Wash your hands thoroughly after handling fish, nets, aquarium water, or containers housing fish.

Working with fish presents no safety or health threats to students. Have students thoroughly wash their hands after contact with aquarium water or containers housing fish.

Make sure collected fish are transported immediately to the classroom in plastic bags with an adequate air supply. Once in the classroom, there are four basic factors to consider for the health and well-being of the fish: (1) suitable water, (2) adequate oxygen, (3) correct temperature and protection from wide temperature fluctuations, and (4) correct kinds and amounts of food.

Use slow, careful movements when handling fish. Frightened fish can injure themselves. Never touch fish with bare hands; use a wet net or nets. Hold a hand over the net when transferring fish to prevent them from jumping out.

Careful attention to the proper setup of an aquarium and to the basic needs of the fish will reward you and your students with a great deal of learning and entertainment.

If you put individual fish in small containers during activities, watch closely for signs of low oxygen such as the fish gulping air from the surface. Leave fish in small unaerated containers for as short a time as possible. Be alert to students

HEALTH AND SAFETY
Teachers

Students

Fish

who might agitate the fish by shaking their container, tapping on the container, or putting objects into the container. If fish in a small space become highly agitated, they could injure themselves or attempt to jump out.

**H1.** *Fish Habitats.* Professor I. M. Scaly needs your students' help in determining the origin of selected fish. Show students pictures, diagrams, and/or slides of as many different kinds of fish as possible from each of the three classes of fish. Have students attempt to explain orally or in written form where each fish would be found and what adaptations it has for its particular habitat.

**H2.** *Glowing Fish.* Some fish that live in the inky black benthic depths of the ocean have chemicals in their skin that make them luminescent (glow-in-the-dark). Have students theorize in what ways this would be an advantage to these fish. (Answer: Such bioluminescent characteristics may enable them to see in dark water, confuse predators, attract curious prey, or find mates.)

**H3.** *Walk a Mile in My Shoes.* Have students try to put themselves in the fish's place by asking them to react orally or in written form to the following question: What specific fish would you be and why?

**H4.** **Challenge:** *Do Fish Prefer Light or Dark Habitats?* Have students devise a way to test this problem. First, word the problem more precisely by specifiying what type of fish will be tested. If possible, have different groups of students test different types of fish. Small glass or clear plastic aquaria about $15 \times 15 \times 27$ centimeters ($6 \times 6 \times 9$ inches) or around 8 liters (2 gallons) work well for testing. Fill the aquaria about three-fourths full of water from the aquarium where the fish to be tested are being housed.

The most satisfactory experimental design is to cover the bottom, sides, and top of one-half of a small aquarium with white paper and the bottom, sides, and top of the other half with black paper. Ideally, students will arrive at this design on their own after realizing that the entire aquarium must be covered or the fish might react to the students' presence (and false data would result). If they miss this point in the design brainstorming, help them "see the light" through investigative questioning; do not simply tell them how to proceed.

Have students predict what they think will happen before they begin. Set up the test aquaria and carefully add one fish to each. Students should determine in their experimental design that they should test only one fish at a time. Several fish together may react more to each other than they do to the color of the habitat, resulting in "muddy data." Allow the fish several minutes to calm down before taking data. Strategically placed slits in the paper on both halves of each aquarium will allow the students to see the fish without the fish seeing them. Using two stopwatches, have students record how much time the fish spends in each half of the tank over a set period of time. Then have students record their data in appropriate data tables, construct charts or graphs, and draw conclusions.

**H5.** *Population Growth in Fish.* Scientists have developed mathematical formulas for growth of natural populations. Two types of population growth can be described: r-selected populations and K-selected populations. K-selected organisms are large, slow growing, and long lived. They produce few young and generally give some care to their young. On the other hand, r-selected organisms are small, have short lives, and produce large numbers of offspring with little or no parental care given to the young.

Based on what they know about fish, have students theorize whether bony fish are K-selected or r-selected and whether sharks are K-selected or r-selected. (Bony fish are r-selected and sharks are K-selected.) Pose this question to students: Humans are thoughtlessly overexploiting all types of fish. Which type—bony fish or sharks—faces the greatest danger from humans? (In general terms, sharks are in the greatest peril because of their slow growth, few offspring, and long generation time.)

**H6.** *Fish Food Chains.* With few exceptions, fish are simultaneously predator and prey in their natural environment. Relatively few fish are exclusively herbivores or scavengers. Thus fish are important components of aquatic food chains. Challenge student understanding of aquatic food chains by using the illustrations as a reference. Describe or provide pictures of the organisms involved in each food chain and ask students to determine the proper sequence of the food chain.

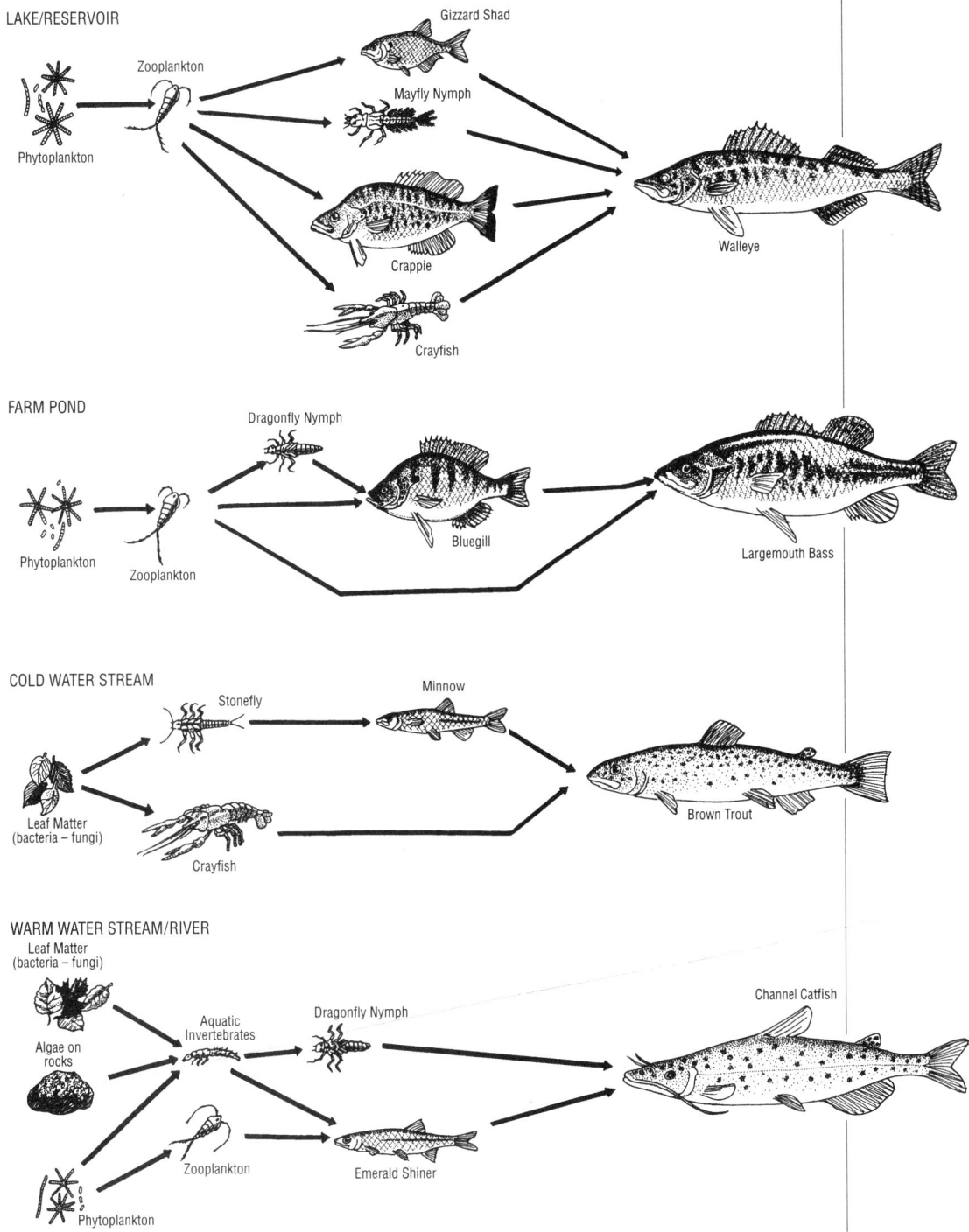

LAKE/RESERVOIR

Phytoplankton · Zooplankton · Gizzard Shad · Mayfly Nymph · Crappie · Crayfish · Walleye

FARM POND

Phytoplankton · Zooplankton · Dragonfly Nymph · Bluegill · Largemouth Bass

COLD WATER STREAM

Leaf Matter (bacteria – fungi) · Stonefly · Crayfish · Minnow · Brown Trout

WARM WATER STREAM/RIVER

Leaf Matter (bacteria – fungi) · Algae on rocks · Aquatic Invertebrates · Dragonfly Nymph · Zooplankton · Emerald Shiner · Phytoplankton · Channel Catfish

**H7.** *Mabel's Aquarium Calculations.* Have students perform the necessary calculations detailed in the following scenario: At a garage sale, Aunt Mabel bought a used aquarium and the necessary equipment to set it up. However, she has no idea how many gallons it can hold nor how many fish she can safely put in it. The tank's dimensions are 48 inches long, 20 inches wide, and 14 inches high. Can you help her figure it out? (First determine the volume of the aquarium by taking length × width × height, or $48 \times 20 \times 14 = 13,440$. Divide 13,440 by 231 to determine the volume in gallons: $13,440 \div 231 = 58$ gallons. As a general rule you need 1 gallon [4 liters] of water for each 1 inch [2.5 centimeters] of fish [excluding tail fin], so Mabel could safely put 58 one-inch fish in this aquarium, or 29 two-inch fish, or 19 three-inch fish, and so on.)

**H8.** *Camouflage-a-Fish.* Have students imagine that the classroom is under water. Challenge them to design and construct a fish to live anywhere in the classroom they choose—the wall, the floor, the top of a desk, the ceiling, or other area. Each fish must be protectively colored to camouflage itself and shaped to adapt itself to the surface where it lives. Let students see how well they met the challenge by having other students, teachers, or an administrator play the role of a predator and come into the room after the students have placed their fish in their habitats. How many of the fish can the "predator" find?

## Structure

**S1.** *Fish Structure Comparisons.* Have students compare and contrast the structure of the various classes of fish by constructing and filling in a blank table similar to the following one. For your convenience the table has brief answers included. Students could work with live specimens, pictures, and/or preserved specimens of the lamprey, hagfish, shark, skate, ray, and assorted bony fish on this activity.

|  | Agnatha | Chondrichthyes | Osteichthyes |
|---|---|---|---|
| **Skeleton** | (cartilage) | (cartilage) | (bone) |
| **Covering** | (slimy skin) | (denticles) | (scales) |
| **Fins** | (1—fleshy) | (many but stiff) | (many but flexible) |
| **Gill covers** | (absent) | (absent) | (present) |
| **Swim bladder** | (absent) | (absent) | (present) |

Older or more advanced students could accomplish the same task in a more challenging manner by constructing a dichotomous key of fish characteristics. A dichotomous key requires a choice between successive pairs of characteristics. Each subject is identified by separating out the characteristics unique to that subject. Again, live specimens, pictures, and/or preserved specimens of the lamprey, hagfish, shark, skate, ray, and assorted bony fish would be needed.

One possible dichotomous key to fish structure might look something like this:

1A. Skeleton of cartilage, no swim bladder or gill covers . . . . . . . . go to 2
1B. Skeleton of bone, swim bladder and gill covers present . . . . . . . go to 5
2A. No paired fins . . . . . . . . . . . . . . . . . . . . . . . . . . . . . . . . . . go to 3
2B. Paired fins . . . . . . . . . . . . . . . . . . . . . . . . . . . . . . . . . . . . go to 4
3A. Large, disk-shaped mouth and large eyes . . . . . . . . . . . . . . . Lamprey
3B. Small mouth with barbels and tiny eyes . . . . . . . . . . . . . . . . Hagfish

4A.  Pectoral fins small, mouth at end of body . . . . . . . . . . . . . . . . . Shark
4B.  Pectoral fins large, mouth beneath body . . . . . . . . . . . . Skate or ray
5A.  Scales present . . . . . . . . . . . . . . . . . . . . . . . . . . . . . . . . . . . . . . Bass
5B.  Scales absent. . . . . . . . . . . . . . . . . . . . . . . . . . . . . . . . . . . . . Catfish

   The number of bony fish pictures or specimens you have available would dictate how much farther students would need to carry out the key beyond number 4.

**S2.** *Structure of a Bony Fish.* Have students diagram and label a bony fish and its parts: mouth, eye, operculum (gill cover), scales, caudal (tail) fin, dorsal fin(s), pectoral fins, pelvic fins, anal fin, and anus.

**S3.** *Parts of a Fish.* Have students respond to the following questions: What are the main divisions to the body of a fish? (Answer: The body is divided into the head, trunk, and tail.) What constitutes the head, trunk, and tail of a fish? (The head is the section from the mouth to the gill covers, the trunk is from the gill covers to the anus, and the tail is from the anus to the other end.)

**S4.** *Design-a-Fish.* Life in the water puts many severe constraints on the design of a fish. Based on body shape, there are several broad categories of fish: rover-predator, lie-in-wait predator, surface fish, and bottom fish. Have students diagram a fish of their own design to fit any or all of the categories listed. (Rover-predators are usually streamlined with a pointed head and forked tail. Lie-in-wait predators usually have an elongated body, large mouth with teeth, and a large tail fin with the dorsal and anal fins far back on the body. Surface fish usually are small with an upward-pointing mouth, flattened head, and large eyes. Bottom fish usually have a body flattened in one direction or the other and a mouth turned down or on the underside of the body. These categories are merely general groupings. Many fish have shapes that are difficult to categorize.)

**S5.** *Fish Swimming Action.* Place a fish in a container by itself and have students observe the action of the fins and the general movement of the fish. If the container is large enough, have students describe the swimming action of the fish viewed from above.

   **Challenge:** What is the function of each type of fin on a fish? (Fins can function in one of four possible manners: balance, power, steering, or combinations of those three.) Have students observe the action of each type of fin and attempt to determine the function of each type. Ask students to keep their observations in table form.

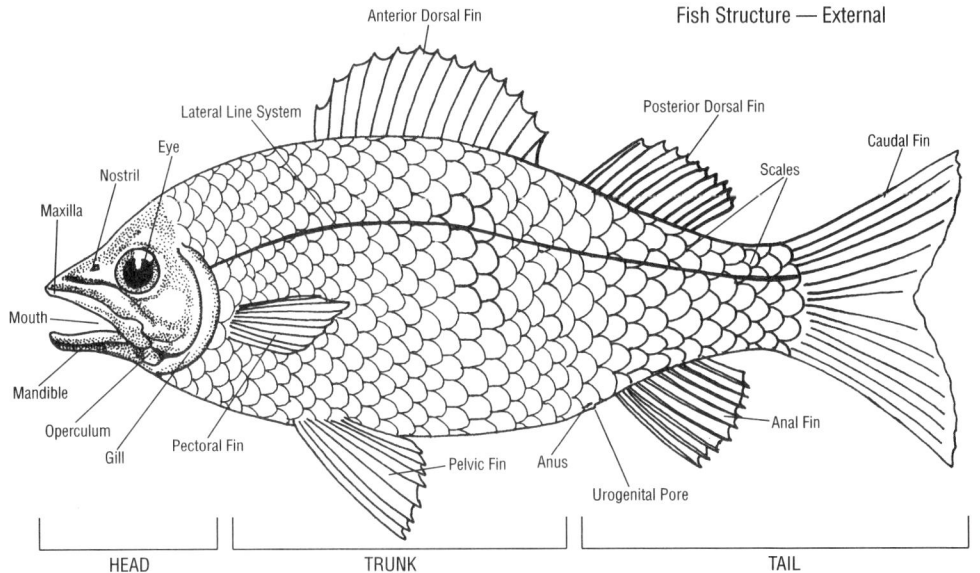

Fish Structure — External

Anterior Dorsal Fin

Posterior Dorsal Fin

Caudal Fin

Lateral Line System

Scales

Eye

Nostril

Maxilla

Mouth

Mandible

Operculum

Gill

Pectoral Fin

Pelvic Fin

Anus

Urogenital Pore

Anal Fin

HEAD          TRUNK          TAIL

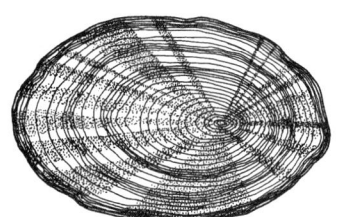

Scale Showing Growth Rings

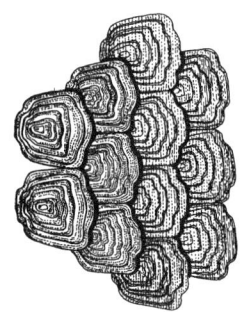

Cycloid Scales

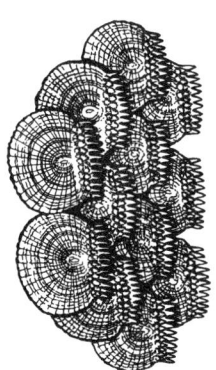

Ctenoid Scales

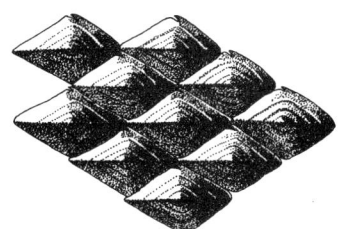

Ganoid Scales

Placoid Scales

**S6.** *Swimming Abilities Comparisons.* Have students compare and contrast the swimming abilities of the various classes of fish. (Agnathans are weak swimmers that wriggle laboriously through the water. The sharks, skates, and rays are powerful and even graceful swimmers, but they are not particularly agile. They cannot stop very well once moving forward and they cannot swim backward. The many flexible fins of the bony fish allow them to swim powerfully and gracefully with amazing agility.)

**S7.** *How Old?* Pose this question to students: Would it be possible to tell the approximate age of a fish by counting the total number of scales on the fish? (No, but it is possible to determine the approximate age of the fish by counting the rings on its scales. Scales grow as the layer of skin that covers them on the outside forms around the edges. Since scales grow as the fish grows—more in summer and less in winter, especially in temperate zones—they leave a distinct record of age and season.)

There are several categories of fish scales based on their structure and appearance—cycloid, ctenoid, ganoid, and placoid.

Obtain several different types of fish scales. The suppliers listed in Appendix B sell sets of fish scale types. Have students view the different types of scales with a hand magnifier or preferably a dissecting scope and try to determine the approximate age of the fish from which the scales were taken.

**S8.** *In Goes the Good Air, Out Goes the Bad Air.* Like all other animals, fish need oxygen to sustain life. Most fish get their oxygen by drawing water in through their mouth, passing the water over the gills, and expelling the water out through openings on the side of the head. Blood vessels in the gills absorb oxygen from the water and dump carbon dioxide into the water as the water passes over them.

Place a fish in a container by itself and have students observe and describe the movements of the gill covers and mouth as the fish breathes. Have students attempt to determine the respiratory rate—the number of breaths per minute of the fish. (The mouth and gill covers alternately open and close, pumping water over the gills. Count each opening of the gill covers as one exhalation in determining respiratory rate.)

**Challenge:** What effect does raising or lowering the water temperature have on the respiratory rate of a fish? Have students devise a way to test this problem.

One design would be to put a single fish in a container about half full of aquarium water. Allow the fish and water to remain undisturbed for at least five minutes. Then record the water temperature and consider that temperature the initial temperature. Now determine the respiratory rate of the fish a total of four times. Average the respiratory rates and consider that number the base respiratory rate. Have students record their data in a table.

Now gently place the container with the fish in it into an ice-water bath. Do *not* add ice directly to the water containing the fish. When the water temperature around the fish is 5 degrees fahrenheit cooler than the initial temperature, record this temperature and determine the respiratory rate of the fish a total of four times. Compute the average respiratory rate for that temperature.

Gently place the container with the fish in it into a warm-water bath. Do *not* add hot water directly to the water containing the fish. When the water temperature around the fish is 5 degrees fahrenheit warmer than the initial temperature, record this temperature and determine the respiratory rate of the fish a total of four times. Compute the average respiratory rate for that temperature.

Have students graph their results with temperature on the horizontal (X) axis of the graph and average breathing rate on the vertical (Y) axis of the graph. Have students draw conclusions from their data table and graph.

The rate at which fish consume oxygen can be affected by a number of factors. Have students examine the graphs at right and answer the questions.

a. What is the relationship between oxygen consumption and swimming velocity? (The higher the velocity, the more oxygen consumed.)

b. Explain the relationship shown on the graph. (A higher velocity requires the fish to work harder. In turn, its muscles demand more oxygen.)

c. What is the relationship between water temperature and oxygen consumption? (The higher the water temperature, the more oxygen consumed.)

d. Do larger fish consume more oxygen than small fish? If so, why? (Yes, because a large body means more cells demanding oxygen.)

**S9.** *Swim Bladder and Gill Covers.* Pose the following question to students: Bony fish have gill covers and a swim bladder. How do these characteristics benefit them? (A swim bladder allows the fish to regulate its buoyancy, thus expending less energy in movement and allowing it to remain motionless at a constant depth. Gill covers allow bony fish to remain motionless and continue to move water over the gills. The poor shark, without swim bladder or gill covers, must constantly keep swimming. To stop is to sink and suffocate.)

**S10.** *Challenge: How Can You Take a Fish's Temperature?* Have students devise a way to test this problem. (Since fish are ectothermic [cold-blooded], their temperature is close to the temperature of the water around them. Hence, to determine the temperature of the fish, take the temperature of the water surrounding the fish.)

**S11.** *Fish Size.* The smallest fish is the Marshall Island goby at 1.25 centimeters (0.5 inches), and the largest fish is the whale shark at 18 meters (60 feet). Have students measure and mark off these distances for comparison. You could also include the measurements of some common aquarium fish or native game fish the students might be familiar with. Use a corridor, hallway, or gymnasium to allow adequate room for your measurements.

**S12.** *Fish Models.* Have students make a model of any fish of their choice using colored modeling clay or bread dough (Recipe in Chapter 3, activity S9).

When observing fish behavior, cover the container housing the fish in such a way that you and your students can see the fish but the fish cannot see you. The fish may react to your presence, and their reaction will invalidate whatever factor you are testing. Make sure students understand that the way a fish behaves in a container is not necessarily the way it would behave in its natural surroundings.

**B/R1.** *Touch Reponse.* Place a single fish in a container about three-fourths full of aquarium water. Have the students carefully investigate whether the fish is sensitive to touch and if so, which areas seem to be the most sensitive. Students should use a blunt probe for this activity. Have them bring the probe toward the fish's body slowly, carefully, and deliberately.

**B/R2.** *Lateral Line.* Students may notice from the previous activity that the fish can seemingly detect the presence of the probe even when it cannot fully see the probe. Ask these questions: How can the fish detect the probe? How can some fish swim in large schools and make intricate, organized

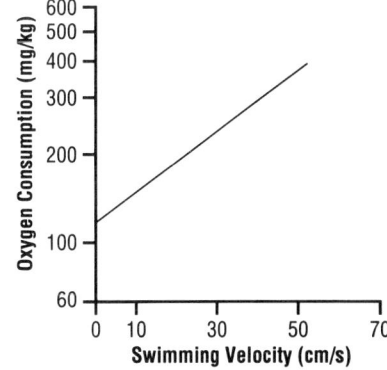

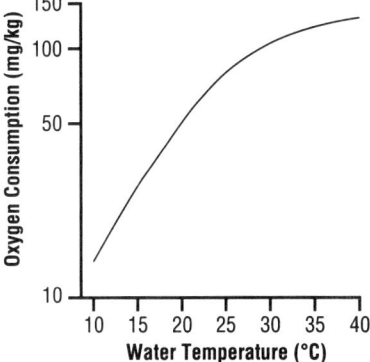

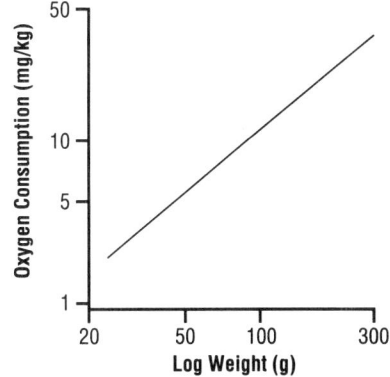

## Behavior/Response

group movements without colliding with one another? Why don't fish in murky or dark water bump into things? Why don't blind cave fish, commonly seen in aquarium stores, never run into the sides of the aquarium? (The answers lie in the lateral line system, a series of pits and canals running the length of the fish. The lateral line allows the fish to detect low-frequency vibrations and the pressure waves from stationary or moving objects [like the probe] in the water.)

Ask students, How does the lateral line benefit fish? (This system helps fish find food, detect predators, and avoid objects in the water even when it cannot see these things with its eyes.)

**B/R3.** *Can Fish Taste/Smell?* Have students put a chemical such as vinegar near the head of the fish and observe its reactions. Use caution about which chemicals or substances are used, and for the safety of the fish, introduce them in very dilute amounts only. (Fish vary in this ability, but most do have a sense of taste. The sense of smell, however, seems to be more important. Fish can smell to a high degree. Some eels can smell certain chemicals in concentrations of 0.0000000000001 moles! Salmon can literally smell the stream from which they migrated as young smolts when they return to breed in these streams. Sharks can smell blood from a great distance and seem to materialize out of nowhere to attack bleeding animals.)

**B/R4.** *Can Fish Hear?* Have students visualize the following scenario: You are going fishing with your young cousin, Bart Barnacle. Bart is very noisy. He runs screaming down the bank and throws his fishing gear with a clatter into your boat. While out on the lake, Bart constantly sings loudly and restlessly thumps and bangs about the boat. Will you have much luck catching any fish under such circumstances? In other words, could fish hear all this commotion? (Fish probably do not hear in the same sense that we do, but they do perceive sound waves in the form of vibrations. Consequently, your fishing expedition with Bart probably will be fruitless—and fishless.)

**B/R5.** *Fish Eyes.* Have students observe the eyes of a fish and then answer this question: Compared to the size of their head, fish have very large eyes and huge pupil openings. Why? (Even clear water absorbs light quickly so fish constantly inhabit a dim, murky world where they need as large a light-gathering organ as possible.)

Can fish blink? (No, they have no eyelids. They don't need eyelids because the water around them constantly moistens their eyes.)

Can fish see colors? (Considering the brilliance of many fish colors, it is not surprising that most fish have color vision. Fish living in turbid or deep water often lack the ability to see red since very little red light penetrates such environments.)

**B/R6.** *Exploratory Behavior.* Have students investigate the exploratory behavior of fish. In an established aquarium, introduce a new and novel object such as a marble or a shell. Have students note and record the nature of the fishes' response to the object, the frequency of the response, and the duration of the response.

Have students further investigate such behavior:

a. Does the response change if the object is introduced every day for a week but removed after ten minutes?

b. Does the response change if the object is introduced before the fish are scheduled to be fed? After the fish have been fed?

c. Does changing the location of the object in the tank change the response?

Have your students brainstorm further investigations they could make on the exploratory behavior of fish.

**B/R7.** *Schooling Behavior.* Have students investigate the schooling behavior of fish. You will need 9 to 10 fish of the same species for this activity. Native minnows work well because they tend to school at any time of the year. Cover the test tank in such a way that you and your students can see the fish but the fish cannot see you. You want the fish to react to each other rather than the presence of humans.

Place a single fish in a beaker of aquarium water, cover the beaker with a flexible wire mesh, and secure the mesh with a rubber band. Immerse the beaker containing the fish at one end of an aquarium full of aquarium water but nothing else—no other fish, no bottom material, and no plants. This end of the aquarium should be designated side X. As a control, immerse a similarly prepared beaker with no fish in it at the other end of the tank. This end should be designated side Y.

Place one test fish of the same species as the beaker fish into the tank. This is the test fish. Allow the test fish time to adjust to the new conditions. Use a stopwatch to time the number of seconds the test fish spends in each half of the tank during a 5-minute period. Have students record this information in a data table. Repeat this procedure several times, using a different test fish of the same species as the one in the beaker each time.

Now put 5 to 6 fish of the same species in a beaker in the X end of the tank and 1 fish of the same species in a beaker in the Y end of the tank. Add to the aquarium a test fish of the same species as those in the beakers. Time and record as before. Repeat several times using a different test fish of the same species as those in the beakers each time.

From their data have students calculate the percentage of time the test fish spent in each half of the aquarium for each experimental setup. Have students use their data to answer the following questions:

a. In the first setup, does the test fish prefer to associate with the empty beaker or the one containing ? Support your answer with data.

b. In the second setup, does the test fish prefer to associate with the larger group or the single fish? Support your answer with data.

c. Based on your observations, what is the main sense the fish seems to use in schooling? (Vision, but the lateral line plays a role.)

d. How would you define schooling in fish? (The most useful definition explains a school as a group of fish mutually attracted to each other.)

e. Why do fish school? How does schooling benefit fish? (Experts surmise that fish school for increased swimming efficiency, reduced risk of predation, increased efficiency of food-getting, and increased reproductive success.)

Interested, older, or more advanced students could carry these simple schooling experiments further and investigate problems such as species preference or the effects of light intensity, water temperature, water depth, and other factors on schooling.

**B/R8.** **Challenge:** *Can Fish Learn?* Have students devise a way to test this problem.

You can develop a conditioned response in fish by training them to come to a certain corner of the tank when you blow a whistle. Shade the tank so the fish are reacting to the whistle and not your presence. Blow the whistle once for several seconds each time before you feed the fish. In a short time the fish will exhibit feeding behavior when they hear the whistle. While training your fish, never feed them without whistling and never whistle without feeding them. Have students record accurate observations of the behavior of the fish as training progresses and keep track of the time it takes to train the fish.

Once the fish have been trained to the whistle, use another stimulus such as a flashing light to train them to feed in the opposite corner of the tank. If you can accomplish this, you could direct your fish to opposite corners by using the appropriate stimulus, the whistle or the flashing light.

Interested, older, or more advanced students might pursue other problems along these lines. For example: Do some species learn faster than others? How soon will fish forget their training? Do environmental factors such as light intensity or temperature affect the rate of learning?

Many species of fish can learn to solve underwater mazes. Such investigations are very interesting and enlightening, but they do require a great deal of construction, and rather large tanks are needed to hold the mazes.

## Feeding

**F1.** *Feeding Comparisons.* Have students compare and contrast the various types of food fish eat and the various ways fish get their food. (See the "Specific Class Characteristics" section of this chapter and consult other appropriate references.)

**F2.** *Feed a Fish.* Have students observe and describe the feeding behavior of an individual fish. Place a single fish that has not been fed for 24 hours in a container about three-fourths full of aquarium water. Add the appropriate food for the type of fish you are observing. Have students carefully observe and record the fish's feeding behavior while considering the following questions:
a. How did the fish position its body while feeding?
b. How did the fish position its fins while feeding?
c. How did the fish take the food into its mouth—gulp, suction, or tear?
d. Did the fish swallow the food whole, or did it chew the food and then swallow?

**F3.** *Feed a Bunch of Fish.* Have students observe and describe the feeding behavior of several fish of the same species they observed feeding singly. Have students observe and note any differences in feeding position or feeding action compared to the fish feeding alone.

**F4.** *Feeding Hierarchy.* Have students observe the feeding behavior of a group of fish and try to determine if there is a feeding hierarchy among the fish. While observing have students consider the following questions:
a. Does one fish or do several fish dominate over the others?
b. Is the dominant fish male or female? (In some live-bearing fish such as guppies, the sexes are easily distinguished, but in most egg-laying tropicals, goldfish, and native fish, only the fish know for sure.)
c. Is the dominant fish larger or simply more aggressive than the others?
d. How does removing the dominant fish affect the hierarchy?

Some native fish such as the sunfish family—bass, crappie, bluegill, and sunfish distributed over most of North America—show strong territorial tendencies and develop a definite feeding hierarchy when placed in an aquarium. However, use caution and do not keep members of the sunfish clan together for very long as one will quickly become dominant and harass the others to death in a short time.

**F5.** **Challenge:** *How Do Environmental Conditions Affect the Feeding Rate of Fish?* Have students devise a way to test this problem.

Your students should recognize that their first step is to rewrite the problem to make it more specific. You must determine specifically what environmental factor—light intensity, temperature, and so on—is to be tested.

You will need two tanks to conduct this activity, one for the experimental conditions and one to act as a control. Goldfish, guppies, or small native fish make excellent test subjects. Set up both tanks identically except for the factor to be tested.

Feed the fish in both tanks a measured amount of food daily and record the time necessary for the fish to consume the food. Have students predict what they think will happen before they begin. Make sure they keep data in appropriate tables, charts, and graphs and draw conclusions from their data.

Interested, older, or more advanced students might use this activity as a springboard into investigating whether feeding rate is directly proportional to growth rate.

**F6.** *Design-a-Fish.* Have students create, illustrate, and label a fish with unusual feeding adaptations such as gulping large quantities of algae, getting prey from tiny cracks and crevices in a coral reef, getting prey buried in bottom sediments, filtering plankton from the water, or getting insects off of tree branches hanging over the water. You could also have students create, illustrate, and label a fish with unusual camouflage or unusual defenses that help prevent it from being eaten by predators.

**R1.** *Reproductive Comparisons.* Have students investigate the various reproductive behaviors of courtship, nest-building, egg-laying or live birth, and parental care in fish by having individual students or groups of students research specific types or groups of fish and report their reproductive strategies to the rest of the class.

**R2.** *Observing Fish Reproduction.* Have students observe the reproductive behavior of fish. Live-bearing tropical fish make the best subjects for an activity of this type. Goldfish or egg-laying tropicals do not reproduce readily in the typical classroom aquarium. Guppies are especially suited to this activity because they are inexpensive and easy to obtain and maintain, the sexes are easy to distinguish, they give birth to live young, and they reproduce rapidly.

Isolate male and female guppies into separate containers and have students carefully describe each sex. Male guppies tend to be smaller and more brightly colored than the females. Male guppies may also be distinguished by a tubular structure near the anus called the gonopodium. Female guppies are larger and drab colored compared to the males. The female has a fan-shaped fin near the anus.

Place the guppies together in an aquarium and have students carefully observe and describe any mating behaviors that occur. A positive mating response in male guppies involves vibrating the dorsal fin and maneuvering the gonopodium in an attempt to inseminate the female. Have a ratio of about three females for every one male or the males will run the females ragged. Have students make observations daily and note any changes in the appearance of male and female and any changes in behavior that may occur. As students are carrying out their observations have them consider the following questions:

a. How does the male entice the female to mate?
b. What is the body position and fin position of both the male and female during mating?
c. What is the sequence of events leading up to mating? following mating?
d. Do males defend a mating territory, and/or do they defend certain females against male rivals?

When the female's abdomen becomes enlarged and an area called the gavid spot near the anal fin becomes dark, she is ready to drop her young. Guppies will eat their young, so make some accommodation to protect the

## Reproduction and Development

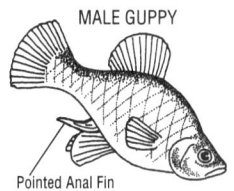

MALE GUPPY

Pointed Anal Fin

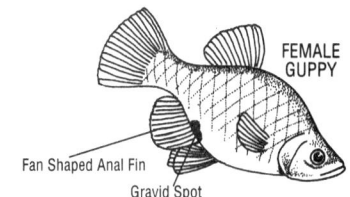

FEMALE GUPPY

Fan Shaped Anal Fin

Gravid Spot

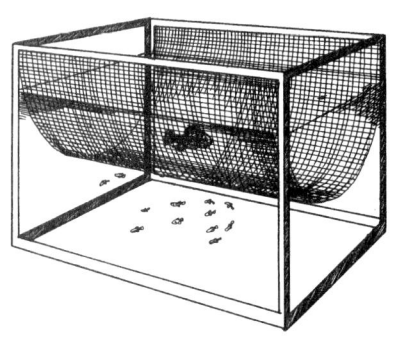

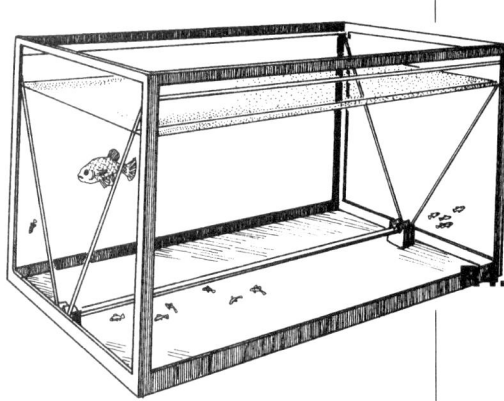

Guppy Breeding Trap Types

young guppies. The female may be removed to a tank with plenty of vegetation where there are no other fish, or she may be placed in a breeding trap.

After giving birth the female should be removed immediately to a tank by herself and kept away from male guppies for a few days. When guppies are given adequate food and kept in a heated aquarium they will bear young every four to six weeks.

The young fry should be left in a tank of their own. They are fairly hardy and can eat finely powdered food immediately. You may purchase suitable food at any aquarium store or pet shop. If properly cared for, these young fish will reach reproductive age in about four months.

**R3. Challenge:** *What Is the Effect of Environmental Factors on Fish Reproduction?* Have students devise a method to test any or all of the following specific problems (or brainstorm and come up with some problems of your own):

a. What is the effect of temperature (or light intensity or food availability) on the reproductive behavior of fish?

b. What is the effect of temperature (or light intensity or food availability) on the gestation period of fish?

c. What is the effect of temperature (or light intensity or food availability) on the number of live offspring born?

d. What is the effect of temperature (or light intensity or food availability) on the survival rate of fry for one week (or a time period of your choice) after birth?

You will need several tanks and a healthy stock of fish to conduct any of these activities. Guppies would be the fish of choice for this activity for reasons stated in activity R2. Control your variables. One tank and set of fish should be the control and kept as normal as possible. Another tank and set of fish should be the experimental group. The only difference between the tanks should be the environmental factor you are testing.

Have students predict what they think will happen before they begin; keep data in appropriate tables, charts, and graphs; and draw conclusions from their data.

*Fish Embryology.* Conduct a study of fish embryology by having students watch the final development and hatching of fish eggs. Carolina Biological Supply Company, listed in Appendix B, sells kits for hatching fish. The kits contain necessary apparatus, instructions, and coupons for fish eggs. Redeeming the coupon will bring you the ready-to-hatch eggs of the annual killifish (Notobranchlus guentheri).

Killifish are from the tropical and subtropical regions of Africa and South America. During the dry season, adult female killifish lay eggs at the bottoms of puddles. As the puddles turn to dry holes, the eggs survive for days, months, or even years in a state of suspended animation called dipause. When the rains return, the eggs hatch. The eggs you will receive will be in diapause. When you add water, they will begin to hatch, sometimes within minutes.

The eggs are about the size of a pinhead, and microscopes will be necessary for students to adequately appreciate the structure of the embryo and its emergence on hatching. Using diagrams and descriptions, students could keep a developmental diary of the hatching and maturation processes of these amazing little fish.

Unfortunately, killifish eggs come to you in the very final stages of development. To study the development of a fish in totality from just-laid egg to hatched fry, consider using a fish called the medaka (Orizias latipes). These hardy fish can be maintained easily in a classroom setting and reliably bred year-round. Natural breeding occurs from April to October but can be induced any time by regulating the period of light the fish receive. Breeding females produce clusters of eggs that cling to her body. The optically clear eggs, which may be removed, give an excellent view of organ formation and overall embryo development. Several of the suppliers listed in Appendix B handle the medaka and Carolina Biological Supply Company has produced a very useful pamphlet on these fish, *The Japanese Medaka: Its Care and Development*. As with the killifish, students need access to microscopes to adequately view and appreciate the marvelous changes occurring within the medaka eggs. Suppliers will provide information on maintenance of adults and fry. Neither killifish or medaka are native to North America and should not be released into the wild.

**R5.** *Fish Genetics*. Have students conduct a study of fish genetics. It is beyond the scope of this book to give a detailed account of genetic principles in general or fish genetics in particular. If you are interested in pursuing such activities, local aquarium stores, fish fanciers, or geneticists at local colleges or universities may be able to help with the details of conducting such investigations. The book entitled *Guppies*, by Wilfred L. Whiten (listed in Appendix F), has an excellent chapter on inheritance in guppies.

Goldfish and egg-laying tropical fish are difficult to breed in the small aquariums often found in classroom situations. Live-bearing tropicals, especially the guppy and the platy, are much more suited to breeding and genetic studies.

Use fish genetics to challenge students' understanding of certain genetic principles such as dominance. When breeding fish of different colors or color patterns, does one color or color pattern dominate over others? If so, what pattern is dominant? Have students take on more advanced genetic challenges by trying to purposefully develop a certain color, color pattern, or fin shape through selective breeding. Advanced genetic activities such as these require males and females from pure breeding stock, and the females must never have mated before (virgin females) as female fish who have mated can store sperm in their bodies for up to six months.

**In1.** *Writing:*

a. Have students write a formal library report on the sea lamprey (Ptromyzon marinus) and the problems it has caused in the Great Lakes.

b. Have students discuss in writing the many ways fish are important both in general and specifically to humans. (See the section "The Importance of Fish" in this chapter and use other appropriate sources.)

c. Have students react in writing to this quote by John Ruskin: "No human being, however great or powerful, was ever so free as a fish."

**In2.** *Fine Arts:*

a. Use your study of fish to introduce your students to gyotaku, Japanese fish printing. Purchase a whole fish about the size of your hand. Wash the fish well with soap and water and dry thoroughly. Place the fish on a pad of newspaper supporting the fins and tail with lumps of clay. Brush on ink or paint against the grain of the scales. Then carefully press a piece of unglazed paper over the fish and pat it down gently with your fingers. Using this technique, students can print a variety of fish species and produce bulletin board displays or notebooks of their work. By using insoluble ink, prints can be made onto T-shirts— a great way to promote your class and the study of fish.

b. Have students choreograph and perform a dance depicting the schooling behavior of fish such as their reaction to predators and/or feeding.

Integration
with Other
Subject Areas

c. Have students draw a cartoon depicting the disadvantages of being a shark with no swim bladder or gill covers.

**In3.** *Social Studies:*

a. *History.* Throughout history humans have been matching wits with fish in an attempt to catch them. Bring to class natural objects such as pieces of bone, long straight sticks, sticks with a Y-shaped end, pieces of animal skin, fibrous plant material, and so on. Have your students imagine that they are an ancient tribe of humans called the Troglodytes and that they are very hungry. Challenge them to devise as many ways as possible to catch fish using only the natural materials you have presented.

b. *Geography.* Have students bring in recipes for fish dishes. Try to get as many recipes as possible from different cultures and countries. This task should present no problem if you have a mixed ethnic group of students. Some of your students might have pen pals or relatives in other countries; have them write for recipes. You might contact the United Nations or various foreign embassies, as well. Have students keep track on a map of the country of origin for each recipe. A class meal featuring a few of these aquatic appetizers would be a great closure to your study of fish.

A health note about eating fish: The risk of becoming ill from eating cooked seafood is one in 2.5 million according to the National Academy of Science, and that risk comes from food poisoning caused by improper handling and storage rather than chemical contaminants. The risk of illness from eating raw seafood is relatively high—about one in 1,000.

**In4.** *Societal/Environmental Issues:*

a. In remarks made to an 1883 International Fishing Exhibition, Dr. Thomas Huxley stated, "I believe that the cod fishery and probably all the other great sea fisheries are inexhaustible; that is to say, that nothing we do seriously affects the number of fish." Have students investigate modern fishing practices and yearly yields and react orally or in written form to Dr. Huxley's comment.

b. The shark has been and continues to be one of the most persecuted and unreasonably feared creatures on this planet. The truth is, far more people are killed by bee stings and snake bites worldwide than by shark attacks. The attitude that "the only good shark is a dead shark," commercial exploitation for fins and meat, fishing, and accidental catches in fishing nests have pushed many shark species to the brink of extinction. Have students write a defense of the shark and incorporate into this defense a plea for conservation of these ancient and magnificent beings. If you wish, add a twist by having the students use the shark's viewpoint to defend itself in its own words.

c. After the Asian walking catfish was imported to a fish farm in Florida, some escaped to spawn in the canals of Florida, where they have no natural enemies. Have students investigate this fish and the effect it has had on the new environment into which it escaped and adapted. You could expand this activity to include investigations of other similar situations with introduced species worldwide such as the English sparrow in North America, the rabbit in Australia, and "killer" bees in South America.

## RELEASE OF SPECIMENS

Native fish may be released back into the ponds, lakes, or streams from which they were collected. Take precautions to provide adequate space and aeration for the fish on the way to the release site. Place the container with fish in it into the water at the release site for several minutes to allow temperature equalization and avoid a possibly lethal shock to the fish's system when released.

Never release any commercially purchased fish into the wild.

# 9. AMPHIBIANS

| | |
|---|---|
| **Kingdom:** | Animalia |
| **Subkingdom:** | Metazoa |
| **Phylum:** | Chordata |
| **Subphylum:** | Vertebrata (possessing a backbone) |
| **Class:** | Amphibia (amphibians) |
| | Orders: Apoda (caecilians) |
| | Urodela (salamanders and newts) |
| | Anura (frogs and toads) |

## DIVERSITY AND DISTRIBUTION

These unusual vertebrates chirp, whistle, and croak from a variety of habitats: ponds and road ditches, swamps and treetops.

What makes the amphibians so unusual? Although they spend a great deal of time on land as adults, they have never totally broken their bond to water and become true land vertebrates (Greek—*amphi*, dual + *bios*, life). Nearly all are restricted to living near water or in damp areas, and their eggs are nearly always laid in water.

The amphibians are the smallest group of vertebrates, with only about 4,015 living species. They are restricted mainly to water or moist places, and none are found in salt water. Amphibians are most common in moist temperate ranges, but some are tropical and one type ventures as far north as the Arctic Circle. Some tree frogs are found at 3,600 meters (12,000 feet) in the Sierra Nevada mountains. Some toads live in desert areas where they hide underground during the day and emerge only in the cool of the night.

The hellbender, mud puppy, and amphiumas ("congo eel") are strictly aquatic. Most frogs live in or close to water, although the toads usually range farther afield. The tree frogs and tree toads have taken partially to the trees, with some tropical types living a completely aboreal life. Land salamanders commonly hide under stones or logs, and the strange legless caecilians burrow into the moist earth of tropical areas.

The amphibians range in size from the Brazilian rainforest frog of about 1 centimeter (0.4 inches) from snout to rump to the Columbian caecilians and Asian salamanders, both over 1.5 meters (5 feet) long.

## General Class Characteristics

**Digestive System and Feeding.** Adult amphibians and the larvae of salamanders are carnivores that eat only live moving animals such as insects, worms, small crustaceans, and small mollusks. Salamanders and caecilians can only snap their jaws shut to capture prey, but the frogs and toads have long, sticky tongues to help them snare prey. Large aquatic species take small fish, and the bullfrogs sometimes catch small fish, birds, mammals, or other amphibians.

The aquatic larvae of frogs and toads (often called tadpoles) are typically filter feeders that strain algae or bits of organic matter from the water. Some tadpoles eat so much so quickly that up to half their body weight is in their digestive system. Some tadpoles can extract food particles such as algae as small as one tenth of a micrometer (0.000004 inches) in diameter—an efficiency that rivals the best mechanical sieves produced by humans.

From the mouth, food passes through the esophagus into the stomach. The stomach opens into the small intestine. Also attached to the small intestine are other digestive organs, the liver and gall bladder. The small intestine leads to the large intestine, which ends in a muscular cavity called the cloaca, where wastes are stored until they can be expelled.

**Circulatory System.** The adult amphibian has a three-chambered heart: left atrium, right atrium, and ventricle. The heart moves red blood through a double-loop system of closed vessels. The first loop carries oxygen-poor blood from the heart to the lungs and takes oxygen-rich blood from the lungs back to the heart. The second loop transports oxygen-rich blood from the heart to the rest of the body and oxygen-poor blood from the body back to the heart.

Young amphibians or larvae have a two-chambered heart and a single-loop circulatory system similar to that of the bony fish. As the larvae mature into adults, the circulatory system changes dramatically.

Like fish, amphibians are ectotherms. Amphibians produce some internal heat by metabolism, but they are dependent primarily on environmental sources of heat to regulate body temperature. Because of this connection between body temperature and surroundings, amphibians can endure extremes of heat and cold but are also greatly influenced by them. At low temperatures during temperate zone winters, amphibians cannot remain active and enter into a state of torpor (often called hibernation). During hot spells or droughts, many amphibians seek shelter and become inactive.

**Respiratory System.** Amphibians exhibit more means of respiration than any other animal group. Adult amphibians breath with their lungs, mouth cavities, and skin. The frogs and toads have lungs that are fairly well developed, but some land salamanders have no lungs at all. The mouth cavity and skin of amphibians are richly supplied with blood vessels and serve as areas of gas exchange, either under water or in air. Larvae and a few types of adult salamanders breath primarily through gills and expel carbon dioxide through their skin.

Since they lack well-developed chest muscles, many species of amphibians are mouth breathers. They fill their mouth with air, close the mouth, and force the air back through an opening called the glottis into the lungs.

Vocal cords in frogs and toads make the distinctive calls so familiar during spring mating rituals. Some species have large, expandable vocal sacs that amplify the sound and allow the animal to croak even underwater. Salamanders lack vocal cords, but a few types make faint squeaks.

**Muscle System and Movement.** Amphibians are equipped with a complex muscle system. Aquatic salamanders swim fishlike with a side-to-side S-shaped flexing of the body. Frogs and toads, with their short, inflexible bodies, swim by means of simultaneous thrusts of the hind legs. Land salamanders move by undulating the body and advancing diagonally opposite feet each time the body bends. On land, frogs and toads are noted for their explosive jumps (but clumsy landings). The burrowing caecilians move by alternately folding and extending from points where body bends make contact with the wall of the burrow.

**Skeletal System.** The skull of modern amphibians is flattened and connected to the backbone in such a way that the head cannot be moved from side to side as it can in reptiles.

The limbs of the salamander stick out from the side of the body. Consequently, salamanders are "belly-draggers" that must lever themselves over the ground slowly and clumsily. The limbs of the frogs and toads are positioned more under the body than salamanders, and they can raise themselves more upright than salamanders. Aside from their explosive leaps, frogs and toads are slow and rather clumsy on land.

**Body Covering.** Amphibians are covered by a thin, moist, glandular skin without scales (some caecilians have internal scales and some frogs have external bony plates) or true claws. A thin, moist skin works well for gas exchange, but water is constantly lost by evaporation. Death due to drying is an ever-present threat to amphibians.

Many amphibians have brightly colored skin. Color is used for camouflage and sexual attraction and to warn predators about the poisonous nature of amphibians possessing such bright colors. Many amphibians can change color by concentrating or dispersing pigments in skin cells called chromatophores. Color change is under hormonal control and happens rather slowly. The skin of most amphibians also contains glands that produce bitter-tasting or even toxic mucous coatings. The poison-arrow frogs of Central and South America develop some of the most lethal biological toxins known. One type, the Kokoi poison-arrow frog of Colombia, produces skin secretions so deadly that a mere 0.00001 grams (0.0000004 ounces) is enough to kill a man. The Choco Indians poison the tips of as many as 50 arrows with the secretions of one tiny frog and then use the arrows to bring down large game such as jaguars, monkeys, and birds.

**Excretory System.** Amphibians use kidneys to filter wastes from the blood. The finished excretory product of the kidneys, called urine, travels directly to the cloaca for expulsion or may be stored in the urinary bladder and then passed to the cloaca, where it is expelled.

**Brain and Nervous System.** Amphibians have well-developed nervous systems and sense organs. Their bulging eyes (except in the caecilians) are large and very movable and provide them with an excellent view of their world.

Anurans have an external eardrum called the tympanic membrane. This structure is quite sensitive as hearing plays an important role in survival and reproduction.

Many amphibian larvae and adults possess a lateral line system similar to fish for detecting water movement.

**Reproduction and Development.** Amphibians exhibit the most diversity of reproductive methods of any vertebrate group. Mating in frogs and toads may be preceded by a chorus of calls distinctive to each species. Salamanders often engage in courtship dances that range from simple movements to elaborate ceremonies.

Fertilization of eggs may be internal or external. With few exceptions, frogs and toads fertilize externally. The male clasps the female from behind with his forelegs and releases sperm as she releases the eggs. Most salamanders transfer sperm in small packets that are picked up into the body of the female during courtship rituals.

Amphibians' eggs are covered with a jellylike layer that dries quickly. Most amphibians deposit their eggs in water or in very damp places on land—in still or running water, beneath logs, on leaves overhanging water, in water-filled areas in plants, and even in frothy foam nests on tree branches. In a few types, the female retains the eggs in her body, where they are nourished by yolk within the egg or directly by the mother. Frogs and toads lay egg masses that range from a single egg to over 25,000 eggs, depending on the species. Salamanders generally lay no more than a few dozen eggs. Caecilians have internal fertilization; some lay eggs (7 to 20) and others retain the eggs in their body.

Amphibians exhibit some degree of parental care. The most common form is the male frog's protection of eggs laid in his territory. In some amphibians, such as the midwife toad of Europe or the Australian pouched frog, the eggs may be carried on the male's body. In the mouth-brooding frogs of South America, the male carries as many as 20 larvae in his vocal cords. The eggs of the Surinam toad of South America develop in packets on the back of the female and emerge as tadpoles or fully developed young, depending on the species. The most bizarre example of parental egg brooding must be the Australian gastric-brooding frog. The female ingests the eggs, which develop in her stomach and are vomited back up as tadpoles.

Wherever the eggs of amphibians are laid or brooded, they all undergo complete metamorphosis from egg to larvae to adult. Amphibians are the only four-legged animals in which this remarkable transformation occurs. Metamorphosis is under the control of hormones secreted by the pituitary and thyroid glands. The time required to complete metamorphosis can vary enormously. Some desert toads complete the transformation in a few days; in other species the larvae overwinter and totally transform the following summer.

Metamorphic changes are the most dramatic in frogs and toads. The large tail of the tadpole is totally absorbed, lungs replace gills, the larval "teeth" are shed, the mouth enlarges greatly, the intestine shortens, and limbs develop. Larval salamanders look like miniature adults with external gills. Metamorphosis for them is a more subtle loss of gills and acquisition of lungs, absorption of tail fins, and changes in the thickness and permeability of the skin. Some salamanders, such as the axolotl and the mudpuppy, retain their larval characteristics yet become sexually mature and reproduce.

Amphibian Reproduction and Metamorphosis

## Specific Order Characteristics

**Order Apoda.** This group, collectively known as the caecilians, consists of about 163 species found in the tropical areas of Central and South America, Africa, and Southeast Asia. With their long, ringed, legless bodies, caecilians are more likely to be taken for large worms than amphibians. The bones, teeth, and other structures of the caecilians, however, show that they are more closely related to amphibians than any other animal. Biologists are just beginning to understand the lives of these secretive burrowers.

Most caecilians are a uniform blue-gray color, but they vary greatly in size. The smallest is mature at 7 centimeters (2.7 inches), and the longest grows to 1.5 meters (5 feet).

Caecilians burrow in soil or in the bottom sediments of bodies of water. They use their heavily boned heads as trowels for digging or poking around in the mud and soil. Caecilians are opportunistic feeders on earthworms and insects. They employ a modified "sit-and-wait" feeding strategy, approaching their prey slowly and then quickly seizing it with a strong grab of the jaws. All caecilians have teeth on the upper and lower jaws.

All species internally fertilize. The male directly transfers sperm by inserting part of his cloaca into the vent of the female. Live birth is the most striking feature of caecilian reproduction. In nearly half of the species, the developing young are retained in the female's oviducts and nourished with uterine milk (rich secretions from glands in the oviducts) through metamorphosis until they are born fully formed.

Caecilian

**Order Urodela.** This group is composed of about 358 species, including the salamanders and newts. Salamanders and newts live in cool, shady places and can be found in North, Central, and South America; Europe; Africa; and Asia. These secretive amphibians hide under rocks and logs during the day and are active at night. Unlike frogs and toads, they do not advertise themselves by making loud sounds.

Salamanders and newts typically have elongated bodies, long tails, and two pairs of legs roughly the same size (although some forms have lost one pair of limbs). They live in a variety of habitats ranging from wholly aquatic to totally terrestrial, and some divide their time between land and water. Aquatic forms are found in lakes, ponds, swamps, rivers, and underground pools. Land types commonly live under rocks and logs, although some burrow while others climb trees.

Salamanders and newts display a wide range of colors, including green, brown, black, red, orange, and yellow. They range in size (snout to tip of tail) from 3 to 160 centimeters (1.2 to 63 inches), but most are in the 5 to 15 centimeter (2 to 6 inch) range.

The term "salamander" is applied generally to any tailed amphibian but especially those with terrestrial (land) preferences. The term "newt" refers broadly to three genera (one in Europe and two in North America) that return to water each spring to breed.

All salamanders, adults and larvae, are carnivorous; they feed on small snails, worms, and insects.

Salamander

**Order Anura.** This largest and most diverse group of amphibians has about 3,500 species, including the frogs and toads. The members of this group blanket North, Central, and South America; Europe; Africa; Asia; and Australia. The greatest variety (80 percent of species) is found in the tropics and subtropics. They occupy deserts, grasslands, mountains, ponds, swamps, and rainforests. Most live both on land and in water, but a few types are entirely aquatic or terrestrial.

The main features that distinguish frogs and toads are the absence of a tail in the adult stage; a much shorter body than other amphibians; and large, powerful hind limbs.

Frogs and toads range in size (snout to vent) from 1 to 35 centimeters (0.4 to 14 inches), but most fall in the 2 to 12 centimeter (0.8 to 5 inch) range. Frogs especially occur in vivid colors of green, brown, black, red, orange, yellow, and white.

Functioning as both predator and prey, amphibians are very important parts of food chains in the habitats where they are found. Frogs are eaten by humans in many parts of the world but are considered a delicacy rather

Toad

# The Importance of Amphibians

than a major food item. Axolotl salamanders from lakes near Mexico City are also used as food by people.

In tropical rainforests, native hunters tip their arrows and blowgun darts with the toxic skin secretions of the poison-arrow frogs. Scientists are studying these secretions for possible future use as anesthetics, muscle relaxants, and heart medications and to increase our understanding of strokes and seizures. Amphibians are also the subject of research on regeneration. Why salamanders can regenerate lost limbs but frogs cannot remains a mystery. Solving that mystery may have applications to humans who have lost limbs due to accidents or birth defects.

Frogs are probably the most extensively studied animals on earth. Legions of school children and future doctors and researchers have been introduced to vertebrate anatomy by these creatures. They have added greatly to our knowledge of life on this planet and may even help us live in space (they have been rocketed into orbit to study the effects of weightlessness).

In the 1930s the large cane toad (often the size of a pie plate) was introduced into Australia to control sugarcane pests. Their numbers exploded out of control due to lack of predators and they have become a serious pest. The resourceful Australians are fighting back by using large quantities of toads for educational and research purposes in schools, universities, and hospitals; developing trade markets with China, where the toads are used for medicinal and therapeutic purposes; and marketing of wallets, purses, and vests made from toad skin leather.

Perhaps the most important service amphibians provide is to serve as environmental monitors. Amphibians may amplify environmental problems because of their position in the food chain and their dependence on clean air and water. Many scientists believe that amphibians could be an early warning system signaling imbalances or degradation in the environment, both in local areas and worldwide.

## COLLECTION OF SPECIMENS

Many states have laws regulating the collection of amphibians. Some amphibians are endangered and protected by state and federal laws, and others are considered game animals with bag limit restrictions. Some states also regulate the collection of hibernating amphibians and the collection of eggs and tadpoles. Check with the appropriate wildlife authorities for your area, listed in Appendix C, before collecting. I strongly recommend that you purchase a good field guide to amphibians with color pictures and range maps before setting out to collect.

## Salamanders and Newts

The salamander that you are most likely to encounter in North America is the tiger salamander (Ambystomia tigrinum). These salamanders have a bulky body, broad head, small eyes, and a variable color pattern of yellow blotches against a black background.

The newts are restricted to the eastern half of the U.S. and extreme southern Canada around the Great Lakes. In those areas you will encounter the eastern newt (Notophthalmus viridescens), also known as the red-spotted newt. There are several different races of this newt within its range. Use appropriate field guides to identify the other types of salamanders and newts in your area.

Land salamanders can be captured by day by overturning rocks and logs. Quickly grasp any found there around the top of the middle portion of the body. At night or during cloudy rainy periods, you may find them wandering in more open areas.

To collect the aquatic newts, use a coarse net to remove them from weedy ponds, lakes, or backwaters.

Transport aquatic types in containers of water. Land forms should be transported in closed ventilated containers with damp leaves or moist paper towels in the bottom. Dehydration and wide temperature swings can be fatal to amphibians, so avoid both by transporting specimens to the classroom immediately.

# Frogs and Toads

The most common frog you will encounter is the leopard frog (Rana pipens). It ranges over most of the U.S. and far up into Canada. The most common toads are the American toad (Bufo americanus), common toad (Bufo woodhousei), Great Plains toad (Bufo cognatus), and western toad (Bufo boreas). Use appropriate field guides to identify the other types of frogs and toads in your area.

Collect frogs with a coarse net. Collect at night if possible. You can get quite close to frogs by turning on a flashlight or spotlight to locate them and then turning off the light to approach them. Repeat this on-off process until you are close enough to momentarily blind them with the light and net them. Note: Local and state laws may regulate capturing animals at night with a light, regardless of the purpose. Check with the proper authorities before collecting in this manner.

Toads are easier to catch than frogs because they can be found on land away from water. At night, look for them with a light in gardens or flowerbeds or near porch lights or street lights, where they feed on the insects attracted to the light. Handle toads with caution, as the mucous from the epidermal glands in their skin may be strongly irritating to a person's hands, mouth, and eyes. Toads often will release fluids (urinate?) when grasped, so be prepared for this.

Tree frogs are difficult to capture because of their small size and their ability to conceal themselves in trees and shrubs often far above the ground. Try to collect them carefully in a small net with a long handle.

Transport frogs and tree frogs in covered ventilated containers with damp leaves or moist paper towels in the bottom. Toads can be transported in a closed ventilated container. Damp packing for toads is not necessary unless they are to be kept in the container for an extended period such as one or two days.

From early March to midsummer, amphibian eggs often can be collected in still ponds and marshes. Some kinds of amphibians attach their eggs to floating or underwater vegetation; others lay a floating raft of eggs along the edge of the water.

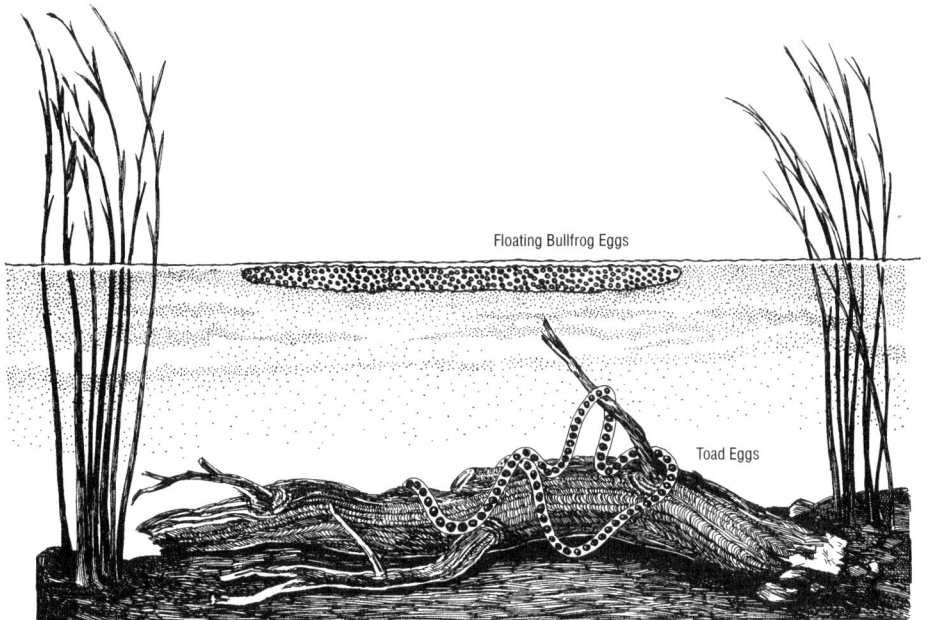

Floating Bullfrog Eggs

Toad Eggs

Collect floating eggs by maneuvering them into a large plastic bucket along with plenty of water. Collect attached eggs by cutting the vegetation above and below the egg mass. Transport eggs to the classroom in large ventilated covered plastic buckets about two-thirds full of water from the collecting site. The most common mistake in transporting and rearing amphibian eggs is putting too many eggs in too small a container, which results in a diminished oxygen supply. Bring plenty of water back from the collecting site to establish rearing containers in the classroom.

The suppliers listed in Appendix B sell adult frogs, toads, salamanders, and newts as well as larvae (tadpoles) and eggs. Aquarium stores and pet shops often sell aquatic newts and frogs, and live salamanders often can be found in fish bait shops.

The suppliers listed in Appendix B also can provide the African clawed frog (*Xenopus laevis*) and complete instructions for maintaining it. These hardy frogs are easily maintained and feed on a dry staple diet available from the suppliers. They also can be induced to mate and produce fertile eggs in the classroom any time of the year (although breeding adults can be expensive to purchase initially). Several states require permits before *Xenopus* can be shipped in; suppliers can give you more details about the requirements of your particular area. Widespread use of *Xenopus* in the classroom and laboratory may help alleviate the pressure on native species. However, *Xenopus* must *never* be released into the wild under any circumstances.

The main factor to consider in the care of amphibians is providing sufficient moisture to prevent dehydration.

Aquatic newts can be housed in a minimum aquarium (see Chapter 8 for guidelines on establishing a minimum aquarium). Feed them a variety of small aquatic invertebrates such as daphinia, insects, crustaceans, and worms or finely cut meat or liver three times a week. Take care not to overfeed and foul the water.

Adult land salamanders tend to burrow and will uproot plants if kept in a regular terrarium. Therefore, a modified terrarium is better. Use a 20- or 40-liter (5- or 10-gallon) aquarium to construct a modified terrarium. Place 5 to 8 centimeters (2.5 to 3.5 inches) of damp soil in the bottom of the aquarium. Place a small, shallow dish of pond, spring, or aged tap water at one end of the aquarium with the top of the dish level with the soil. Change the water regularly and keep the dish full at all times. Cover the soil with a layer of damp peat moss. Place several large pieces of bark on top of the peat moss for the salamanders to hide under. Maintain a high level of humidity in your modified terrarium by misting the peat moss with water regularly and keeping a glass or plastic cover over the terrarium.

Feed salamanders mealworms, earthworms, and insects such as crickets and small beetles. Salamanders will quickly learn to accept food held in forceps. Once trained to this, they can also be fed strips of raw meat and fish.

Toads may be kept in the same modified terrarium setup as that recommended for salamanders. Toads are voracious eaters and feed primarily on insects, spiders, earthworms, and other small invertebrates. Their food must be alive, as the movement of the prey is what signals them to feed. If you offer a dead insect or insect-sized bit of meat by loosely tying it to a thread and jiggling it in front of them, it may be eaten.

Frogs can be kept in elaborate terrariums, but such lavish quarters are not necessary. Frogs can be adequately housed for a short time in a plastic dish pan, aquarium, or sink. Fill the pan, aquarium, or sink with pond, spring, or aged tap water deep enough to just cover the frogs. Place several bricks or flat stones in the container with their top surfaces out of the water so the frogs can crawl on them and be completely out of the water. Frogs cannot remain in water indefinitely and need access to a dry place. Place a few broken clay pots in the container for the frogs to hide under. Change the water at least every other day, rinsing off the frogs and bricks or stones each time. Keep a secure ventilated cover such as a screen over the container as frogs can and will jump out. Feed frogs live insects, spiders, and earthworms, or try dangling dead insects or strips of meat on a thread in front of them.

## MAINTENANCE OF SPECIMENS

### Salamanders and Newts

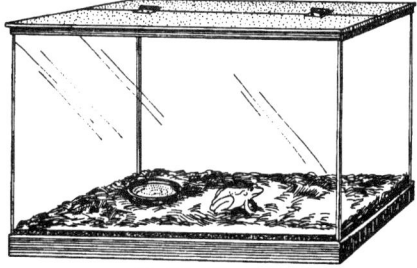

Modified Terrarium

### Frogs and Toads

Frog Holding Chamber

Tree frogs can be housed very temporarily in nothing more than a ventilated covered glass jar with moist towels or damp leaves in the bottom and a few large sticks added for climbing. Tree frogs are relatively inactive so the size of the container is not of major importance for temporary housing.

Keeping native adult amphibians for long periods in the classroom is difficult and time-consuming because of their demand for live food and lots of it. In addition, they often refuse to feed in captivity at all. The best strategy is to keep them only as long as necessary to conduct the teaching activities you have designed and then release them back to the collecting site as soon as possible.

If you have collected amphibian eggs, separate the eggs from the main mass by cutting through the clear jelly-like material surrounding them with a razor knife or sharp scissors. Give each group of students their own eggs by placing 5 to 10 eggs per quart of water in shallow containers (a large surface area for oxygen exchange is more important than volume or depth of water). Healthy eggs darken as the mature. Discard white eggs, as they are infertile, and any eggs with cottony fibers attached, as they have died and are beginning to mold.

At room temperature most amphibian eggs will hatch in five to seven days. After hatching, transfer the larvae to an aquarium of spring, pond, or aged tap water. About 200 tadpoles can be sustained in a 20-liter (5-gallon) aquarium if the water is continually but gently aerated.

Tadpoles of the frog and toad can be fed on pieces of lettuce that have been boiled for about one minute to soften them, small bits of boiled egg yolk, or finely powdered fish food. Salamander larvae require daily feeding of live aquatic organisms such as daphinia. You should be able to determine which type of larvae—frog, toad, or salamander—you have about five days after hatching, when the external gills of the frog and toad tadpoles will shrivel as the internal gills take over; salamander larvae retain their external gills. If you have salamander larvae, I suggest that you release them back to the collecting site unless you have the time and tenacity to provide the constant supply of live food they require.

If you have frog or toad tadpoles, feed them daily only what they will consume in several minutes. Do not overfeed, as it will foul the water and the resulting drop in oxygen levels could be fatal to the tadpoles. Remove about one third of the water in the container housing the tadpoles each day and replace it with clean spring, pond, or aged tap water. If the water ever becomes cloudy or smells bad, replace all of it immediately.

After several weeks of this routine, the tadpoles will be mature enough to be cared for as one might care for goldfish, feeding them daily only what they will consume in a few minutes and changing the water only as necessary.

Depending on the species, tadpoles grow and develop for two or three months before transforming into adult frogs or toads (unless you have bullfrog tadpoles, which won't mature until the following spring).

Collecting amphibians will put you around water, so follow good safety procedures and be especially cautious if collecting at night. Dress appropriately and be alert to contact with poisonous plants or stinging, biting, or parasitic animals.

Wash your hands thoroughly after handling amphibians, pond water, or containers housing amphibians. Be especially careful when handling toads to keep your hands away from your eyes and mouth.

Due to the toxic epidermal mucous on toads, avoid letting students directly handle live toads. Have students thoroughly wash their hands after contact with amphibians, pond water, or containers housing amphibians.

Leave collecting sites as you found them by replacing overturned logs and rocks.

HEALTH AND
SAFETY
Teachers

Students

Amphibians

Make sure that adequate levels of moisture and humidity are maintained to prevent the amphibians you collected from dehydrating. Have students moisten their hands before touching or handling any amphibian, and keep such contact to a minimum. Make sure students handle amphibians gently and correctly. Cup frogs in the hands and grasp salamanders or newts by wrapping the fingers gently but firmly around the middle of the body. Never grab or allow students to grab a salamander or newt by the end of its tail. If a frog jumps to the floor, drop a damp towel over it and recapture it.

Many students are afraid of or repulsed by amphibians. Do not force these students or let other students force them into handling amphibians against their will. These actions may result in a traumatic experience for a student and injury or death to the amphibian from being dropped or thrown by a frightened student.

Frogs in captivity sometimes develop a disease known as redleg as a result of heavy bacterial infection. Consult a veterinarian for treatment with antibiotics. It usually can be avoided by preventing overcrowding, giving the frogs the opportunity to crawl completely out of the water, changing the water at least every other day, and releasing the frogs as soon as possible.

## TEACHING ACTIVITIES
## Habitat

**H1.** **Challenge:** *Design Amphibian Habitats.* Have students imagine they are the chief habitat engineer for Amphibian Acquisitions, a company that specializes in collecting and maintaining amphibians for supply houses and research laboratories. They have been assigned the task of designing appropriate habitats for the long-term maintenance of the following amphibians: leopard frogs, green tree frogs, American toads, tiger salamanders, eastern (red-spotted) newts, and caecilians.

Consult the "Specific Order Characteristics" section of this chapter, appropriate field guides, and other references. Have students diagram and explain their designs. This activity will give students an understanding of amphibian habitat requirements and allow them to compare and contrast the various amphibian habitats.

**H2.** *Home, Home on the Range.* Ask students to imagine that they are now the head collector for Amphibian Acquisitions and have been given the task of collecting the following North American amphibians (add to or delete from the following list as you wish): hellbender, mudpuppy, striped newt, Jefferson's salamander, tiger salamander, red salamander, plains spadefoot toad, red-spotted newt, green treefrog, barking treefrog, mountain chorus frog, leopard frog, and wood frog. Have students color in the range of each amphibian type on a blank map.

Students will need appropriate field guides to do this activity. Some field guide series are listed in Appendix F. In addition, field guides may be purchased from the suppliers listed in Appendix B. This activity will give students a better understanding of the types and distribution of amphibians in North America, provide some familiarity with field guides and their use, and help them review or develop geography skills.

**H3.** *Walk a Mile in My Shoes.* Have students try to put themselves in the amphibian's place by responding orally or in written form to the following question: What specific amphibian would you be and why?

**H4.** *Salamander Stealth.* In some mountain forests of eastern North America, biologists estimate that the total mass of woodland salamanders exceeds all of the woodland birds and mammals put together. Yet most people are never aware of their presence. Have students attempt to explain why we overlook the salamanders. (Your students may conclude that salamanders seem invisible because (1) they hide under rocks, logs, and leaves during the day to avoid drying; (2) they are active at night when they are hard to see; (3) many are small and easily overlooked; (4) some are well camouflaged and difficult to see; and (5) they do not advertise their presence with loud calls as do frogs and toads.)

**H5.** *Amphibian Colors—Camouflage and Communication.* The color of an amphibian's skin is often vital to its survival. If possible, show students examples of amphibians using their colors to camouflage themselves. Ask students to speculate about why some amphibians try to blend into their surroundings. (Answer: Such coloration helps hide them from predators and from potential prey.)

Other amphibians are so brightly colored that they are very easy to see. If possible, show pictures of the brilliant colors of the poison-arrow frogs and have students speculate about why some amphibians advertise rather than hide their presence. (Answer: Some amphibians use bright colors to warn predators that their toxic skin secretions make them distasteful or even lethal to eat.) Explain that some amphibians are not poisonous but are colored like those that are poisonous. Biologists call this mimicry.

**Challenge:** Have students imagine that they are genetic engineers in the future and must design new species of amphibians to live in the following habitats (add to or delete from the list as you wish):

a. on the floor of a forest in dead, brown leaves
b. on blackish-gray rock outcrops over a river
c. on and in the sands and gravel of a desert
d. on mats of floating algae along the edge of a pond
e. on the bark (but not leaves) of trees in a forest

Have students brainstorm and then diagram and explain their new amphibians on a large sheet of blank paper. Make sure they consider body shape and behavior as well as body color in their design. Have them present and explain their design to the rest of the class.

Another challenge you might present to students is to design a brightly colored amphibian with toxic skin or a nonpoisonous type that mimics the colors of a poisonous type. Students should brainstorm and then diagram and explain their new amphibians on a large sheet of blank paper. Make sure they consider body shape and behavior as well as body color in their design. Have them present and explain their design to the rest of the class.

**H6.** *Froggie Chorus.* Frogs and toads can make an amazing array of sounds, including clicks, whistles, chirps, trills, and barks. Choruses of thousands of male frogs from as many as two dozen species can be heard more than 1 kilometer (0.6 miles) away. The champion "sound-for-pound" amphibian caller has to be the tiny coqui frogs of Puerto Rico. Although they are less than 5 centimeters (2 inches) long and weigh only a fraction of an ounce, these tiny croakers have a call that reaches 108 decibels—louder than a low-flying jet or a subway train. Their call is a two-note whistle that states their name: Ko-Kee!

Have students imitate any frog or toad calls they may know. If possible, play recordings of real frogs or toads making different calls. Carolina Biological Supply Company (see Appendix B) offers a record called "Voices of the Night" that contains the calls of 36 different species of frogs and toads of eastern North America. The recording comes with narration. The zoology department of local colleges or universities, public libraries, or local zoos and nature centers also may have amphibian call recordings.

Once students have heard frog and toad calls, ask the following question: How do frogs and toads call? (Calls are generated by pushing air back and forth over the vocal cords causing them to vibrate and produce sound. The size of the frog or toad, the number of vibrations, and the way the vocal cords vibrate affect the type of sound produced.)

Many frogs and toads have vocal sacs that amplify their sounds. These sacs, inflatable pouches of skin around the neck or head, are inflated as air is pushed into them through slits in the floor of the mouth. The inflated sacs resonate and greatly amplify the sound. If possible, show students pictures of frogs or toads with inflated vocal sacs calling.

Now have students consider the question: Why do frogs and toads call? (Frogs and toads make four basic kinds of calls: (1) Mating calls are made by males to attract females for mating. Females don't make mating calls. Each species has its own distinct call and specific places where it calls. (2) Territorial calls made by some males during breeding warn other males away. In some types, the mating and territorial calls are the same. (3) Release calls are made during the frenzy of mating when males may grab anything that moves, including other males or unreceptive females. The offended party vibrates its body and makes a release call to convey to the male that he should let go. (4) Distress calls, often referred to as screams, are made by some frogs when they are grabbed by predators. Such calls may startle the predator into dropping its victim and/or may warn other frogs of danger. In most species, both males and females make distress calls. The distress call is the only type of call made with the mouth open.)

If practical and possible, take a night hike to a local pond or marsh to hear a live performance. The following tips will help make such a trip safe and worthwhile:

- A damp, warm night in spring or early summer is the best time. However, frogs and toads in your area may call at other times of the year as well; check with local wildlife authorities.
- Visit the area in the daytime and familiarize yourself with it. Find safe spots where the students can get close to the water's edge. Try to go out the night before you plan to take students there to make sure the frogs and toads are actually calling.
- Instruct students to dress appropriately in old clothes and rubber boots or old sneakers. Wet feet are to be expected.
- Students may want to bring along some insect repellent to counteract mosquitoes.
- All students should have flashlights to help them find their way around and to view the frogs and toads they hear calling.
- Take along appropriate field guides so the students can identify the frogs and toads they hear calling.
- Bring a tape player and blank tapes to record the calls.

Such a field experience can be quite rewarding but demands extra work on the teacher's part:

1. Get signed parental permission slips from the parents of each student before the trip.
2. Get approval from school authorities ahead of time.
3. Arrange for suitable transportation.
4. Arrange for parent volunteers to help supervise.
5. Bring along plenty of flashlights or spotlights (make sure they work beforehand). Each adult supervisor should have a light.

6. Discuss rules, regulations, and safety precautions with students ahead of time and again the night of the trip. Make sure students are fully aware of what is expected of them.

7. Bring along a good first-aid kit, just in case.

After the trip, play your recordings and see if the students can match the calls to the type of frog or toad that made the call. You could also have students develop their own frog chorus (see the "Integration with Fine Arts" section later in this chapter).

**H7.** **Challenge:** *Do Amphibians Prefer Light or Dark Habitats?* Have students devise a way to test this problem.

Begin by wording the problem more specifically to the actual type of amphibians you will be testing. If possible, have different groups of students test different kinds of amphibians.

One design might be to cover the sides and top of one half of a modified terrarium with black paper and the sides and top of the other half with white paper. Both halves of the terrarium on the inside should be as identical to each other as possible. Place a single amphibian in the terrarium and use stopwatches to determine how much time it spends in each half of the terrarium during a five-minute span of time. Repeat several times using as many different amphibians of the same species as you have available. Students should position themselves so they can see the amphibian but it cannot see them. Have students predict what they think will happen before they begin; keep data in appropriate tables, charts, or graphs; and draw conclusions from their data.

**S1.** *Amphibian Structure Comparisons.* Have students compare and contrast the structures of the various orders of adult amphibians. They might use a blank table similar to the one shown. For your convenience, the table includes brief answers. Live specimens, pictures, and/or preserved specimens of caecilians, frogs, toads, and salamanders are needed for this activity.

# Structure

|        | **Apoda**    | **Urodela**        | **Anura**      |
|--------|--------------|--------------------|----------------|
| **Limbs** | (none)    | (4 equal)          | (4 unequal)    |
| **Toes**  | (none)    | (no webs)          | (hind webbed)  |
| **Skin**  | (thin moist) | (thin moist)    | (thin moist)   |
| **Tail**  | (present) | (present)          | (absent)       |
| **Eyes**  | (very small) | (small to medium) | (large)       |

Older or more advanced students could accomplish the same task but in a more challenging manner by constructing a dichotomous key of amphibian characteristics (see Chapter 8, activity S1, for an example of a dichotomous key and how to construct one). Again, live specimens, pictures, and/or preserved specimens of caecilians, frogs, toads, and salamanders are needed.

**S2.** *Amphibian Structure.* Have students diagram and label a frog (or toad) and its parts: mouth, nostrils, eyes, tympanic membrane (external eardrum), front limbs, and hind limbs.

Have students diagram and label a salamander and its parts: head, trunk, tail, mouth, eyes, nostrils, front limbs, and hind limbs.

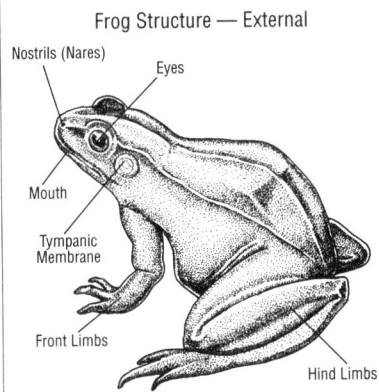

Frog Structure — External

Nostrils (Nares)

Eyes

Mouth

Tympanic Membrane

Front Limbs

Hind Limbs

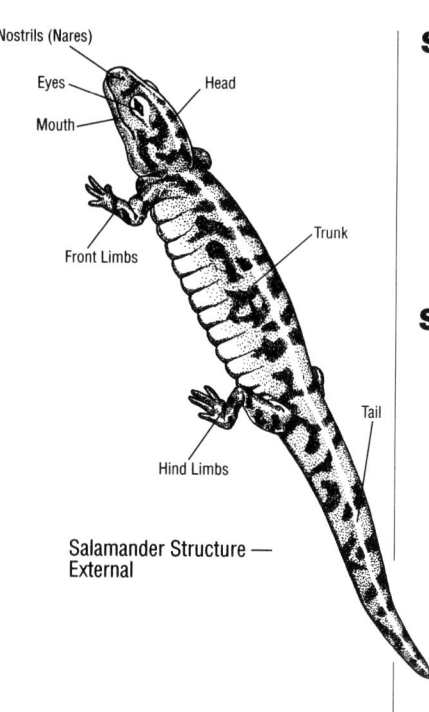

Nostrils (Nares)

Eyes

Head

Mouth

Front Limbs

Trunk

Tail

Hind Limbs

Salamander Structure —
External

**S3.** *Caecilians—What Are They?* Give students the following imaginary scenario: Trudy Tumtater and Morty Mugwump are arguing about the caecilians. Trudy says they are obviously large segmented worms; Morty says they are snakes. Have students explain in oral or written form how they would solve this argument. Who is correct? (Answer: Neither is correct. Caecilians have a backbone, so they are not segmented worms. They lack the scales, well-developed eyes, and internal structures of the reptiles, so they are not snakes. They may be bizarre amphibians, but they *are* amphibians.)

**S4.** *Amphibian Observations.* Have students observe a live frog and/or salamander and answer the questions and do the activities that follow. Some manipulation of the live amphibian will be required, so the use of live toads is not recommended because of their irritating skin secretions. To observe, place a live amphibian in a small glass or clear plastic container with moist towels in the bottom. If your frogs are quite active, a cover may be needed to prevent them from jumping out of the container.

a. Carefully observe the eyes of the frog. What is their shape? (Spherical.) Estimate in fractions how much of the frog's head is occupied by the eyes. Compare and contrast this to the human head and eyes. Why do frogs have such large eyes? (The eyes are their main sense organ for finding food and avoiding predators.)

   Does a frog have eyelids? (Technically, yes, but they do not cover the eye as human eyelids do.) Very carefully touch the frog's eye with the eraser end of a pencil. Describe what happens. (A clear membrane called the nictitating membrane will be pulled up over the eye.) What is the function of the nictitating membrane? (This membrane covers and protects the eye under water.)

   Compare and contrast the eye of the frog to that of the salamander. (Salamander eyes are usually smaller than frog eyes.) How can you account for any differences between the eyes of frogs and the eyes of salamanders? (Both are active mainly at night, so perhaps salamanders depend more on their senses of touch and smell than do frogs.)

b. Observe the frog as it breaths. Notice the nostrils, floor of the mouth, and torso (chest). Describe the breathing pattern of the frog. (Air is pumped in and out of the nostrils by the muscular action of the floor of the mouth.) Compare and contrast the breathing pattern of frogs with that of humans. (Breathing in humans involves increasing or decreasing the size of the chest cavity to pump air in and out. Frogs, lacking ribs, cannot enlarge the cavity containing the lungs. They must use the muscles of the mouth to move air in and out. Humans can breath through their mouth but frogs cannot.

   Observe the breathing pattern of a salamander and compare it to that of the frog.

c. Observe and describe the structure of the skin of the frog and the salamander. (An amphibian's skin is thin, smooth, and moist and only loosely attached to the underlying muscles.) Carefully touch the skin of the frog and salamander. Are amphibians slimy? (Yes, amphibian skin contains small mucous glands over practically the whole body. Some types, especially toads and salamanders, have poison glands in their skin as well.)

   An amphibian's skin has been described as "an open bucket of water." Why? (When submerged in water, amphibians can absorb water through their skin. In the air, they constantly face the threat of dehydration due to evaporation because they have no physical ability to control evaporation off their skin. Occasionally dead toads or frogs that are dry and stiff can be found around buildings or in road ditches. Show these specimens to demonstrate the threat that amphibians face from dehydration. I demonstrate a dried specimen I once found in the hallway of our school during the summer months. Because it looks mummified, I jokingly refer to it as the mummy of the toad pharaoh—Toad-anhkamen.)

Describe the color pattern of the frog's skin. (Splotchy greens and browns on the dorsal [top] side but an off-white on the ventral [bottom] side.) How is this color pattern beneficial to the frog? (The frog is camouflaged from above against the background of green water plants and dark, murky water and from below against the sunlight coming down into the water. Biologists call such coloration countershading.) Compare the color patterns of several frogs. Are they exactly similar? Could we consider the color pattern of the frog as unique to that animal as fingerprints are to humans?

d. Fill a 20-liter (5-gallon) or 40-liter (10-gallon) aquarium about three-fourths full of water and carefully put the frog in it. Observe and describe the frog as it floats quietly. (The frog will float with limbs outstretched and only the top of the head above water.) As the frog floats, what part of its body is exposed, and how does this benefit the frog? (With only the top of the head out of the water, the frog can see and breath without easily being seen.) Carefully put the salamander in the water with the frog and compare the way it floats to the way the frog floats.

e. Describe the swimming action of the frog and the salamander. Compare and contrast the swimming motion of the frog, the salamander, and the fish. (Frogs swim by thrusting with their hind webbed feet. Salamanders, like fish, propel themselves forward with their tail by bending their bodies back and forth.)

f. Remove the water from the container the amphibians are in. Let the frog and salamander sit quietly in the bottom of the container on moist towels. Compare and contrast the front limbs and the hind limbs of the frog. (The front limbs are short and stubby with small unwebbed toes and the hind limbs are long and muscular with long webbed toes.) Measure the length of the front and hind limbs of the frog and the length of the front and hind limbs of the salamander. Compare and contrast the limbs of the frog to those of the salamander both in structure and in length. (The legs and toes of a salamander are all approximately the same size and none of the toes are webbed.)

g. Moisten your hands and then carefully cup the frog in your hands and place it on the floor. Gently prod the frog into making several jumps. Describe the take-off, flight, and landing of the frog. Measure the distance the frog jumps. (For the frog's health and well-being, make sure that students handle it correctly and prod it to jump in as gentle a manner as possible. Allow each frog to take only several jumps and then return it to its container. Repeated landings on a cold, hard, dry classroom floor and the elevated evaporation rate due to handling and jumping can quickly take their toll on the frogs. Make sure that students do not step on the frogs.

The illustration shows the jumping pattern of the frog and explains what happens at each phase of the jump:

You might mix up the illustrations and explanations and have students put them in the proper order. If you have access to the proper equipment and your students have the expertise, challenge them to try

**Phase 1:** Elevation. Forelimbs elevate the front part of the frog; ankles lift the hind legs off the ground.

**Phase 2:** Take-off. Hind legs push off; upper and lower legs extend and ankles and hind legs roll off the ground.

**Phase 3:** Flight. Flight path follows a curve of approximately 45°; eyes are shut and withdrawn.

**Phase 4:** Landing. Front limbs break the fall and the chest hits the ground.

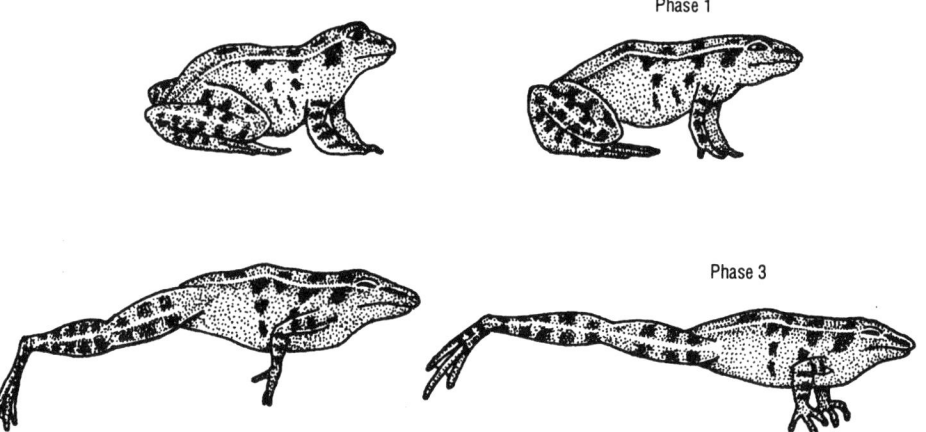

to film the jumping action of the frog. Show the film in slow motion and have students describe what happens at each phase of the jump.)

Compare the leg lengths of the frogs that jumped to the distance they jumped. Does a correlation appear to exist between the length of the leg and the length of the jump? Cricket frogs are about 4 centimeters (1.5 inches) long yet can jump 40 times their length. Compute your own length in centimeters and then calculate how far you would have to leap to match the cricket frog. (Note: Students may want to have a frog jumping contest. I strongly advise against it because it puts the frogs under serious stress. The risk of possible harm to the frogs is greater than any educational benefits that can be derived from such an activity.)

Would a tail be a help or a hindrance to the adult frog? (It would be a hindrance to jumping because the frog could not properly elevate and the tail would add a lot of extra weight.)

Moisten your hands, carefully grasp a salamander, and place it on the floor. Describe the pattern of locomotion (movement) in the salamander when viewed from above. (Follow the same safety guidelines as with frogs.)

(The illustration shows they typical movement pattern of a salamander: right front limb, left hind limb, right hind limb, and so on.)

h. Structurally, amphibians are ectothermic (cold blooded). What does this mean? (They cannot regulate their body temperature so it varies with the temperature of the surroundings.)

Examine the graphs and answer this question: Which graph shows the daily body temperature of an amphibian such as the frog, and which shows the daily body temperature of a mammal such as the gerbil? How

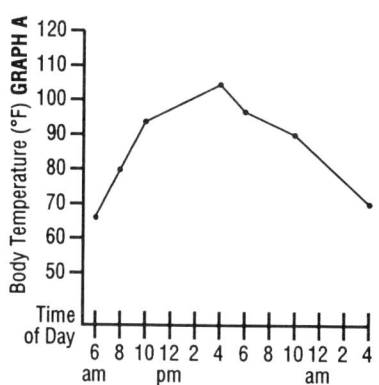

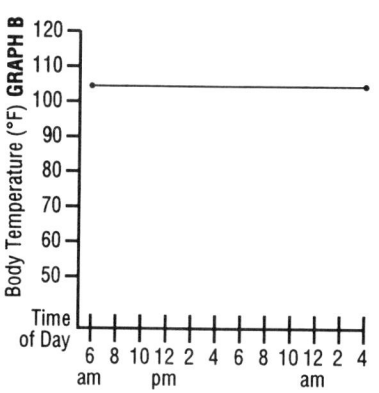

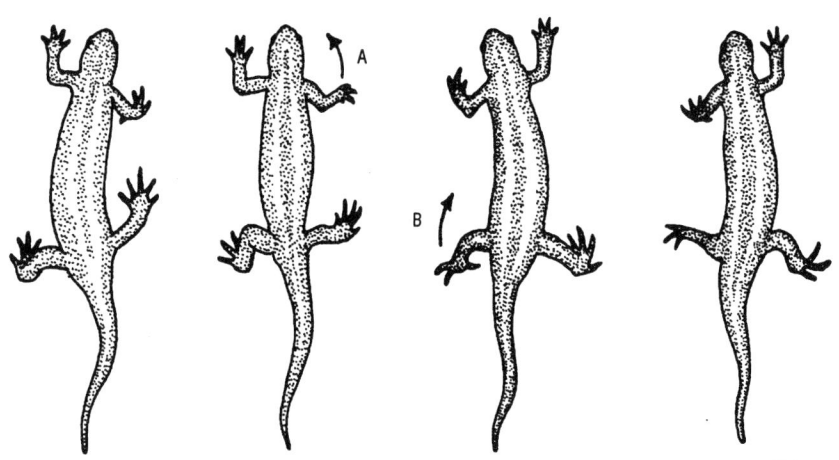

Salamander

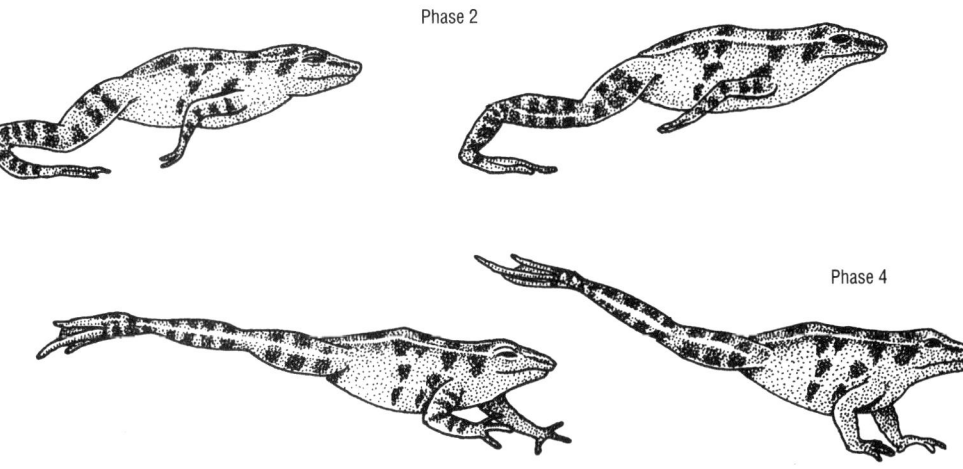

Phase 2

Phase 4

did you decide? (Graph A shows the daily body temperature an amphibian because it varies so much. Graph B shows the temperature of a mammal because it remains fairly constant and stable.)

i.  Locate and describe the tympanic membrane (external eardrum) of the frog. (The tympanic membrane is a round area behind and slightly below the eye.) What is the function of the tympanic membrane? (These membranes are the visible external structure of a well-developed internal sense of hearing.)

**S5.**  **Challenge:** *What Are the Effects of Environmental Conditions on the Rate of Regeneration of Salamander Toes?* Have students devise a method to test this problem.

In both larvae and adult salamanders, the power to regenerate lost parts is very great. Toes, limbs, and tail will be reproduced perfectly if damaged or bitten off by a hungry predator. In frogs and toads, only the larvae have the power of regeneration.

Students will recognize that the first step will be to rewrite the problem to make it more specific. They must determine specifically which environmental factor—light intensity, light color, temperature, and so on—is to be tested.

You will need two modified terrariums to conduct this activity, one for the experimental group and one to house the control group. You will also need salamanders of the same species. Set up both terrariums as identically as possible except for the factor to be tested.

Use fingernail clippers or small, sharp scissors to totally remove some of the toes of the salamanders. Remove the same number of toes, all toes from the same position, from all salamanders.(Don't worry—the loss of some

Movement Pattern

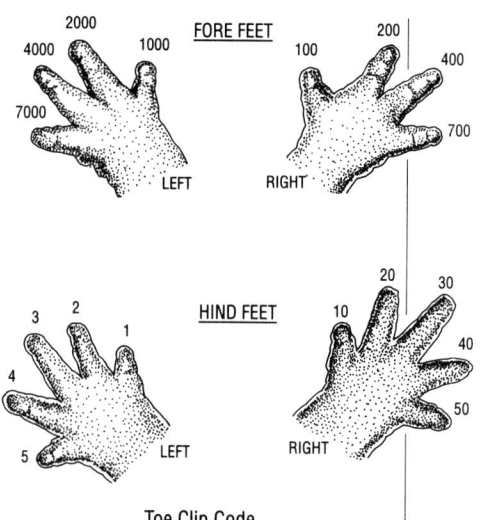

FORE FEET
2000
4000  1000
7000
LEFT

200
100
400
700
RIGHT

HIND FEET
3  2
1
4
5
LEFT

20  30
10
40
50
RIGHT

Toe Clip Code

toes is not a traumatic or harmful experience for salamanders.) Have students predict what will happen before they begin.

Instruct students to measure the length of regenerating toes every several days (or whatever time period is practical and appropriate for you). Have students keep their data in appropriate tables, charts, and graphs. They should draw conclusions from their data.

If larval amphibians are available, they can be used in this activity as well. In fact, larvae may be more satisfactory than adults because they regenerate missing parts more rapidly. Instead of removing toes as with the adults, have students clip a measured amount from the tip of the tail of the larvae. If both salamander and frog larvae are available, one might do some comparisons between the two groups of the rate of regenerate under different environmental conditions.

Biologists mark individuals when studying salamanders in the wild by clipping their toes. One possible system of toe-clip coding used to mark individual animals for recognition on recapture is shown here. The next illustration shows how one would clip the toes of salamander #2372. Give the students several identification numbers and have them diagram how the toes of the salamanders bearing those numbers should be clipped.

**S6.** *Amphibian Models.* Have students construct a model of a frog, a toad, or a salamander using colored modeling clay or colored bread dough. Models could be constructed as external views, or students could recreate internal struture with appropriate organs. Such models could serve as alternatives to dissection. Students with sewing skills could develop external or internal amphibian models of cloth.

## Behavior/Response

**B/R1.** *Touch Response in Amphibians.* Have students touch various areas of an amphibian's body with a blunt probe or the eraser end of a pencil and respond to the question, Is the amphibian sensitive to touch? If so, are some areas of its body more sensitive than others? If you have access to different types of amphibians, have students compare and contrast the sensitivity of each type of amphibian to touch. (You will find that the skin of an amphibian is an organ of unusual sensitivity.)

**B/R2.** *Body Orientation in Amphibians.* Place an amphibian in a large, clear, ventilated jar. When the amphibian is resting quietly on the bottom of the jar, have students slowly tilt the jar in various orientations and describe how the amphibian reacts. Pose these questions to students: From your observations, can the amphibian determine changes in the orientation of its body? (It can.) Would you hypothesize that amphibians possess an organ of balance in their inner ear as humans do? (They do.)

If you have access to different types of live amphibians, have students compare and contrast the reaction of each type to changes in the orientation of its body.

**B/R3.** Challenge: *Can Frogs Hear?* Have students devise a way to test this problem. (Frogs have a well-developed sense of hearing. However, they do not usually exhibit clearly evident signs of being able to hear). Students may devise the following or similar activities to test a frog's hearing ability. All sounds should be made out of sight of the test frogs as their behaviors or reactions may be influenced by what they see as much as by what they hear.

a. Often if you hold a frog and rub its sides it will croak. How does a test frog respond to the croaking of another frog? Have students imitate the croaking of a frog. How does a test frog respond? Does it appear that the test frog could discern the difference between a real croak and an imitation one?

b. Make a splashing sound by dropping something in water. The splash sound is significant to frogs and puts them on their guard. How does the test frog respond? Let a frog jump from your hands into water. How does the test frog respond? Does it appear that the test frog could discern the difference in the splashing sounds?

c. Try sounds that vary in loudness and pitch: Ring a bell, blow a shrill whistle, or strike several different pitches of tuning forks. Have students describe how the test frog responds to each sound.

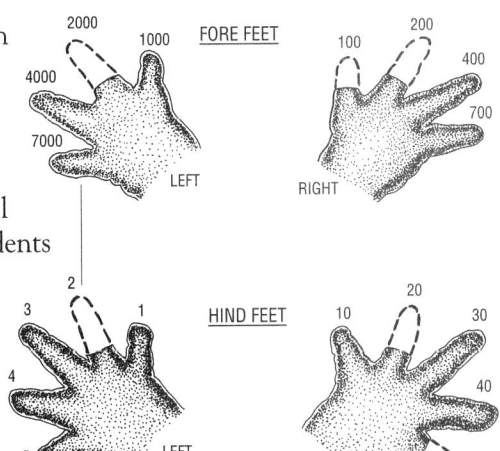

Toe Clip Code for #2372

Have students try to draw conclusions from their observations. Beware of cloudy conclusions with this activity! Students should not infer that frogs do not hear well or cannot hear a wide variety of sounds simply because they manifest attention only to a few sounds of particular interest to them.

If you have access to different types of amphibians, have students compare and contrast their hearing abilities to that of the frog.

**B/R4.** **Challenge:** *Does a Frog React More to Movement or to Shapes?* Have students devise a way to test this problem.

Have students cut out silhouettes of creatures that the frog would regard as enemies in its natural habitat (for example: snakes, birds, and fish). All silhouettes should be dark in color and all the same color. The only difference should be their shape.

Place a frog on moist towels in a large container such as a 20-liter (5-gallon) aquarium. Darken the room and place one of the silhouettes in position. Frogs are myopic (near sighted) out of water. They do not possess a high degree of binocular vision and thus cannot see very well directly in front of them. Position the silhouette outside the aquarium off to either side of the frog and close enough for the frog to see it.

Have students back away from the container so the frog cannot see them but they can see the frog. Now turn the lights on and have students observe and describe how the frog reacts to the silhouette. The silhouette should remain moitionless and there should be no movement of any kind within the frog's field of view. Repeat the process using the other silhouettes one after the other. Have students predict what will happen before they begin.

Next, attach the silhouettes to long sticks such as meter sticks. Darken the room and position students where they can see the frog but it cannot see them. Keep the silhouettes down and out of the frog's sight. Turn the lights back on and have the students thrust the silhouette toward the frog quickly and in a menacing manner. The frogs should see only the movement of the silhouette, not the movement of the students. Repeat using each silhouette. Have students predict what will happen before they begin.

Data collected by students will be mainly observational. Have them attempt to draw conclusions from their observations.

It is usually evident that frogs respond more to the perception of movement than to form. Have students respond to these questions: Why does the frog respond only to movement? (Large moving objects usually mean enemies to a frog, regardless of their form, and the necessity of getting out harm's way.) Is it an advantage or disadvantage to the frog to be myopic (near sighted) in air? (A case could be made either way. It is advantageous to need to see only those objects near enough to be eaten but it is a disadvantage to not be able to see lurking predators at some distance.)

**B/R5.** *Hypnotize a Frog.* Your students will enjoy a demonstration of frog hypnosis. A frog can be placed in a so-called hypnotic state in several ways. If it is laid on its back and held firmly in a person's hands until it ceases to

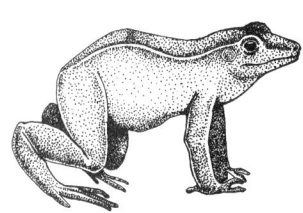

| Wind direction | Frogs migrating in that direction |
|---|---|
| N | 3 |
| NNE | 0 |
| NE | 0 |
| ENE | 0 |
| E | 4 |
| ESE | 6 |
| SE | 0 |
| SSE | 25 |
| S | 32 |
| SSW | 7 |
| SW | 21 |
| WSW | 1 |
| W | 6 |
| WNW | 0 |
| NW | 3 |
| NNW | 4 |

struggle, it usually will remain motionless for a considerable time, sometimes hours. If frogs are in a normal resting postion and their backs or sides are rubbed, they frequently raise up on their legs and remain motionless and rigid for some time.

The muscles of the frog seem to go into a state of tonic contraction as if movement were being inhibited. Frogs can be awakened by any sudden stimulus, and their recovery is usually immediate.

Hypnotic reactions have been noted in such diverse animal groups as insects, crustaceans, fish, reptiles, birds, lower mammals, and primates. The phenomenon seems general throughout the animal kingdom.

**B/R6.** *Response to Light.* How do frogs respond to light? Place a frog on moist towels in a large clear container such as a 20-liter (5-gallon) aquarium. Shine a light on the frog from various angles—directly above, from the left, from the right, directly in front, and directly behind. Have students observe and describe how the frog reacts. (Frogs usually will react by placing their body so they face the direction of strongest illumination; frequently they also move toward the light.)

Have students respond to this question: Based on your observations, would you say that frogs are positivly or negatively phototaxic? (Frogs generally exhibit positive phototaxis.)

If you have access to other types of live amphibians, you might have students compare and contrast their reactions to light with those of the frog.

**B/R7.** *Contact Response in Frogs.* Do frogs respond positively or negatively to contact (thigmotaxis)? Many animals tend to remain in situations that afford contact stimulus over a considerable portion of their body.

Place several frogs in a large clear container such as a 20-liter (5-gallon) or 40-liter (10-gallon) aquarium with about 2.5 to 5 centimeters (1 to 2 inches) of water in it. Place objects in the tank that will allow the frogs to crawl under or between them. Leave the frogs undisturbed for some time, and then have students observe the location of the frogs. Ask: Based on your observations, is the frog positively or negatively thigmotaxic? (Frogs show a propensity to crawl under stones or to get between objects, where they remain quiet.)

Interested, older, or more advanced students could investigate the role of temperature in this behavior, which becomes even more pronounced as temperatures are lowered.

**B/R8.** *Which Way the Wind?* Frog expert Dr. Hip N. Hop has collected data concerning frog migration and wind direction, as shown in the table.

Have students analyze this data by making a bar graph of it. Pose this question to students: What general conclusion can we draw from this data? (A large surplus of frogs migrated when the winds tended to be southerly.) Could these results be a coincidence or chance occurrence? (The actual data from which this table was derived was subjected to a test of significance and was found to be quite significant. Therefore, there is no reasonable possibility that this happened by coincidence or chance.) Would this conclusion hold true for all frogs or other amphibians everywhere? (No. It is valid only for the place, time, and creatures for which the initial data was gathered.)

## Feeding

**F1.** *Adult Amphibian Feeding Comparisons.* Have students compare and contrast what the various types of adult amphibians eat. (See the "Specific Order Characteristics" section of this chapter and consult other appropriate references.)

**F2.** *Adult vs. Larvae Feeding Comparisons.* Have students compare and contrast adult amphibians' food preferences with those of larval amphibians. (See the "Specific Order Characteristics" section of this chaper and consult other appropriate references.)

**F3.** *Feeding an Amphibian.* Have students observe and describe a frog, toad, or salamander eating a mealworm, cricket, or earthworm. The prey must be alive and moving to entice the amphibian to feed; otherwise, lightly tie the prey on a thread and dangle it alluringly before the animal. In my experience, getting frogs and toads to feed in captivity has been difficult. However, I have had success training salamanders to take inseccts and especially earthworms held in forceps.

Have students respond to this question: How are the mouth and tongue of a frog adapted for eating insects or other small invertebrates? (The mouth is large and basket shaped and the tongue is long and sticky.)

**F4.** *No Food = No Toads?* A biologist fenced off a colony of toads in a wire enclosure where the toads sheltered in the turf. The biologist was called away unexpectedly for an extended period but forgot to tell anyone to feed the toads. When the biologist returned, the toads were healthy and fat and the population density was far higher than ever occurs in nature. Have students hypothesize about how this could have happened. (Apparently, enough prey animals flew in or crawled through the fence to keep the toads fat and happy, and the fence evidently kept predators out of the toad colony so that the toads' numbers increased.) Have students respond to this question: In this situation, was food a limiting factor for the toad population? (No.)

**F5.** **Challenge:** *Do Certain Colors Cause a Feeding Reaction in Frogs?* Have students devise a way to test this problem.

Through previous activities, we have established that frogs depend on motion to locate their prey. Students might begin by dangling small bits of colored yarn before the frogs. Make sure the yarn is positioned slighly to the side and close enough so the frogs can see it. Use a variety of brightly colored yarns. Make sure each piece is approximately the same size. Dangle the yarn on clear fish line or neutral-colored thread so that the frog reacts to the yarn and not the movement of the line. Use the same pattern of movement for each color of yarn.

Have students predict what they think will happen before they begin and draw conclusions from their data, which will be mainly observational.

**R1.** *Metamorphosis Mix-up.* Mix up the illustrations of the various stages of frog metamorphosis shown and have students sort them out into their proper sequence.

**R2.** *Jumping Gender.* Orchids do it, shrimp do it, and even some fish do it. Now biologists have discovered that some amphibians do it. Do what? Change sexes. A German research team reported female amphibians becoming males without hormonal or surgical intervention. Have students hypothesize about why frogs would change gender. (Biologists believe it happens when an excess of females exists. Some females may possibly change to increase their chances of mating.) Pose this question to students: Why don't more animals undergo sex reversal? (Biologists speculate that the energy expenditure may be too high in species with more pronounced differences between the sexes.)

**R3.** *Which Gender?* If you have frogs available, have the students carefully examine them to see if there are any external clues that would denote the gender of the frog. (Male frogs usually have a lump near the "thumb" of the front limbs. This pad helps the male grip the female during fertilization.)

# Reproduction and Development

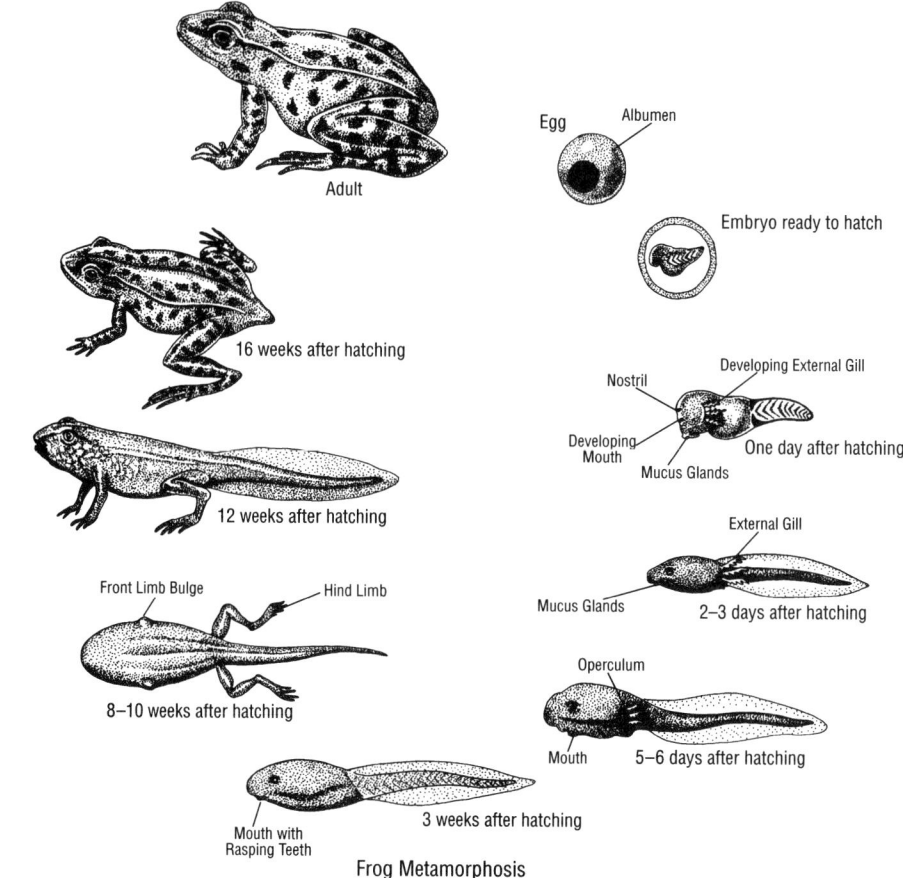

Frog Metamorphosis

**R4.** *Amphibian Embryology.* Have students observe the development of amphibian eggs and metamorphosis to adults if possible. Have students keep observations and diagrams of the changes that occur in a developmental diary. Strong magnifiers or stereo dissecting scopes will be needed for this activity.

There are several sources for amphibian eggs. You could collect the eggs yourself in the early spring. You might also consider purchasing fertile eggs (frog or toad) from the suppliers listed in Appendix B. These suppliers also handle induced breeding sets as well as amphibians for breeding in the classroom such as Xenopus (African clawed frog).

See the "Collection of Specimens" and "Maintenance of Specimens" sections in this chapter for hints on collecting eggs, rearing larvae, and breeding Xenopus.

**R5.** *No Place Like Home.* Do newts return to breed in the same place every year? To answer this question, a biologist worked for five years capturing, marking with toe clips, and releasing all the male newts that entered a 50-yard stretch of a small stream. The capture-and-release area was designated Station 9. The graph shows the number and location of captured males four years later in relation to Station 9.

Have students analyze the graph with the original question in mind. Ask: What has been graphed? According to the graph, do newts return to breed in the same place yearly? (Yes, and in significant numbers, although, as the graph shows, some venturesome individuls traveled farther afield to breed.)

**R6.** *Challenge: Does Sense of Smell Play a Role in Male Newts Locating Female Newts for Breeding?* Share the following background information and illustration with students: Newts breed in the water. Male newts are

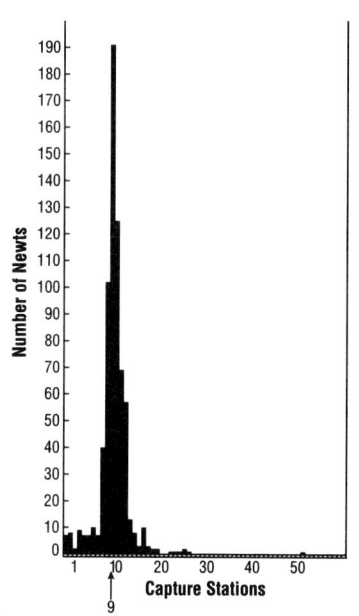

attracted upstream by receptive females but are not attracted by receptive females downstream.

Now have students devise a way to test this problem. Students should realize that the purpose of this exercise is experimental design, and unless you have access to a stream with newts, it will not actually be carried out. Ideally, students will hypothesize from the background information that the female newts are giving off odors that the males can smell and are attracted to.

How do we test that hypothesis? Biologists who conducted this experiment soaked some sponges in water containing females (experimental) and other sponges in sterile distilled water (control). The sponges were anchored into a small stream. Challenge students to explain what kind of data they could collect from such an experiment. (They should reply that the males on or in close proximity to both kinds of sponges could be counted. From these numbers graphs could be drawn and appropriate conclusions derived.)

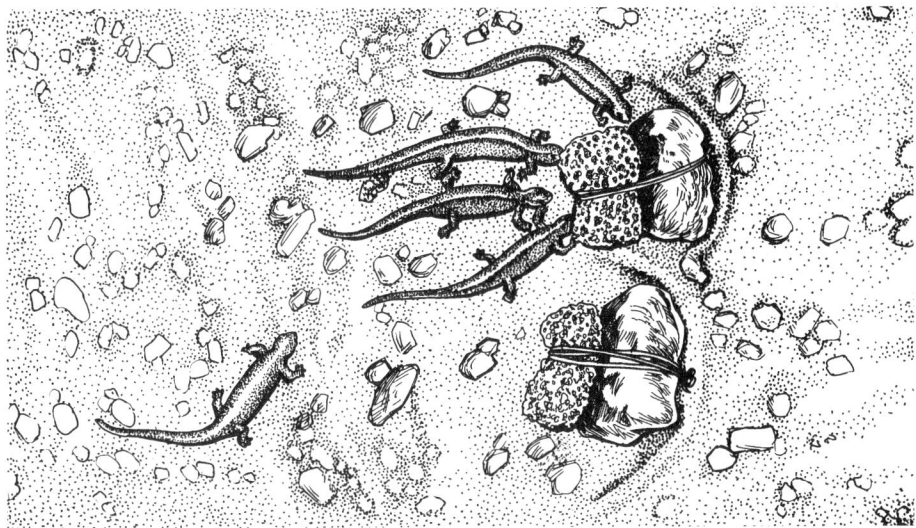

Have students view the illustration showing the male newts and sponges and ask: What conclusions can you draw from this picture? (The males seem to cluster around the sponge soaked in water containing females [experimental] more than around the sponge soaked in sterile distilled water [control].)

Students may also suggest plugging the nose of the newts with something like petroleum jelly. (Biologists tried this but weren't sure whether the results they observed were due to the newts' inablility to smell or their inability to breath properly due to blocked nasal passages.)

Another course of action students may suggest is to destroy the sense of smell by surgical means. (This also was tried by biologists, but the results were not conclusive.) Biologists do believe that olfaction (smelling) is an important factor in the breeding of newts.

**In1.** *Writing:*
  a. Have students respond in writing to this statement: Amphibians are to the animal kingdom what mosses and liverworts are to the plant kingdom.
  b. From Mark Twain's celebrated jumping frog and Mr. Toad of *The Wind In The Willows* to Kermit the Frog, amphibians have found a place in literature, song, and film. Have students write a short story or play with a frog, toad, or salamander as the main character.

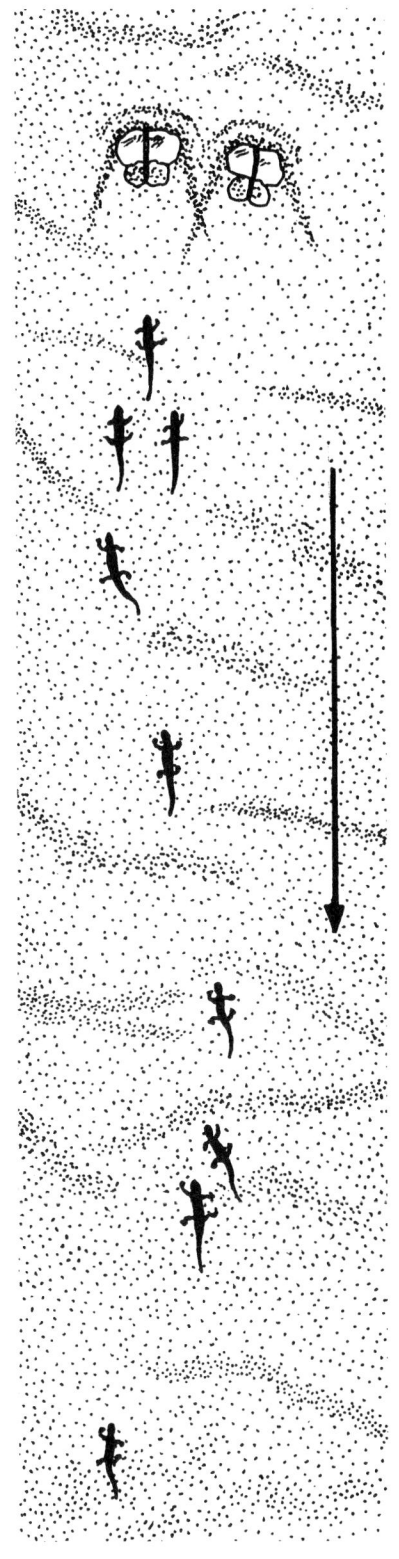

Integration with Other Subject Areas

c. Challenge students to learn more about amphibians by having them do a formal library report on the specific amphibian of their choice.

**In2.** *Fine Arts:*

a. Frogs make an unbelievable array of sounds:
- Gray tree frog: flute-like trill
- Spotted chorus frog: *wrrank, wrrank*
- Stecker's chorus frog: two sharp, clear whistles per second
- Northern cricket frog: *gick, gick, gick*, one per second
- Cricket frog: cricket-like cheeps
- Wood frog: quacks like a duck
- Bull frog: deep-throated rumble like "jug-o-rum"
- Great Plains narrow-mouthed toad: high pitched nasal *neeeeee*

Explain that usually only male frogs and toads call and that salamanders make no sounds.

Assign or have students pick certain sounds. Let each group practice their calls, separately if possible. Now bring the entire group together and create a mixed chorus by having all the groups call at once. Encourage students to call clearly but not to shout and scream. Use a tape recorder to record the calls. Replay the tape and see if they can pick out their own species over the din. Pose this question to students: Why is it imperative that female frogs and toads be able to hear the call of the male of their species? (If they cannot, mating will not occur and no young would be hatched.)

b. Have students compose a song or poem entitled (with apologies to Kermit the Frog), "It's Tough Being Green" (or "Warty" if they want to make it about toads).

c. Have students draw or paint a picture of any amphibian of their choice and its habitat.

**In3.** *Social Studies:*

a. *History.* Frogs and other amphibians have figured into fact and fable for thousands of years. Ancient Egyptians believed frogs could enhance human female fertility. Some South American tribes thought frogs could bring rain, and one tribe even sacrificed women to a divine frog. Generations of biologists and surgeons have been introduced to vertebrate anatomy by probing a frog's insides, and amphibians have been rocketed into space to test the effects of weightlessness. See the section "The Importance of Amphibians" in this chapter for other ways in which humans have historically benefited from amphibians. Share this information with your students.

Now challenge your students to make history by thinking up new ways amphibians could be useful to humans. Encourage students to devise novel but humane ways of using amphibians.

b. *Geography.* Have students study the map of amphibian distribution and question them about where they would or would not go to find the amphibians shown on the map.

**In4.** *Societal/Environmental Issues:*

a. Have students discuss the pros and cons of the traditional use of frogs for dissection activities in life science classes. This discussion could take the form of a position paper prepared by each student or a classroom debate. If you have a debate, establish a set of rules beforehand and make sure to enforce the rules.

b. For some time biologists have had a suspicion that amphibian populations have been declining on nearly every continent. The evidence

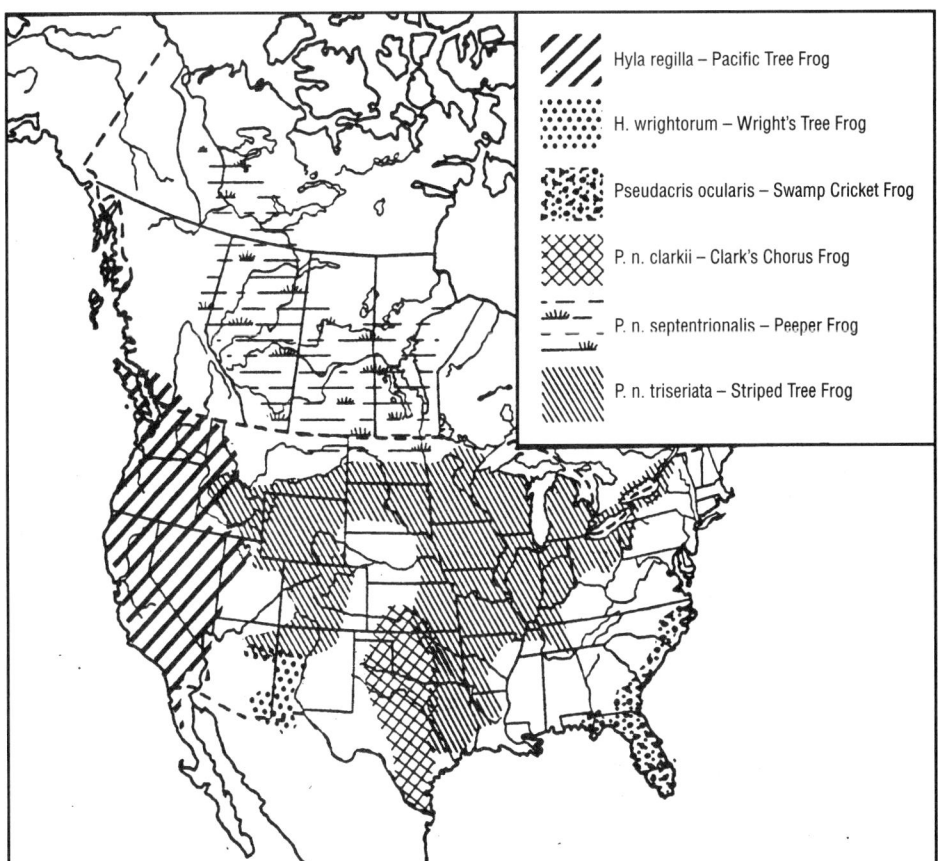

Hyla regilla – Pacific Tree Frog

H. wrightorum – Wright's Tree Frog

Pseudacris ocularis – Swamp Cricket Frog

P. n. clarkii – Clark's Chorus Frog

P. n. septentrionalis – Peeper Frog

P. n. triseriata – Striped Tree Frog

seems mainly anecdotal at this point, however, and scientists are calling for long-term studies to provide convincing evidence. Some species disappearing in certain regions are doing well in other places. Other species appear totally unaffected by the declines. Such variations complicate any analysis of the problem. Even skeptical scientists agree that something is happening to amphibians, and we need to find out what it is because it may be an early warning sign of the world's increasing environmental degradation.

Have students investigate their own community and region to discover what human activities have occurred or are occurring that negatively impact amphibians or their habitats. Have your students consult zoologists, herpetologists, and ecologists at local colleges and universities as well as area wildlife authorities. Invite these experts to your school as guest speakers. They can give you and your students a better understanding of any amphibian problems in your area and, as an added benefit, serve as positive career role models for students.

If it becomes apparent that there are problems in your area with declining habitat or pollution of suitable habitat for amphibians, challenge your students to do something about the problems. Should you and your students take on the challenge, and if so, how do you proceed? I cannot give you specifics. Such questions would have to be answered by you and your students based on your own situation.

Student activists have made a difference in the past and continue to make an impact on the quality of life around them. Kids care but they need a cause to focus on and proper leadership to tackle that cause. What better cause is there than defending the unappreciated and defenseless amphibians?

# RELEASE OF SPECIMENS

Frogs may be released back into the ponds or marshes from which they were collected. Put toads and salamanders back under the rocks or logs where you found them.

Do not release commercially purchased amphibians, eggs, or larvae unless you can absolutely verify without doubt that they are native to your area. *Never release Xenopus (African clawed frog) into the wild under any circumstances.*

# 10. *REPTILES*

| | |
|---|---|
| **Kingdom:** | Animalia |
| **Subkingdom:** | Metazoa |
| **Phylum:** | Chordata |
| **Subphylum:** | Vertebrata |
| **Class:** | Reptilia (reptiles) |
| | Orders: Rhynocephalia (tuatara) |
| | Squamata (lizards and snakes) |
| | Crocodilia (crocodiles, alligators, caimans, and gharials) |
| | Chelonia (turtles and tortoises) |

## DIVERSITY AND DISTRIBUTION

The 6,547 living species of modern reptiles that slither, swim, and scurry (Latin—*reptum*, creep) over the earth today are mere shadows of a group that once dominated the land, seas, and sky with their numbers and size. Fossils indicate that around 65 million years ago most reptiles disappeared into extinction. What happened to them? Some 90 different causes have been proposed, but none satisfactorily explains the extinction of most of the reptiles. The truth about their demise remains a mystery. As with amphibians, the majority of reptiles that ever lived are extinct.

Living reptiles have adapted to a true terrestrial existence living and reproducing on land. The reptiles have managed to accomplish what the amphibians never quite managed for several reasons: (1) a dry, scaly body sealed to prevent dehydration; (2) limbs suited for rapid movement; (3) advanced heart and lungs; (4) internal fertilization; and (5) eggs covered and sealed with membranes and shells suited for development on dry land.

Most reptiles, both species and individuals, live in tropical and subtropical regions; their numbers decline rapidly toward the poles and in high altitudes. The lizards and snakes are by far the most numerous and widely distributed of living reptiles. Both occur in a great variety of habitats and climatic conditions, ranging from deserts to tropical rain forests. There are no fully aquatic lizards but several groups of snakes, such as sea snakes, are highly aquatic.

Turtles are amphibious, with both fresh- and saltwater species, but the tortoises are highly terrestrial. Turtles and tortoises are more abundant and diversified in the tropics and extend into both the north and south temperate zones.

The crocodilians are quite restricted in diversity and distribution. They are limited to the tropics and a few warm temperate areas. They are all amphibious, with most being found in fresh water, although a few are tolerant of salt water.

The tuataras are the most extremely limited of living reptiles. The one living species survives only on remote islands off the main island of New Zealand. Unfortunately, the tuatara is near extinction.

Living reptiles range in size from the Panamanian lizard at 5 centimeters (2 inches) to the regal python of Malaya, which grows to 9.7 meters (32 feet). The monitor lizards reach 2.9 meters (9.5 feet) or more, the marine leatherback turtle may exceed 2.1 meters (7 feet) in length, and there are reports of large crocodiles of 7 meters (23 feet).

## General Class Characteristics

**Digestive System and Feeding.** Most reptiles are carnivorous and eat all types of other animals such as worms, crustaceans, snails, spiders, insects, fish, amphibians, other reptiles, birds, mammals, and eggs depending on the size of the individual and its species. Land tortoises, some turtles, and lizards such as the chuckwalla, desert iguana, and Galapagos iguana eat vegetation.

As a group, carnivorous reptiles are stalkers. They make slow, deliberate movements until they are within striking distance of their prey and then suddenly snap and grab it.

Reptiles, especially snakes, have extremely flexible and elastic muscles and ligaments around the jaws and throat that allow them to swallow objects bigger than their head. The powerful muscles give reptiles great gripping, snapping, slicing, and tearing strength. Interestingly, the muscles that close an alligator's jaws are powerful enough to break your arm, but the muscles that open the jaw are so weak that a person can hold the alligator's jaws shut with one hand (I don't recommend testing it, however).

Because reptiles swallow their food whole or in large chunks, they have a long digestive system with powerful digestive juices. The digestive acids of crocodiles have dissolved iron spearheads and six-inch steel hooks.

**Circulatory System.** Reptiles have a well-developed double-loop circulatory system. Reptile hearts are either modified three-chambered or, as in crocodilians, four-chambered hearts similar to those of birds and mammals.

Like fish and amphibians, reptiles are ectothermic (cold blooded). However, unlike the fish and amphibians, which are at the mercy of the environment, reptiles have developed numerous strategies to actively regulate their body temperature: (1) They may be active only when the temperature is favorable.

Many desert reptiles are active at night or in the early morning and avoid the scorching heat of midday. (2) They alternate between basking in hot, sunny areas to warm up and moving to shady areas to cool down. (3) They burrow into the ground or move back and forth between shallow, warm water and deeper, cool water. (4) They position their body to receive the maximum heating from the sun's rays or raise their legs and possibly their tail up off of warm rocks or sand to cool down. (5) Some types can change their color: darkening early to absorb radiant energy and later in the day becoming lighter to reflect radiant energy. Control of body temperature is possible because the hypothalamus of the brain acts like a thermostat and stimulates the reptile to seek either heat or cold. Proper temperature regulation promotes growth, reproduction, and survival by controlling the rate of food processing. A snake denied access to heat may die because the food in its stomach becomes cold and rots.

Being ectothermic presents serious survival challenges daily, but it does have one advantage—slow metabolic rates (about one-tenth that of birds and mammals). This results in a slower but longer life for reptiles than for birds and mammals. In captivity, several tortoises have survived beyond 100 years, and there are historical accounts of tortoises possibly living to be 200 years old. Some species of lizards have lived more than 50 years in captivity. Large snakes may reach 40 years and crocodilians 100 years under such conditions.

**Respiratory System.** The lungs of reptiles are larger and better developed than those of the amphibians, and there is no skin breathing with reptiles as there must be with amphibians. However, some turtles can remain submerged in water for extended periods by extracting oxygen from water they pump into their pharynx or cloaca. Reptiles have ribs with attached muscle and, except for turtles and tortoises, breathe by expanding or collapsing the chest cavity.

Most reptiles have two lungs, but some snakes, in an adaptation to their long, slender bodies, have only one. Snakes also have a special tube in the floor of their mouth through which they can breathe during the extended time it may take them to swallow large prey. Some crocodilians have flaps of skin that separate the mouth from the nasal passages and allow them to breathe through their nostrils while opening their mouth underwater to feed.

**Muscle System and Movement.** The reptilian muscle system exhibits many advances over that of the amphibians. Reptiles have larger, stronger limbs whose movements are well-regulated.

Flying Dragon

Amphibian Limb Position

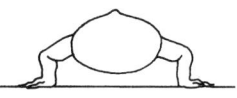

Reptile Limb Position

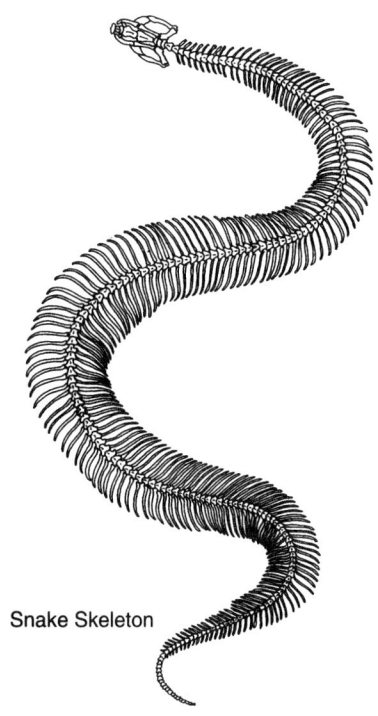

Snake Skeleton

The legs of a reptile, with their powerful clawed toes, can be adapted to walking, running, burrowing, swimming, and climbing. The flying dragons of Southeast Asia glide from perch to perch by extending a large, thin fold of skin between the legs and supported by the ribs.

**Skeletal System.** The skeletal system of reptiles is more advanced than that of the amphibians. The limbs of a reptile are positioned in a manner that raises the body farther off the ground than do amphibian limbs. Thus, reptiles can move more rapidly and efficiently than the belly-dragging amphibians (although some lizards would also have to be considered belly-draggers).

Due to modifications of their pelvis and hind limbs, reduction in size of the front limbs, and development of an extra-long tail for balance, some lizards, such as the crested dragon and frilled lizard of Australia, can run upright on their hind legs.

The snakes have no limbs, limb girdles, or sternum, but they do have greatly increased numbers of vertebrae and ribs all practically alike in structure.

All reptiles except turtles and tortoises have teeth. In turtles and tortoises, a hard, bony beak functionally replaces the teeth. Crocodilians have conical teeth set in sockets, as are the teeth of mammals. Snakes have long, sharp, backwardly curving teeth arranged in rows on the upper and lower jaws. Most lizards have small marginal teeth attached without sockets to the biting edges of the jaws.

Some reptiles, such as pythons, crocodiles, and giant tortoises, lack points of fusion in their bones and grow continually throughout their life, often reaching giant size. In addition, reptiles do not lose their teeth in old age as mammals do. Their continuous lifelong tooth replacement contributes to their longevity and potential size.

**Body Covering.** All reptiles have a dry skin consisting of several layers. The horny outer layer, or epidermis, is thick and composed of layers of flat, dead cells filled with keratin. The scales of a reptile are localized thickenings of this keratin connected by hinges of thinner material often folded back so they overlap each other. Unlike the scales of a fish, reptile scales are not separate and detachable structures; they are part of a continual epidermal sheet.

Periodically, the keratinous outer layer is shed and replaced in a process called molting. In snakes and some lizards, the skin is often shed in one piece. In others species, it may come away in large flakes. The rattlesnake's rattle is a unique epidermal structure composed of interlocking horny segments; a new segment is formed at each molt, although the end segments tend to break off when the rattle gets very long. The frequency of molting varies with the species and with age. Young reptiles generally shed more than adults, snakes and lizards may shed several times a year, and some turtles shed once annually. The outer layers on the box tortoise, crocodilians, and some others are not shed but wear off and are replaced from underneath.

The lower layer of skin, or dermis, consists mainly of connective tissue, blood vessels, and nerves. In some reptiles, such as the crocodilians and many lizards, bony plates in the dermis reinforce the epidermal scales. The remarkable shell of a turtle consists of thin epidermal scales over an oval box-like layer of bony dermal plates.

The dermis also contains pigment cells. Many of them contain black pigment, but there may be white, yellow, violet, and red pigment cells as well. Interaction between these cells produces a variety of colors. The most colorful of all in terms of variety and brilliance are the snakes and lizards. In fact, the true chameleons are famous for their ability to change both the shade and the pattern of their skin coloration.

Amphibians have an abundance of skin glands, but reptiles almost totally lack them. The few that do occur usually are scent glands for repelling predators or for sex discrimination during breeding.

**Excretory System.** Reptiles eliminate liquid wastes in the form of urine, which is filtered from the blood by the kidneys. In some reptiles, urine flows directly into a cloaca similar to that of amphibians. In others, a urinary bladder stores urine before it is expelled.

**Brain and Nervous System.** The brain of a reptile is organized along the basic vertebrate plan. Despite its small size, it is significantly advanced over the brains of amphibians and fish, with the cerebrum and cerebellum somewhat larger in the reptile brain.

Most reptile sense organs are well developed, but vision is the dominant sense. Reptile eyes are, depending on the species, adapted for day vision (diurnal) or night vision (nocturnal), and some lizards, crocodiles, and turtles have color vision at least as good as the human eye. The tuatara and some lizards have what is called a third eye in the top of the head. Known more correctly as the pineal body, it does not form images but may act as a light meter.

As in most higher vertebrates, the reptilian ear serves as an organ of both hearing and balance. In most reptiles other than snakes, the tympanic membrane (eardrum) is visible on the surface of the head. In turtles it is thin and transparent, but in tortoises it is thick and covered by skin. Some lizards and crocodilians hear through external ear holes leading to the tympanic membrane. Snakes lack a tympanic membrane but can sense vibrations through bones in their skull.

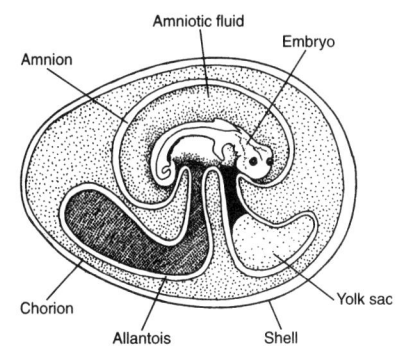

Tuatara

The nasal region of reptiles is more complicated than in amphibians and allows the reptiles a greater development of the sense of smell. However, crocodilians have little if any sense of smell and in turtles the sense is poorly developed. The sense of smell in reptiles achieves its greatest development with the lizards and snakes. Specialized organs in the roof of the mouth aid the nose in smelling. When the tongue is flipped out, molecules (odors) from the air gather on it. When it is drawn back into the mouth and onto these special smelling organs, information about the environment is gathered. The sense of taste is relatively poor in reptiles compared to amphibians and fish.

**Reproduction and Development.** In most reptile species, the two sexes differ to some extent in adult size, shape, and/or color. Sexual reproduction is the rule, although some rock lizards and the whiptail lizard of North America are all females that give birth to young through a process called parthenogenesis (reproduction without fertilization). All sexually reproducing reptiles practice internal fertilization by introducing the sperm directly into the cloaca of the female. Fertilization is usually preceded by courtship rituals that may be quite elaborate and lengthy. In the tuatara, fertilization is achieved by cloacal contact, but in all other reptiles, the males have specialized organs for insemination. Some female snakes, lizards, tortoises, and turtles can store sperm for a year or more.

Most reptiles lay their eggs, which, unlike amphibian eggs, are resistant to drying. The eggs of snakes, most lizards, and turtles are covered by a tough, flexible, leathery shell; those of the tortoises, crocodilians, and many gecko lizards are hard and calcified somewhat like birds' eggs. The number of eggs produced annually by a female varies from nearly 400 in some sea turtles to a single egg in the house gecko. Small pond turtles lay 5 to 11 eggs, snakes and lizards about 10 to 20, and the American alligator 30 to 60. Upon hatching, the young resemble the adults except in size and become independent at once.

Reptile Egg — Internal

Some reptiles, such as garter snakes, rattlesnakes, sea snakes, and some lizards, hold their eggs inside their body until they hatch, thus producing live young. Some garter snakes have produced over 70 living young in a single brood. A few snakes have a primitive placenta that permits the exchange of nutrients between the mother and the embryos developing within her.

Parental care of the young varies among reptiles. It is the most highly developed in the crocodilians, which may build elaborate nests of rotting vegetation to provide warmth. The female lays the eggs there and then faithfully guards the nest. Peeping calls uttered by the young just before emergence signals the female to uncover the nest and assist the young to water. Female Nile crocodiles take the young hatchlings into their mouths and transport them to the water. The female may stay in the vicinity of the young for several weeks after hatching. Snakes exhibit little parental care. Some female pythons coil around their eggs and incubate them, and some female cobras guard their clutch of eggs. Among lizards, some types guard the eggs but little other care is provided. In turtles and tortoises, the female lays the eggs and goes on her way,

## Specific Order Characteristics

**Order Rhynocephalia.** This order is made up of only one living species, the tuatara. Living tuataras, thought to be similar in structure to a form that existed millions of years ago, are studied for clues of ancient reptile physiology and anatomy. They are found only on about 30 small islands off the coast of New Zealand.

Superficially, tuataras resemble lizards, but several internal features of the skull, vertebrae, ribs, and heart place them in a group of their own.

Tuataras are night-active burrowers often found in association with burrowing sea birds. The tuatara's diet includes spiders, earthworms, slugs, snails, lizards, and the eggs and chicks of sea birds.

Adults have a background color of olive green, gray, or dark pink with an overall speckling of gray or white. Males range up to 61 centimeters (24 inches) long, with an average weight of around 0.15 kilograms (1.1 pounds).

**Order Squamata.** This order comprises two groups; lizards and snakes. The approximately 3,751 species of lizards are found nearly from pole to pole around the world. They are scattered over the islands of the Atlantic, Pacific, and Indian oceans and on the island continent of Australia. Species occur from the sea up to 5,000 meters (16,500 feet) in mountains. Their habitats range from terrestrial to tree dwelling and from burrowing to amphibious.

A lizard's body is long and cylindrical (flattened horizontally) or compressed (flattened vertically), depending on the species. Lizards typically possess a blunt head with eyelids and external ear openings, four legs with five clawed toes on each leg, and a long tail. Some lizards, such as the glass snake, worm lizard, and slowworm, have no legs at all.

The trademark tail of the lizard has three primary uses: grasping, balance, and storage. Reserves of fat can be stored in the tail—an important feature in those lizards that remain inactive for long periods in cold climates. Several species, but especially the true chameleons, are noted for their prehensile (grasping) tail, which they wrap around vegetation to steady themselves as they climb.

**Striped Whiptail Lizard**

**Horned Lizard**

The balance function of the tail is the most important, and individuals that have lost their tails run or climb clumsily. Many species of lizards have a fragile tail that, if seized by a predator, separates easily from the rest of the body. Thus the lizard can make its escape while the predator is preoccupied with the wriggling tail piece. The lizard slowly regenerates a new tail, but it will not be quite the same as the original; some individuals generate forked tails from the spot of detachment.

All lizards possess a well-developed tongue that can be extended to varying degrees. Probably none do it so dramatically or from such long range as the Old World chameleons.

Most lizards are predators that feed mainly on insects, worms, birds, mammals, and other reptiles. About 2 percent of all known species are herbiverous and eat plants. The iguanas consume a wide variety of plant material. The marine iguana of the Galapagos Islands dives 15 meters (50 feet) or more under water to nibble algae off rocks. The diet of lizards may shift with maturity and seasonal changes.

Most lizards are colored in varying shades of greens, browns, and black, although some sport dazzling reds, yellows, oranges, blues, and white,

Lizards range in size from the Panamanian lizards at 5 centimeters (2 inches) to the giant monitor lizards (often called Komodo dragons after the place in Indonesia where they were first discovered), which can reach 3 meters (10 feet) in length and weigh over 165 kilograms (364 pounds). Adult monitors regularly kill prey as large as pigs and small deer and have been known to bring down water buffalo. They also will attack and kill humans.

The only poisonous lizards are the Gila monster and the Mexican beaded lizard, found only in the southwestern United States and Pacific slopes of Mexico. These lizards grind their venom into the skin of the victim as the lizard chews. Their bite is painful but only mildly venomous and rarely fatal to healthy human adults.

The other group of the order Squamata is the approximately 2,398 species of snakes. Snakes are distributed worldwide except in the Arctic, Antarctica, Iceland, Ireland, New Zealand, and some small oceanic islands. Snakes occupy a wide variety of habitats. Most are terrestrial, but some climb trees and rocks. Some occupy the burrows of other animals, some burrow into the sand, and some live in the water.

Snakes possess the organs typical of other vertebrates, but their internal structures have been modified to accommodate a long, cylindrical body; the habit of swallowing prey whole; and the need for rapid locomotion without limbs. The body has been lengthened by the addition of extra vertebrae, and many paired organs have been reduced or offset. For example, in most snakes the left lung is greatly reduced or absent, and the female thread snake has only one oviduct.

Snakes are able to make use of several alternative modes of locomotion to move powerfully, gracefully, and rapidly on land, through the water, and even up and across tree branches: (1) With serpentine movement, the body literally swims along in a series of curves and gains traction from exerting pressure against sticks, pebbles, vegetation, and other surface irregularities. (2) With concertina movement, the body coils and then grips the ground, pulling the rest of the body forward into the next compression. (3) With sidewinding, the snake touches the ground only at two points and unrolls its body until the head is extended enough to touch down for the beginning of another loop. (4) The caterpillar crawl allows some large snakes such as constrictors to crawl straight ahead. The broad belly scales (scutes) slide forward and catch the ground like tire treads, allowing the body to be pulled up. This action may alternate at several points along the snake's body.

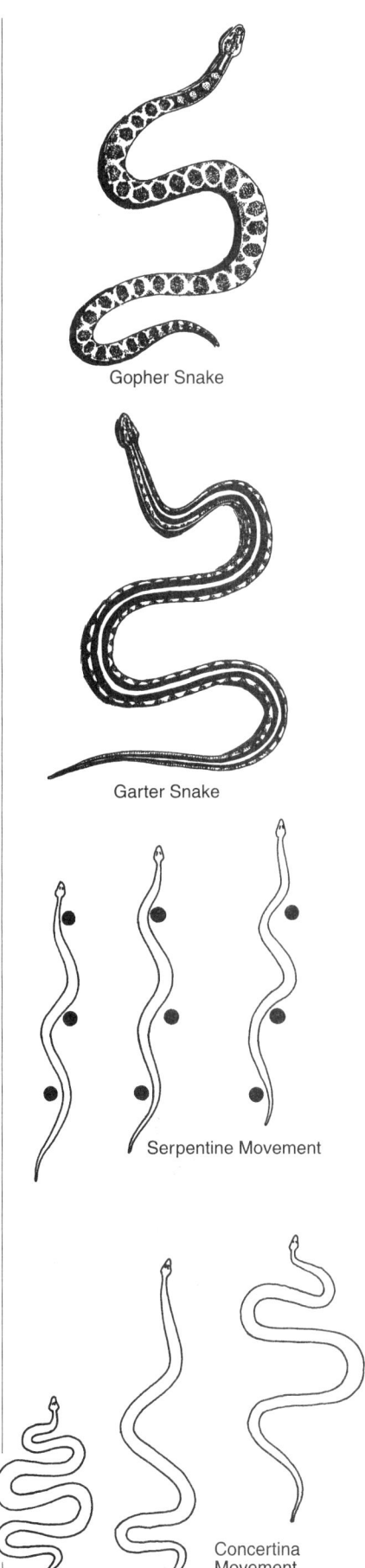

Gopher Snake

Garter Snake

Serpentine Movement

Concertina Movement

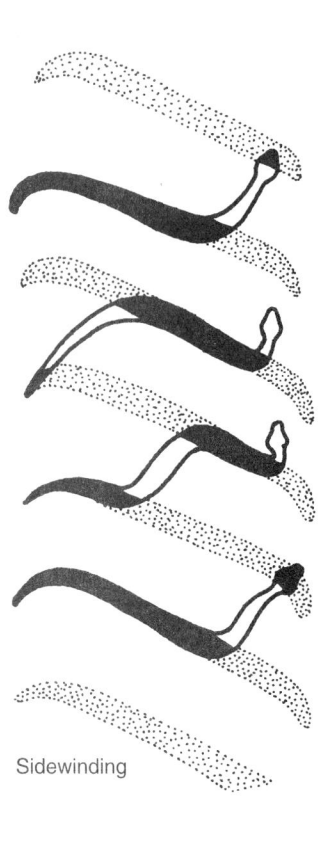

Sidewinding

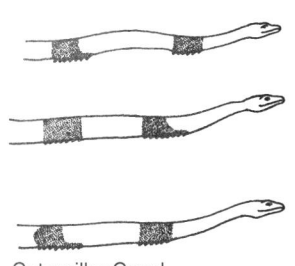

Caterpillar Crawl

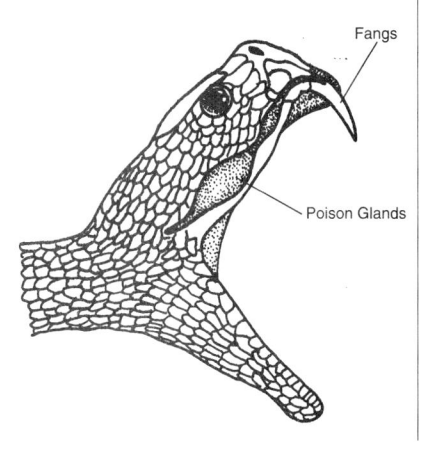

Fangs

Poison Glands

Snakes do not travel as fast as they appear to. Rattlesnakes have been clocked at 3 kilometers (2 miles) per hour, and even racers never reach 6.5 kilometers (4 miles) per hour. The record is held by an African black mamba clocked at 11.2 kilometers (7 miles) per hour while chasing a man who had been teasing it.

The sensory capabilities of snakes are considerably different from those found in most vertebrates. Snakes lack an eardrum and cannot hear airborne sounds, although they can detect low-frequency sounds or vibrations of the surface they are resting on. All snakes have eyes but, unlike lizards, lack eyelids and thus seem to have a menacing stare. The day-active terrestrial and tree-dwelling types have acute vision, but the "blind snakes" can only distinguish light from dark. With a flick of their tongue, snakes pick up chemical scents in the air and use these molecular trails to track prey, avoid predators, and find mates. Pit vipers have heat-sensitive pits on each side of their head with which they can detect not only the direction of an object but also its distance. These are the most sensitive receptors in the animal kingdom; pit vipers can sense changes of less than 0.001°C (0.002°F). This sense is extremely important for night hunters stalking warm animals such as mammals.

All snakes are predatory, and there are no known examples of vegetarians among them. Worms, insects, spiders, fish, amphibians, birds, mammals, and other reptiles are among the usual fare, although some snakes have developed specialized tastes for exclusive diets of snails, eggs, and certain insects. Although most smaller and weaker prey can be swallowed without great difficulty, larger and more active animals need to be subdued. The snakes use two methods: constriction and venom. Some snakes constrict or hold their struggling victims by looping one or two coils of their body around the prey and maintaining this grip until the process of swallowing is well advanced. The true constrictors throw many body coils around their prey and keep tightening the coils until the victim suffocates. As soon as the victim is insensible or dead it is released, reexamined with the tongue, and then swallowed. The swallowing reaction is automatic once begun but can be reversed and the meal regurgitated if the snake is disturbed. (The appearance of regurgitated prey, mangled by the jaws and teeth and covered in saliva and mucous from the mouth, has led to the erroneous belief that constricting snakes crush their victims into pulp and cover them with slimy mucous for ease of swallowing.)

Venomous snakes have special poison glands and specialized teeth called fangs for delivering the poison into their victims. In some poisonous snakes, such as the cobras, mambas, and coral snakes, the fangs are short, fixed, and erect at all times. In the rattlesnake and others of its kind, called vipers, the long fangs fold back when the mouth is closed. Most venomous snakes have their fangs in the front of the mouth, but in the back-fanged snakes, the fangs are to the rear of the mouth.

The clear to amber venom of poisonous snakes can be grouped into a limited number of categories according to its effects: (1) substances that cause the disintegration of tissues, (2) anticoagulants that destroy the clotting capacity of the blood and result in heavy bleeding, and (3) neurotoxins that act on the nervous system, especially the nerves of the respiratory system and the heart.

Venom is an effective offensive weapon for securing prey and can also play a defensive role in deterring enemies. The most lethal snake venoms are those of two Australian land snakes, the desert taipan and Eastern brown snake, and Dubois' reef snake. The poisons of these three species are fatal to a 20-gram (0.7-ounce) mouse at a dosage of 1 microgram (1 millionth of a gram). However, some experts say the sea snakes could be considered more deadly because their venom is so concentrated.

More than 50 species are reported to have poisoned humans from very mildly to fatally. World Health Organization statistics indicate that 30,000 to 40,000 deaths occur annually worldwide due to snakebite.

Most snakes are colored in drab browns, grays, or black. Some have bright red, yellow, or green markings in arrangements varying from blotches to rings, crossbands, and stripes. Snakes cannot change color to any great degree the way many lizards can.

The smallest snake is the tiny burrowing thread snake, only 15 centimeters (6 inches) long and no bigger around than a matchstick. The largest snake is more difficult to determine as all records are based on field observations (often with the snake going one way and a panicked observer the other) and not actual specimens. The reticulated pythons of Southeast Asia grow over 6 meters (20 feet) in zoos, and a 10-meter (33-foot) specimen was reported on the island of Celebes. In weight, the record belongs to the anaconda from South America; a 6-meter (20-foot) anaconda weighs more than a 10-meter (33-foot) python due to the greater girth of the anaconda. Unfortunately, all records of snakes over 10 meters were made early in this century. Given the current commercial value of snake skins and the human attitude toward these animals, it is unlikely any snake now living will live long enough to reach record size in the wild.

**Order Crocodilia.** This order is composed of only 22 species, including alligators (7 species), crocodiles (14 species), and gharials (1 species).

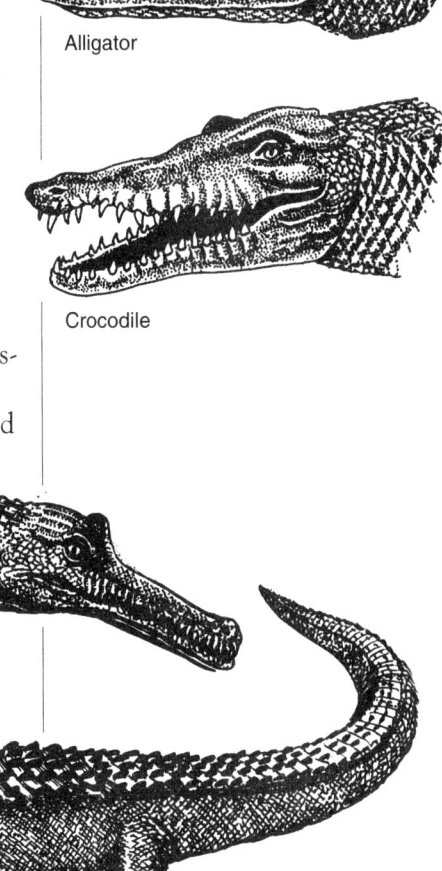

Alligator

To see an alligator slowly drifting through the rising mists of early morning in a tropical swamp is to look back in time millions of years to the Age of Reptiles. No other reptiles and perhaps no other animals have such an aura of antiquity. However, these reptiles are more advanced than other reptiles in several ways. They have a four-chambered heart like birds and mammals, and their brain has a true cerebral cortex, which allows for learned rather than strictly instinctive behavior.

Crocodile

Crocodilians are found in waterways throughout the tropical and subtropical areas of the world. The tropic regions are especially favored, but the American alligator, Chinese alligator, mugger, and some gharials can be found in areas with winter temperatures that other types of crocodilians could not tolerate.

All members of this order are easily recognized by their appearance: a massive, elongated head armed with many pointed teeth; short, sturdy legs; a long, heavy tail; and tough, leathery skin sculpted into rectangular scales. The tail and webbed hind toes propel the animal while swimming and the legs lift the body clear of the

Gharial

Alligator

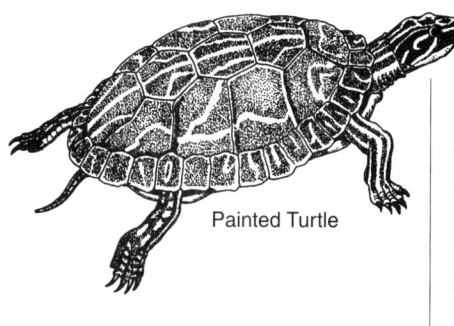

Painted Turtle

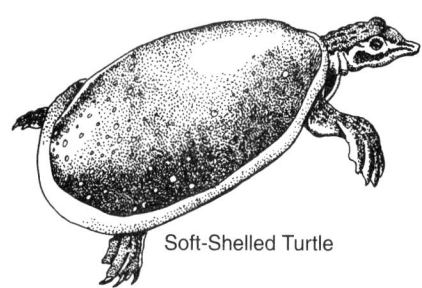

Soft-Shelled Turtle

Sea Turtle

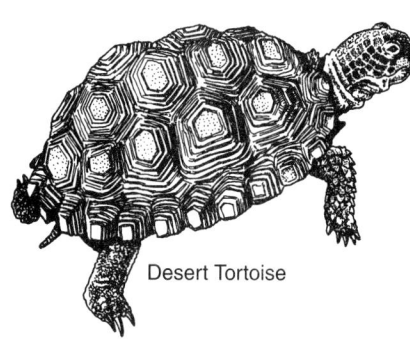

Desert Tortoise

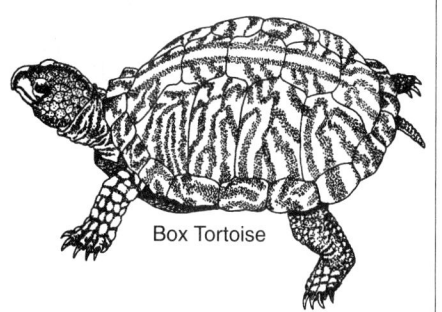

Box Tortoise

ground on land. Crocodiles often exhibit a strange gait called the "high walk." The Australian freshwater crocodile has been seen actually galloping across land.

The gharials (also known as gavials) vary from the general crocodilian plan in one respect—a slender, elongated snout. Gharials also have rather weak legs and seldom move more than their own length from the water's edge.

The extremely elongated snout, equipped with long, piercing teeth, is adapted to a diet consisting mainly of fish. The snout offers little resistance to the water as these animals slash back and forth through a school of fish.

The alligators and the crocodiles are the most numerous, widely distributed, and familiar members of this order. The alligator has a broader and rounder snout than the crocodile, and the fourth tooth on either side of the alligator's jaw is enlarged but hidden when the mouth is shut. The head of the crocodile, by contrast, tapers to a point. Its enlarged teeth stick out and are clearly visible even when the mouth is closed.

Most of a crocodilian's day may be spent basking on the bank, mouth agape, but it becomes active, especially for feeding, in the early evening. Crocodilians are carnivores that will eat any animal they can overcome. Prey preferences change with age. Small, young individuals eat insects, amphibians, fish, mollusks, and crustaceans. Older, larger ones eat fish, turtles, birds, and small to large mammals.

Most crocodilians use surprise to capture their prey. The adults of most species are well camouflaged in drab greens, browns, and black. They may lie almost totally submerged and wait or move very slowly toward their prey. Once in range, a quick lunge, a powerful snap of the jaws, and a trip to the bottom seals the fate of the prey. To dismember very large prey that cannot be swallowed whole, crocodiles perform violent rolling motions that aid their teeth in ripping off large chunks of flesh. On land, the powerful tail can sweep careless creatures who have wandered too close into the water, where they are helpless against the attacker. There are no poisonous crocodilians.

Crocodilians make the most noise of any reptile, and the American alligator is the loudest. They can let loose a rumbling roar that can be heard for over a mile.

Reports of monster-sized crocodilians are common but seldom authenticated. Exceptionally large American alligator males reach about 5.5 meters (18 feet). The record for a gharial is 6.6 meters (21.5 feet), and calculations made on the skull of one saltwater crocodile indicate it may have been 7.46 meters (24.25 feet) in length. Girth must also be considered as well as length. A 4.2-meter (14-foot) crocodile with a 2.1-meter (7-foot) girth could weigh up to 1,800 kilograms (2 tons)!

**Order Chelonia.** This group consists of about 244 species of turtles and tortoises. These animals are found in temperate and tropical regions on all continents except Antarctica and in all oceans. Some are marine or freshwater aquatic; others are more amphibious or highly terrestrial.

All living shelled reptiles are technically turtles, but the term *turtle* generally refers to the members of this order found in or around water; for example, the painted turtle, soft-shelled turtle, and sea turtle. The term *tortoise* generally refers to the members of this order found mainly on land, such as the desert tortoise and the box tortoise.

A turtle's signature is its shell. No other vertebrate has developed anything quite like it structurally. Composed of 59 to 61 flattened bony plates, a turtle shell consists of two parts: the domed carapace covering the top and the flattened plastron covering the bottom. These are connected on the side by a bony

bridge formed by extensions at the sides of the plastron. Covering the bony plates in a thin layer are large scales called scutes.

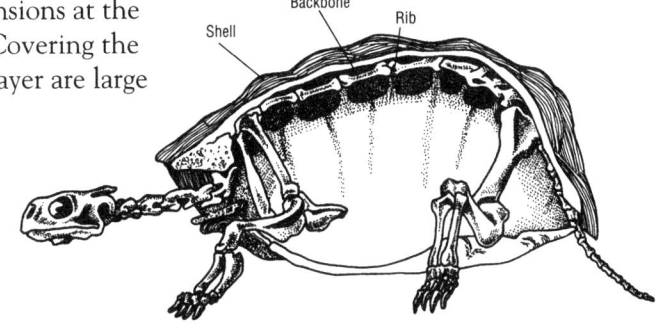

Shell

Backbone

Rib

The size and structure of turtles' shells vary greatly. Large tortoises have huge shells of surprisingly light weight due to pronounced thinning of the shell bones. Strength is provided by the durable scutes and the shape of the shell rather than by thick, heavy bone. The leatherback sea turtle has a shell of leathery skin covering only a few bony platelets that are not connected to the skeleton at all. The soft-shelled or pancake turtles have only a rubbery skin covering. Highly aquatic turtles often have smaller, streamlined shells that offer less resistance while swimming. Some species, such as the mud turtle and the box tortoise, have hinges in the plastron that give them the capability of drawing all body parts inside and tightly closing the shell. Lie-in-wait hunters like the matamata and the alligator snapping turtle have shells that are camouflaged with bumps, ridges, and covering growths of algae.

The shell provides great security and protection but it is cumbersome and not an easy thing to live with. Skeletal accommodations have had to be made: The turtle is the only creature past or present to have its shoulder girdle and hips shifted up inside its ribs. The shell also has dictated a change in the method of breathing. Since a turtle cannot expand its chest, it breathes by pushing the internal organs forward to squeeze against the lungs. The sheer size and weight of the shell precludes any running, jumping, or flying and severely limits the diversity of this group. The desert tortoise moves at speeds of 0.22-0.48 km/hour (0.13-0.3 mph). Giant tortoises have been clocked at 6.4 km (4 miles) per day. However, sea turtles swimming at speeds in excess of 30 km/hour (18.6 mph) can move through the water as fast as humans can run on land.

Protruding between the two parts of the shell are the head, limbs, and tail. Turtles have a large, heavy head set at the end of a long and flexible neck. In most turtles, the head and neck can be retracted in a vertically folding S-curve to pull the head inside the shell for protection. The strange side-neck turtles, such as the matamata, fold the neck in sideways and tuck it up under the eaves of the shell. Turtles are toothless creatures equipped with a powerful, horny beak with sharp, slicing edges. There are no poisonous turtles.

The limbs of a turtle are a good indicator of its habitat and means of locomotion. The terrestrial tortoises have thick, stumpy legs with short toes, and the amphibious turtles have flattened limbs and long, webbed toes to aid in swimming. The highly aquatic sea turtles have no toes and limbs that have been flattened into powerful flippers.

Life in a shell also has influenced the feeding behavior and diet of turtles. Lacking the speed and agility necessary to catch fast-moving prey, turtles feed mainly on vegetation or slow-moving animals such as mollusks, worms, or insect larvae. Some turtles, such as the bizzare matamata, use camouflage and lie in wait on the muddy bottom to ambush unsuspecting prey. The shell of the matamata is ridged, lumpy, and algae covered. The broad head has an enormous mouth, and the long muscular neck has flaps that can detect slight disturbances prey might make in the water. Once prey is in range, the matamata strikes quickly, expanding its mouth to pull in the day's meal. Matamatas have been seen herding fish into shallow water where they could be more easily captured.

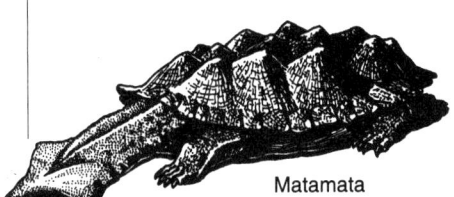

Matamata

The alligator snapping turtle of the United States increases its chances of capturing prey by using a lure to attract victims closer. With its jaws open wide, a small, pink worm-like projection on its tongue begins to quiver enticingly, luring fish closer to investigate. If the prey is small enough, it is swallowed whole. Larger prey is held in the beak and torn apart with powerful clawed front limbs.

Most turtles are colored in dull and dark greens, browns, and black. Some have brighter patterns of browns, olives, yellows, reds, oranges, and gray on the upper shell with browns, black, and white predominating on the underside.

Turtles range in size from the tiny mud turtle at 10 centimeters (4 inches) to giant sea turtles at 1.8 meters (6 feet). These giant sea turtles may weigh over half a ton. On land, the Galapagos tortoises reach weights over 180 kilograms (400 pounds). Turtles often were more gigantic in the past. Fossils of Archelon, the largest turtle that ever existed, show it was almost 3.3 meters (11 feet) long and 3.5 meters (12 feet) across at the flippers.

## The Importance of Reptiles

Reptiles are important predators in their habitats. Many help keep animals we regard as pests under control. Small turtles in turn provide food for other animals.

Humans have exploited reptiles throughout history in a variety of ways, but mainly as food. Sea turtles, lizards, snakes, and their eggs have been fried, broiled, stewed, and eaten raw with great relish by humans worldwide for centuries. Humans collect reptiles for the pet trade, education and research uses, leather products, shell products, and even religious and fertility ceremonies. In medical technology, snake venom is being used to develop pain-killing drugs, ointments for cuts and burns, and toothache remedies.

Every order of reptiles contains some threatened species due to the rapid decline in their numbers. Some are so depleted that they can be considered endangered with extinction imminent. At least 28 reptile groups are thought to have become extinct since 1600; 36 percent were slaughtered for meat and 46 percent were lost through predation by feral animals, habitat loss and destruction, and habitat pollution. On the bright side, the American alligator and the green sea turtle are rebounding and legislation is being passed worldwide to protect various species of reptiles. If we continue the way we are going, however, there could one day be a world without reptiles.

Many states and the federal government have laws regulating the collection and possession of various reptiles. Check with the appropriate wildlife authorities for your area, listed in Appendix C, before collecting. I strongly suggest that you purchase a quality field guide with color pictures and range maps for the reptiles of your area before setting out to collect. Crocodilians and poisonous snakes and lizards are not practical to collect or maintain for classroom study due to legal and safety considerations.

Lizards can be collected with a long-handled net or a looped snare. Quietly approach the animal from behind and quickly lay the net over it. A snare can be made by dangling a heavy cord from the end of a 0.9- to 1.2-meter (3- to 4-feet) stick. If approached quietly and slowly, lizards seldom suspect the noose. Slowly work the snare loop over the animal's head, pull the loop backward over the head, and tighten it around the neck. Trying to catch lizards by hand or by running them down is usually a waste of your energy and may injure the lizard.

Transport lizards back to the classroom in closed, ventilated containers with secure lids. Avoid temperature extremes during transport. Do not crowd the lizards and do not put large lizards in with small lizards as the large ones may attack and kill the small ones. For the same reason, it is best to put only lizards of the same species in a container.

Some types of lizards can be purchased commercially from the suppliers listed in Appendix B.

A long-handled net, a looped snare, or a snake stick are effective tools for capturing snakes. If using a net, quickly cover the snake and keep the net pressed firmly down. Cautiously move the net hoop so that the entire snake is caught up in the net. When snaring, approach the animal quietly from behind and place the loop quickly around the snake's head. In open areas, a snake stick can be used to pin a snake behind the head. The snake then can be carefully grasped behind the head and placed into a bag or container. All snakes bite, so consider wearing thick gloves when handling snakes. Transport snakes in a bag with a drawstring top that can be tightly and securely tied or in a closed, ventilated container with a very secure and tight-fitting lid.

*Never* collect, transport, or attempt to maintain poisonous snakes. Their educational value is not worth the potential risks to your students and to you.

The suppliers listed in Appendix B handle the common garter snake. However, they are available only at certain times of the year and must be shipped air freight, with charges running from $45 to $60 per shipment.

Turtles in water can be taken in a long-handled net. Tortoises can be picked up by hand. If you are hand-collecting, wear heavy gloves, approach the tortoise from behind and grasp it on either side of the carapace midway between the legs. Transport turtles in closed, ventilated containers with a secure lid.

The suppliers listed in Appendix B handle the common painted turtle and box tortoise. They are available only seasonally, however, and may have to be shipped air freight.

Keep lizards of the same species and same approximate size together. A 40-liter (10-gallon) aquarium makes an ideal home for several small lizards for a short time. Crowding can be harmful, so a good rule of thumb is one square foot of bottom space for each lizard. Do not use cages with screen floors or walls as they can damage the animals' noses and feet. For woodland lizards such as the green anole (often called the American chameleon), construct a planted terrarium by placing 2.5 to 5 centimeters (1 to 2 inches) of soil in the bottom of an aquarium. Plant any suitable house plant or place a small potted plant at one end of the aquarium. Try to pick a plant that will remain bushy and

# COLLECTION OF SPECIMENS

## Lizards

## Snakes

Looped Snare

## Turtles and Tortoises

# MAINTENANCE OF SPECIMENS
## Lizards

Snake Stick

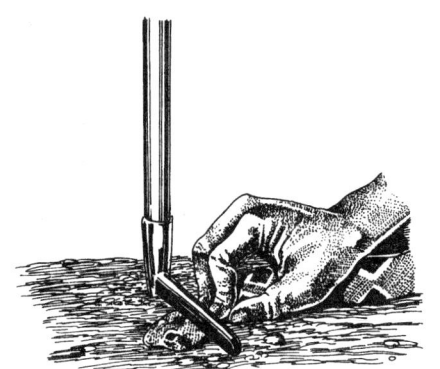

## Snakes

Planted Terrarium

Snake Container

not outgrow your terrarium. Provide a sturdy branching stick for perching and basking. Cover the surface of the soil with a thin layer of peat moss or dead leaves. Purchase or construct a tight-fitting screen cover for the terrarium to prevent escape.

Anoles will not drink standing water from a dish. Do not give them sugar water, as is sometimes suggested. In their natural habitat they lap water from leaves after a rain or during a heavy dew, so you should provide a constant supply of water by a daily sprinkling or misting of leafy twigs. I also have trained them to accept water from a dropper placed near them.

For lizards from more arid environments, construct a bare terrarium by adding sand instead of soil. Add a sturdy, branching stick for perching and basking and several rocks and large pieces of bark for hiding under. Provide a constant supply of drinking water on a moistened sponge in a dish.

Lizards must be maintained at warm temperatures—22° to 27°C (72° to 80°F) for most and 26° to 29°C (79° to 85°F) for desert types. Use incandescent bulbs of varying wattage and distance to maintain proper temperature. Keep a thermometer in the cage and check it often. Pet stores and the suppliers listed in Appendix B can supply synthetic stones with heating elements inside that provide a warm area for basking and congregating.

Lizards require live food several times weekly. Suitable foods include fruit flies, houseflies, spiders, mealworm larvae and adults, waxworm larvae and adults, and crickets. Maintaining lizards in a healthy condition for long periods requires attending to their daily needs and culturing two or three varieties of insects continuously to provide an adequate and varied diet.

As with lizards, house snakes of the same species and same approximate size together. A 40-liter (10-gallon) aquarium provides enough space for short-term care for several small snakes. Do not use wire screen cages as the snakes can injure their noses on the rough surface. Place paper towels on the bottom of an aquarium. Do not use sand, soil, or wood chips as they may get into the animal's mouth and they make cleaning the cage difficult. Paper towels are absorbent and can be changed easily when they become soiled.

Provide a sturdy, branched stick for climbing, a rough rock to two for rubbing against when shedding, and several pieces of bark for the snake to hide under. Fresh water for drinking and soaking should be provided daily in an open, shallow dish heavy and broad enough to resist tipping.

Snake containers should be closed with a tight-fitting ventilated cover. Snakes are amazingly strong and can push the cover off a cage or escape through very small cracks. A secure cover can be made by drilling many small holes in a clear piece of heavy plastic cut to overlap the top of the snake container. Place a brick or heavy object on the cover to prevent the snake from pushing its way out.

Keep the cage at 24° to 30°C (75° to 86°F). You can allow the temperature to fall at night, but not below 21° to 24°C (70° to 75°F). Incandescent bulbs can provide adequate temperature control. Adjust the number and wattage of bulbs and their distance from the cage to achieve the ideal temperature ranges. You might also consider putting an old heating pad in the bottom of the cage under the paper towels. Keep a thermometer in the cage and check it often.

Snakes need to be fed only once or twice weekly if kept that long. Garter snakes will quickly learn to take earthworms from forceps, or you can simply place the worms in front of the snake one at time. Other types of snakes may require larger prey such as amphibians, rodents, birds, or birds' eggs. Avoid the problem of finding and maintaining food for such snakes by releasing them back into the wild as soon as possible after you conclude your studies of them.

Tortoises require land with a water supply for drinking and bathing, and amphibious turtles need standing water with a few rocks for them to crawl out on.

Aquariums make the best containers, but a wooden box or a child's wading pool can provide suitable temporary housing for tortoises. To prepare a bare terrarium for tortoises, place 5 to 7.5 centimeters (2 to 3 inches) of moist sand in the bottom of an aquarium. Sink a water dish into the soil until the top of the dish is level with the sand. The water container should be larger than the tortoise's body, but if the dish is more than 5 centimeters (2 inches) deep, put rocks or gravel in the bottom of the dish to assist the tortoise in climbing out. Keep the water clean by changing it daily. A cover on the cage is not necessary if the container is more than three times the height of the tortoise. Plants can be added, but the tortoise may eat them or uproot them with its tendency to burrow and bury itself.

Turtles can also be housed satisfactorily in an aquarium. Put 8 to 13 centimeters (3 to 5 inches) of pond or aged tap water in the aquarium. Arrange large flat rocks in such a way that the turtles can crawl onto a dry area.

Tortoises are mostly vegetarian but are opportunistic feeders and will consume a variety of plant and animal material. In captivity, tortoises may accept live food such as earthworms, crickets, and mealworms. They also may take small strips of raw lean meat (but not fatty meats like pork or hamburger). They should also be given pieces of lettuce, apples, and bananas.

Turtles tend to be more carnivorous than tortoises. In captivity, turtles may accept live food like earthworms, mealworm larvae, and waxworm larvae. They may also take small pieces of raw lean meat. Place the food near the water's edge or float it on a small piece of lettuce. Turtles can be messy eaters, so you may wish to feed them in a separate container to keep their home cage clean.

Turtles thrive at temperatures of 21° to 27°C (70° to 80°F). Again, use incandescent bulbs to provide temperature control. Do not use aquarium tank heaters for the water in turtle cages. If using incandescent bulbs as a heat source, the turtles will need part of their cage shaded so they can escape the heat.

Collecting reptiles may put you around water, so follow good safety procedures. Dress accordingly and be alert to possible contact with poisonous plants or stinging, biting, or parasitic animals.

Never collect or attempt to maintain poisonous reptiles. These creatures are truly fascinating, but the risks involved are just too great. There are several types of poisonous reptiles in North America: The Gila monster lizard, the beaded lizard of Mexico, the rattlesnake, the water moccasin (cottonmouth) snake, the copperhead snake, and the coral snake. Use a quality reptile field guide with colored pictures and range maps to familiarize yourself with any poisonous reptiles in your area.

The American Red Cross tells us that about 9,000 Americans per year are bitten by poisonous snakes. However, more people die of bee sting each year than snakebite. The venom from the poisonous snakes and lizards of North America is usually not fatal if appropriate action is taken. The bitten person should be kept calm and lying down, as any activity can speed the poison more rapidly through the body. If possible, the bitten area should be kept below the level of the heart. Medical help should be obtained as quickly as possible. Do not cut or suck on a snakebite area or apply ice or a tourniquet. A constricting bandage could be applied between the bite and the heart if possible. Even though they are seldom fatal, poisonous snakebites can result in severe tissue and muscle damage and produce extremely painful and slow-healing wounds. Avoid being bitten in the first place by learning which poisonous reptiles are found in your area and by being very cautious when in their habitat.

# Turtles

Tortoise Container

Turtle Container

# HEALTH AND SAFETY
## Teachers

Proper Lizard Handling

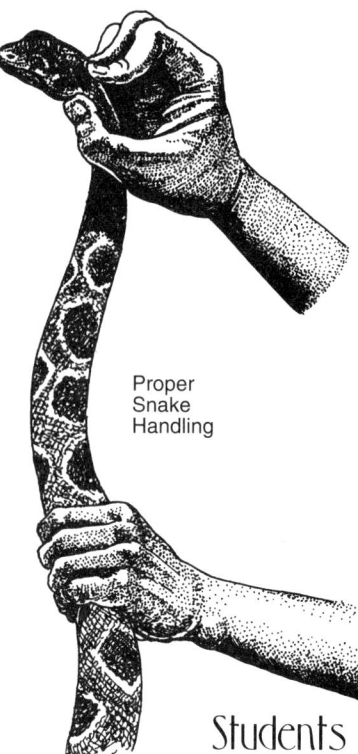

Proper
Snake
Handling

Students

Reptiles

Turtles can carry salmonella bacteria, the cause of salmonellosis in humans. Because of this potential threat, restrictive legislation was passed in 1975 that completely banned the shipment of live turtles with a shell length of less than 10 centimeters (4 inches) and viable turtle eggs. Three simple rules can prevent any health problems associated with turtles: (1) Keep your hands away from your face when handling turtles, their cages, or water dishes; (2) wash your hands thoroughly and immediately after handling turtles, their cages, or water dishes; and (3) never bring human food or drink close to turtles, their cages, or water dishes.

All reptiles can bite, and you may want to wear heavy gloves when field collecting specimens. However, small snakes such as garter snakes, small lizards like the green anole or fence lizard, and small turtles or tortoises really present little threat of biting if handled carefully and respectfully.

Proper handling is important to the safety of the reptile itself. A small lizard can be held by pressing a thumb gently behind the head and grasping it in the middle of the body between the legs. Never grab a lizard by the tail as many have fragile tails that break off easily. Grasp snakes carefully behind the head with one hand while supporting the rest of the body with the other hand. Turtles and tortoises should be handled by holding onto the upper shell behind the head and over the tail.

I have had students handle small lizards, snakes, and turtles many times with no problems, but for the safety of the student and reptile, make sure students handle reptiles in the manner illustrated in the previous section. Make sure students wash their hands thoroughly and immediately after contacting any reptile (especially turtles or tortoises) and handling their cages or water dishes.

Poisonous snakes and large, fierce crocodilians fascinate students. These creatures are not practical to collect or maintain, but you do not need to deprive students of learning more about them. Use appropriate audiovisual materials and field trips to area zoos to acquaint students with these awe-inspiring reptiles.

Reptiles (especially snakes) generate more misunderstanding and misplaced fear than any other animal group. You can help change such attitudes through patience, understanding, and enlightenment. Fearful students should never be bullied or belittled into touching or even coming close to reptiles against their will. This will only serve to reinforce, not change, fears and negative attitudes.

I strongly urge you to collect reptiles locally and avoid commercial purchase if possible. It may help reduce the pressure from overcollection that many reptiles face, and you will avoid regulations requiring that some commercially purchased reptiles be sent air freight at prohibitively high rates.

Make sure reptiles are handled properly (as previously illustrated) and that proper conditions of housing, temperature control, water, and food are maintained. Experts estimate that each year millions of green anoles alone are doomed to a few months' meager subsistence before they decline and die due to poor care in pet shops, homes, and classrooms.

Maintaining an adequate and varied diet of living prey to feed reptiles can present time, financial, and logistical problems. Furthermore, many reptiles are reluctant to eat in captivity. Most reptiles can survive without food for a short time, so the best plan is to study and release them before they need to be fed.

Keep containers housing reptiles away from high student traffic areas. Lizards and snakes often panic and may injure themselves if their cage is approached suddenly or if students tap on the cage.

**H1.** *Designing Reptile Habitats.* Read students the following imaginary scenario: Your school has received a huge sum of money to build a reptile facility on school grounds to house the following reptiles: American alligator, snapping turtle, painted turtle, box tortoise, green anole lizard, fence lizard, horned lizard, garter snake, and any one type of poisonous North American snake. Your class must design the facility with the appropriate habitat for each species.

You might want to assign groups of students each a specific reptile and have them design a habitat for it. Add or delete specific examples from this list as you deem necessary. Have students consult the "Specific Order Characteristics" section of this chapter, field guides, and other appropriate references as guides. Have students make a detailed diagram of their design and present their ideas to the rest of the class. This activity will give students a better understanding of reptile habitat requirements and allow them to compare and contrast the various reptile habitats.

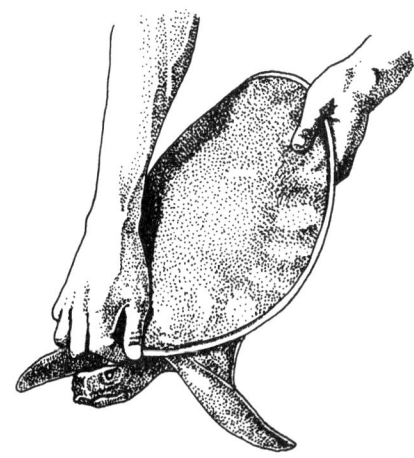

Proper Turtle Handling

**H2.** *Give Me a Home Where the Reptiles Roam.* What reptiles are found in your area? Have your students draw on their own experiences, field guides, and other appropriate references to determine what specific reptiles are found in your area. You might assign different groups of students different orders of reptiles to investigate. For example, one group could determine what lizards are found in your area, and another group might determine what turtles or tortoises frequent your vicinity. Have students share their findings with the rest of the class in some manner you deem appropriate. Colored posters and pictures would be an eye-catching and memorable way of presenting this information.

If possible, take a field trip to a local zoo or nature center to see reptiles of your area and perhaps those of other habitats worldwide.

**H3.** *Walk a Mile in My Shoes.* Have students try to put themselves in the reptiles' place by having them respond orally or in written form to the following question: What specific reptile would you be and why?

**H4.** *How Warm Is My Form?* Have students study the graph showing the range of body temperatures of various groups of reptiles and then answer the following questions and consider the following problems:

a. Based on temperature requirements, which group would be the most limited in its geographic distribution and why? (The crocodilians, because the temperature conditions necessary for their survival are found only in a narrow band along the equator.)

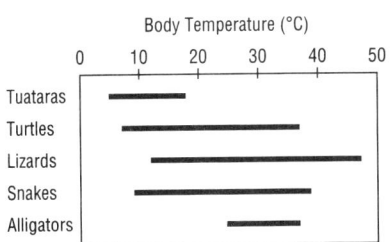

b. Which group or groups would be the most widely distributed and why? (Snakes and especially lizards, because they can withstand a wide range of temperatures compared to the other types of reptiles.)

c. What areas of the earth are devoid of reptiles and why? (The Arctic and Antarctic regions have no reptiles. Being ectothermic, the reptiles cannot develop enough body heat in those regions to survive.)

d. Giant tortoises are often kept outdoors in zoos in Europe. They survive but fail to grow or breed. Hypothesize why they do not thrive. (Temperatures are too low.)

e. Some reptiles in zoos are maintained under artificial conditions in tropical houses, yet they also experience problems with growth and reproduction. Speculate why. (Temperatures are too high and/or too uniformly maintained.)

**H5.** *Temperature Tactics.* Reptiles use different combinations of tactics to stay within their preferred temperature range. Give students the following temperature tactic phrases (or come up with your own) and have them explain how reptiles might use these tactics to regulate their temperature:

a. "Timing's the thing." (Many reptiles are active when the temperature is best. For example, many desert reptiles are active at night or early morning to avoid the searing heat of midday.)

b. "Get down underground." (Many reptiles retreat to cool burrows during the heat of the day or warm burrows during the cool of the night.)

c. "Sun and shade." (Reptiles bask in the sun to warm up and move to the shade to cool off.)

d. "I'm in hot water." (Turtles and crocodilians may warm up in shallow water but move to deeper, cooler water to keep cool.)

e. "Color me cool." (Some lizards can change the color of their skin from lighter to darker shades and back again. Dark surfaces absorb heat while light-colored surfaces reflect heat.)

f. "Body language." (Some reptiles adjust the position of their bodies to heat up or cool down.)

**Challenge:** Can you keep a thermom-a-lizard alive? Share the following background material with your students: Many reptiles, especially some lizards, have narrow optimum temperature ranges and use the tactics listed previously to keep their bodies at or near a constant temperature. As endothermic (warm-blooded) creatures, we humans give this problem little thought, but it controls every aspect of reptiles' lives.

Now divide the class into teams and give each team a thermometer (thermom-a-lizard) and a slip of paper with the temperature range at which they must keep their thermom-a-lizard for it to survive. Temperature ranges you might use (in Fahrenheit): 55-59, 60-64, 65-69, 70-74, 75-79, 80-84, 90-94, and 95-99.

If weather permits, conduct this activity outside. but it can be done inside also. To make the activity more relevant to actual reptiles, affix the thermometers to green construction paper cut-outs of lizards. Give students the following instructions:

1. Do not touch the bulb of the thermometer.

2. Keep the thermometer close to the ground or other surface to avoid taking air temperatures.

3. Leave the thermometer in place for at least a minute so it will register an accurate reading.

4. Use the temperature tactics previously discussed. Some teams may be able to use one tactic and stay put in one spot, and others may have to keep moving and use a variety of tactics.

Set a time limit of about 10 minutes for the teams to get within their assigned range. Then challenge them to stay within that range for 20 or 30 minutes.

Once time is up, bring the teams together and place their results in a table that shows their group designation, their assigned temperature range, the tactics they used, and whether they were successful and their thermom-a-lizard lived.

Based on all teams' results, have students respond to the following questions: Which thermom-a-lizards would have a tough time surviving in this area at this time of year and why? Are the temperature ranges realistic? (Some are not. Lizards don't have ranges as low or as high as some on the chart. These ranges were added to make the activity more challenging.)

Take the temperature of a small reptile by pressing a liquid-crystal temperature strip against the reptile for a short time.

**H6.** *Habitat Habits.* To survive in its natural habitat, any creature needs certain skills and adaptations. Have students explain how each of the following skills or adaptations aid the reptiles that possess them:

a. In the laboratory, chameleons are particularly good at detour problems and negotiating complex mazes. (Chameleons live in a complex jungle of limbs, leaves, and vines and are frequently required to make detours among branches to get within striking distance of their prey.)

b. The tuatara has an eye with a retina that allows it to see by night as well as by day. These animals are active mainly at night. (Nocturnal activity allows the tuatara to better avoid predators and stalk prey.)

c. Snakes have no legs. (This unique adaptation allows snakes to occupy and investigate areas of their habitat such as nooks, crannys, cracks, and holes that other animals cannot enter. Thus snakes avoid larger predators that cannot follow into such areas and can follow and snare their prey in practically any situation.)

d. The box tortoise (as well as several other types) has a hinged plastron, and the carapace and plastron have wide outer edges. The movable plastron can be drawn up tightly against the carapace. (Tortoises can draw in their head, tail, and limbs and seal the shell to make a nearly impenetrable obstacle for predators. Turtles lack this ability, and their head and limbs are more exposed.)

e. Crocodiles have their eyes and nostrils set high on the head, and they can close off their mouth from breathing passages with a flap of skin. (Crocodiles can see and breathe while floating nearly completely submerged—a great advantage for stealthfully approaching their prey. Once the prey is captured, they can feed while submerged without the risk of swallowing water and drowning.)

**H7.** *Habitat Quote.* Have students react orally or in written form to the following quote by Ian Spellerberg in his book *Biology of Reptiles: An Ecological Approach*: "It is the habitat of reptiles rather than the species of reptiles which must be safeguarded." (Dr. Spellerberg continues, "As is the case of thousands of species of wild animals and plants, the changes in land use by humans have resulted in the fragmentation of reptile populations and so the status of many reptiles has declined.")

**H8.** *Challenge: Do Reptiles Prefer Light or Dark Habitats?* Have students devise a way to test this problem. They should begin by wording the problem to specify the actual type of reptile(s) you will be testing. If possible, have different teams of students test different types of reptiles.

One design might be to cover the sides, top, and bottom of one half of an aquarium with black paper and the other half with white paper. Place a single reptile in the aquarium in the middle and use stopwatches to determine how much time it spends in each half of the aquarium over a 5-minute time span. Repeat several times using as many different reptiles of the same species as you have available. Students should position themselves to they can see the reptile but it cannot see them and thus react to their presence. Have students predict what they think will happen before they begin. Make sure they keep data in appropriate tables charts, and graphs and draw conclusions from their data.

Interested, older, or more advanced students might take this activity a step further and see what (if any) role temperature plays in light versus dark preference.

## Structure

**S1.** *Reptile Structure Comparison.* You could have students compare and contrast the structure of the various orders of reptiles by filling out a table similar to the one in Chapter 9, activity S1. For a different approach, divide your class into teams and assign each team a different group of reptiles to investigate. Have the teams research the structure, common and unique, of their assigned reptile group. Then have the teams report their findings to the class. The team reports will be much more interesting and entertaining if you require them to be oral first-person presentations—that is, as if the

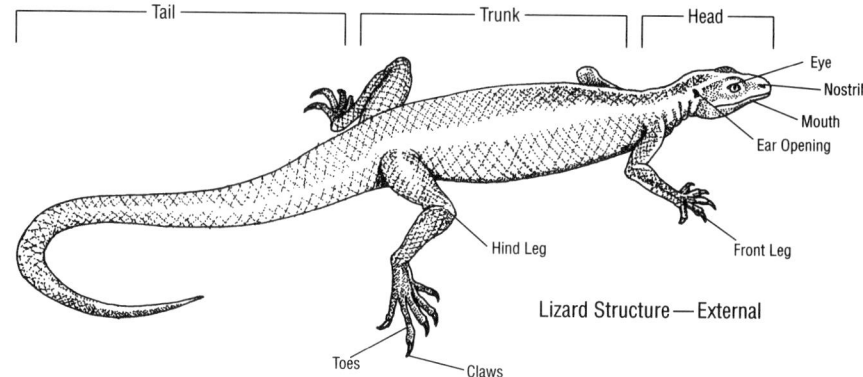

Lizard Structure—External

reptiles themselves were talking. Props such as cardboard scales, turtle shells, and so on will also add interest to this activity.

**S2.** *Reptile Structure.* Have students diagram and label a lizard and its parts: head, trunk, tail, front legs, hind legs, toes, claws, eyes, nostrils, mouth, and external ear opening.

Have students diagram and label a snake and its parts: head, trunk, tail, eyes, mouth, tongue, nostrils, dorsal (top) scales, and ventral (bottom scales).

Have students diagram and label a turtle or tortoise and its parts: carapace (upper shell), plastron (lower shell), head, eyes, mouth (beak), tail, front legs, hind legs, and claws.

**S3.** *Reptile Observations.* If possible, have students observe a live lizard, snake, and/or turtle or tortoise and answer the questions or do the activities that follow:

a. Reptile head
1. Carefully observe the general structure of the head of a lizard, snake, and/or turtle or tortoise. In what ways are they alike and different?
2. Imagine you are taking an exam for an advanced college degree in life science. You are given two containers, one holding a living snake and the other holding a living legless lizard. You must identify which is which and explain how you decided. (Look at the head of each animal. Lizards have eyelids and external ear holes; snakes have neither.)

b. Reptile eyes: Carefully observe the eyes of a lizard, snake, and/or turtle or tortoise. In what ways are they alike and different? (These reptiles have large, well-developed eyes and a keen sense of vision. There is some evidence to indicate color vision in some lizards and turtles. Lizards and turtles have eyelids but snakes do not.)

c. Reptile breathing
1. Carefully observe the nostrils and breathing pattern of a lizard, snake, and/or turtle or tortoise. Compare and contrast the breathing pattern of a reptile to that of an amphibian. (Amphibians move air in and out by expanding and contracting the floor of the mouth. Snakes and lizards breathe by expanding and contracting their chest area. The shell of the turtle and tortoise forces it to take a totally different approach and move air in and out by squeezing the internal organs against the lungs.)

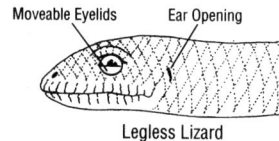

Legless Lizard

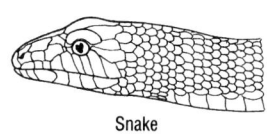

Snake

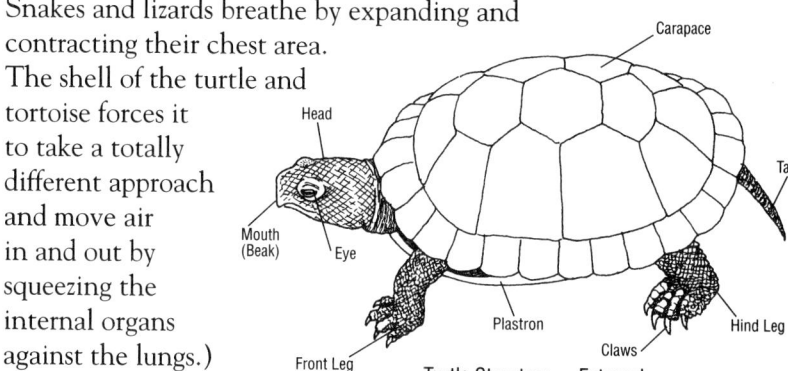

Turtle Structure—External

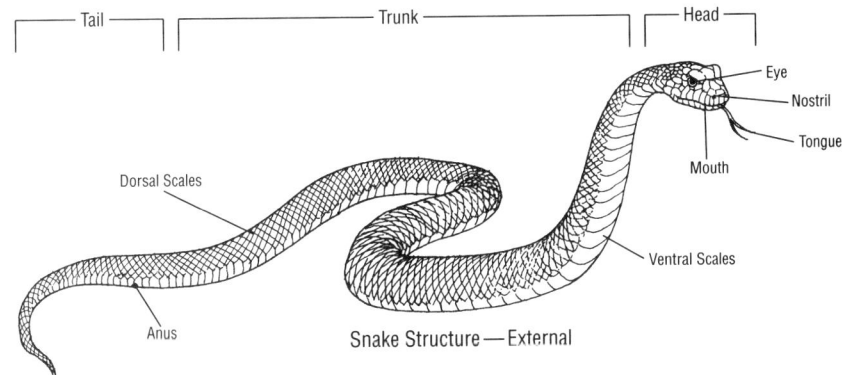

Snake Structure—External

2. Can reptiles supplement their oxygen intake by skin breathing as amphibians can? (Being sealed with dry, scaly skin, most reptiles cannot supplement their oxygen intake by skin breathing. Many freshwater turtles supplement their oxygen supply while submerged from water drawn into the pharynx or cloaca, and soft-shelled turtles can take in 70 percent of their oxygen when submerged through the leathery skin forming the carapace).

3. Which group, reptiles or amphibians, has the largest and most complex lungs? (Reptiles, because they must take in all the required oxygen through the lungs.)

4. How can a snake take many minutes to swallow prey much larger than its own throat without suffocating? (Snakes are able to extend the tubelike opening of the air passage, called the glottis, outward so that it is clear while they are swallowing prey. It is much like a diver breathing through a snorkel.)

5. How can crocodilians open their mouths under water to tear prey and feed without drowning? (These reptiles have a flap of skin they use to close off the air passages from the mouth.)

d. Reptile mouth and tongue

1. Carefully observe the mouth area of a lizard, snake, and/or turtle or tortoise. In what ways are they alike/different? (The most noticeable differences are internal. Snakes and lizards have teeth while turtles and tortoises have a toothless, bony beak.) Most reptiles will not willingly open their mouths and let students peer inside so you will need to supplement this activity with pictures. Do not attempt to force open the mouth of any reptile as you may injure it in the process.

2. How can snakes swallow prey that is often many times bigger than their own head? (The secret is in the jaws. The quadrate bone connecting the lower jaw loosely to the skull works like a double-jointed hinge so that the lower jaw can be dropped at the back as well as the front of the mouth. In addition, the lower jaw can be stretched sideways as it is connected in the front by an elastic muscle.)

3. How can snakes swallow large prey that is often alive and struggling without limbs to hold and guide the prey into the mouth? (Sharp, backward-curving teeth hold the prey while the snake, moving first one side and then the other side of its jaws, works its mouth forward around its food.)

4. Why does a snake flick its tongue in and out? What does a snake use its tongue for? (Here is a good place to dispel some erroneous notions students may have about snakes. Snakes cannot sting, bite, or poison with their tongues. Snakes flick out their tongues to sample chemical "odors" in the air or on the ground. The tongue, covered

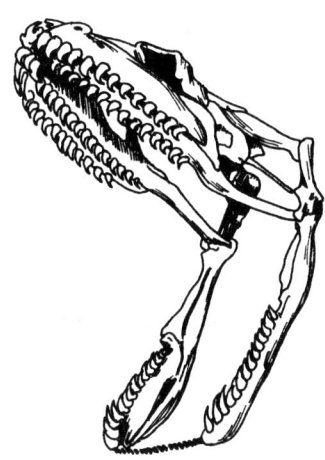

with chemical signals, is then pulled back into the mouth and placed in a special chemical receptor called Jacobsen's organ. Thus snakes can use their tongues to trail prey, sample food, and locate mates. Some rattlesnakes also use it as a warning device, brandishing it stiffly at enemies.)

5. What are the tongues of other reptiles like? (Turtles, tortoises, and crocodilians have relatively simple tongues. Lizards have unforked tongues used in picking up, tasting, and swallowing food. Some geckos use their tongues to lick their eyes and keep them clean, and some skinks flash a large, brilliant blue tongue to confuse and intimidate predators.)

6. How can a chameleon extend its tongue out so far? (The firing of the chameleon's tongue is controlled by two sets of muscles. One set runs the length of the tongue and keeps it tightly packed into pleats on a pointed bone in the back of the mouth like a coiled spring on a stick. A second set of muscles circles the tongue like tiny automobile tires. The chameleon fires its tongue by suddenly relaxing the long muscles and rapidly contracting the ring muscles.)

e. Reptile parts, limbs, and movement

1. Carefully observe the limbs of a lizard, turtle, or tortoise. How are they alike and different? (Lizards tend to have long, slender legs with long, clawed toes. Turtles and tortoises have short, stocky legs. As an adaptation for swimming, the legs of a turtle are somewhat flattened and have webbing between the hind toes. The tortoises are better equipped for a land and walking existence with round, stumpy legs with reduced claws and no toe webbing. Sea turtles have limbs modified totally into flippers with no toes.)

2. Carefully observe a lizard, snake, and/or turtle or tortoise and describe how each moves. (You usually can simply put a small snake, turtle, or tortoise on the floor and have the students observe and describe its locomotion, although turtles may refuse to come out of their shells and perform. Small lizards can run very rapidly and may quickly get under an object or into a space in the classroom where you cannot get them out. The most secure and safe method for observing lizard locomotion is to keep lizards in a large enclosure where they can move freely but not escape. A child's wading pool or a very large aquarium makes an ideal lizard locomotion laboratory.)

3. **Challenge:** Is a rough surface necessary for snake locomotion? Have students devise a way to test this problem. They could develop surfaces with different degrees of roughness and test the snake's ability to move over each type of surface. Experts tell us that snakes have a very difficult time making progress across polished glass.

   Have students predict what will happen before they begin. Data collected will be mainly observational. Have students draw conclusions from their observations.

4. Measure how far a turtle or tortoise walks in one minute. Use this figure to determine how long it would take the turtle or tortoise to walk around a 400-meter running track. (See Chapter 5, activity S8, for the procedure to make the necessary calculations.)

   If you have enough individuals and if the turtles or tortoises will cooperate, it might be interesting at this point to hold turtle/tortoise races.

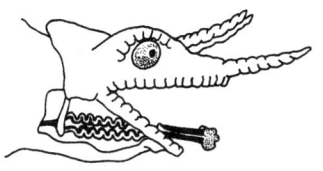

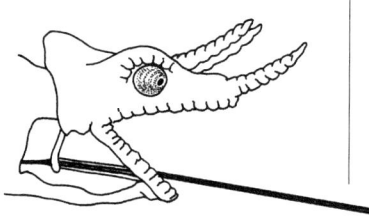

5. **Challenge:** How does the Pull Power Index of a turtle/tortoise compare to that of a snail? Have students design a pulling sled to hold weights and figure out ways to attach the sled to the shell of a turtle or tortoise. (See Chapter 6, activity S2i, for how to determine a Pull Power Index.) A class competition to determine whose turtle or tortoise has the highest Pull Power Index is always interesting. Once this activity is complete, pose this question to students: Based on your observations and calculations, which animal, the snail or the turtle/tortoise, has the greatest Pull Power Index? If you have both turtles and tortoises available, you might compare the Pull Power Index between them.

6. How can snakes move without limbs? (See the "Specific Order Characteristics—Order Squamata" section of this chapter.)

7. How can some gecko lizards scurry easily up trees and smooth walls and even dash across ceilings? (On the underside of the gecko's toes, clinging pads, consisting of a series of plates equipped with many tiny hooklike cells, allow the gecko to get a grip on practically any surface, rough or smooth.)

8. Many lizards have the ability to lose part of their tail and then regenerate the lost portion. How is this a benefit to them? (A logical place for a predator to grab a lizard is by the tail. If the tail breaks off, the lizard may be able to make its escape while the predator is distracted by the squirming tail piece.)

f. Reptile body covering

1. The trademark of a reptile is its scales. Observe and describe the scales of a lizard, snake, and/or turtle or tortoise. How are they alike and different? (Lizards tend to have small, beadlike scales roughly the same size over the entire body. Snakes have small, overlapping, diamond-shaped scales on top and flat, U-shaped scales on the bottom. The scales of a turtle or tortoise are formed as a thin layer over the large bony plates of the shell.)

2. Touch a live reptile, preferably a snake, and describe the sensation. (Reptiles, being ectothermic, tend to feel cool and the scales feel hard and slick. Have only *willing* students touch the reptile.)

3. Are reptiles slimy? (Cool and slick? Yes. Slimy? No.)

4. Do reptiles really shed their skin? (See the "General Class Characteristics—Body Covering" section of this chapter. If possible, show students a shed snake skin.)

5. The green anole (often called the American chameleon) has the ability to change the color of its skin. Have students observe this ability by placing an anole in a ventilated jar and setting the jar on a sheet of white construction paper. Observe the proper techniques for handling lizards. These animals are easily frightened and often will leap violently around a planted terrarium as you attempt to catch and remove them. Grasp them around the shoulders but not by the tail as the tail will pop off. Repeat, placing the anole on colored sheets of paper of varying degrees of light and dark shades. Have students record their observations in a table.

   Once this activity is complete, have students respond to the following questions:
   - In general, what color does the anole become when placed against dark backgrounds? Against light backgrounds? (They tend to darken against dark backgrounds and lighten against light backgrounds.)

• How does the ability to change color and shade benefit the anole in its natural environment? (This ability allows the anole to blend in with the foliage, light, and shadows in its environment to successfully approach prey and to hide from predators.)

Interested, older, or more advanced students could be challenged to design an experiment that tests the role temperature plays in the color change of anoles.

**S4.** *Reptile Models.* Have students construct a model of any reptile of their choice. Students might use colored modeling clay or colored bread dough or sew models out of cloth. Have students use materials such as sunflower seeds or rice to represent reptilian scales.

## Behavior/Response

**B/R1.** *Touch Response in Reptiles.* Have students touch various areas of a lizard, snake, and/or turtle or tortoise's body with a blunt probe or the eraser end of a pencil. Have students respond to the following questions: Is the reptile sensitive to touch, and if so, do some areas seem to be more sensitive than others? How would you compare the sensitivity of touch of the reptile to the amphibian? (Reptile scales are not as sensitive to touch as the thin skin of amphibians.)

**B/R2.** *Body Orientation in Reptiles.* Place a lizard or a snake in a large, ventilated jar. When the reptile is resting quietly in the jar, slowly tilt the jar in various orientations and have students describe how the reptile reacts. Once observations are complete, have students consider these questions: Based on your observations, would you say the reptile can determine changes in the orientation of its body? (It can.) Would you hypothesize that reptiles possess an organ of balance in their head as humans do? (They do.)

If a turtle or tortoise is available, place it on its back and have students observe and describe its struggle to right itself. If the turtle cannot right itself after a short time, assist it or turn it over yourself. Once observations are complete, have students respond to the following questions: Would you say that the turtle reacted positively or negatively to being positioned upside down? (If it cooperates, the turtle or tortoise will react very negatively and attempt to turn back over.) What techniques does a turtle use to right itself?

**B/R3.** **Challenge:** *Can Reptiles Hear?* Have students devise a way to test this problem. Use turtles, tortoises, or lizards for this investigation, as snakes have no ears. Turtles have well-developed middle ears, and lizards have external ear holes, suggesting they can hear well. Turtles have been shown to quickly perceive slight vibrations transmitted through solids or liquids to their skin or shell.

Students might suggest making a loud sound such as blowing a whistle and noting the reaction of the reptile. If you take this approach, make sure that the students can see the reptile but that it cannot see them. You want the reptile to react (if it can) to the sound and not to the sight or movement of someone around them. Make sure that the sound travels through the air and not through solids or liquids. Hitting the table the reptile container sits on with a hammer would make an audible sound, but it would also transmit vibrations and you could not determine exactly which stimulus the reptile responds to. Have students predict what they think will happen before they begin. Data collected will be mainly observational. Have students attempt to draw conclusions from their observations.

**B/R4.** **Challenge:** *Do Reptiles Respond to Visual Threats?* Have students devise a way to test this problem. One way of testing would be to cut out silhouettes of animals that the reptile would regard as enemies in its natural environment; for example, hawks and owls. Place the reptile to be tested in a con-

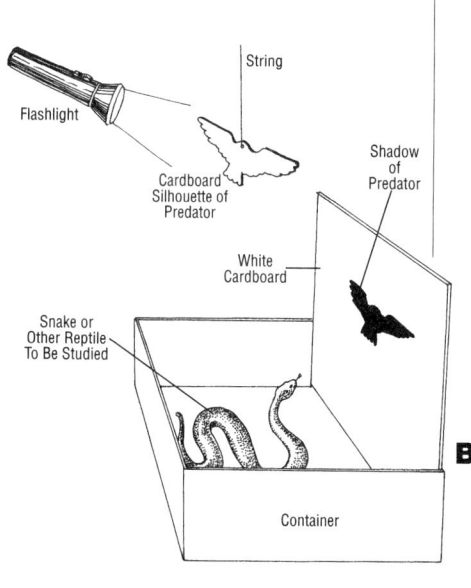

Flashlight

String

Cardboard
Silhouette of
Predator

Shadow
of
Predator

White
Cardboard

Snake or
Other Reptile
To Be Studied

Container

tainer along with a piece of white cardboard. Hold the silhouette and shine a light on it so that its shadow falls on the white cardboard. Make sure the reptile cannot see or react to the silhouette, the light, or the students. Have students predict what they think will happen before they begin.

Repeat using different types of reptiles, if possible, for comparison. Make sure that the size of the silhouette shadow remains approximately the same for all tests.

Repeat again, moving the silhouette so that the shadow approaches the reptile menacingly. Again, use different types of reptiles for comparison.

Data collected from these trials will be mainly observational. Have students attempt to draw conclusions from their observations. Ask the the following questions: Did the reptiles seem to be able to visually detect threatening objects? (They should be able to.) Why is this ability important for their survival? (Reptiles have many hungry enemies, and they need keen senses, especially sight, to avoid them.)

Interested, older, or more advanced students could be challenged to expand this activity into other areas. For example: Do reptiles respond to shape or just movement? Can reptiles perceive color?

**B/R5.**  *Response to Light.* How do reptiles respond to light? Place a live reptile in a large container such as a 40-liter (10-gallon) aquarium. Shine a light on the reptile from various angles—directly above, from the left, from the right, directly in front, and directly behind. Have students observe and describe how the reptile reacts. Do not place the light source so close that the reptile may react to the heat rather than the light from the light source. Position students so they can see the reptile but it cannot see and react to them.

Once this activity is complete, have students respond to the following questions: Based on your observations, was the reptile positively or negatively phototaxic? Did changing the position of the light change the reaction of the reptile? Why did we stay out of sight as we tested the reptile? (You want the reptile to respond to the light and not to distracting movement or objects in its field of view.) Why did we keep the light source away from the cage? (You want the reptile to react to the light, not the heat from your light source.)

**B/R6.**  *Social Hierarchy in Lizards.* Using a group of anoles or fence lizards, have students observe social relationships such as aggression, subordination, and courtship rituals.

This activity will require an enclosure providing about 480 square centimeters (6 square feet) of floor space. A child's wading pool with a screen cover or a 200-liter (50-gallon) aquarium will provide suitable room. Set up and maintain this lizard laboratory according to the directions given in the "Maintenance of Specimens" section for lizards in this chapter. This activity could be conducted over a period of several weeks to several months. I would suggest using native lizards collected from your area for this activity due to the expense of purchasing a large number of lizards and the time and costs involved in long-term care of a large number of lizards that cannot be released after the study is over.

Depending on the number of lizards you have to work with, individuals may need to be marked for identification. Place tiny spots of nontoxic enamel paint of different colors in different arrangements on different parts of the lizards' bodies. These marking will be lost at each molt.

Have students observe the social interactions in the lizard community with the goal of being able to answer the following questions at the end of the study: Is there a dominant lizard or lizards? Is there a dominant member of each sex? How do subordinate lizards behave? Is there a correlation between body size and social position? Do courtship displays occur? Where do courtship displays occur? What movements and body postures accompany courtship displays? (Add to or delete from this list of questions as you wish.)

## Feeding

**F1.** *Reptile Feeding Comparisons.* Have students compare and contrast what and how the various kinds of reptiles eat. As with activity S1 of this chapter, you could divide the class into teams and have each team investigate the food sources and feeding behaviors of different kinds of reptiles and then present an oral first-person report of their findings to the class. See the "Specific Class Characteristics" section of this chapter and other appropriate references.

**F2.** *Feeding a Reptile.* Have students observe and describe a reptile eating a prey animal. If various types of reptiles are available, have students compare and contrast how reptiles eat. (I have the best luck with this activity using lizards, which readily take live insects, and small snakes, which can be trained to take earthworms from forceps. I seldom can get turtles to eat on demand. Be aware that seeing a reptile eat something alive might be a stressful and upsetting experience for younger students especially. The smaller the reptile and the smaller the prey, the less upsetting the sight of predation will be. Avoid showing students large snakes eating rodents or birds. If you feel that demonstrating any sort of predatory feeding activity will be a problem, consider using a tortoise, if you can collect or obtain one, as they readily feed on plant material, especially fruit.)

**F3.** *Do They Spit Out the Seeds?* Have students react orally or in written form to the following imaginary headline on a supermarket tabloid paper: "Woman Wakes To Find Entire Watermelon Patch Eaten By Marauding Band Of Snakes!" (Snakes are carnivorous without a known example of a vegetation-eating type.) Now challenge students to write their own headlines, some accurate and some not. Have students share their headlines with the class and try to separate fact from fallacy about reptiles and their feeding behaviors.

**F4.** *Feed Me! (But Only Occasionally).* Mammals and birds eat many times a day, but some large snakes eat only several times a year. In general, why do reptiles need to eat less often than birds and mammals? Have students attempt to explain. (Some reptiles can eat up to one-quarter of their body weight in one meal, so they do not need to eat as often. Reptiles do not require as much energy to maintain their ectothermic metabolism as birds and mammals do to maintain their endothermic metabolic rates.)

**F5.** *Wood Turtle Stomp.* Have students visualize this actual scenario: You are a biologist studying wood turtles. One day after a heavy rain, you observe wood turtles stomping bare, muddy ground with their front feet, alternating left and right. Then suddenly a turtle jabs its head at the ground and snaps at something. Offer possible explanations about what is happening. (Wood turtles stomp in this fashion to stimulate earthworms to the surface where they can be snapped up for food. No one knows why vibrations in the soil cause earthworms to emerge.

Humans also use this method to gather worms. Depending on where you are from, it is called grunting or sounding for worms. A wooden stake is set in the ground and a notched stick is used to rasp the stake. The vibrations drive nearby worms up and out and send them wriggling across the surface. The U.S. Forest Service allows controlled grunting on national forest lands, and an annual worm grunting championship is held in Florida. Zoologist John Kaufman, who brought this turtle feeding behavior to light, has imitated the turtle stomp by tapping the soil with two fingers. He has raised six worms from a one-square-meter area; four of them within fifteen seconds.

**R1.** *Internal Is Essential.* Have students respond to the following questions: Why must reptiles, which lay shell-covered eggs, have internal fertilization? (The egg must be fertilized before the shell is formed around it and the egg passes out of the body.) Why must an egg that is laid on land be covered with a shell? (If an egg laid on land were not protected by a shell, it would quickly dry and die.)

**R2.** *Amphibian vs. Reptile—A Comparison of Eggs.* Have students compare and contrast amphibian eggs with reptile eggs and explain why reptile eggs are more suited to be laid on land. (Amphibian eggs are covered by a soft, gelatinous layer, and reptile eggs are covered by a leathery shell and associated membranes. Reptile eggs can survive the drying effects of land, but amphibian eggs cannot.

**R3.** *Which Gender?* Most reptiles show very few external differences between the sexes. If green anoles are available, have students carefully examine them to see if they can discover any external clues to the sex of each individual anole. (Male anoles are usually larger than females and possess a flap of skin under the chin, called a dewlap, that is often brightly colored when extended.)

**R4.** *Turn Up the Thermostat (Unless You Want Females).* The famous crocodili-ologist, Dr. Croc O. Dile, has gathered his recent data regarding the effects of temperature on the eventual sex of developing crocodilian eggs into a graph. Have students analyze this graph and interpret the data. (In general, as incubation temperature increases, so does the percentage of male crocodilians hatched.)

**R5.** *The Hole Thing.* When a female leatherback sea turtle crawls up on a beach to lay eggs, she digs a deep hole, lays her eggs, and covers them with sand. She then crawls about 100 meters (330 feet) and digs another hole. She lays no eggs in the second hole but merely covers it back up with sand. Have students speculate on the purpose of this behavior. (One possibility is that the empty holes may confuse and distract predators from the holes actually containing eggs.)

**In1.** *Writing:*

a. Challenge students to learn more about reptiles by having them do a formal library report on a specific reptile of their choice.

b. Have students write, conduct, and analyze a survey concerning the true facts about reptiles and peoples' attitudes toward reptiles. Have students write both facts and misconceptions into their survey questions. Students might use some of the following misconceptions:

- All turtles are slow. (Most are, but giant sea turtles weighing more than a horse can swim faster than most humans can run.)
- Reptiles are slimy. (Wrong. They are cool, dry, and slick but definitely not slimy.)
- Rattlesnakes always rattle before striking. (Wrong. If startled, they can strike silently.)
- Snakes can sting, bite, or poison with their tongue. (Wrong. The tongue is a harmless sense organ.)
- Crocodiles are slow and clumsy on land. (Wrong. For distances of up to 150 feet, crocodiles can outrun most humans.)
- Most snakes are poisonous. (Wrong. Less than 10 percent of all snakes have venom capable of harming people.)
- Crocodiles shed tears before they kill a victim. (Wrong. This is an old belief that has no basis in fact.)
- Snakes "walk" on their ribs. (Wrong. The muscles and large bottom scales provide the power and traction for snake movement.)

## Reproduction and Development

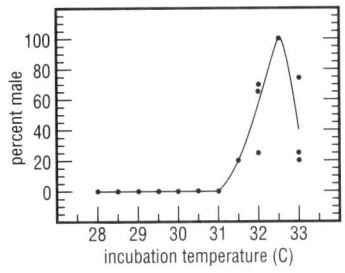

## Integration with Other Subject Areas

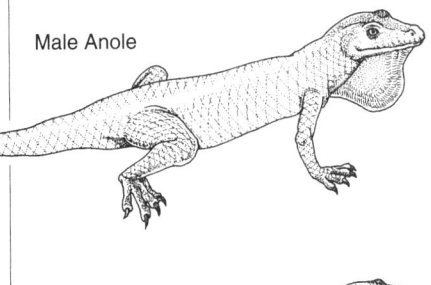

Male Anole

Female Anole

geckos - squeak
crocodiles - roar
snakes - hiss
turtles - grunt

Surveys could also include questions to determine peoples' attitudes toward reptiles and efforts to conserve them and their habitats.

Have students survey fellow students, teachers, other school staff, parents, and community members. Once the survey is complete, have students analyze their results by using math skills to calculate percentages.

c. Have students write a short play in which the only actors are reptiles.

**In2.** *Fine Arts:*

a. Although most reptiles are voiceless, some can make rather startling sounds:

Have students write a song or compose a poem in which the sounds of reptiles are used at appropriate places for emphasis or humor. This can be quite entertaining if students present their work to the rest of the class.

b. Have students imagine they are a company of snakes called "Reptilian Rodent eRadicators" (or something similar) who wish to sell their services as rodent exterminators. They should write a classified ad for their services that could be run in a newspaper. If you have the necessary equipment, you could have older or more advanced students do an actual television commercial for their services. As part of the activity, have students develop a company logo and slogan.

c. Have students draw or paint a picture of any reptile of their choice and its habitat.

**In3.** *Social Studies:*

a. *History.* Throughout history, reptiles have been feared, revered, and symbolized. Challenge students to find historical examples of how humans have expressed fear or reverence toward reptiles and how we have used them as symbols in the past. A few examples:

- Snakes got their first "bad press" in the oldest book, the Bible.
- The intertwined snakes of the Greek caduceus are still used as a symbol of healing by the medical profession.
- In Mexico, a rattlesnake represented an Aztec god.
- The American colonists had a flag with a snake on it admonishing, "Don't Tread On Me."
- More than 2,000 years ago, Hannibal had his men throw pots of snakes onto Roman ships in battle, causing the Romans to panic and surrender.
- St. Patrick supposedly drove the snakes from Ireland.
- According to Hindu legend, the world rests on the backs of four elephants who are in turn standing on the back of a giant turtle.

If you have students delve into this, you and they will be surprised at how many references to reptiles and reptile symbols appear in history. You might challenge students to take world events or well-known people of today and symbolize them in cartoon or poster form using the appropriate reptile(s).

b. *Geography.* Have students investigate where reptiles are found. For a general activity, have students color in on blank world maps where the various orders of reptiles are found. With appropriate references, you could get more specific. One of many specific possibilities would be to show the ranges of the various types of poisonous snakes in North America on a blank map. Have students consider how reptiles are adapted to live where they are found and why some areas of the world have no reptiles.

**In4.** *Societal/Environmental Issues:*

   a. Divide students into teams and have them debate the question, Is the survival of reptiles worth the cost of preserving their habitat, the inconvenience of having them where we don't want them, and the threat they pose to human life worldwide?

   b. Have students role-play how best to protect a beach for nesting green sea turtles. Conduct this activity as a hearing by the County Planning Commission. Assign or let students pick the following roles: county commissioners (4 or 5 needed), surfers (1 or 2 needed), a housing developer who wants to build condominiums on the beach (1 needed), a turtle biologist (1 needed), a beach homeowner (1 or 2 needed), a beach concession stand owner (1 needed), and a state wildlife protection officer (1 needed).

     Have the commissioners listen to the testimony of each interested party. Encourage students to do research and prepare their testimony beforehand. Caution them to present solid facts to support their position rather than rely on emotion and rhetoric.

     As each interested party testifies, encourage the commissioners to ask them questions. Once the commissioners have no further questions, allow others to ask questions of the person or people testifying.

     Once testimonies and questions are complete, have the commissioners present a proposal of action based on the facts given during the hearing.

   c. Use activity In4b in Chapter 9 as a model to investigate what problems reptiles might be having in your area and what you and your students might do about these problems.

Reptiles may be released back into the habitats from which they were collected. Do not release commercially purchased reptiles unless you can absolutely verify without doubt that they are native to your area.

# RELEASE OF SPECIMENS

# SECTION FOUR:
# UPPER VERTEBRATES

## 11. BIRDS

**Kingdom:** Animalia
**Subkingdom:** Metazoa
**Phylum:** Chordata
**Subphylum:** Vertebrata
**Class:** Aves (birds)
**Orders:** 24 to 34 orders (depending on the authority). See Appendix A for a partial listing.

CLASSIFICATION

Filling the sky with graceful flight, dazzling our eyes with brilliant plumage, and soothing our ears with melodious songs, birds are regarded by many as the most beautiful and distinctive of all the vertebrates.

The nearly 8,600 species of birds on earth today have developed aerial highways to every possible habitat on earth. Birds are at home in polar regions and in the tropics; in forests, deserts, and grasslands; on mountains and swimming on and under the ocean and other bodies of water. Yet, few species are truly cosmopolitan. Some shore- and seabirds are worldwide in their distribution, but land birds have a seemingly haphazard distribution. Why does South America have 300 species of hummingbirds while Africa, with similar habitats, has not a single one? Why are finches found on even the most remote oceanic islands yet not on Australia? Why is the Laysan teal found in the smallest range of any bird, the shores of a marshy lagoon of about 5 square kilometers (2 square miles) on the small island of Laysan? These and many other oddities of bird distribution have long perplexed ornithologists and ecologists.

Depending on the authority consulted, there are 24 to 34 orders of birds, with about 15 families arranged into 8,600 to 9,000 species. But just how many birds are there? By some estimates, there are 100 billion birds in the world, roughly 20 billion of them in North America alone. The world's most abundant birds are oceanic. A single flock of shearwaters off Australia once was computed to number more than 150 million birds. Penguin colonies often number hundreds of thousands, and an estimated 5 million Adelie penguins have been recorded on a single group of small islands. The Atlantic puffin has been estimated to number 15 million, and the guano birds on islands off Peru gather in aggregations more than 10 million.

In North America, the domestic chicken is probably the most abundant species. Among wild birds, arguments are made for starlings and the American robin. English sparrows also exist in large numbers, and recently exploding populations of red-winged blackbirds may make it the most abundant bird south of the Canadian border.

DIVERSITY AND
DISTRIBUTION

Flamingo
(Straining Beak)

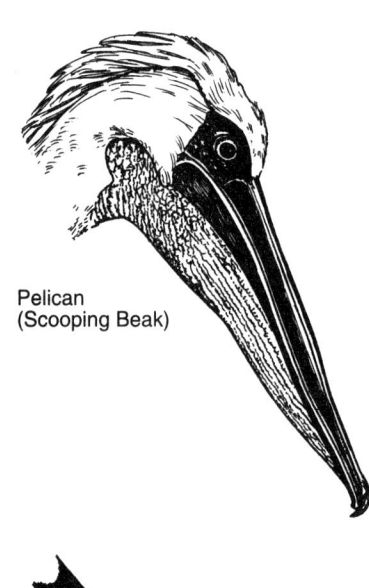

Cormorant (Grasping Beak)

## General Class Characteristics

Pelican
(Scooping Beak)

Anhinga
(Spearing Beak)

Hawk (Tearing Beak)

Many bird species are nearing extinction. The least common North American bird may be the ivory-billed woodpecker, the California condor, or the eskimo curlew. A few sightings of single birds or a few individuals keep hope alive that some of these birds may still be with us.

Birds range in size from the Cuban bee hummingbird, weighing less than 2 grams (0.70 ounces) and measuring less than 6.1 centimeters (2.5 inches) in length (counting the bill), to the ostrich, which weighs 160 kilograms (350 pounds) and stands about 2.5 meters (8.25 feet) tall. Birds with the widest wingspan are the marabou stork of Africa and the wandering albatross of the southern hemisphere, with wings stretching almost 3.6 meters (12 feet).

**Digestive System and Feeding.** Birds have a high metabolic rate, which means they burn food quickly and must feed often to refuel. The smaller they are, the faster they use energy. Land birds weighing 100 to 1,000 grams (0.25 to 2.5 pounds) eat approximately 5 to 9 percent of their body weight each day. Birds weighing 10 to 90 grams (0.34 to 3.2 ounces) may have to eat 10 to 30 percent of their body weight each day.

Among birds there are herbivores, carnivores, omnivores, and scavengers. The digestive system must be structured to the type of food eaten and to the lack of teeth. Herbivorous birds feeding on seeds, fruits, buds, leaves, nuts, and other tough plant material have a more complex digestive system than do carnivorous birds. Herbivores have a storage sac, called the crop, leading to a two-part stomach where food is mixed with digestive juices in the first part and then ground to a pulp in the second part, the thick-walled, muscular gizzard. Studies on turkeys have shown that they can grind up 24 walnuts, shell and all, in just four hours and can even grind steel needles to pieces. To aid this grinding action, herbivorous birds often swallow small stones. Carnivorous birds feeding on insects, fish, amphibians, reptiles, mammals, or other birds usually do not have a crop (or have only a small one) and their gizzard functions as a normal stomach.

The powerful and swift action of a bird's digestive juices can be seen in the speed with which foods are digested. A shrike can digest a mouse in three hours. A thrush fed elderberry fruits will defecate the seeds 30 minutes later, and seeds of berries eaten by waxwings appear in their feces in as little as 16 minutes. Owls do not attempt to digest the bones and fur, feathers, or skin of their prey; they regurgitate this material in the form of a compact pellet.

Some birds have very specialized diets. Hummingbirds live primarily on nectar from flowers, but some larger types feed extensively on insects as well. Tree sap is the specialty of the aptly named sapsuckers, and the wax from beehives is a major part of the diet of honeyguides (thanks to a special bacteria in their digestive system that make them the only vertebrate able to digest wax).

The need for constant food is so critical that birds must be perfectly structured and adapted to getting it. The form and structure of the beak proclaim the nature of a bird's food. The toothless, lightweight beak is composed of a layer of hard keratin over the bones of the upper and lower jaws or mandibles. Unlike mammals, birds can move both the upper and lower jaws.

The beaks of birds are adapted for many purposes:
- straining
- catching fish by grasping, scooping, or spearing
- crushing seeds and nuts
- tearing flesh
- sipping nectar
- sweeping for insects
- chiseling for insects
- probing

Grosbeak (Crushing Seeds and Nuts)

Many birds could be said to have nondescript, multipurpose beaks adapted to picking and probing a wide variety of plant and/or animal material. One bird, the woodpecker finch of the Galapagos Islands, even manipulates tools with its beak. Using a twig or thorn, the finch pries insects out of cracks and holes, then drops the tool and catches the insect.

**Circulatory System.** Birds have a well-developed and powerful four-chambered heart that moves red blood through two separate circulatory loops. Powerful flying birds have larger hearts than nonfliers, weak fliers, or soaring birds.

The heartbeat is extremely rapid in birds, especially the smaller species. The hummingbirds have a rate that ranges from 500 beats per minute at rest to 1,200 beats per minute during extreme activity. The ostrich may have a range of 38 to 176 beats per minute.

Birds are endothermic (warm blooded) and maintain a steady temperature independent of the external environment (although their body temperature can vary as much as 10° under different conditions). Their normal body temperature is between 38° and 40°C (100° to 112°F), depending on the species. It is highest in the passerines (perching birds).

Young birds born without a covering of down have almost no ability to regulate their body temperature and thus require brooding by the parents.

Some birds, such as swifts and swallows, can lower their body temperature, heartbeat, and breathing rate during short cold periods and enter a state of torpidity in which they consume practically no energy. Hummingbirds use this ability at night to use less fuel from food consumed during the day and thus avoid starving to death overnight.

In hot weather, birds have several cooling strategies. They may become less active, move into the shade, depress their feathers to reduce their insulating powers, and pant. Birds also lose heat through unfeathered legs and feet. Storks and the New World vultures defecate on their legs, which are then cooled by evaporation and the drying process.

**Respiratory System.** The high metabolic rate required to maintain an endothermic body and the rigors of flight require a rapid and efficient uptake of large amounts of oxygen. A bird's respiratory system shows several adaptations that allow it to meet these demands and fit into a small, streamlined body. The lungs, although not particularly large, are divided into many air passages, each exposed to blood vessels. This arrangement presents a large surface area for gas exchange while occupying a small space. The lungs are supplemented by a series of air sacs that allow the bird to intake more air than the lungs can hold at one time.

Like heart rate, breathing rate varies among species. Most small birds breathe between 100 and 200 times per minute, and very large birds breathe 6 to 12 times per minute but faster during strenuous activity.

Hummingbird (Sipping Nectar)

Nighthawk (Sweeping for Insects)

Woodpecker (Chiseling for Insects)

Kiwi (Probing Beak)

Woodpecker Finches

**Muscle System, Movement, and Migration.** Most birds have about 175 different muscles to perform their variety of movements. Bird muscles come in two main types: one designed to provide explosive bursts of speed for short distances and others structured for long endurance. Ground birds such as the quail, turkey, and domestic chicken have flight muscles that tire easily (this muscle is light colored when cooked—white meat) but powerful leg muscles for walking and running (this muscle is dark colored when cooked—dark meat). In birds that are strong fliers, somewhat the reverse is true.

The size of leg muscles depends on how a bird uses its legs and feet. Active swimmers, runners, and climbers have larger, stronger muscles than species who do none of those things. The legs of the highly aerial whippoorwills and swallows are so weak and tiny that these birds find any walking difficult; such activity for the hummingbird is almost impossible.

Because of lack of lower leg musculature, the legs are controlled by a series of tendons from the muscles at the top of the legs. When a bird stands, these tendons are relaxed and the toes spread out. However, when a passerine (perching bird) perches by squatting and bending its legs, tension is applied to the tendons and the toes lock in a grasp so firm and tightly curled that these birds can sleep on the perch without falling.

The most remarkable movement birds are capable of is the ability to fly. The simplest form of flight is gliding. Gliding flight—several strong wing strokes and then a glide—saves energy, but gravity and air conditions determine how far a bird can skim before flapping again. Pheasants and quail beat their wings rapidly to gain altitude and then glide on stiff wings. Many other birds use the glide when they have gained enough height and speed and want to save energy on descent.

Some birds have elevated gliding to a specialized skill called soaring. Hawks, eagles, and vultures with broad wings and tails search for food from high in the air and must be able to spend hours aloft. These birds travel by riding on rising thermal currents over land to great heights, then gliding down to be carried up by another column of rising air.

The long, narrow wings of the albatross, shearwaters, and frigatebirds and the lack of thermal air currents over water have forced these soaring seabirds to develop a different kind of soaring. Their flight requires continuous winds that do not carry them high but give them enough lift over waves to make a long, wind-pushed glide until they descend to wave level, where they turn into the wind and are lifted like a kite for the next glide.

Released Tendons

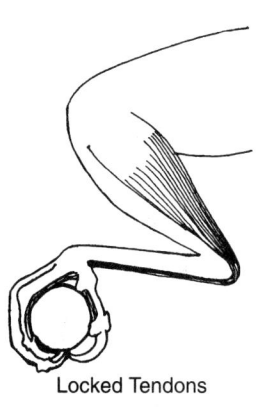

Locked Tendons

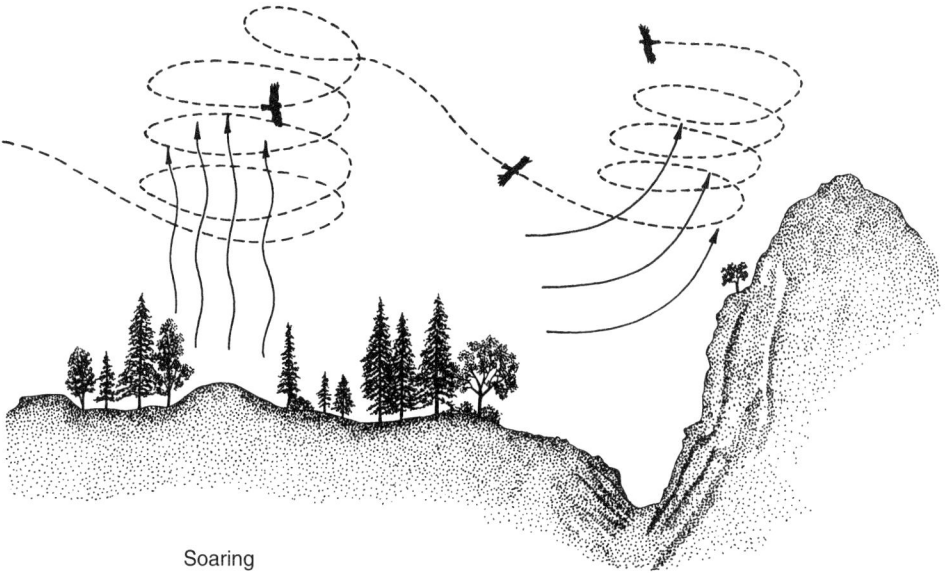

Soaring

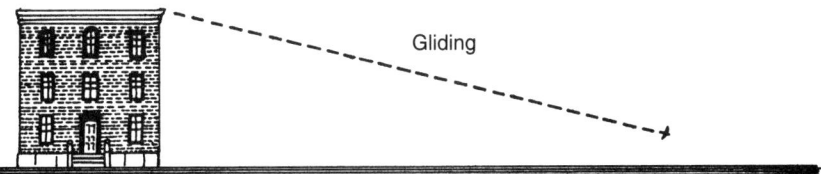

Gliding

Sustained or flapping flight involves an up-and-down motion of the wings to keep the bird aloft and a nearly imperceptible forward-and-backward motion to make it move forward. The power is applied on the downstroke. The large primary feathers on the wingtips are bent upward and twisted into the air; as they are brought down, they pull the wing and the entire bird with them. On the upstroke the primaries separate to permit easy passage of air between them, and the wingtips move upward and backward, still providing slight propulsion. Then the cycle begins again.

The most remarkable aerial acrobats are the hummingbirds. Their tremendous wing speeds of 50 to 200 beats per second (so fast the wings produce a humming sound, which gives these birds their name) and their swiveling and sculling action allow these "feathered helicopters" to fly straight up, hover, and even fly backwards.

In level flight, most perching birds fly at 22 to 40 kilometers (15 to 25 miles) per hour, geese and ducks travel between 65 to 100 kilometers (40 to 60 miles) per hour, and some shorebirds have been clocked from airplanes at 176 kilometers (110 miles) per hour. In a dive, the peregrine falcon is in a class alone. It climbs high above its prey, folds its wings, and drops for a thousand feet or more at speeds of about 320 kilometers (200 miles) per hour before slashing into its victim.

The highest flying birds ever recorded were a flock of geese over Dehra Dun, India, at an altitude of 9,000 meters (29,700 feet). Even small birds such as warblers and vireos have been known to fly as high as 6,364 meters (21,000 feet) during migration—a remarkable physical feat for such small birds considering the cold temperatures and reduced oxygen levels at that altitude. Going the other direction, emperor penguins dive as deep as 265 meters (875 feet) in Antarctic waters to feed on squid.

The longest sustained flights may be made by sooty terns. Like some other seabirds, the terns spend years at sea and do not come to land until maturity. However, unlike some other seabirds, terns quickly become waterlogged and cannot come to rest on the water. Thus they spend virtually all of their first six to eight years in ceaseless flight.

**Flapping Flight**

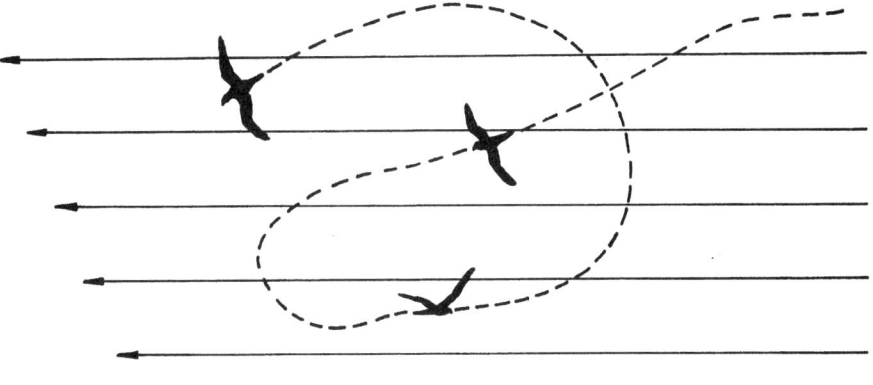

Dynamic Soaring

ATLANTIC

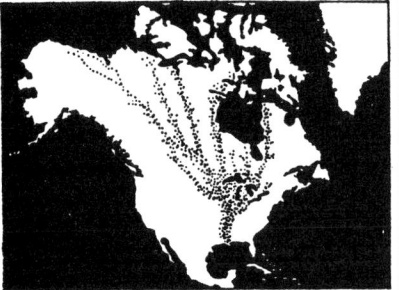

MISSISSIPPI

CENTRAL

PACIFIC

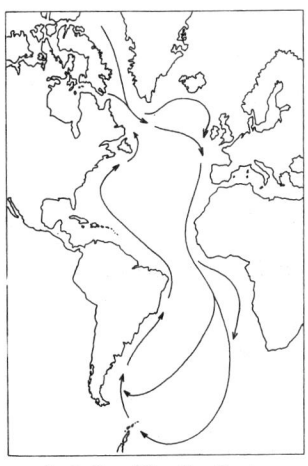

Arctic Tern Migration Routes

No aspect of bird flight is so awe-inspiring as the mass movements of birds we call migration. What is the destination or the origin of that whirling cloud of dark, winged bodies against a gray autumn sky? What forces drive those winged silhouettes flashing across the face of a full moon on a bright September night? Of all known bird species, more than half migrate regularly. Other types of animals migrate, but only birds do it in such epic proportions (the total number of birds migrating each season estimated to be in the billions). Migration can be a short trek up and down a single mountainside or an intercontinental journey. Some types of birds migrate in flocks while others make solitary journeys.

Why do birds migrate? Food, water, and a suitable breeding place are vital to a bird's survival. Changing seasons can transform a safe and comfortable habitat into a hostile, forbidding one. When this happens, two choices are available: go dormant and hibernate or migrate. Most birds opt for migration; only a very few, such as the common poor-will, hibernate. Some migration schedules do not always closely follow seasonal changes. For some nomadic species like the crossbills and redpolls, fluctuations in food supply may force migration in some winters but not in others.

Each migratory species chooses a well-defined route of travel between its nesting site and winter range. These migration routes are usually quite broad. Waterfowl tend to be confined to narrower migration corridors by the availability of suitable habitat.

Certain routes are used by so many birds in both spring and fall that they are called flyways. These flyways should be considered only very broad and general paths, however. Some scientists beleive the whole concept of flyways is inaccurate because birds from one nesting area have been found migrating in several different flyways. North America has four major flyways that follow prominent geographical features running north and south on the continent:

- Atlantic
- Mississippi
- Central
- Pacific

Migration cues such as the changing length of day and internal migration clocks trigger a bird's metabolism to store fat under the skin for the strenuous journey ahead. Species that make long, nonstop flights may increase their body weight by half again with stored fat. As the birds take wing, most must stop occasionally to replenish their fuel reserves. For this reason, suitable stopover sites providing food and cover are as important as suitable nesting and breeding grounds.

The champion long distance migrator is the arctic tern, which flies a 35,400-kilometer (22,000-mile) loop each year between the top of the northern hemisphere to the bottom of the southern hemisphere.

The highest migrators are bar-headed geese, which fly over Mount Everest at altitudes exceeding 9,000 meters (30,000 feet). However, most migration occurs much lower, with exact altitude determined by wind direction, wind speed, and cloud cover.

Despite the advantages of flight, about 40 species of birds have given up an aerial existence for life on the ground. Birds that have adapted to a running or swimming existence are penguins, the ostrich, the rhea, cassowaries, the emu, and kiwis.

**Legs and Feet.** Nothing so clearly reveals the habitat a bird occupies as the form and structure of its legs and feet. Feet serve feeding birds in two ways: getting to food and catching and holding food. In general, the legs and feet of birds are covered with reptilelike scales. Each toe has a claw at the tip. Most birds have four toes, some have three, and a few, such as the ostrich, have only two. The length of the toe and claw, the position of the toes, the number of toes, the thickness of the toes, and the presence of webbing are specific adaptations related to habitat, feeding, and locomotion.

Wading birds have long, slender toes to support them on mud or vegetation.

Nearly all swimming birds use their feet for propulsion, although some ducks and the penguins move underwater using their wings. The toes of swimming birds may be lobed, as in grebes, or fully webbed, as in ducks.

The predatory raptors have long, sharp claws called talons that help them grasp, kill, and carry their prey. Ospreys have rough, scaly soles to aid in grasping the slippery fish on which they feed.

The largest order of birds, the passerines or perching birds, have slender toes suited for wrapping around branches and twigs. Most perching birds have three toes in front and one in the back. The woodpeckers have two in front and two in back to act as a brace as they peck at trees.

Ground-dwelling birds that depend mostly on running, such as the grouse, have short, thick toes. Others, such as the flightless ostrich, have only two huge, muscular toes with very reduced claws.

**Skeletal System.** Compared with mammal or reptile skeletons, there are far fewer bones in a bird's skeleton. Flying animals need a light but rigid skeleton, and this has been accomplished in birds by the fusing of some small bones and the elimination or reduction of other bones. For example, birds lack a heavy tail, heavy jaws, and teeth. Many birds have bones containing air spaces or hollow bones stiffened by internal struts (see illustration page 184). The skeleton of a frigatebird of 1.4 to 1.8 kilograms (3 to 4 pounds) with a 2.1-meter (7-foot) wingspan would weigh only 112 grams (4 ounces)—less than the weight of the feathers.

Unlike all other vertebrates, a bird must support itself by its wings and its legs. Consequently, the shoulder and hip girdles are strong to provide the support needed. The sternum is modified into a flat keel in most birds to provide a greater surface area for the attachment of flight muscles.

The skull of a bird consists of little more than huge eyesockets and a beak. Even the cervical vertebrae are unusual. Mammals have 7 such vertebrae no matter how long their neck, but most birds have from 13 to 25 such neck bones. The common sparrow has more neck bones than a giraffe.

**Body Covering.** If it has feathers, it's a bird. No bird is without them, and no other animal possess anything similar to them. Feathers are horny, keratinous outgrowths from specialized areas of the skin called papillae. Early development of a feather is similar to that of a reptile's scale. However, feathers continue to grow outward, eventually loosing their blood supply and becoming a dead structure that receives nothing from the body except physical support.

In time, as feathers become worn, they loosen and drop out and are replaced through a process called molting. There is much variation in the pattern of molting. For example, penguins shed their old feathers nearly simultaneously so that they come off in sheets, and many water birds lose all their primary wing feathers at once so the birds are flightless for several weeks after molting. Most birds lose and replace a few feathers at a time in regular sequence. Most species of birds renew their wing feathers only once a year even though other feathers may be renewed twice a year.

Molting is connected with age and the breeding cycle. As many birds mature, successive molts bring different plumage colors and patterns. Once adulthood is reached, plumage is often determined by the breeding cycle. Male birds especially tend to have bright-colored feathers during breeding and then molt to drabber colors after breeding.

The feathers of birds perform five functions: (1) They insulate and hold heat around the body by their own weight or thickness and by trapping air underneath.

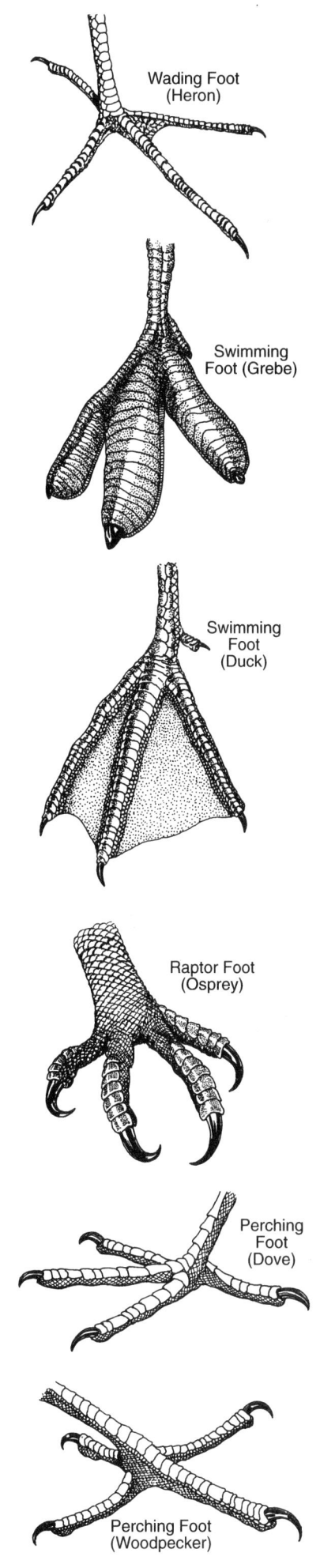

Wading Foot
(Heron)

Swimming
Foot (Grebe)

Swimming
Foot
(Duck)

Raptor Foot
(Osprey)

Perching
Foot
(Dove)

Perching Foot
(Woodpecker)

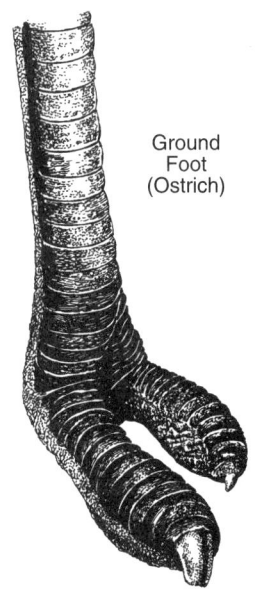

Ground
Foot
(Grouse)

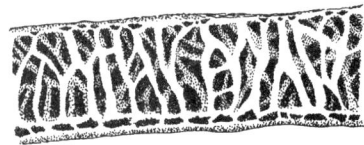

Ground
Foot
(Ostrich)

Bird Bone — Internal

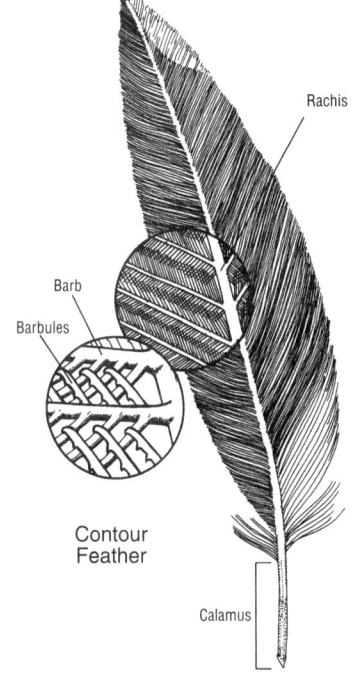

Rachis

Barb

Barbules

Contour
Feather

Calamus

Muscles attached to each feather allow birds to pull them up and trap more air during cold weather. Penguins, which live in very cold climes, have very thick layers of puffy and highly insulating feathers, which they coat with a thick layer of oil to further seal, waterproof, and insulate them. The oil gives them the deceptive appearance of having a slick covering that resembles skin more than feathers. (2) Feathers create wing and tail surfaces essential for lift and control during flight. (3) Feathers waterproof the body. This is accomplished in most birds by taking oil on their beak from a gland at the base of the tail and applying it to the feathers. Strangely, a few water birds, such as the cormorants and the anhinga, lack waterproofing and must spread their soaked wings to dry after swimming. (4) Feathers are colored to camouflage birds by blending with the background of their habitat. (5) Feathers are important in species recognition. The plumes, crests, and brilliant patches on male birds shown during courtship displays enable the females to select a mate of the same species and the best possible mate from those assembled.

Birds are the most brilliantly colored members of the animal kingdom. Their feathers appear colored because they contain structural elements that reflect light in different ways, as a film of oil on water, and because of actual pigments in the feathers. Structural colors are either iridescent or noniridescent. Iridescent colors give the feather a metallic appearance and change according to the angle at which light strikes the feather surface. Noniridescent colors are produced by the scattering of light through minute air-filled cavities in the feather; they do not change with changing angles of light. Pigments are not limited to the plumage but may also be found on the beak, legs, feet, and sometimes neck and head. The pink color of the flamingo comes not from pigments in the feathers but from the food it eats.

To serve all the functions required of them, feathers have been specialized into several categories:

*Contour feathers* are made up of a stiff, hollow central shaft. On each side of the shaft is a flat surface made of interlocking rows of barbs.

Contour feathers are the large feathers that cover a bird's body, wings, and tail. The long, stiff contour feathers of the wing and tail are called flight feathers, and those covering the rest of the body are known as general body feathers.

*Down feathers* grow underneath and between the contour feathers. They are short and fluffy and function to trap air and thus insulate the bird.

Young birds are covered by down feathers before they develop adult plumage. Down is the best protection against cold ever developed. Humans never have improved on it and use bird down in coats, vests, sleeping bags, and comforters.

Powder down is a light dusting of powder on some birds probably derived from disintegrating down feathers. This powder, especially thick in herons and bitterns, may help remove fish slime from the feathers.

*Semiplume feathers* are a type of contour feather with no firm vane.

*Filoplume feathers* are very specialized hairlike feathers with a few barbs at the top. They occur among the contour feathers. Their exact function is unknown, but it may be decorative or sensory.

Feathers require a great deal of daily care to keep them in good condition. All birds preen, using their beak to reattach separated barbs and smooth the feathers into place or combing the feathers with their feet. Bathing in water or dust also helps keep the feathers clean and in good condition. One of the strangest forms of feather care is practiced by some of the jays. They find a suitable ant nest and spread themselves out over it so the ants will crawl into their feathers. They often pick up individual ants and pass them across their feathers. It is believed that formic acid produced by the ants helps kill parasitic fleas and feather lice on the bird.

**Excretory System.** Birds eliminate nitrogenous wastes by filtering them from the blood in the kidneys. Urine flows to the cloaca, where most of the water is reabsorbed. What is left are uric acid crystals in a white pastelike form—the familiar bird droppings.

**Brain and Nervous System.** Birds have larger and more complex brains than reptiles. The large optic lobe gives them the acute vision necessary for flight and food-getting. Birds have a large cerebrum controlling most instinctive behavior patterns, and the cerebellum controlling their precise skills and movements is also comparatively large.

The brain is especially well developed in parrots, owls, and woodpeckers, but proportionately largest in crows, ravens, jays, and magpies—a family of birds known for their so-called intelligence.

The eyes of a bird are enormous. The European buzzard and some hawks, eagles, and owls often have eyes as large as or larger than humans' eyes. In fact, the eyes of a bird may weigh more than the brain. The eyes of most birds are located on the side of the head, allowing them to see over a larger area than humans can. Most of what birds see is perceived with only one eye; the fields of vision overlap only in a small area in front. Owls have excellent overlapping vision, but penguins have none at all.

Vision in birds is the most highly developed of any animal. Birds' eyes can detect the direction, distance, size, shape, color, brightness, three-dimensional depth, and motion of an object often at great distances. The predatory birds or raptors who live by scanning vast distances for prey have the keenest eyesight of all. A red-tailed hawk soaring 450 meters (1,500 feet) above the ground can see a field mouse scurrying through underbrush; a human eye would see only an indistinct jumble of shapes and colors. Microscopic examination of the fovea, the region of visual acuity within the eye, shows 1,000,000 visual cells per square millimeter in hawks but only 200,000 visual cells in the same area in humans.

Birds are so completely covered by feathers that there are few places exposed enough to feel things, although their vigorous scratching shows they feel minor skin irritations. Certainly the feet must feel the surfaces on which they walk or perch and the food they grasp, and the beaks of some birds have sensory nerves used in probing for food they cannot see.

The variety of bird songs and calls indicates that bird hearing is acute. In fact, some owls locate their prey at night entirely by sound. Birds have external ear openings, called auriculars, hidden by feathers. The horns or tufts on some owls play no role in hearing.

In most birds the sense of smell is barely developed. The kiwis of New Zealand have poor vision but the strongest sense of smell of all birds. With nostrils at the tip of their long probe-like bill, they seem to sniff the ground for earthworms and other concealed food.

Birds have very few taste buds. Most swallow their food quickly, giving little indication of taste discrimination. Insect-eating birds do learn to avoid the foul-tasting monarch butterfly and other bitter-tasting or poisonous insects.

One of the most amazing senses birds possess is the ability to navigate and find their way during migration. Various techniques of observing bird migration (banding of individual birds, direct observation of day and night movements, radar observations, and controlled experiments) have shown that migratory birds use a variety of navigation techniques. Day migrators use the sun as a visual compass to determine direction. Night migrators orient themselves to certain star patterns and can become disoriented on cloudy nights. Some birds seem to possess a magnetic compass. Laboratory experiments with birds in orientation cages show that birds do respond to magnetic direction and that their orienta-

Down Feather

Semi-plume Feather

Filoplume Feather

tion can be shifted by changing magnetic directions. No field studies, however, have found a clear indication of magnetic influence on migratory birds in the wild. Birds also may rely on some sort of biological map to find their way. Studies have shown that young pigeons learn odor maps by smelling different odors that reach their home loft on winds from varying directions. Birds may use a magnetic compass for direction but a magnetic map is thought to help determine location. The main support for this theory comes from observations of pigeons released in areas of magnetic anomalies (places where the magnetic field is disturbed by large iron ore deposits near the surface). These ideas are still controversial, and none have been proved to the satisfaction of all the experts, so new and different experiments continue to be performed.

**Reproduction and Development.** There are almost as many different reproductive strategies as there are types of birds. All birds share certain reproductive features: the sexes are separate, male and female mate to fertilize the eggs inside the female's body, the eggs always pass outside the mother's body, the eggs are covered by a thin and brittle shell, the eggs are laid in a safe place where they will be warmed, and the young must receive enough food to grow until they become independent.

The breeding cycle of birds is timed to take place at the season when the maximum amount of food is available to the female forming eggs inside her or when the maximum amount of food is available for feeding the young. Sometimes the breeding season represents a compromise between these two periods.

Most North American birds do not winter where they breed. In spring, migrants return to the region where they were born or to the territories they previously occupied. As males begin to come into the spring breeding area, they quickly establish and begin to defend some territory. The territory may be no larger than the area within the reach of their beak (colonial birds) or it may be as large as several square miles (raptors). Territorial ownership is most frequently conveyed and contested by songs and feather displays but, if necessary, fights and chases may develop. Establishing territories serves several functions: (1) it spaces out the pairs of birds and provides each with a place to mate, (2) it spaces out the nests and makes them harder for predators to find, and (3) it spaces out the birds over the available habitat and thus reduces competition for food for the young.

Ducks and geese that nest in the Arctic arrive already paired and lose none of the little nesting time available in preliminaries like courtship. However, with most birds, once territories have been established and females begin to arrive, the competition of courtship begins. Courtship is a necessary prelude to establishing the bond between male and female that will result in fertilization of the eggs.

For most birds, the bond between male and female is established after courtship rituals in the male's territory, whether nesting takes place there or not. In all species studied to this point, the female selects the male on the basis of his displays or suitability of his territory.

Courtship rituals may be one sided, with the male displaying or dancing. The male sage grouse strut, dance, and make booming sounds with air sacs on their necks while the females calmly circle them. The male birds of paradise are without equal in the brilliance and oddity of their displays. The display often involves the erection of brilliant iridescent plumage accompanied by bizarre cracking or whirring sounds and frequently culminates with the male hanging upside down on its perch.

In some birds, courtship involves rituals in which both sexes participate. Western grebes throw their heads back in unison and run along the top of the water side by side. Cranes bow to each other, jump into the air with outstretched wings, and then bow again. Storks face each other, throw their heads back, and make loud clapping noises with their bills. Many birds of prey swoop and dive at each other high in the air.

Many smaller birds establish a monogamous bond, with the pair remaining together for only one breeding season. Some may nest together in following years, but only because they both returned to the same territory. The loyalty is to the territory, not the mate. Among larger birds that live longer, such as geese, swans, raptors, and many seabirds, pairs often bond for as long as both partners live. Crane researcher George Archibald tells a story about a wild female sandhill crane that was hit and killed by a car in Wisconsin. After her untimely death, her mate spent hours every day all summer and fall standing in solitary loneliness by the roadside where she had been killed.

In a few monogamous birds that raise more than one brood per mating season, the females may switch mates between broods. The briefest kind of monogamous pairing is found in birds that come together to mate but leave the raising to the young to the female. There are also types of birds in which the male bonds and mates with more than one female (polygyny) or in which the female mates with several males (polyandry) and leaves the male to incubate the eggs and raise the young.

In birds, sperm must be transferred by contact of the cloaca of the male with the cloaca of the female. In order for this to be achieved, the male must mount the female and she must move her tail to one side. The positioning is delicate, and the male is dependent on the full cooperation of the female. Many attempts at copulation appear to be unsuccessful because the male fails to get in the proper position. Some species, such as the common swift, copulate while in flight. As far as is known, the females of most species do not store sperm for long periods. A series of copulations may be required to successfully fertilize a large clutch of eggs. In some ducks, however, one successful copulation seems to be all that is necessary.

Once the eggs have been fertilized, the next order of business is nest building. Birds seek to protect their nests by concealing them or by building the nests in inaccessible places. Most birds build a familiar nest of twigs and plant fibers in an open-topped cup design. There are many variations, however. Birds such as the orioles and weavers weave elaborate and complex chambers from strands of grass or other plant material. The swifts and swallows use mud and saliva to cement their nests in place. The nest of the plover is a slight depression in the sand. Some birds build no nest at all. The fairy tern lays a single egg on a horizontal tree branch, from which it never seems to roll. The male emperor penguin incubates a single egg on the top of his feet and hatches out a youngster in the dead of the Antarctic winter. Some cuckoos and the cowbirds have an audacious reproductive plan. The female lays her eggs in other birds' nests and then departs, leaving the foster parents to incubate her eggs and raise her young.

The smallest nest is built by the hummingbird; it is a scant 2.5 centimeters (1 inch) across. Raptors build huge nests of limbs and sticks and add to them year after year. A bald eagle nest in Ohio measured 2.5 meters (8.5 feet) across and 3.5 meters (12 feet) deep and weighed 3,600 kilograms (2 tons).

Once nest building is complete, the female lays the eggs in it. The size, shape, color, and markings of birds eggs are consistent within each species but vary greatly from one species to the next. All birds lay eggs and all birds' eggs are covered with a thin, brittle shell.

The tiniest eggs are those of the hummingbirds. They are pea sized and always white and always number two. The largest are those of the ostrich, at 13 to 18 centimeters (5 to 7 inches) across and weighing 1.5 kilograms (3.3 pounds).

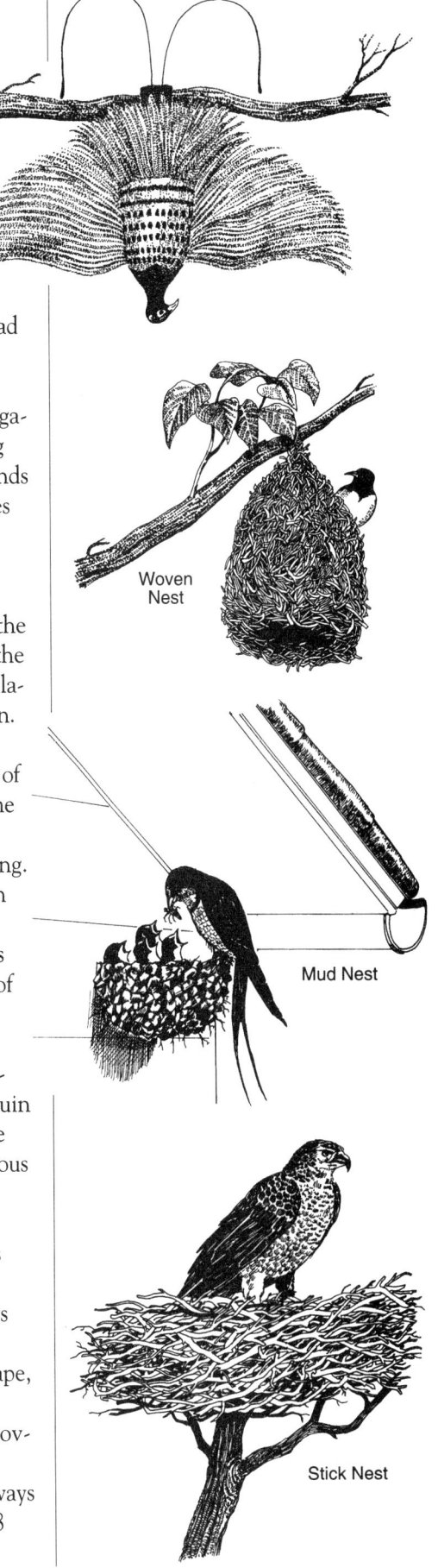

Woven Nest

Mud Nest

Stick Nest

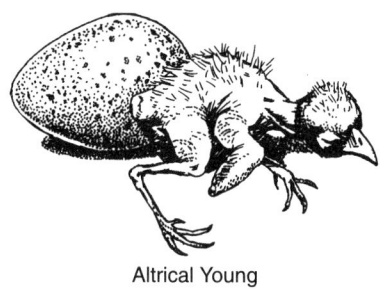

Altrical Young

Precocial Young

Female birds can lay fertilized or unfertilized eggs, but only those that are fertilized will develop into young.

Some birds are determinate layers. That is, they always lay a certain number of eggs and then stop, even if some of the eggs are taken. Indeterminate layers keep laying eggs if their eggs are taken. A flicker whose eggs were removed each day laid 71 eggs in 73 days! Domestic fowl fall into this category. The record for a chicken is 361 eggs in a year and for a domestic duck 363 eggs in 365 days.

Birds' eggs must be kept warm to develop properly, so one or both parents must maintain proper temperature through incubation. Merely sitting on eggs does not ensure warmth, and incubating birds often develop brood patches, or places where the feathers fall out on the underbody to expose warm, bare skin that can be pressed directly against the eggs. Not all types of birds develop these patches.

Eggs need not be covered constantly. In most perching birds where the female alone is responsible for incubation, 6 to 10 minutes may be spent off the eggs feeding for every 15 to 30 minutes spent on the eggs in incubation. Incubation to hatching may take as little as 11 days in some perching birds and as long as 80 days in the albatross.

Newly hatched young fall into two categories. Those that are helpless, blind, naked, and feeble, like the meadowlark, are called altrical. Those that are fully feathered with down, bright eyed, and able to run and peck at food almost immediately after hatching, like the killdeer, are called precocial.

Young, growing birds place extreme demands on their parent(s) to supply enough food. One pair of phoebes was reported to make 845 trips to their nest in one day. A larger bird like the eagle may make only two or three trips daily, but the prey it brings to its hungry young consists of large animals.

Once the young birds are mature enough to fend for themselves and have been abandoned by their parents, a crucial point in their survival has been reached, as mortality is the greatest in the first year of their life.

**Songs and Calls.** The songs and calls of birds serve a variety of functions: (1) They advertise nesting territories and attract mates, (2) they assemble gregarious species, (3) they serve as directional calls between parents and young, (4) they serve as threat calls to warn others of danger, and (5) they can play a role in

Nuthatch

Wren

Vireo

food-getting. Some songs are used at all times of the year, some only during breeding season, and a few only during migration.

The rule of thumb seems to be that the drab-colored birds are the most gifted singers. Brightly colored birds use their colors and not their voice to advertise themselves, but the camouflaged birds of thicket and plain can make their presence known only by warbling tireless torrents of song.

How do birds know what to sing? Some birds, such as the chirping sparrow or least flycatcher, have an unvarying song pattern that seems to be instinctive. Young of those species raised artificially without the chance to hear their own kind sing as they should when they reach proper age. The more gifted singers, such as the nightingales and mockingbirds, must learn their art from older birds. There are still as many questions as answers about the songs and calls of birds.

It is beyond the scope and intent of this book to give a detailed description of each of 24 to 34 bird orders. Instead, a few of the more familiar orders are discussed.

**Order Passeriformes.** This is the largest order of birds. It contains more than a third of all living families and over half of the living bird species. Included in this order are flycatchers, larks, swallows, shrikes, waxwings, wrens, creepers, mockingbirds, thrushes, sparrows, warblers, nuthatches, chats, vireos, orioles, birds of paradise, starlings, crows, jays, and magpies—to name just a few.

The passerines are commonly referred to as the perching birds because they have feet that are adapted to cling to branches, reeds, and human-made objects

Grouse

Turkey

Quail

## Specific Order Characteristics

Gull

Plover

Puffin

Falcon

Owl

Wood Duck

Canada Goose

The Importance
of Birds

like wires. Passerines include all birds noted for their singing ability and are also commonly referred to as songbirds as a result.

**Order Galliformes.** This order contains many of the ground-dwelling birds that are often hunted as game, including grouse, pheasants, quail, and turkeys.

These birds have feet adapted for running and scratching and fly only for short distances. They feed mainly on seeds, nuts, berries, and other plant material.

**Order Charadriiformes.** This order includes waders and shorebirds such as the plovers, sandpipers, phalaropes, gulls, terns, auks, and puffins.

The waders have long, slender legs suitable for wading in shallow water and long, slender necks and bills suited for probing shallow water for food.

The gulls are solidly built with strong legs and webbed feet for running or swimming. They have a stout bill with a tip adapted for tearing. The auks and puffins have large heads on a compact body. Their powerful webbed feet allow them to dive and swim after fish, their main prey.

**Order Falconiformes and Order Strigiformes.** These orders include the hunting and flesh-eating birds known as raptors or birds of prey. The Order Falconiformes includes the vultures, hawks, eagles, osprey, and falcons. The Order Strigiformes includes the owls.

The raptors all possess sharp, curved beaks for tearing prey and powerful feet with long talons for grasping prey. The birds in these orders are renowned for their powers of flight and sight.

**Order Anseriformes.** This order, collectively known as waterfowl, includes ducks, geese, and swans. Waterfowl are excellent swimmers, with short, powerful legs and strong webbed toes. Most have relatively long necks and flattened, broad bills. Depending on the species, waterfowl feed on grass, seeds, aquatic vegetation, fish, mollusks, crustaceans, and insects.

**Order Piciformes.** This order includes the woodpeckers, among others. The woodpeckers have strong, tapering, often chisellike bills and short, stiff tail feathers used as props against the bark of trees. They pound, pry, probe, and excavate trees for insects and to build their nests.

**Order Apodiformes.** This order includes the swifts and hummingbirds. The swifts, the most aerial of birds, are capable of rapid flight for days on end. Their wings are long, pointed, and powerful, their neck short, and their tail streamlined. They feed entirely on insects or spiders caught in the air.

The hummingbirds are tiny, nectar-sipping birds of the New World. They are mainly aerial and, like the swifts, have short, weak legs and tiny feet. Hummingbirds are the most versatile of flyers; they are able to fly forward, up, down, and backward and to hover in one spot.

**Order Ciconiiformes.** This order includes the herons, storks, ibises, spoonbills, and flamingos. These birds eat fish or strain their food from the water. They have very long necks and bills as well as very long legs for wading in shallow water.

In their habitats, birds consume immense quantities of insects, rodents, and weed seeds and in turn are an important part of the food chain. The meat and eggs of birds provide around 15 percent of the total animal protein consumed by humans worldwide. Domestic poultry accounts for most of this, but significant amounts of meat and eggs of many other species also serve as food.

The decorative properties of feathers have attracted our attention for ages. Very few of the world's peoples are without some tradition of feather decoration for fashion and finery. Fortunately, the worldwide slaughter of certain birds for the use of their feathers in the millinery trade is a thing of the past, but the feathers of rare birds are sought still in some cultures. Around 1800, 80,000 Hawaiian mamos, extinct since 1899, were sacrificed to make the royal cloak worn by King Kamehameha I. Soft down feathers are used to make warm comforters, jackets, coats, and sleeping bags.

Guano, the droppings of fish-eating birds, has been recognized as the best organic fertilizer since the days of the Incas in Peru. This resource has been exploited and in most parts of the world the birds that produce it have been severely depleted.

From pigeon racing to falconry, birds have had a strong role in many traditional recreational pursuits. According to a survey by the United States Department of the Interior, watching, feeding, and attracting birds ranks second only to gardening as America's favorite pasttime. This interest is due mainly to the fact that birds are the most visible and accessible forms of wild animal life on the planet.

Biomedical research on hair cell regeneration in birds' ears may one day aid humans who are hearing impaired. The way damaged brain cells of birds behave may lead to a better understanding of our own brain.

By their visibility and because of the high esteem with which we regard them, birds aid all animal life, including humans, by serving as monitors of global environmental quality. For example, in the 1960s falcons and eagles warned us of DDT pesticide contamination. In present times, one of the best indicators we have of the level of oil pollution in the ocean is the grisly toll of bird bodies washed up on beaches.

Recent research by the International Council for Bird Preservation (ICBP) concludes that more than 1,000 bird species are threatened with extinction today. Many scientists believe the situation may be even worse than this shocking figure implies. The family with the most threatened species (more than 70) is the parrot family, Psittacidae. Birds on small oceanic islands face the greatest threat, followed closely by those in tropical rainforests. In addition, many of the world's poorer economic nations have the highest total of threatened bird species.

The factors causing the decline of birds are varied, complex, and interrelated:

1.  Habitat destruction. To cite one example, the tropical rainforests have been reduced by 44 percent of their original area, and this destruction continues with up to 20.4 million hectacres (78,700 square miles) lost each year.
2.  Introduced species. Introduced predators such as cats, rats, snakes, fish, and mongooses have been the major cause of extinction of island birds. Introduced herbivores such as rabbits and goats can be as damaging as predators with their destruction of native vegetation.
3.  Human predation. A well-known example is that of the passenger pigeon, extinct since 1914. Once they numbered in the millions, but, relentlessly pursued by armies of hunters, within 40 years they were gone. Bird hunting continues today. Some species can make up the losses, but others are seriously reduced.
4.  International trade. Prized types of rare wild birds tempt trappers and dealers with rich rewards. Parrots are the most popular, and the trade has had devastating effects on them. Spix's macaw has been illegally trapped to the last bird in the wild, and the only hope for the species lies with the 150 or so individuals held in captivity and a carefully planned captive breeding program.
5.  Pesticides and pollution. The DDT alarm of the 1960s has resulted in restricted use of chlorinated hydrocarbons, but new classes of deadly chemicals have emerged to take their place. In addition, herbicides, oil, acid rain, industrial chemicals, and nuclear contamination threaten birds and their habitats worldwide.

Woodpecker

Swift

Hummingbird

# COLLECTION OF SPECIMENS

Heron

Flamingo

Stork

# MAINTENANCE OF SPECIMENS

Collection of wild birds is not appropriate for several reasons. First, from a legal standpoint, almost all native birds (and some introduced ones) are protected by federal and state laws. It is illegal to possess them, their nests, or their eggs without special permits. Second, from an ecological and conservation standpoint, wild birds are inappropriate for the classroom. Finally, from an education and maintenance standpoint, wild birds are difficult to work with in the classroom.

A variety of birds are available through the pet trade, but most of these— canaries, finches, and parakeets—are nervous birds that are easily alarmed and do not adjust well to the hustle and bustle of the classroom. Furthermore, these birds are susceptible to crowding diseases; they require stable temperatures, especially in the winter; and they can be very noisy and distracting. Larger birds like parrots and macaws have the same drawbacks as smaller types, plus they require much more room to house and special knowledge to properly maintain. Furthermore, some birds of this type are bred in captivity, but most are netted or trapped in the wild and then sold on the open market. To purchase such birds is to sanction and support their devastating exploitation.

You might consider borrowing birds for your students to observe. I have borrowed a small parrot on occasion from a school patron who has had the bird for many years. Pet stores may lend you a bird for a small fee or free for the publicity value. To even recommend this approach makes me uneasy, however. By bringing these birds into the classroom we may giving students the unspoken and certainly unintentional impression that we condone the commerce in birds. Furthermore, I worry that something might happen to such rare, beautiful, and expensive birds while in our care.

None of the suppliers listed in Appendix B sells live birds, but some do handle fertile chicken eggs.

Some animal care authorities and books on the subject recommend ring-necked or white doves as suitable classroom birds. Doves resemble pigeons but are smaller and have a long, pointed tail. Doves adjust well and can be kept easily at normal classroom conditions of temperature, light, and humidity. They may even reproduce, lay eggs, and hatch young. Doves do not peck or bite, but they are nervous birds and should be approached slowly and handled gently. They are not noisy, but they do create a mess with their droppings (although not of the magnitude of some larger types of birds).

Doves can be purchased at pet shops and feed stores or from hobbyists who have organized local breeding associations.

I have had the most success introducing live birds for short periods in my classroom by borrowing chickens or ducks from area poultry farmers or fanciers. Domestic fowl are grown for meat and eggs in large numbers all over North America (in fact, only domestic dogs may outnumber them on this continent), and hobbyists and fanciers often raise rare and exotic breeds of these birds. I prefer to bring the exotic varieties of poultry into my classroom if possible, as they tend to be smaller and easier to work with than normal domestic fowl. The exotic types are more personable and brightly colored and thus resemble wild birds more than the varieties raised for slaughter.

A decision to keep doves in the classroom should be carefully considered, as these birds and their cage(s) require lots of room. The birds need daily maintenance and care, and the cage needs frequent cleaning. The ultimate fate of the birds must be considered as well. Doves should never be released into the wild for humane and ecological reasons. They are so tame and dependent that release would nearly guarantee their death. Furthermore, because they are not native to North America, their release would be ecologically unsound.

If, in spite of the drawbacks, you opt to keep doves in the classroom, you will need a large wire cage. You should try to achieve at least 0.6 square meters (2 square feet) of cage space per dove, and the larger the space the better. A perch or two about the diameter of a broomstick (doves have large feet) should be securely attached to the side of the cage. Cover the bottom of the cage with multiple layers of newspaper. Water should be provided with a water fountain. These watering devices can be purchased from pet shops, farm supply stores, or hatcheries.

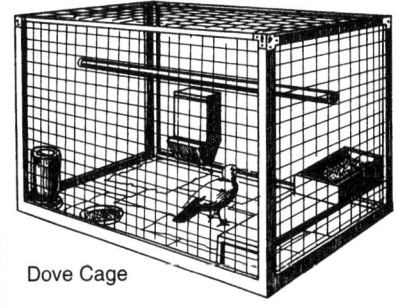

Dove Cage

Doves should be fed once each day. Dove ration in the form of pellets or mixed grain is usually available from pet shops or farm supply stores. Doves do best on a varied diet, so you may want to supplement standard rations with finely chopped vegetables and fruits, earthworms, crickets, moths, and mealworms. Doves can be messy eaters and fling food all over, so do not overfeed. Doves also need a source of calcium for egg production as well as a source of grit to aid digestion. Both of these needs can be met by providing commercial bird grit (calcium based). Grit also is available from pet or farm supply stores. Food and grit can be dispensed in a hopper or chick feeder.

Doves can be kept at usual classroom temperatures and humidity but to avoid cold drafts at night, cover the cage with a towel or sheet.

If a breeding pair is being kept, a bowl of 10 to 12.5 centimeters (4 to 5 inches) in diameter or a shallow wooden box should be provided for a nest site. This may be placed on the floor of the cage or securely attached to a shelf in the cage. Straw, fine twigs, pine needles, or dried grass should be provided for nest building.

The cage should be cleaned with a wire brush and a strong disinfectant at least twice a week, and newspaper in the bottom of the cage should be changed daily.

Domestic fowl or rare breeds of fowl may be kept in a large cardboard box for several days. To prevent possible escape, cover the box with a larger piece of ventilated cardboard held in place with a brick. Put plenty of newspaper in the bottom of the box as these birds seem to produce more wastes than the actual food they take in. Supply water with a water fountain and commercial chicken feed in a heavy, shallow dish.

Adult fowl tolerate normal classroom temperatures and humidity, but to avoid cold drafts at night, cover the box. If the fowl crow and become noisy during the day, covering the box will quiet them.

Health factors to consider are not from the hazards associated with the collecting of wild birds, as that is not recommended and may be illegal, but from handling birds, cages, feeders, waterers, and soiled paper. Few diseases and parasites are common to birds and humans and handling live birds such as doves or domestic fowl involves little health risk. As usual, practice good hygiene by thoroughly washing your hands after contact with birds, cages, water and food dispensers, and soiled paper. Keep birds away from your eyes and face, and never put feathers in your mouth.

The same basic rules of hygiene around birds apply to students as to teachers. Watch for possible allergic reactions by students, as feathers may produce violent asthmatic attacks in some individuals.

If raising doves in a long-term situation, provide adequate space, food, and water as detailed in the "Maintenance of Specimens" section of this chapter. Doves are nervous birds, so approach them slowly and grasp them gently but quickly, pinning their wings against their body. Keep dove cages away from high traffic areas of the classroom to reduce stress on the birds.

Domestic fowl and exotic breeds kept for a short period should be provided with adequate space, water, and food as detailed in the "Maintenance of Specimens" section of this chapter.

Water Fountain

HEALTH AND SAFETY
Teachers
Students
Birds

Hopper Feeder

Chick Feeder

Occasionally students may bring you an orphan bird. Explain that young birds are almost always better off in the wild than they are in a box under human care. Educate your students not to bring in what appear to be abandoned young birds. Many birds assumed to be orphans are not. Their parents are frequently nearby, deliberately apart from the young avoiding predators. Advise students that if they find a bird that has obviously fallen from a nest to replace it, as the parents cannot do so. There is no truth to the old belief that young birds handled by humans will be rejected by their parents. If they find an unaccompanied nestling on the ground and cannot spot a nest from which it may have fallen, tell them to do what they can to protect it from predators and leave it alone. If an entire nest has fallen, recommend that they put the young birds back in it and put the nest back in the tree as near to the location of the original nest site as possible.

If students bring you an injured bird, put it in a warm, dark spot and reach for the telephone. Caring for injured wildlife requires considerable training and experience. Many communities have wildlife conservation officers, humane societies, and bird clubs that know the local licensed facilities for treating injured wildlife. Do not handle or attempt to feed or water an injured bird while you are waiting for help to arrive. To do so may add enough extra stress to kill it.

Birds do not lend themselves as well to detailed hands-on classroom study as other animals, so a great deal of teaching and learning about birds should occur in the field.

Amateur ornithologists contribute a great deal of knowledge about birds. By having students make careful records, observations, and descriptions and by accumulating and adding to these each year, you and your students can establish an important and ever-increasing base of knowledge about birds. Many of the activities in this section would be suitable as independent projects for interested individuals or small groups.

## TEACHING ACTIVITIES

## Habitat

**H1.** *Designing Avian Habitats.* Give students the following imaginary scenario: Your school has received a huge sum of money to build aviaries to properly and humanely house the following types of birds: common loon, blue heron, American bittern, sandhill crane, coot, Canadian goose, mallard duck, wood duck, sandpiper, ring-billed gull, red-tailed hawk, golden eagle, great horned owl, screech owl, ring-necked pheasant, turkey, hummingbird, downy woodpecker, crow, vireo, cliff swallow, chickadee, wren, robin, warbler, red-winged blackbird, oriole, finch, and sparrow. You might want to assign groups of students to each specific type of bird or assign several types of birds to each student group. Add or delete from the list as you deem necessary. Challenge students to design a suitable habitat for their assigned bird(s). Students should consult field guides and other appropriate references. Have students make a detailed diagram of their design and present their design ideas to the rest of the class. This activity will give students a better understanding of the great variety of bird habitats.

**H2.** *Sharing Our Habitats.* Which types of birds are found in your area? Have students draw on their own experiences, field guides, and other appropriate references to determine what specific birds are found in your area. Local wildlife authorities (see Appendix C) and groups listed as Friends of Birds in activity In4c of this chapter may be able to provide lists of the birds in your area. You might assign different groups of students different categories of birds to investigate. Categories could be shorebirds and wading birds, predatory birds, ground-dwelling birds, swimming birds, and perching birds. Perching birds is a large category, so you will need several groups of students working on that one. Have students present their findings to the class in whatever manner you or they chose.

**H3.** *What Bird Is That?* Now that students have some idea about which birds are found in your area, take them bird watching to see which birds you can find and identify. Your trip could be a simple walking tour close to school or a trip to a specific habitat such as a marsh or wooded area. Local wildlife authorities and/or local birding groups could advise on the best locations and might agree to conduct such a tour for your students.

You and your students should dress apprpropriately and take along the necessary items to ensure an interesting, rewarding, and comfortable trip:

- Good-quality binoculars. Seven- and eight-power binoculars are the most popular for bird watching. They offer good magnification at reasonable cost and are light in weight. A pair of binoculars with a wide field of view can be helpful because they make finding the bird easier. Prices range from around $100 to about $400. Shop around, consult and question the experts, and then buy the best binoculars you can afford.
- Field guides with colored pictures. Good and accurate field guides are indispensable in bird watching.
- Notepad and pencil for recording observations, making diagrams, or compiling lists of birds.
- Tape recorder and blank tapes for recording bird songs and calls.
- Camera for snapping the portraits of birds you encounter.
- Insect repellent (depending on the time of year).
- Canteen or water bottle.
- Lunch or snack. Consider bringing along something appropriate to feed the birds. Many types can be lured quite close with the right tidbits.

There is more to bird-watching than merely knowing a bird's name, so here are a few tips to make your bird-watching activities more meaningful:

- Try to estimate the size of the bird compared to common reference birds like sparrows, robins, and crows. Note the shape of the bird. Is it plump or slender?
- Notice the color and markings of the bird, especially any unusual patterns and any distinct body parts such as a head crest, very long legs, or forked tail that stand out.
- Note the structure of the beak. Is it long and dagger shaped, short, stout and conical, small and pointed, or large and curved?
- How a bird flies can help identify it. Does it fly in a straight line or up and down? Is it swooping, gliding, or hovering? Note the shape of the bird's wing. Some birds have long, slender wings and others have wings that are shorter and rounder.
- Some birds have characteristic mannerisms or behaviors that help identify them.
- Occasionally you will hear or partially see birds so well hidden you can't identify them. Try luring them out with an old bird-watcher's trick called spishing. Make a *pssst* noise like a loud whispering to a friend and the hidden bird may come out in the open to investigate.

Conducting bird watching activities will give students a better understanding and appreciation of birds and provide them with a leisure activity and interest they may adopt for the rest of their lives. You might also consider taking your students to a local zoo or nature center to see the birds of your area and perhaps those of other habitats worldwide.

An interesting and beneficial extension of this activity would be for you and your students to participate in the National Audubon Society's annual Christmas count. Your local Audubon chapter could provide more details. The facts and figures gathered by amateurs and enthusiasts on

Hat to keep off sun & insects

Backpack

Long pants for wading through tall grass, shrubs and woods

Sturdy walking shoes and/or rubber boots for walking through wet areas.

these counts are important in determining current population levels of many types of birds.

**H4.    Challenge:** *How Many Birds?* Have students attempt to count the birds in a given area. Several techniques exist for censusing birds, but none is completely satisfactory. Census by direct counting is possible only in certain situations; for example, with colonial birds or birds of very restricted habitat. The simplest procedure is to use what is called a strip census, which is taken by counting and identifying all the birds in a strip of measured width through an entire area. Extrapolating the number of birds in the strip to a larger area gives an approximation of the total number of birds in the larger area. If applicable, have your students perform the following calculations to illustrate how strip censusing works.

You are counting the birds in a strip of wooded area that is 10 meters (33 feet) wide by 300 meters (990 feet) long. The entire wooded area is 600 meters (1,980 feet) wide by 300 meters (990 feet) long. How large an area does your census strip occupy? ($10 \times 300 = 3,000$ square meters or 9,900 square feet). How large an area does the entire wooded area occupy? ($600 \times 300 = 180,000$ square meters or 594,000 square feet) In your census strip you identify 7 downy woodpeckers. Approximately how many downy woodpeckers are there in the entire wooded area?

$$\frac{7 \text{ woodpeckers}}{3,000 \text{ sq. meters}} = \frac{x}{180,000 \text{ sq. meters}}$$

Cross multiply: $3,000x - 1,260,000$

To solve for $x$, divide both sides by 3,000

$x$ = approximately 420 woodpeckers

The total area surveyed and the size of strip you have your students census will be dictated by your particular circumstances. A heavily wooded area is much more difficult to census than an open, grassy area so set a reasonably sized strip to census.

Make sure students keep accurate records. When the activity has been completed, have them prepare a bar graph showing the approximate number of each type of bird in your entire survey area.

Conducting this activity in the spring, fall, and winter is a dramatic way of showing the seasonal variations in birds that occur in most areas of North America. In addition, keeping accurate records of the fluctuations of bird types and numbers in a specific area year after year would add to ornithological data.

A note of caution: Avoid field work during hunting seasons. Even people brightly attired and clearly marked have been shot by hunters who mistook them for game animals.

**H5.    *Beaks, Feet, and Food—a Comparison.*** The habitat a bird occupies determines the form, structure, and function of its parts. This is most evident in the structure and function of the beak and feet of birds.

Have students match the beaks and feet of some common birds to their habitat and the type of food eaten. Use illustrations in this chapter or your own pictures.

Have students make and fill out a chart showing and comparing different birds, beak types, foot types, habitat, and types of food.

Once their chart is complete, have students respond to the following questions: Why is it vitally important that a bird's beak and feet be perfectly matched to its habitat and food source? What would be the wrong habitat for each of the following birds: pelican, robin, hawk, and sparrow? What type of beak and feet would the following birds have?

a. a bird that runs over desert sands eating insects, reptiles, and rodents
b. an aquatic bird that dives down and snatches fish
c. a bird that perches in trees and catches insects while in flight

**H6.** *Walk a Mile in My Shoes*. Have students try to put themselves in the bird's place by having them respond orally or in written form to the question, What specific bird would you be and why?

**H7.** A *Poisonous Bird?* Yes! Share the following information with your students:

Researchers trying to capture the bird of paradise in New Guinea also trapped an orange and black jungle songbird named the pitohui as well. The sharp beaks and claws of these birds cut and scratched the researchers as they removed them from the nets. One researcher licked his wounds and felt his mouth and tongue immediately go numb. Curious, other researchers put pitohui feathers on their tongues and suffered immediate reactions of numbness, burning, and sneezing on contact with the feathers.

Feather samples analyzed by the National Institutes of Health and the Smithsonian Institution were found to contain a poison called homobatrachotoxin. The only other creature known to possess this poison is the poison-dart frog of South America—although the concentration of the poison in the frogs is about 1,000 times higher. Extracts of the skin, feathers, and muscles of the pitohui injected into mice caused the mice to convulse and die within two minutes. There are several types of pitohuis. The New Guinea pitohuis seem the most poisonous with two other types, the variable and the rusty, less so.

Now have students respond to the following questions: What is the advantage of poisonous feathers and skin? (Predators would avoid you, and if they did snap you up would probably spit you out immediately.) Is the poison of the pitohui a defensive or offensive weapon? (Defensive.) Why is this bird aptly named? (Its name is the sound an animal might make as it spits this foul-tasting bird out—pit-a-who-ee.)

**H8.** *Poles vs. Trees*. Woodpeckers are damaging power company poles in many states. Recently, Alabama Power spent more than $1 million replacing poles. To date no knows why woodpeckers prefer power poles to natural trees. As an exercise in hypothesizing and experimental design, challenge your students to design an experiment to determine why woodpeckers seem to prefer poles to trees.

**S1.** *Strange Bird Contest*. Students see birds every day and are familiar with the generic structure of birds. But how familiar are your students with the many variations? To illustrate the great variety in birds, conduct a strange bird contest. Have students work individually or in teams to discover what they consider the strangest bird on earth. Suggest that they consult appropriate references and tap local wildlife and ornithology experts. Once they have made their selections, have them present their choice and defend it before the rest of the class. Students might want to conduct an election campaign before the presentations. Once the presentations are complete, select a winner and runners-up. You can judge these yourself, but it might be more interesting and impartial to let a panel of judges composed of school staff members, wildlife authorities, and/or noted area bird watchers

## Structure

or ornithologists make the selections. Award gag gifts or some memento relating to birds to the winners.

**S2.** *Bird Structure*. Give students a diagram of the external anatomy of a bird similar to the one shown. Have students locate and, where appropriate, explain the function of the bird's parts. Live birds such as doves and/or domestic fowl would be preferable, but this activity could be conducted with stuffed birds or bird skins obtained from local museums, zoos, nature centers, or college ornithology departments.

**S3.** *Bird Observations*. Have students observe a live bird if possible and answer the questions or do the activities that follow:

a. Bird eyes
   1. Carefully examine the eyes of the bird and note their position. Determine how much of the bird's head is occupied by its eyes by first carefully measuring the width of the eyes and totalling these. Then measure the circumference of the bird's head (not counting beak) with a piece of string. Express these numbers as a fraction.

   For example, a red-tailed hawk would have the following measurements:

$$\frac{\text{eyes (2 cm each)} = 4 \text{ centimeters (1.6 inches)}}{\text{head} \qquad = 20 \text{ centimeters (8 inches)}}$$

   Now make the same measurements on a human and compare them. A human would have the following measurements:

$$\frac{\text{eyes (3 cm each)} = 6 \text{ centimeters (2.4 inches)}}{\text{head} \qquad = 56 \text{ centimeters (22 inches)}}$$

   For birds the ratio of eye to head is 1:5 and for humans nearly 1:10. Some birds have eyes that are larger than the human eye.
   2. Why do birds have such large eyes? (Sight is the main sense in birds; it takes sharp vision to fly, find food, and avoid predators.)
   3. Note the large pupils in the bird's eye. Which type of birds would have the largest pupil and why? (Owls and other night hunters have eyes that are nearly all pupil to capture all the light possible for their nocturnal activities.)
   4. Owls have wide-ranging binocular vision, but their eyes are nearly immovable in the sockets. Therefore, owls constantly turn their head from side to side, often giving the illusion of turning in a full circle. Is there any truth to the old belief that if you rapidly run around a perched owl it will wring its own neck? (No. When an owl turns its head it reaches a halfway point and quickly pivots back to the other side.)

b. Bird beaks
   1. Carefully observe and describe the beak of the bird.
   2. From your observations, is this statement true? "Beaks are modified jaws, hardened epidermis, forming a

Lesser Primary Coverts
Lesser Coverts
Primaries
Secondaries
Greater Coverts
Median Coverts
Tertials

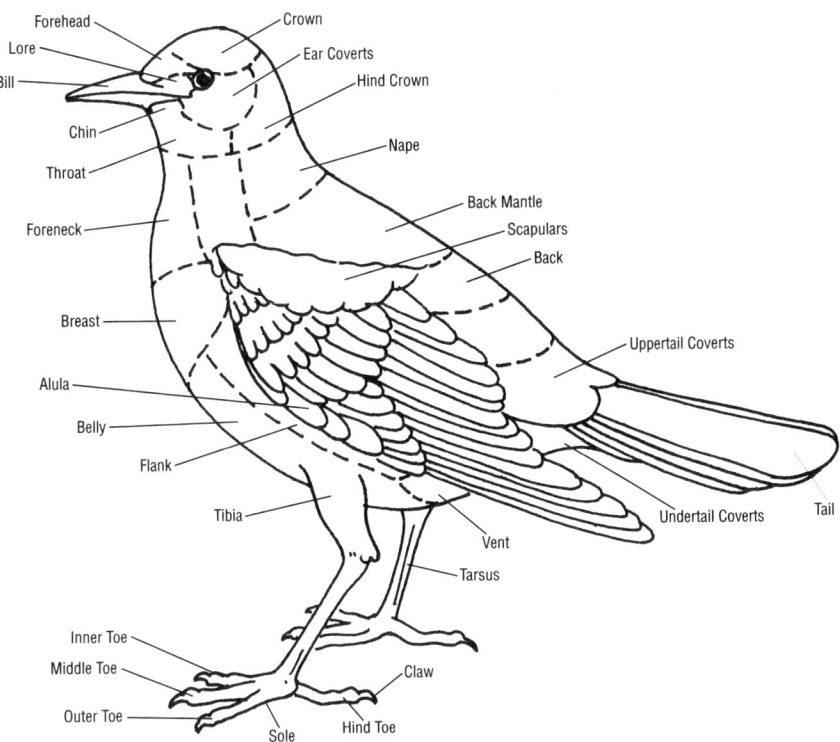

horny sheath over bony projections of the lips." (No, but if you inter-change the words *jaws* and *lips*, it will be true.)

3. Look at the various objects and tools supplied by the teacher. Explain which bird(s) would have beaks similar in function to each object or tool. (Put out a hammer, chisel, tweezers, soda straw, pruning shears, nutcracker, strainer, large fish hook, a small basket, and other appropriate objects and let students match the form of the object or tool to the function of a particular bird's beak.)

4. Is the old saying "scarce as hen's teeth" accurate? (Yes, because no birds have teeth.)

5. Discuss the advantages and disadvantages to the bird of having no teeth.

6. What are some of tasks birds must do with their beaks that we do with our hands or other animals do with their legs? (With their beaks birds pick up and manipulate objects, catch prey or get food, dress their plummage, care for their young, and defend themselves. Challenge students to do a simple task like picking up a pencil and writing their name with their "beak"—their lips and mouth.)

c. Bird legs and feet

1. Carefully observe and describe the legs and feet of a bird.

2. In what ways are the legs of a bird similar to those of a reptile? (They are covered with scales and the toes are tipped with claws.)

3. What are some of things that birds do with their feet that humans do with their hands? (A chickadee firmly grasps a seed with its feet while it hammers the seed open. A hawk grips its prey with its feet while the beak tears flesh away. Parrots, which grip branches and are quite dexterous, are "left handed" or "right handed." Herons comb their feathers and scratch themselves with a toothed comb on their second toe.) Have willing students remove their shoes and socks. Give them a simple task to perform (picking something up off the

floor and putting it on the table or scratching their ear) using only their feet and toes.

4. How can birds grasp small branches and even wires and not fall off even while sleeping on these perches? (The toes lock and curl tightly. See the illustration in the "General Class Characteristics—Muscle System, Movement, and Migration" section of this chapter.)

5. Look at pictures or diagrams of an ostrich's foot and toes. How are they different from the foot and toes of other birds and why? (Use the illustration in the "General Class Characteristics—Legs and Feet" section of this chapter. The ostrich has only two large toes adapted for running, not perching, swimming, or wading.)

6. Carefully work the legs of a live bird up and down. Does the bird's knee bend backward compared to the human knee? (The bare visible joint between the feet and the bird's body is actually its heel. The knee is the fleshy end of the "drumstick" attached to the sides of the body and covered with feathers.)

d. Bird feathers and wings

1. Using magnifiers or microscopes, observe and describe the main types of feathers. In what ways are they alike and different? (Provide students with the long, stiff flight feathers from wing or tail, smaller general body feathers from back or breast and puffy down feathers. Be advised that collecting wild bird feathers is against the law. Sources for feathers are poultry farms and butcher shops. Carolina Biological Supply and Connecticut Valley Biological, listed in Appendix B, sell prepared microscope slides of various feather types. See the illustrations of feather types in the "General Class Characteristics—Body Covering" section of this chapter.)

2. What role does each type of feather play for the bird? (Flight feathers provide lift for flying; general body feathers cover, insulate, and protect; and down feathers further insulate the bird by holding in its precious body heat.)

3. Explain bird preening in light of feather structure. (Birds preen or draw their feathers through their beak to "zip" the barbs back together and get them back in shape for flying.)

4. Which type of feather do humans use in sleeping bags, jackets, and comforters and why? (We use down feathers because their lack of a central shaft makes them fluffy. This fluffiness makes a soft stuffing and helps trap air, which also makes down a good insulator.)

5. Carefully observe the teachers's demonstration on waterproofing and answer the following questions. (Cut two 15 × 30 centimeter [6 × 12 inch] strips of cotton cloth. Apply baby oil to one piece only. Dip the

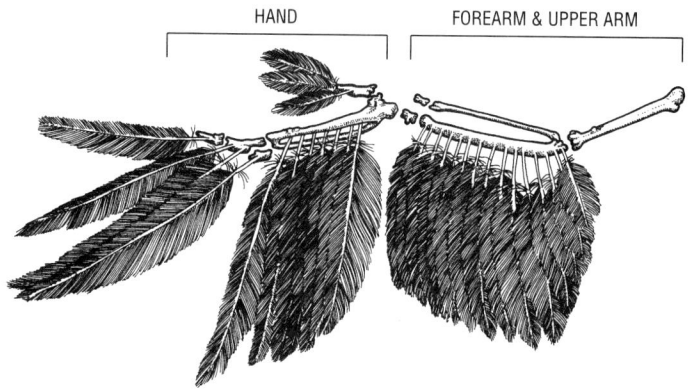

HAND          FOREARM & UPPER ARM

pieces of cloth in water and pull them out. The water will soak into the cloth without oil but run off the cloth soaked in oil.) What is the significance of this for birds? (Oily feathers keep the bird dry and hold in body heat. Penguins living on ice and swimming in icy water are so oily that they look like they have slick black and white skin rather than feathers.) Where does the oil on bird feathers come from? (The oil is produced in an oil gland on the rump near the base of the tail. Birds squeeze this gland with their beak and then wipe the oil on their feathers.)

6. Measure the wingspan of a live bird. Estimate your "wingspan" and then measure it. Was your prediction close? Mark your wingspan on a wall with masking tape. For comparison, measure out and mark on the wall beneath your own the following wingspans: eagle—2.1 meters (7 feet); Andean condor—3 meters (10 feet); albatross—3.6 meters (12 feet).

7. Carefully extend the wing of a live bird. Compare and contrast it to the human arm and hand.

8. Try out your "wings" by extending your arms and flapping away. How long can you keep up an easy pace (one flap per second) before you get tired? (As students are flapping tell them that some birds, such as the lesser golden plover, can fly for 48 hours straight, flapping the entire time.) What muscles became tired and sore on your body rather quickly? (The chest and arms.) What does this tell you about the chest and arm muscles of birds? (They have more muscles in those areas than we do and a type of muscle that does not become tired. Because we are walking creatures, our leg muscles are more fully developed than our chest and arm muscles.)

9. Look at the wingbeat chart. What rate do you think you can keep up with? Put the wingbeat chart on a large piece of paper or a chalkboard. Have younger students start with the crow and try to work up. By the time you get to starlings, it will be impossible for most kids to keep up.

10. Your friend, Boomer Bolinski, has really been "pumping iron" and has tremendously large chest and arm muscles. Boomer has also built a pair of wings out of ultralight materials and covered them with feathers. He tells you he plans to jump off a tall building and use his big muscles and light wings to fly away. What advice would you give him? (Don't try it! He will surely be killed or severely injured in the fall. And he will fall because even with the added muscle bulk, he does not have the power to overcome his own weight. A bird's entire body from the skeleton out is designed to be lightweight, but Boomer's isn't. In addition, a bird's flight muscles are powerful and do not become fatigued. Even if Boomer could manage a few flaps of his homemade wings—which he won't—his arm and chest muscles will tire and cease functioning.)

11. Wingbeat Math. Look at the wingbeat chart and calculate:
    a. How many wingbeats in one minute from:
       • a hummingbird? (4,200)
       • a chickadee? (1,620)
       • a crow? (120)
    b. Which combination would make the most flaps?
       • a hummingbird flapping for 45 seconds
       • ten crows flapping for 60 seconds

| The Wingbeat Chart | |
| --- | --- |
| *Bird* | *Wingbeat/10 seconds* |
| Crow | 20 |
| Robin | 23 |
| Pigeon | 30 |
| Starling | 45 |
| Chickadee | 270 |
| Hummingbird | 700 |

- sixteen starlings flapping for 1 minute
- a pigeon, chickadee, and robin flapping for 3 minutes
  (The pigeon, chickadee, and robin—5,814.)

  c. If a crow, a robin, a pigeon, and a starling each flew 48 kilometers per hour (30 miles per hour), how many times would each one flap if
- the crow flew 16 kilometers (10 miles)? (2,400 flaps)
- the robin flew 64 kilometers (40 miles)? (10,800 flaps)
- the pigeon flew 128 kilometers (80 miles)? (28,800 flaps)
- the starling flew 8 kilometers (5 miles)? (2,700 flaps)

e. Bird body temperature

1. Carefully hold a live bird and gently work your fingers down through the feathers so you touch the skin. Compare and contrast the bird's temperature to your temperature and to a snake's temperature. (The bird's temperature will be somewhat warmer than a human's and much warmer than a snake's temperature.)

2. Birds are endothermic. What does this mean? (They have a constant body temperature that does not fluctuate with changes in the temperature of the air or water around them.)

3. The normal range of body temperature for birds is between 38°C (100°F) and 45°C (112°F). However, body temperature in birds varies by several degrees during a 24-hour period. When birds are active, their temperature increases; when they are at rest, their temperature decreases. Look at the data table comparing the active and inactive temperatures of several common birds.

  Use the data in this table to prepare a bar graph. Use a shaded bar to represent the active temperature and an unshaded bar to represent the inactive temperature for each bird listed in the table. Once you have completed your bar graph, answer the following questions:

  a. Suggest several hypotheses to explain why birds' temperatures vary during the day. (Accept any reasonable hypothesis. High temperatures are probably a result of activity during waking hours.)

  b. If the air temperature drops, what can a bird do to compensate? (Birds can ruffle their feathers to trap even more air and further insulate the body.)

  c. If the air temperature rises, what can a bird do to compensate? (Birds flatten their feathers to reduce their insulating properties, move into shade or protected areas, and may pant to release heat.)

f. Bird bone structure

1. Examine a bird bone and a mammal bone that have been cut open to reveal their internal structure. In what ways are the bones alike and different? (As a source of bones for this activity, save the leg bones from a chicken dinner and get some cow or pig bones from a butcher shop. Use a hacksaw to cut the bones open, preferably lengthwise.)

2. How does a bird's bone structure benefit it? (By having hollow bones, the bird reduces bone weight for flying without sacrificing bone strength.)

g. Bird songs and calls

1. Listen to recordings of bird calls and songs and learn the songs of the more common species. (Carolina Biological Supply and Connecticut Valley Biological, listed in Appendix B, handle a wide variety of bird songs and calls on records, cassettes, and compact discs with some sets designed to accompany field guides. Local libraries, zoos, or college ornithology departments may also be a source for such recordings.)

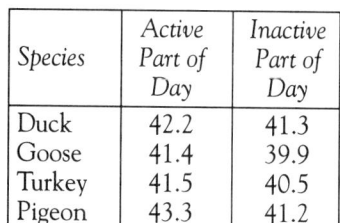

| Species | Active Part of Day | Inactive Part of Day |
|---------|--------------------|----------------------|
| Duck    | 42.2               | 41.3                 |
| Goose   | 41.4               | 39.9                 |
| Turkey  | 41.5               | 40.5                 |
| Pigeon  | 43.3               | 41.2                 |

2. If possible, go bird-listening and practice identifying birds by their songs and calls as well as by their appearance. (More variety of songs and calls can be heard in most areas in the spring when birds are mating and establishing territories.)

**S4.** **Challenge:** *Do Big Birds Bully (Dominate) Smaller Birds?* Have students devise a way to test this problem.

The idea that animal societies possess hierarchies of dominance was first supported in domestic chickens several decades ago. We now know that dominance occurs not only within species (intraspecific) but also between species (interspecific). A good time to observe dominance in birds is when they are feeding, and species coming to a feeder in the winter make excellent subjects for this investigation.

One design would be to use two large square boards of the same size as feeders. Place one on the ground and one approximately 1 meter (3.3 feet) off the ground on a post. To concentrate the effect, nail a jar lid to the center of each board and put food only in the lid on each board. More birds will frequent the feeders if they are placed close to trees and shrubbery. Have students predict what will happen before they begin. Have students note when one bird displaces another from its position at the feeders. This is known as supplanting and can be used as a measure of dominance; the supplanter is dominant and the supplanted is subordinate.

Have students prepare a chart or data table to record supplanting and the relative size of the supplanter compared to the relative size of the supplanted. In winter, feeders will be busy, so a few minutes of observation will yield much data. Have students draw conclusions based on their data.

**S5.** *Bird Models.* Have students construct a model of any bird of their choice. Students might use colored modeling clay or colored bread dough or sew models of colored cloth.

**B/R1.** *Defense Mechanisms.* Here are some of the ways birds protect themselves and their young:

- Safety in numbers. A predator has a difficult time singling one animal in a flock.
- Blending in. The color and pattern of many birds allow them to camouflage themselves by blending into the environment.
- Mobbing. A group of smaller birds attacks flying or perched predatory birds such as hawks or owls and drives them off with dives, pecks, and scolding calls. Crows, jays, and some songbirds take part in mobbing.
- Sound the alarm. Birds often use loud, sharp calls to warn each other when they spy a threat in their area. On hearing this call, most birds will scatter, freeze, or hide.
- Freezing. When birds catch sight of a predator or even its shadow, they often instantly become still. Predators often key on movement, so freezing helps hide the bird from the predator's view.
- Big and mean. Some birds try to bluff and intimidate if threatened. They ruffle their feathers to appear larger, hold out their wings, open their bill menacingly, and/or make hissing noises.
- I'm hurt. Some birds act as if they are injured, flopping and fluttering about to distract a predator and lure it away from the nest and young.

List each of the defensive behaviors on a large sheet of paper or a chalkboard. List only the name and not the description of each behavior. Divide the class into teams and secretly assign each team a

## Behavior/Response

specific behavior. No team should know what behavior any other team was assigned. Give each team a description of the particular behavior they have been assigned. Ask each team to present the appropriate actions, movements, and sounds of their behavior to the class and challenge the class to guess what bird defense behavior each team is exhibiting. Once the teams have made their presentations, challenge them to invent and present to the rest of the class new behaviors for self-defense, territorial defense, attracting a mate, or defending food. Again, see if the rest of the class can guess what bird behavior is being exhibited.

**B/R2.** **Challenge:** *Does Size Determine Individual Distance?* Have you ever noticed the measured spacing of birds on a wire? It seems as if the birds measure the interval and space themselves accordingly. Does size determine this spacing? Have students devise a way to test this problem.

Students may hypothesize that individual distance and spacing are determined by the reach of a perching bird's beak and that no other bird is permitted inside that space. Thus, the bigger the bird, the farther from its neighbors it perches or stands.

Arrange for students to observe birds perching or standing in groups. Have students record in data tables the approximate body width of the birds and the approximate distance of the birds from each other. Try to observe and record data on as many types of birds as possible. Remind students that their data is not rock solid as they are estimating body width and spacing distance. From their data tables have students prepare a line graph with body width on the horizontal axis and spacing distance on the vertical axis. If the points on the graph are arranged in a narrow band from lower left to upper right, it would seem to indicate that bigger birds do space farther apart. From their graph have students draw conclusions.

**B/R3.** *Season Determines Behavior.* Birds exhibit different behaviors at different times of the year. Have students examine the behavior calendar for a common bird, the American robin, and answer the questions that follow:

a. Your neighbor calls you on the phone and informs you that a pair of robins has laid eggs and is incubating them in a nest in a tree in your backyard. You look at the calendar and note it is October. Possible? (No. Early August marks the end of the breeding and nesting season.)

b. Your neighbor calls again and says that a baby robin has fallen from a nest in a tree in your backyard. The calendar says June. Possible? (Yes.)

c. You look out your window and see an adult robin in your backyard. The calendar says January. Possible? (Yes. Behavior calendars are approximations of the cyclic behavior of birds. The robin might be a very early migrator returning, or perhaps a mild winter has caused the robin to stay in the area and not migrate.)

Older, more advanced, or interested students could develop their own behavior calendars of selected birds.

**B/R4.** *Hypnotize a Chicken.* In Chapter 9 instructions were given for hypnotizing a frog. The same thing works for chickens. If you have access to a live chicken, hypnotize it by drawing a white chalk line down the middle of a black piece of paper. Gently grasp the chicken and push its head down until the beak rests on the white line. Hold the chicken firmly in this position for several minutes and then very slowly release your grip on the chicken. I have seen chickens stand, beak down on the line, motionless for many minutes before eventually toppling over in a stupor. As with frogs, the chicken's nervous system goes into a state where muscle movement seems to be inhib-

**BEHAVIOR CALENDAR**

| | TERRITORY | COURTSHIP | NEST-BUILDING | BREEDING | PLUMAGE (MOLTS) | SEASONAL MOVEMENT | SOCIAL BEHAVIOR |
|------|---|---|---|---|---|---|---|
| JAN | | | | | | | ■ |
| FEB | | | | | | | ■ |
| MAR | | | | | | ■ | ■ |
| APRIL | ■ | | ■ | ■ | | ■ | |
| MAY | ■ | | ■ | ■ | | | |
| JUNE | ■ | | ■ | ■ | | | |
| JULY | ■ | | | ■ | ■ | | |
| AUG | | | | | ■ | | |
| SEPT | | | | | ■ | | ■ |
| OCT | | | | | | ■ | ■ |
| NOV | | | | | | ■ | ■ |
| DEC | | | | | | | ■ |

ited. Chickens can be awakened by removing them from the paper and gently shaking them. Their recovery is usually immediate. Note: Convey to students that such behavior does not reflect stupidity on the part of the animal affected. You do not want to foster an attitude that could lead to cruelty. Many types of animals, including humans, can be hypnotized.

**B/R5.** *Building Nests: Learned or Instinctive Behavior?* One of the most remarkable bird behaviors is nest building. Share the following information with students and then have them respond to the question that follows:

- Birds of the same species build nests that look exactly alike generation after generation.
- Four generations of weaver birds were reared completely isolated from nesting materials. The fifth generation had access to nesting materials and wove perfect examples of their species' elaborate nests.
- Introducing eggs and young into an unfinished nest does not interrupt the normal course of nest building activity.
- When surplus moss was placed in front of the nest burrows of Wilson's petrels, they carried so much inside that they left hardly any room for themselves.

Based on this information, does it seem that birds must learn to build their nests or is it an instinctive behavior? (Nest building is primarily an instinctive behavior, but experimentation and observation have shown that birds are very adaptable and not totally slaves to instinct in this behavior.)

**B/R6.** **Challenge:** *Can Birds Hear?* Ask students if birds can hear. Most will answer that they can, and some sharp student undoubtedly will note that they wouldn't make such a wide variety of songs and calls if they couldn't hear them. Tell the students you don't believe it because you can't see any ears on birds. (Birds do have ears but the external ear holes are covered with feathers.) Challenge them to prove that birds can hear.

Use a live bird as a subject, students might suggest making a loud noise such as blowing a whistle and noting how the bird reacts. Others might suggest playing recordings of bird songs and calls and seeing how the bird reacts. If using this approach, make sure the students can see the bird and note its reactions but the bird cannot see and thus react to the presence of the students or their movements. Have students predict what they think will happen before they begin. Data collected will be mainly observational. Have students attempt to draw conclusions from their observations.

**B/R7.** *Migration Maniacs.* Migration has been studied perhaps more than any other aspect of bird behavior. For over 100 years humans have studied bird movements with every tool from eyes to satellites. Yet we cannot today state with assurance why birds migrate, how they navigate, or how such behavior originated.

Share the information on migration in the "General Class Characteristics—Muscle System, Movement, and Migration" section of this chapter. Divide the class into pairs. Assign each team a place in school or, weather permitting, on school grounds and challenge them to migrate to that spot and back to your classroom. No problem, right? Wrong! They must do it blindfolded. Allow students to walk their "flyway" to their target site and back home (classroom) once without blindfolds. Encourage them to make measurements and observations that will aid them in navigating when blindfolded.

Once the teams have scouted their "flyways," securely blindfold one team member of each team. The other team member may walk with the blindfolded person but cannot touch or speak to the blindfolded person except to prevent possible harm or injury. Once they reach the target site, the team members should reverse roles and head back home (classroom). Time the round trip for each team and declare those with the shortest migration time as Migration Maniacs. Gag prizes or small bird mementos would be a great way to climax this activity.

This activity will give students a better appreciation of the ability that some birds have to navigate very long distances often in bad weather and at night. When the activity as been completed, have students respond to the following questions:

a. Some birds migrate by day and some by night. Discuss the advantages and disadvantages of each strategy.

b. Some birds migrate in compact flocks and some in V formations, and others go it alone. Discuss the advantages and disadvantages of each strategy.

c. Name five birds native to your area that migrate.

d. Name two birds native to your area that do not migrate.

## Feeding

**F1.** *Feeding a Bird.* Have students observe and describe, if possible, a live bird eating and drinking. (Domestic chickens usually cooperate well, but to ensure success try withholding food and water overnight before the day you want to watch them feed and drink.)

**F2.** *What's on the Menu?* An interesting way of determining the diet of a bird is through the use of owl pellets. Owls eat rodents or other birds whole and later cough up their fur, feathers, and bones in a compact pellet. You or knowledgeable students may be able to collect some of these pellets from around trees frequented by owls in your area. The suppliers listed in Appendix B sell owl pellets and owl pellet study kits.

Small pellets can be dissected dry, but large ones should be soaked for an hour or so in a dish of warm water. Put the pellets on paper towels. Gently separate the hard bones and teeth from the soft fur or feathers using tweezers or dissecting needles. Use field guides of birds and mammals to identify what the owl ate.

Soaking Owl Pellets

**F3.** *Fill My Bill.* Put a few raisins on a paper towel for each member of your class and then challenge them to eat the raisins using only their mouth and lips. Use this to lead into an activity on matching beak type to food eaten.

List the following birds on a large piece of paper or a chalkboard: warblers, toucans, nighthawks, swallows, pelicans, cardinals, sparrows, ducks, hummingbirds, curlews, and snipes. Have students consult field guides for pictures of each type of bird on the list.

Set up eight stations each with a special food and an array of tools, one of which represents the type of beak that eats that food and two that don't fit.

Station 1:   Food—whole nuts representing seeds with hard coverings

Beaks—nutcracker or pliers, tongs, and chopsticks

(Correct beak: nutcracker or pliers. Examples: sparrows and cardinals)

Station 2:   Food—small pieces of wood floating in a pan of water to represent fish or other aquatic animals

Beaks—straw, chopsticks, and scoop or slotted spoon

(Correct beak: scoop or slotted spoon. Example: pelicans)

Station 3:   Food—small fruits like grapes hanging from a string to represent fruit hanging from a branch

Beaks—straw, tongs, and strainer

(Correct beak: tongs. Example: toucans)

Station 4:   Food—water in the bottom of a very tall vase representing nectar in a flower

Beaks—small fish net, straw, and scoop or slotted spoon

(Correct beak: straw. Example: hummingbirds)

Station 5:   Food: cooked macaroni on a piece of bark representing insects and grubs

Beaks—straw, nutcracker or pliers, and tweezeers

(Correct beak: tweezers. Example: warblers)

Station 6:   Food—small marshmallows tossed in the air to represent insects caught when flying

Beaks—small fish net, tweezers, and straw

(Correct beak: fish net. Examples: nighthawks and swallows)

Station 7:   Food—puffed rice floating on the water in a pan to represent tiny water plants and animals

Beaks—chopsticks, strainer, and nutcracker or pliers

(Correct beak: strainer. Example: ducks)

Station 8:   Food—rubber or candy worms buried under dry oatmeal to represent worms buried in mud

Beaks—scoop or slotted spoon, chopsticks, and straw

(Correct beak: chopsticks. Examples: curlews and snipes)

Have students move from station to station deciding which type of beak should be used to eat the food at each station. Ask them to match the birds from the list to the appropriate type of beak at each station.

**F4.** *Who Gets Which Meal?* Give students the following imaginary scenario: You are the assistant curator in a large aviary. Your boss has left on vacation and told you to feed the birds while she is gone. She gave you several diets but forgot to tell you which diet goes with which bird. The birds to be fed are hawks, hummingbirds, chickens, and robins. Match the diets with the correct birds.

Diet A:   raw ground meat, oystershell flour, powdered skim milk iodized salt, mineral mixture, and A-D feeding oil.

Diet B:   honey, sweetened condensed milk, vitamins, and almond oil.

Diet C:   minced cooked meat, ground carrots, and ground hard-boiled eggs with shell.

Diet D:   ground milo, ground corn, ground whole wheat, ground barley, ground oats, soybean meal, alfalfa meal, and vitamins.

(Diet A: hawk; Diet B: hummingbird; Diet C: robin; Diet D: chicken)

**F5.** *So Many Birds, So Little Space.* Give students the following imaginary scenario: You are attending a lecture by the famous bird expert, Dr. Bob White. After the lecture you approach Dr. White with a question that has been puzzling you for a long time. You ask, "How can so many birds be packed into such small areas yet all find sufficient food?" Being in a hurry,

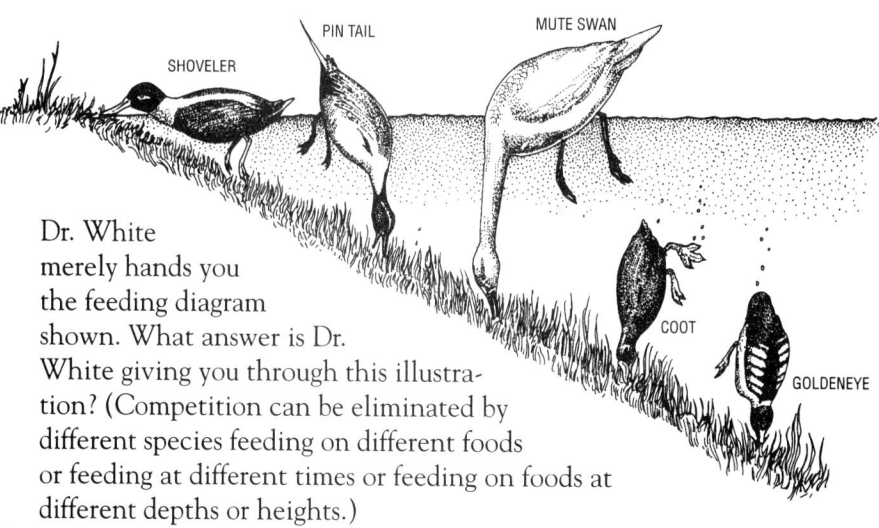

Dr. White merely hands you the feeding diagram shown. What answer is Dr. White giving you through this illustration? (Competition can be eliminated by different species feeding on different foods or feeding at different times or feeding on foods at different depths or heights.)

**F6.** **Challenge:** *How Do Robins Search for Food?* On an early evening in April after a gentle rain, robins are everywhere, engaging in a tug-of-war with their favorite food, earthworms. After eating a worm, what does the robin do next? Worms are not scattered about at random due to various factors. How do robins search for worms?

Give students the hypothesis that robins search more carefully in an area when they find a worm than when they don't. Have students observe robins feeding, positioning them so they can observe without disturbing the robins. If enough robins are available, have each student focus on a separate bird.

Have students pay careful attention to the robin's movements after it successfully captures a worm. They will notice that the robin makes a short run before trying to capture another worm. Have students estimate and diagram the lengths of these runs using the robin—about 21 centimeters (8.2 inches) long—to estimate distance (see example diagrams).

Initially, have students record only the length of the first run after a stop when a worm has been caught and the length of the first run after an unsuccessful stop. Try to obtain a large amount of data for both categories—worms and no worms.

When observations are complete, average each column. If the average length is smaller after a successful stop, the hypothesis may be correct. Older, more advanced, or interested students could extend this study to include angles as well as run lengths after successful and unsuccessful stops or investigate the effect of the size of the worm on the next run length and angle.

## Reproduction and Development

**R1.** *Which Gender?* Explain to students that birds are examples of animals that exhibit dimorphism. That is, the sexes usually differ markedly in appearance. Show students colored pictures of brightly colored male and drab-colored female birds but do not tell them which are males and which are females. Field guide pictures will suffice if necessary. Have students predict which ones pictured are males and which are females. Then ask this question: What function might dimorphism have in birds? (It plays a role in courtship and warns other males away from previously occupied territory. Not all birds are dimorphic, and of the many that are, the male's bright feathers molt to drabber ones after the breeding season.)

**R2.** **Challenge:** *Design a Courtship Ritual.* Courtship rituals in birds help establish a bond between them to ensure successful fertilization, nest-building, and rearing of young. Courtship rituals range from simple to elaborate.

Divide the class into small groups and challenge each group to develop its own bird courtship ritual. The ritual should include appropriate sounds and movements. Students can simulate feather displays by male birds using pieces of colored paper sacks or colored cardboard pieces. Warn them that no actual mating will take place. Have each group present its courtship ritual to the rest of the class.

**R3.** *My Nest, My Home.* Divide your class into teams of two each (nesting pairs). Let each pair select a nest site somewhere on school grounds or inside if weather demands. Present the class with nesting material—sticks of various sizes, newspapers, rags, and assorted pieces of cardboard or styrofoam. Challenge the pairs to construct a nest from the materials provided at the site of their choice. This activity allows students to model nest-building and will give them an appreciation of the difficulties involved in building a nest. You might make this activity even more challenging by requiring the students to use only their feet, legs, and arms. Do not allow them to use their hands and, for health reasons, the nesting materials should not be put in the mouth.

**R4.** **Challenge:** *Do Members of the Same Species Build Their Nests at the Same Approximate Height?* Assign teams of students certain types of birds to investigate. For example, one team might look for downy woodpeckers, another group robins, and so on. This activity should be done in the spring when nest types can be identified by the types of birds on the nests. It can be quite challenging as birds' nests are difficult to see in trees and shrubs that are covered by leaves.

Students should estimate the height of a nest using their own height as a guide. Students should never climb trees to take measurements. This action could result in serious injury and may cause a nesting bird to abandon the nest.

**R5.** *Read All About It!* Have students react to the following imaginary headline in a supermarket tabloid paper: "Poultry Farmer Has Hen That Gives Birth To Live Chicks!!" (All birds lay eggs. Not one type, including chickens, has been discovered that doesn't.)

**R6.** *How Many Eggs?* Have students examine the table of clutch size and incubation time and answer the following questions:

a. Does there seem to be a connection between the size of the bird and the number of eggs laid? (No. Hereditary patterns and environmental conditions play a bigger role than does the size of the bird.)

b. Does there seem to be a connection between the size of the bird and the length of the incubation period? (Yes. In very general terms, larger birds tend to have longer incubation times.)

**R7.** *Timing Is Everything.* Share the following information with students: Cowbirds and cuckoos often remove the eggs from the nests of other birds and then lay their own eggs in those nests. The cowbirds or cuckoos leave and let the foster parent birds incubate their own eggs, if any remain, and the cowbird and cuckoo eggs. The cowbird or cuckoo eggs hatch earlier than the eggs of the other birds, and the hatchlings are larger and more powerful and often push other eggs or hatchlings out of the nest. Have students respond to the following questions:

a. Can this behavior be considered a form of parasitism? (Yes. Ornithologists refer to it as brood parasitism.)

b. How is this an advantage to adult cowbirds or cuckoos? (They are relieved of the time and energy cost involved in nest-building, incubation, and rearing of young.)

## CLUTCH SIZE AND INCUBATION

| Species | Clutch size (range) | Incubation (days) |
|---|---|---|
| Canada Goose | 4–7 | 25 |
| Mallard | 8–15 | 25–30 |
| Killdeer | 3–5 | 25–28 |
| California gull | 3–5 | 25–29 |
| California condor | 1 | 45–50 |
| Bald eagle | 1–3 | 35 |
| Red-tailed hawk | 1–3 | 30–35 |
| American kestrel | 4–7 | 30 |
| Northern bobwhite | 5–28 | 22 |
| Mourning dove | 2 | 14 |
| Great horned owl | 1–4 | 31 |
| Black-chinned hummingbird | 2 | 14 |
| Barn swallow | 3–7 | 15 |
| Eastern bluebird | 4–6 | 12–14 |
| American robin | 3–8 | 12–14 |
| Red-eyed vireo | 4 | 12–14 |
| Yellow warbler | 4–5 | 11–12 |
| Common yellowthroat | 4 | 11–12 |
| Northern cardinal | 2–5 | 12–14 |
| Song sparrow | 3–4 | 12–14 |

Foster Parent Feeding Young Cuckoo

c. What advantages do the young of the cowbird and cuckoo have over their nest mates? (They hatch sooner and are strong enough to push out all other hatchlings and eggs.)

d. Don't the other birds realize what is going on? (They don't seem to. Even after a young cowbird or cuckoo is nearly full grown, the duped foster parents still instinctively shove food down its gaping mouth. However, when a yellow warbler finds a cowbird egg in its nest, it covers all the eggs with a new nest and starts again. As many as five yellow warbler nests containing cowbird eggs have been found stacked one on top the other.)

**R8.** *Egg Development.* Mix up diagrams of embryonic development in chicken eggs and have students put them in their proper order.

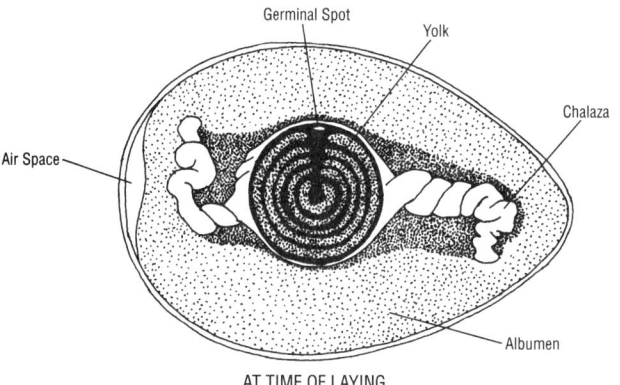

AT TIME OF LAYING

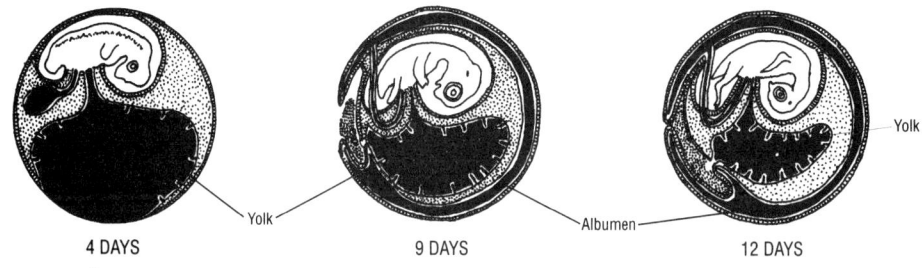

4 DAYS          9 DAYS          12 DAYS

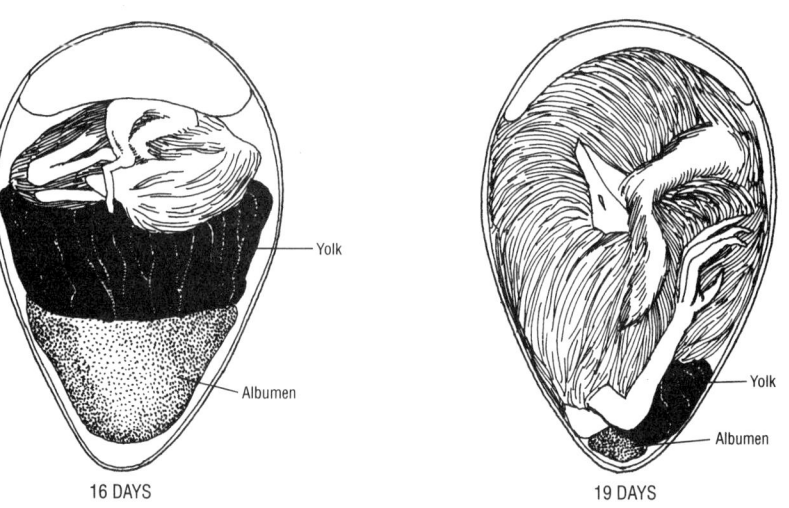

16 DAYS          19 DAYS

Carolina Biological Supply and Connecticut Valley Biological, listed in Appendix B, sell prepared microscope slides detailing the development of bird embryos through various stages.

Hatching eggs in the classroom can be an interesting learning experience. To do so you will need

- fertile eggs. Hatcheries, game farms and the suppliers listed in Appendix B are possible sources. These sources can also provide details on caring for the eggs during incubation.
- a reliable incubator. Eggs will not hatch unless kept at the proper temperature. Beware of trying to cobble up some type of heating apparatus. You don't want to fry the eggs and you may create a fire hazard.
- a way of disposing of the young birds (if any hatch). Poultry farmers and game farms may take your hatchlings, but you should have an outlet for hatched birds before you ever start a project like this.

**R9.** *Active or Helpless? Hatchling Development.* If possible, show your students pictures of both types of young birds—altrical (born blind, naked, and helpless) and precocial (born bright-eyed, covered with down, and able to run and peck for food). Have students speculate where each type would be found, in nests high in the trees or on the ground. If photos for comparison are not available, paint a mental image for your students by describing each type of young bird. See the "General Class Characteristics—Reproduction and Development" section of this chapter. Concerning hatchlings, pose the following questions to your students:

a. In what ways is precocial development of the young an important survival tactic for ground-dwelling birds? (Living on the ground exposes young birds to practically all predators. Being able to flee and hide soon after hatching is the only hope for survival. Because the chicks can move about and feed themselves, they and their parents are not as exposed to predators as they would be if tied to a single nest site for an extended period.)

b. What are the advantages and disadvantages of both altrical and precocial development?

**In1.** *Writing:*

a. Challenge students to learn more about birds by having them do a formal library report on a specific bird of their choice.

b. Bird expressions abound in our language. Have students determine the accuracy or inaccuracy of the following phrases:

"like water off a duck's back" (accurate)

"eagle-eyed" (accurate)

"wise as an owl" (not accurate)

"birds of a feather flock together" (accurate most of the time)

"eats like a bird" (not accurate in the sense of not eating much because birds consume up to 20 percent of their body weight a day in food)

"happy as a lark" (not accurate)

"crazy as a loon" (not accurate)

Now challenge students to write their own bird expressions or phrases, accurate and inaccurate. Students could present their expressions to the rest of the class and have classmates determine which are accurate and which are not.

c. Have students describe the life and times of a bird as seen through the eyes of the bird.

**In2.** *Fine Arts:*

a. Have students compose a song, limerick, or poem about any aspect of a bird's existence. For example, there is a verse that describes the pelican as a bird whose bill can hold more than its "belican."

Integration with Other Subject Areas

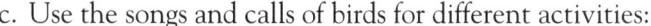

b. Have students paste colored pictures of birds onto heavy paper or thin cardboard and cut around the pictures. Attach the pictures with string to a coat hanger or other wire frame. A silhouette mobile could be a useful bird identification tool.

c. Use the songs and calls of birds for different activities:

1. Have teams of students invent their own songs and calls for the following situations: attracting mates, defending territory, warning of danger, and directing young birds to food or water. Have students present their compositions to the rest of the class and challenge the other students to determine what category of song or call is being presented. Encourage students to incorporate any musical instruments they play along with their own voices in their songs and calls.

2. Hold a contest to see who is the best bird imitator. Play a song or call from a bird recording and have several students try to imitate it. The rest of the class can vote on who did the best job. Pick another song or call, select several new students, and repeat the contest. Make sure everyone who wants to participate gets the chance to "sing like a bird." This would be an appropriate place for older, more advanced, or interested students to investigate why some birds copy the songs and calls of other birds (mimicry).

**In3.** *Social Studies:*

a. *History.* Birds as symbols abound throughout history. For example, the United States is symbolized by the bald eagle and Chile by the Andean condor.

1. Assign individual students or teams specific countries or businesses and have them develop a bird symbol appropriate to that country or business. Have students develop their symbols on posters and present them to the rest of the class.

2. Have each student develop a family coat of arms that features a bird symbol. Ask them to explain their choice of bird(s) and its meaning as a symbol on their coat of arms.

b. *Geography.* Have student research the distribution and migration patterns of birds.

1. Challenge individual students or teams to investigate the distribution of selected birds or types of birds in North America or worldwide. Have students consult appropriate references and field guides. Students could present their findings on posters containing colored pictures of the bird or bird group they investigated along with colored or shaded maps to show its distribution.

2. Challenge individual students or teams to investigate the migratory patterns of selected birds—if possible, birds that migrate through your area. Have students consult appropriate references and field guides. Students could present their findings on posters containing pictures and information about the bird along with colored or shaded maps showing the migration routes of the bird.

3. Assign teams of students to study specific birds that migrate long distances. Challenge each team to prepare a flight plan for its bird. Have them trace on a blank map the route the bird will follow and label all countries, bodies of water, or other natural features the bird will fly over on its journey.

**In4.** *Societal/Environmental Issues:*

a. Use activity In4b in Chapter 10 as a model for a role-playing activity involving birds. Establishing the controversy and patterning the roles to

Homemade Hummingbird Feeders

fit situations in your own area or community will make the activity more realistic and meaningful to your students.

b. Ask students to imagine that a mysterious virus has spread rapidly worldwide, wiping out every single bird on the planet but not harming any other form of animal life. Challenge students to describe what the world would be like without birds.

c. More than 100 species of birds have become extinct in historical times. The list of endangered birds in the United States, Hawaii, and Canada alone should be enough to alarm and anger anyone. Many scientists believe that even common songbirds are showing alarming rates of decline. Among the causes of these declines (discussed in "The Importance of Birds" section of this chapter), the most immediate problem seems to be habitat destruction.

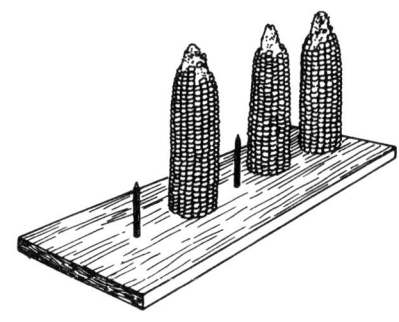

Challenge yourself and your students to do what you can to help the birds of your area. Consider the following actions you could take:

1. Join a group concerned about birds and the conservation of their habitats (see the Friends of Birds list, page 214). With your membership fees these groups purchase and preserve habitat, conduct research, develop educational materials and programs, and attempt to influence and instruct governments at all levels worldwide in developing policies and laws that are ecologically sound.

   My students have had an ongoing membership in several of these organizations for over twenty years. Each fall students voluntarily each contribute less than the cost of a candy bar and a soda pop to renew our commitment. Your students might prefer to raise the money with a bake sale or car wash or some other creative fundraising activity. If your fund raiser is well planned and advertised, you might make enough to pay for one or more memberships and to make a donation to the group(s) of your choice.

   However you go about it, joining these groups will give students a feeling of satisfaction that their time, efforts, and money are helping the planet and the living things on it and foster the attitude that individuals can make a difference.

2. Become involved in local, state, or national issues that affect not only birds but conservation in general. As students write their congressional representatives or address their local city council on issues of concern, they learn how government works.

3. Establish your own bird sanctuary. This could be as simple as hanging a feeder on a tree outside your window or as elaborate as developing an area that has been planted with bird-attracting plants and that provides food, water, and shelter. Your sanctuary could be established on school grounds (even sterile fenced and paved school grounds have a secure corner somewhere that could be a haven for a single bird), in the back yard of a sympathetic and supportive school patron, or in a city park.

   A Variety of Homemade
   Bird Feeders

   When planning a bird sanctuary you must provide for the needs of the birds:

   • Water. Make your own bird waterers and baths or purchase some of the many commercial models that are available.

   • Food. Make your own bird feeders or purchase some of the many commercial models that are available. Not all birds are seed eaters. Insect-eating birds need to be supplied with suet or other animal fat.

# Friends of Birds

American Birding Association
Box 6599
Colorado Springs, CO 80934

American Ornithological Union
National Museum of Natural History
Smithsonian Institution
Washington, D.C. 20560

Ducks Unlimited
One Waterfowl Way
Long Grove, IL 60047

National Wildlife Federation
1412 19th Street, N.W.
Washington, D.C. 20036

National Audubon Society
950 Third Avenue
New York, NY 10022

Sierra Club
730 Polk Street
San Francisco, CA 94109

The Nature Conservancy
1800 North Kent Street
Arlington, VA 22209

World Wildlife Fund
The Conservation Foundation
1255 23rd Street, N.W. Suite 200
Washington, D.C. 20037

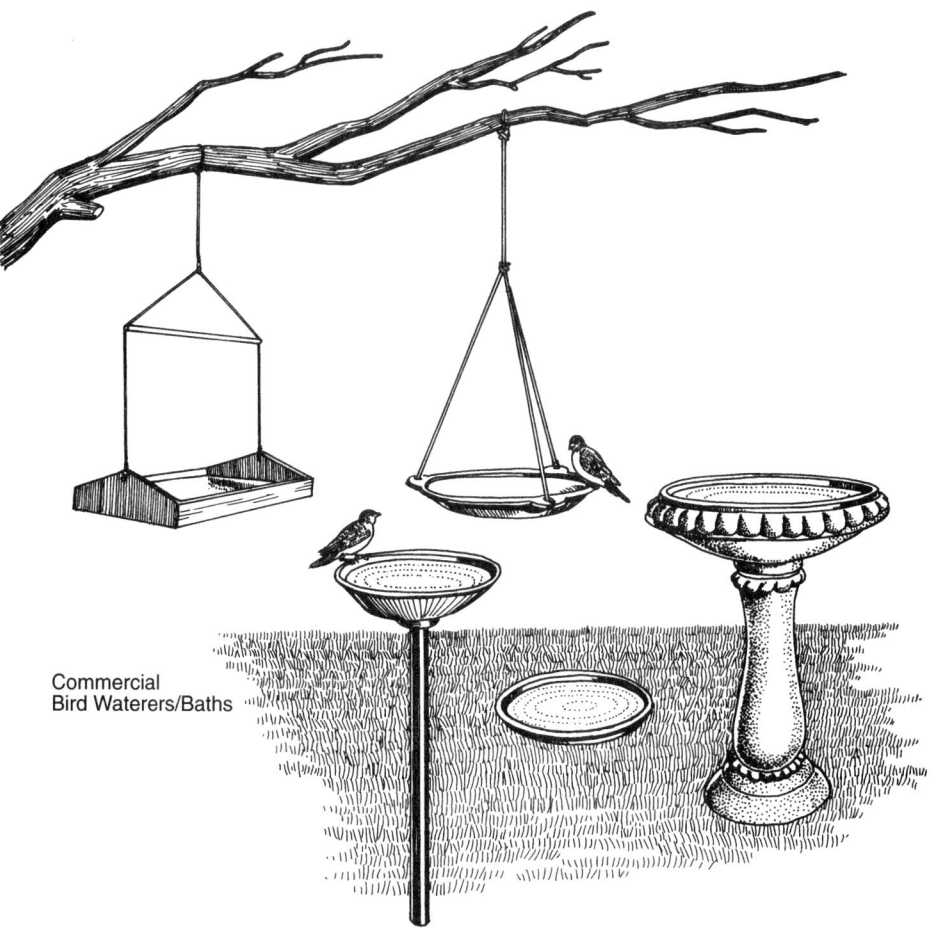

Commercial
Bird Waterers/Baths

Homemade Bird Waterers/Baths

- Nest boxes.    You could make your own or purchase a wide variety of commercial models. If you choose to construct your own, I suggest that you purchase a book showing plans for constructing many types of bird houses. The dimensions of the house and size of the entrance hole are critical for many species.
- Shelter.    An area that combines trees, shrubs, flowers, and grasses with food and water is especially attractive to birds.

The National Wildlife Federation sponsors the Backyard Wildlife Program designed for all backyard bird-watchers, including those with even the smallest backyards. Applicants who agree to provide certain minimums of food, water, and shelter receive a Backyard Wildlife Registration Certificate, an annual newsletter, and a list of publications on a variety of subjects. For further information write: Backyard Wildlife Habitat Program, National Wildlife Federation, 1412 Sixteenth Street, N.W., Washington, DC 20036.

Many books, pamphlets, and videotapes on attracting birds; watering and feeding birds; and building bird houses, feeders, and waterers are on the market. They are available at libraries, book stores, pet shops, hardware stores, discount centers, and specialty shops. Contact your local 4-H chapter, extension service, wildlife authorities, and local chapters of the Friends of Birds groups for further information and guidance.

There should be no animals to release at the end of your activities with birds. Domestic fowl or doves should not be put into the wild, and live wild birds should not have been collected in the first place.

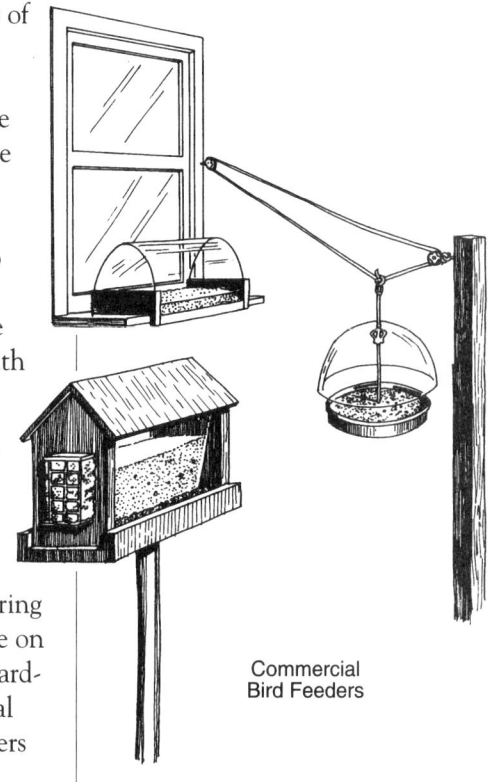

Commercial
Bird Feeders

# RELEASE OF SPECIMENS

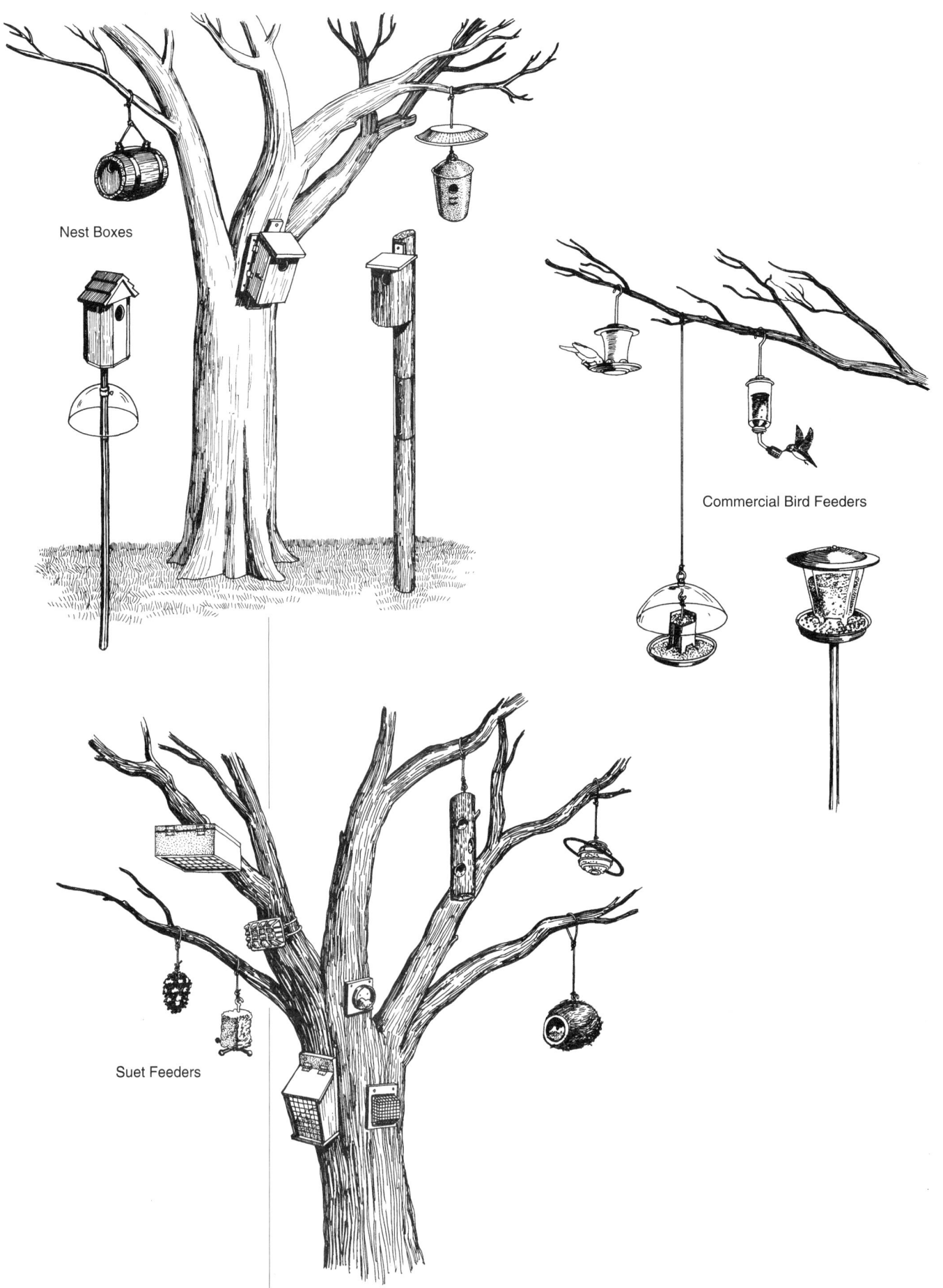

Nest Boxes

Commercial Bird Feeders

Suet Feeders

# 12. MAMMALS

| | |
|---|---|
| **Kingdom:** | Animalia |
| **Subkingdom:** | Metazoa |
| **Phylum:** | Chordata |
| **Subphylum:** | Vertebrata |
| **Class:** | Mammalia (mammals) |
| **Orders:** | 21 orders |

## CLASSIFICATION

## DIVERSITY AND DISTRIBUTION

Humans have developed no closer relationships or bonds of dependence with any other animal group than we have with the approximately 4,070 species of mammals. We even share the physicality of our bodies as humans are, biologically speaking, mammalian in form and structure.

In spite of the many ways our lives are intertwined with and affected by mammals, we do not seem to hold them in very high esteem. Mammals are judged for their usefulness and utility; valued more for what they can do and provide for humans than for what they are. This attitude is unfortunate because the fate of many endangered species may depend on an awakening of greater public interest in and concern for mammals.

Mammals have changed and adapted their basic body plan to an astonishing array of sizes, shapes, and appearances. The smallest mammal in the world is the recently discovered Kitti's hog-nosed bat, which weighs just 1.5 grams (0.05 ounces). The largest, the blue whale, weighs 117 metric tons (130 tons) and may reach 30 meters (100 feet) in length. In form mammals range from the flittering winged bat to the prowling lion, from the long-snouted anteater to the sleek porpoise, and from the hooting howler monkey to the industrious beaver.

By cleverness of adaptation and efficiency of endothermy, mammals have come to dominate nearly all ecosystems on land and in water. They are found from polar ice to steamy tropical jungle. They swim and dive on and under the waters of ocean, lake, and pond. Some burrow ceaselessly into the soil. They stroll, gallop, or scurry across deserts and grasslands and through forests. Some sail through the skies and others swing from tree to tree. In spite of their dominance, mammals constitute a very small class numerically compared to other animal groups. If the total number of species for all major animal groups are compared, the mammals are second from the bottom (above amphibians).

**Digestive System and Feeding.** In the broadest terms, mammals can be classified based on their food intake into three groups: strictly herbivorous, eating only plant material; strictly carnivorous, eating only flesh; and omnivorous, eating both plant and animal food. More specifically, however, the feeding habits and

## General Class Characteristics

exact diets of mammals are an interplay between age, season, health, and environmental conditions and circumstances. Hunger brings necessity, and few mammals are so specialized for one diet that they cannot make do in an emergency with food they normally would not accept.

Most mammals are herbivores, or vegetarians. The plants they eat vary according to the adaptations of their anatomy, especially their teeth, and the availability of plants. Grass, shoots, and leaves are commonly utilized, but some mammals dine on nectar, fruits, bark, fungi, nuts, and seeds. The Egyptian gerbil and the kangaroo rats of the southwestern United States can subsist on seeds as a source of food and water. Drinking very little if any water, these animals prosper on dry seeds with less than 10 percent water content.

In a green world such as ours, a vegetarian existence might seem to be an easy life-style. However, plant-eating mammals must contend with the cellulose armor encasing plant cells and battle a devilish array of spikes, thorns, and poisons that plants use to protect themselves. To counter these problems, herbivorous mammals usually have long intestines and pouched stomachs to provide extended exposure to the rich flora of microorganisms in the gut necessary to fully digest tough plant material. The ruminants, or cud-chewing mammals, such as the cow, grind their food with broad, flat teeth, swallow it, and then later bring the food back up from the stomach for further rechewing. Rabbits chew and eat some of their own fecal pellets, passing them through the body for a second round of digestion. The largest group of vegetarian mammals are the rodents, followed by the ungulates, or the hoofed mammals.

Carnivores must work much harder for food than herbivores—green plants at least are stationary. Great demands are made on the wits, stealth, and precision of carnivores if they are to survive.

The largest groups of carnivores are the cats, such as the lion, tiger, cheetah, and jaguar, and the dogs, such as the coyote, jackal, fox, and wolf. Also included in the order Carnivora are the bears, raccoons, and weasels. Carnivores hunt singly, in pairs, or in packs and depend on speed, cunning, and strength to bring down prey and sharp claws and teeth to tear it into chunks for swallowing.

There are many forms of carnivorous mammals that do not belong in the carnivore order. Seals and sea lions are voracious eaters of fish, squid, and crustaceans. Like seals and sea lions, otters are great fish eaters, and their bodies are similarly streamlined. The toothed whales, such as the dolphins, porpoises, and sperm whales, prowl the depths feeding mainly on fish and squid. Some bats snap insects from the air, and others skim fish from the surface of the water. The vampire bats cut the skin of sleeping animals and lap up the oozing blood. The strange-looking anteater uses its long sticky tongue to snare ants and termites, and the shrew eats its own weight in insects and earthworms every 24 hours. Some shrews are the only type of poisonous mammals. The poison in their saliva can paralyze a small animal in seconds.

The greatest survival asset of the omnivorous mammals is their ability to eat a wide variety of food. Bears eat berries, honey, fish, grubs, insects, frogs, and small mammals. Foxes, coyotes, opossums, raccoons, and humans are accomplished omnivores. The most outstanding omnivore is the brown rat, which will eat practically anything, including its own kind.

**Circulatory System.** In keeping with their active lives and endothermic capabilities, mammals have highly efficient circulatory systems. The four-chambered heart serves as a double pump: the right side of the heart receives venous blood from the body and pumps it to the lungs; the left side receives oxygenated blood from the lungs and pumps it to the body.

Because of the great size differential between the largest and the smallest mammal, the heart rate is highly variable between species. The rate in non-hibernating species varies from under 20 beats a minute in whales to over 1,300 beats per minute in a shrew. Some mammals have the ability to alter heartbeat rapidly. A resting brown bat has a heart rate of around 400 beats per minute, but this rate increases almost instantly to 1,000 beats per minute when the bat takes flight.

Like birds, mammals are endothermic animals. The body temperature of mammals varies from 30°C (86°F) in the platypus to 37°C (98.6°F) in humans to 39°C (102.2 F) in rabbits and cats. Endothermy is a costly metabolic proposition, and some mammals minimize the cost by not maintaining a constant internal temperature. Many bats allow their temperature to fall when at rest. They get so cold that when they awaken, they must move and jerk their wings to raise their temperature enough to fly.

Winter sleep, or hibernation, is practiced by ground squirrels, chipmunks, marmots, and bats to avoid winter food scarcity. During hibernation all bodily metabolism drops to a low level; the heartbeat and respiration are slowed. The heartbeat of the ground squirrel, normally about 150 beats per minute, slows to 5 beats per minute. The animal's respiration also drops, from about 200 breaths a minute to 4 or 5 breaths per minute, and its body temperature may plummet as much as 30 degrees. The temperature of some hibernating mammals may drop to within several degrees of freezing. Excess body fat is accumulated prior to hibernation and serves as bodily fuel through the period of hibernation. Some ground squirrels hibernate for about two-thirds of the year. Bears do not truly hibernate but instead undergo a sort of stupor called dormancy.

The mammals' insulation of hair and/or fat helps retain body heat in cold conditions. During hot periods, mammals are cooled by the evaporation of liquid from the sweat glands off the skin. Species with few sweat glands, such as the cat and dog families, resort to panting and also lose heat by the evaporation of saliva off the tongue and inside of the mouth. Elephants flap their ears to cool off, and other types of mammals slip into cooling water or shade.

**Respiratory System.** In mammals the lungs are large and well developed but lack the accessory air sacs found in birds. Mammalian lungs have a spongy texture because they are filled with innumerable air pockets called alveoli. In humans, the lungs contain about 300 million alveoli, which provide a total respiratory surface of about 70 square meters (6,000 square feet), or roughly the area of a regulation tennis court.

The respiratory rate varies according to the size of the animal, its age, amount of work being done, and other factors. Respiratory rate, expressed in cubic centimeters of air per kilogram of weight per hour, is 200 for a resting human, 460-850 for a rabbit, and over 5,000 for one species of shrew. The rate for a hibernating dormouse is 15.

Sitting on top of the windpipe or trachea is the voice box or larynx. It is made up of several separate cartilages with membranous folds, the vocal cords, lying within it. Air from the lungs passes over the vocal cords and causes them to vibrate. The volume of air expelled from the lungs, the tautness of the cords, the shape of the pharynx, and the position of the mouth and lips modulate the voice. Mammals' voices range from the eerie howl of the wolf to the soft squeak of mice and from the braying of the donkey to the soft lullaby sung by a human mother to her child. In dogs the voice box engages with the nasal passages; to bark, a dog must raise its head to disengage the voice box. Hence, if a dog is placed in a kennel with a low roof so it cannot raise its head, it will be prevented from barking.

Grasping Teeth

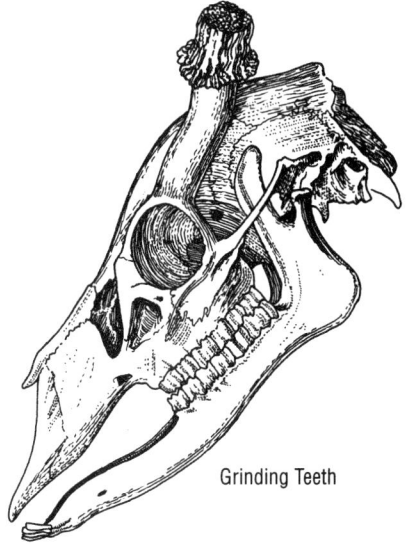

Grinding Teeth

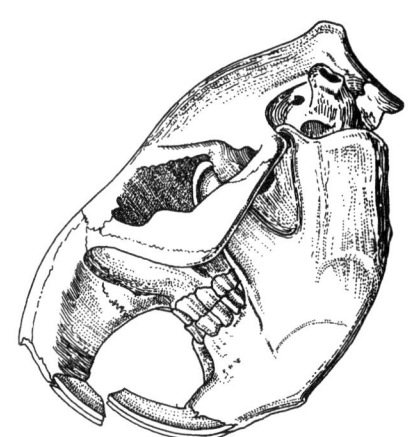

Gnawing Teeth

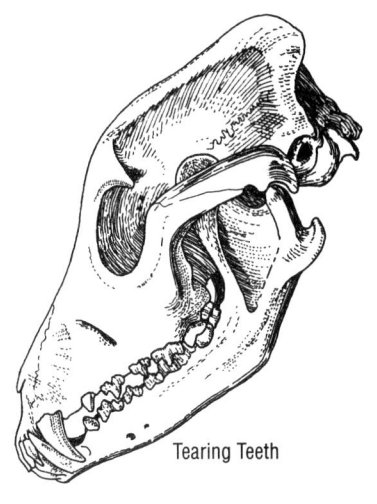

Tearing Teeth

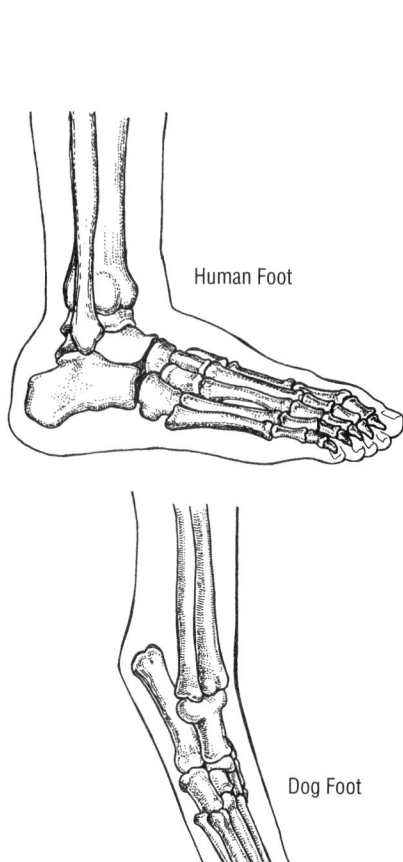

Human Foot

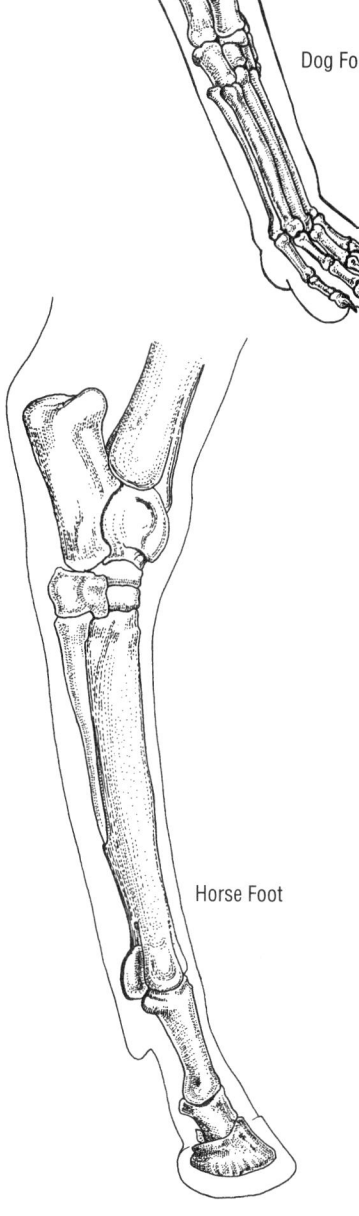

Dog Foot

Horse Foot

The sounds and calls of mammals serve to (1) warn of danger, (2) intimidate or frighten enemies, (3) assemble gregarious species, (4) bring sexes together, and (5) locate and coordinate parents and young.

**Muscle System, Movement, and Migration.** The muscular patterns of mammals are beautifully adapted to diverse modes of locomotion: slicing swiftly through the water, galloping across land, swinging through the trees, and flying through the air.

The most vital muscles are those that circle the mouth and function during suckling of milk from the mother. Mammals also have many finely structured facial muscles to move the ears, close the eyes, and control changes in facial expression—unique to the mammals, especially primates.

Many mammal species are extremely restricted in range and make extraordinary efforts to return to their birth area if removed from it. Studies on marked brown rats showed that most after recapture had moved no more that 40 feet from the place where they were originally marked. In larger species, the range is proportionately increased. The grizzly bear may wander across an area of 19 kilometers (12 miles), and movements of large herbivores and predators such as wolves often encompass as much as 50 kilometers (30 miles) in any one direction.

True migration does occur among many types of mammals. On land the large hoofed mammals show the most striking movements. For example, large herds of the North American caribou travel between 650 to 800 kilometers (400 to 500 miles) on their seasonal journey, pressing onward despite all obstacles.

Sea and air provide fewer barriers to migration than land, and migrations in these environments is particularly common. The movements of gray whales from the Arctic Ocean to sheltered lagoons along Baja California are well documented. The great blue whale makes spectacular journeys. One tagged blue whale traveled 490 kilometers (300 miles) in 32 days; another traveled 800 kilometers (500 miles) in 88 days. Humpback whales and fin whales also are long-distance migrators, and fur seals travel great distances to return to breeding grounds.

Bats also are known for remarkable migrations considering their size and the distance traveled. For example, the tiny European pipistrelle travels 1,000 to 3,000 kilometers (600 to 800 miles) between southeastern Europe and central Russia.

The strangest migration is that practiced by the lemmings. Lemmings are small, largely nocturnal rodents that inhabit the plateaus and mountain slopes of the Scandinavian peninsula. Periodically, and with favorable conditions, their numbers increase dramatically for several years. Every three or four years, the carrying capacity of the habitat is exceeded and a mass migration occurs. The lemmings start traveling one by one but natural barriers and topography funnel them into groups of ever-increasing size. Many perish crossing rivers or in the jaws and beaks of predators. Some march all the way to the sea and swim outward until they become exhausted and drown. These mass movements, apparently triggered by overcrowding, cause thousands to perish. However, not all lemmings are seized by this wanderlust and the cycle begins anew.

The urge to migrate in mammals is based on physiological stimuli. Glandular secretions and other physical transformations operating in a seasonal rhythm trigger and dictate the pattern of migration. As with birds, the exact methods of navigation in migrating mammals is not fully understood.

**Skeletal System.** The active life-style of mammals requires a skeleton that is well braced for attachment by many muscles. To accomplish this, the bones of a mammal are nearly completely ossified (solid) and considerable fusion of bones occurs, as in the pelvic girdle. The flexibility of the mammal skeleton allows the limbs great speed and agility.

Mammals have abandoned the pattern of bone growth typical of reptiles. In many reptiles skeletal growth continues throughout much of their life, but in mammals skeletal growth is generally restricted to the early part of life. This pattern of bone growth is useful in estimating the age of a mammal.

The brain case of the mammalian skull is quite large. Besides protecting the brain, the skull provides an attachment site for the many muscles that control the face, eyes, jaws, and lips of the animal.

Mammalian teeth, unlike most lower vertebrates, are differentiated in form and function. Mammalian teeth are set in sockets and are of a definite number. Each mammalian order has teeth specialized to the type of food eaten:

- teeth for grasping insects and worms
- teeth for grinding tough plant material
- teeth for gnawing and chiseling
- teeth for stabbing and tearing

However, adult monotremes, some whales, and the armadillos and sloths lack teeth entirely. (See drawings on p. 219)

**Limbs and Feet.** The limbs of mammals range from the slender, tapering legs of the agile deer and antelopes to the round, stumpy legs of the elephant; the paddlelike limbs of the seal and porpoises; and the long, delicate forelimbs and fingers covered with skin of the bats.

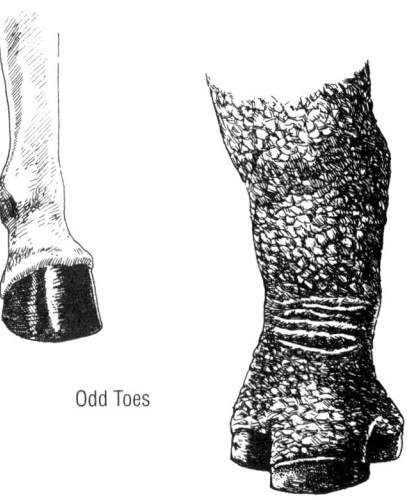

Odd Toes

Typically the limbs of mammals end in a foot with five toes. Humans have a generalized foot and walk with the entire foot touching the ground. Other mammals have four toes. The dog walks on fleshy pads under its four toes with its heel raised. Others, such as the horse, walk on a single toe capped by a hoof over the tip of the toe and with their heel raised.

Some hoofed mammals have an odd number of toes. The horse, for example, has one, and the rhinoceros has three. Other hoofed mammals, such as the sheep, pig, camel, cow, and deer, have an even number of toes. Such mammals are referred to as cloven hoofed. The ends of the digits of most mammals are protected by hoofs, claws, or nails.

**Body Covering.** Hair is to mammals what feathers are to birds and scales are to reptiles. This furry exterior forms an insulating covering that helps the animal retain its body heat. However, some mammals are hairless or nearly so. Some of them, such as the elephant, rhinoceros, and hippopotamus, live in warm areas and have a thick skin and a large body that retain heat. Other hairless mammals that live in cold areas or in the water, such as the whale, are insulated by thick layers of fat beneath the skin.

EvenToes

The hair of mammals varies in length, density, texture, and color in different species. It is heaviest on arctic mammals but often thin and short on tropical species. On many mammals the coat is differentiated into a dense fine underfur for body insulation and a lesser number of heavier and longer guard hairs that protect against wear. Many mammals also have long, sensitive whiskers around their snouts.

The coat of hair is shed periodically, and new hairs grow in. Shedding, or molting, may occur seasonally once or twice a year or may be a continuous process. Color patterns may change with molting. For example, in northern regions the weasels and hares have a brown summer coat but replace it with a white one for winter.

The skin of mammals contains numerous glands not found in other vertebrates. The most important are the mammary glands, from which this group derives its name. All female mammals provide nutritious secretions called milk from these glands for their young during the initial period of development by the young. In most mammals, the openings of the mammary glands are projecting nipples (mammae), from which the milk is sucked by the young. The monotremes lack nipples. Instead, the milk oozes out and the young suck it from tufts of hair on the mammary area.

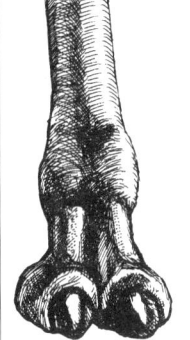

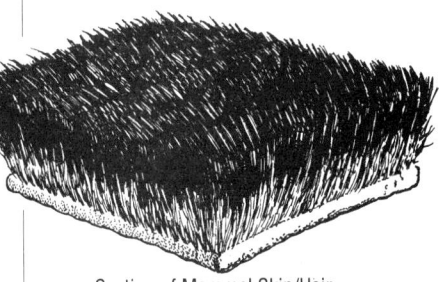

Section of Mammal Skin/Hair

The watery secretions of the sweat glands in the skin help cool the body through evaporation. In humans and hoofed mammals the sweat glands are widely distributed about the body, but in most mammals they are restricted to certain areas. Secretions from the sebaceous glands keep skin and hair soft and oily and provide insulation and waterproofing. Scent and musk glands are used by mammals for attracting mates, marking territories, communicating during social interaction, and protecting themsleves.

Where subject to heavy wear, mammal skin forms a dense cornified coating such as the calluses on human palms or soles and the foot pad of bears, dogs, and mice. The claws, nails, and hoofs of mammals are hard, cornified outgrowths of the skin. The horns of the hoofed mammals are also derivatives of the skin. They grow from bony stumps on the forehead covered by hard, cornified products of the outer layer of skin.

**Excretory System.** Mammals have the most highly developed kidneys of all vertebrates. Mammalian kidneys extract nitrogenous wastes from the blood in the form of urea. Urea, water, and other wastes form urine. Urine flows from the kidneys to the urinary bladder, where it is stored until eliminated from the body. Mammalian kidneys are efficient at controlling the composition and level of body fluids and thus allow mammals to live in hostile environments such as deserts.

**Brain and Nervous System.** The single most important factor that makes mammals the most complex of all animals is the development of the brain. Their large brain and well-developed sense organs give the mammals an intelligence, curiosity, and vitality unmatched by any other animals.

The mammalian brain consists of three parts: cerebrum, cerebellum, and medulla. The large size and complexity of the cerebrum distinguishes the brain of the mammal from that of other vertebrates. The massive, wrinkled cerebrum is the site of thinking, learning, memory, and interpretation of senses. The smaller cerebellum coordinates muscular movements, and the medulla regulates autonomic body functions such as heart rate and breathing rate.

The size of the brain relative to total body weight is not a reliable guide to intelligence. The degree of folding and convoluting on the surface of the cerebrum is perhaps a better indicator.

Mammals are equipped with an impressive array of senses related in degree of development to their necessity for survival in specific situations and habitats. For example, the carnivores, rodents, and hoofed mammals have an acute sense of smell; this sense is reduced in the whales and primates and absent in the porpoises and dolphins.

No other vertebrate seems to depend so heavily on the sense of hearing as do mammals. Mammals alone have an external funnel-like structure (the pinna) that serves to locate and direct sound waves. The pinna is large and well developed in bats but missing entirely in seals and whales. Bats are able to hear and generate ultrasonic frequencies. Dogs, cats, and small rodents can hear high frequencies beyond those the human ear can detect, and elephants and especially whales can hear sounds of very low frequencies, often over great distances.

The eyes of most mammals are large, well developed, and quite sensitive to movement (that is, the brain is quick to perceive such signals coming from the eyes). Many species preyed upon by others react to motion alarms by freezing, but the opposite applies to predators: the slightest movement in the visual field attracts their attention. The retina of most mammals contains few or no cone cells for detecting colors and consequently most are color-blind. This color blindness may be correlated with the fact that most mammals are drab in color. Only the squirrels and the primates enjoy color vision.

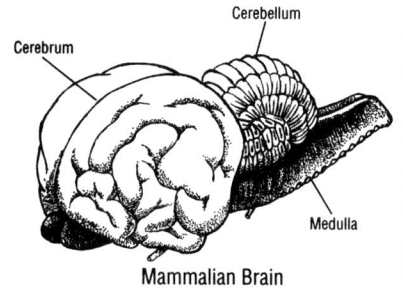

Cerebrum

Cerebellum

Medulla

Mammalian Brain

In mammals active by day, the retina absorbs light, and in mammals active at night, the retina reflects light. This reflection explains the appearance of glowing eyes when car headlights shine on nocturnal mammals along the roadside in the dark.

All mammals have two eyes, but their development in the skull varies widely. In hoofed mammals, which are always on the lookout for predators, the eyes lie on the sides of the head so that a very wide visual field is produced. These animals can see from straight ahead to far behind. In carnivores, on the other hand, the eyes lie more on the front of the face, giving a more extensive stereoscopic view and great sense of depth and distance. The primates, with flattened faces and eyes set relatively close together, have developed stereoscopic vision to its highest level.

The sense of smell is highly developed in some mammals. The hoofed mammals are able to detect the odor of an approaching predator over long distances. The predator must constantly work to stay downwind of its intended victim. Dogs also are noted for their great sense of smell. This remarkable canine abilitiy has been put to use by modern law enforcement officers to detect illegal contraband of all types.

The most striking manifestation of the advanced brain of mammals is in the wide and complex variety of behaviors they exhibit. No other creatures have such varied and complicated behaviors of food-getting, defense, reproduction, and social interaction. No other animals band together in such intimate and intricate social hierarchies.

**Reproduction and Development.** Mammals are separate sexes—distinctly male or female. Most mammals have rather definite mating seasons, often in winter or spring. At these times internal and behavioral changes may occur in both sexes. The primary stimulus to mating in most mammals is the condition of the female, who at certain times enters a state known as estrus, or heat. In most mammals, estrus occurs only during certain breeding seasons. In others, such as primates, bats, cats, whales, and squirrels, estrous cycles occur at regular intervals throughout the year.

Like birds, many mammals possess secondary sex characteristics that are often of great importance in mating behavior. The mane of the male lion, the shoulder cape of some male baboons, the antlers of male deer, and the inflatable nose pouches of the male elephant seal all are important traits distinguishing the sexes. Colored coats, faces, and rumps as well as size also play a role. A bull fur seal may weigh 270 kilograms (600 pounds) and its mate only 34 kilograms (75 pounds). Male weasels and minks may weigh twice as much as their mates.

Courtship displays in mammals generally are less spectacular than in birds but may be quite elaborate. Various rodents engage in rough-and-tumble fights, the male short-tailed shrew emits excited clicks as he approaches his potential mate, the male and female Falkland sea lion engage in long caressing sessions on shore and platypus pairs swim in a tight circle beak to tail.

Humans imagine prolonged monogamous relationships between mammals, but such pairings are extremely rare. Mating in many species, especially rodents and bats, is promiscuous and indiscriminate. Other types, such as seals and deer, practice polygamy, with males gathering and serving harems of females. In some carnivores, the male remains with the female and helps gather food until the young are weaned. Foxes and wolves tend to remain faithful to one mate, and a high degree of fidelity is shown by primates and the American beaver.

The climax of courtship is copulation. This is performed in different ways by different species. Sometimes the period of union is very long. Ferrets may remain in a single union for over an hour and the rhinoceros for several hours.

Platypus and Young

Alternatively, many small rodents will copulate scores of times a day, each act taking only a few seconds. Shaw's jird, a small North American desert rodent, has been observed copulating 224 times in two hours, nearly twice a minute.

Based on what happens to the fertilized egg, mammals can be categorized into three groups developmentally:

1. *The monotremes.* In the platypus and echidna, a reptilelike shell is deposited around the egg, which passes out of the female's body. The platypus lays two or three eggs, each about 1.25 centimeters (0.5 inches) in diameter, in an underground nest about two weeks after mating. Curling about the eggs, the female platypus incubates them for about 10 days until they hatch. Once hatched, the young lap milk that oozes from the mammary glands onto the fur on the female's underside.

2. *The marsupials.* In the opossum, kangaroo, wallaby, koala, bandicoot, and wombat, the fertilized egg develops into an embryo inside the reproductive tract. The embryo does not attach and is nourished by a yolk sac on the egg. The yolk sac is not large enough to nourish the embryo through its entire development, and the tiny, wormlike embryo leaves the womb and enters a pouch, typical of this group of mammals. Gestation, or the period of development, ranges from 12 to 14 days in the American opossum to 38 to 40 days in the largest kangaroos. Climbing with a swimming motion of stubby forelimbs and head through a tangle of fur, the embryo seeks the nipple of a mammary gland. If it finds one, it seizes it and hangs on. If a nipple cannot be located, the embryo dies. The developing young marsupial remains attached, growing sufficiently large and independent to eventually leave the pouch.

3. *The placentals.* Monotremes and marsupials account for only 5 percent of the mammals. In the other 95 percent, the placentals, the developing embryo attaches to and develops a link with the mother. Nutrients, oxygen, carbon dioxide, and water are exchanged between embryo and mother through a network of intertwined blood vessels called the placenta. The placenta allows the embryo to develop for a much longer time inside the mother and frees the mother to move about and feed while still protecting the embryo. The gestation period for placentals ranges from several weeks in some rodents to 36 weeks in humans to as long as 96 weeks in elephants.

Kangaroo and Young

Most placental mammals are born on land and come out head first. However, the porpoise gives birth under water, with the young exiting tail first. Mother manatees give birth under water then maneuver the young to the surface for their first gulp of air while supported on the mother's back.

Some mammals, such as carnivores and primates, give birth to young that are helpless. Others, such as the hoofed mammals, give birth to active, fully furred young able to feed, run, and hide shortly after birth. Bear cubs, for example, born blind and helpless, weigh only 280 grams (10 ounces). A baby giraffe, on the other hand, may weigh 39 kilograms (85 pounds), stand 1.8 meters (6 feet) tall, and be able to stand alone in a few minutes and run efficiently several days after birth. Rodents give birth to blind, helpless young but compensate for this initial disadvantage by speedy maturation. Young field mice, for example, may be weaned before they are three weeks old.

The number of young produced by placental mammals at any one birth varies from one to as many as a dozen or more.

Once the young of any mammal are born, they are nourished by milk from the mother's mammary glands until they are able to feed or hunt for themselves.

Mammals are noted for the length and quality of parental care devoted to their young. Quality lavished on a few offspring has replaced quantity of offspring as the key to survival in mammals. Carnivores often spend months teaching their young the intricacies of hunting and social order. Young elephants may remain with their mother for several years after they are born. Humans are the most spectacular example of parental care. Even in the most primitive societies, young humans do not become truly independent until at least 12 years old, and in more advanced societies with protracted periods of education, youngsters may not be emancipated until the age of 21. Even after that and for the remainder of life, there is a bond of caring, concern, and support between human parent and child.

It is beyond the scope and intent of this book to give a detailed account of all 21 orders of mammals. Instead, some of the largest and most familiar orders are discussed.

**Order Monotremata.** This order of egg-laying mammals is composed of only three species: the short-beaked echidna, the long-beaked echidna, and the platypus.

The monotremes are quite restricted in their range. The short-beaked echidna is found in Australia, Tasmania, and New Guinea; the long-beaked variety is found only in the mountains of New Guinea; and the platypus is distributed from eastern Australia to Tasmania.

Echidnas are readily recognized by their covering of long spines with fur between the spines. The spiny coat provides excellent defense. When disturbed, the echidna coils up into a spiny ball. The snout is bare with a small mouth and large nostrils near the tip. Echidnas have small, bulging eyes but a good sense of hearing. Prey is located mainly by smell as the animal roots through forest litter or undergrowth. Ants and termites, which make up the bulk of the diet, are rapidly taken in on a long, sticky tongue that can be extended up to 18 centimeters (7 inches) in the short-beaked species.

Short-beaked echidnas are about 30 to 45 centimeters (12 to 18 inches) long and weigh 2.5 to 8 kilograms (5.5 to 17.6 pounds). The long-nosed type is about 45 to 90 centimeters (18 to 35 inches) long and weighs from 5 to 10 kilograms (11 to 22 pounds). Echidnas walk with a distinctive rolling gait and take shelter in hollow logs, under brush piles, and in clumps of vegetation. They avoid rain and will remain inactive for days if rain continues.

When the first dried skin of a platypus arrived in Britain from the Australian colonies around 1798, it was deemed a fake. It was thought to be the beak of a bird and various mammal parts sewn together. However unusual its appearance, the platypus does possess the typical mammalian characteristics of hair, mammary glands, and endothermy. The platypus varies in length and weight from season to season and in different areas. Males, which are larger than females, have a head-and-body length of around 45 to 60 centimeters (18 to 24 inches), a bill length of 5 to 8 centimeters (2 to 3 inches), and a tail length of 10.5 to 15 centimeters (4 to 6 inches) and may weigh 1.0 to 2.4 kilograms (2.2 to 5.3 pounds). The body is covered by a dense coat of waterproof fur.

The platypus obtains its food from streams and rivers and is suited for this mode of food-getting. The dense fur insulates the body while the powerful webbed feet provide power for swimming and diving. Closing both its eyes and ears when it dives, the platypus uses its soft, pliable, and highly sensitive bill to find bottom-dwelling invertebrates, particularly insects. The tail is broad and flat and is employed as a fat-storage area. The rear ankles of the male bear a hollow, horny spur that is connected to a venomous gland in the thigh.

**Order Marsupialia.** The marsupials or pouched mammals have a broader distribution than the monotremes. The approximately 266 species of marsupials are found mainly in Australia, Tasmania, and New Guinea (174 species); South America (81 species); Central America (9 species); and North America (2 species).

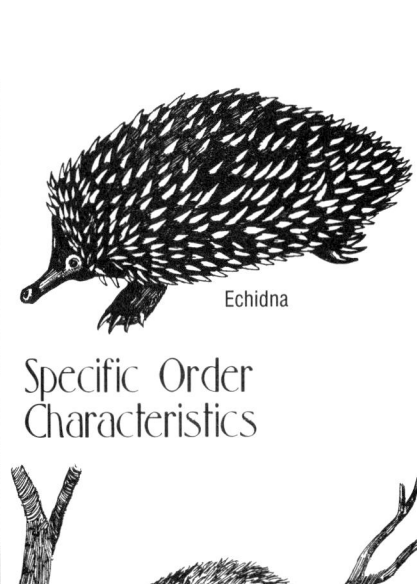
Echidna

## Specific Order Characteristics

Opossum

Kangaroo

Platypus

Grizzly Bear

Polar Bear

Panda

Lynx

In female marsupials that jump or climb trees, the pouch opens toward the head, and in those that run or burrow, it opens toward the tail. The numbat has no pouch, and its young, clinging tenaciously to the nipples, are dragged along underneath the mother as she travels.

The opossum represents the only family of this order found in the Americas. The opossum family includes the common opossum of North and Central America, the Southern opossum of Central and South America, and the white-eared opossum of higher elevations in South America.

American opossums range from the size of a mouse to that of a cat. The nose is long and pointed with stiff, tactile hairs around the snout. The eyes are generally small and somewhat protruding, and eyesight is considered reasonably well developed. The naked ears are constantly in motion as the animal tracks sounds. The body is covered by dense fur, but the tail is usually bare and prehensile. That is, the tail can be used as a grasping limb as the animal climbs trees. The feet also are adapted for climbing and grasping. Each foot has five digits, and the big toe on the hind foot is opposable.

The opposums are opportunistic feeders that vary their diets depending on what is seasonally or locally available—fruit, insects, earthworms, and small invertebrates.

Opossums cope with danger by employing several defense mechanisms, the most famous of which is playing dead. This may seem a rather foolish strategy as it leaves the animal open to easy attack, but many predators refuse to eat something they haven't killed, and others give up the chase because the stimulus (a fleeing animal) that triggers the hunt-and-kill response is no longer available. Recent research has shown that the feigning of death is actually a physiological faint triggered by fear. The opossum goes into a comatose state and loses all responsiveness to external stimuli. It can be dropped, prodded, thrown, and even cut without response. Opossums may remain in this state for only seconds or for as long as six hours. Most opossums never use this defense and prefer to flee or bluff by hissing, baring their teeth, or releasing noxious gland secretions.

The best known of the Australian marsupials is the kangaroo. Kangaroos have adapted to a wide variety of habitats, including open plains, woodlands and forests, and rocky outcrops, slopes, and cliffs. The short-nosed kangaroo lives underground in burrows, and the improbable tree kangaroo has taken to an aboreal life, leaping from limb to limb.

Kangaroos are distinguished by their large, powerful hind legs and long, heavy tail. Using the legs for power and the tail for balance and thrust, kangaroos are capable of attaining speeds of 48 kilometers (30 miles) per hour and making leaps of over 8.5 meters (27 feet). Kangaroos use their tail when walking slowly by alternately placing their weight on the tail and hind legs.

Kangaroos browse on plants and are the ecological equivalent to such hoofed mammals as antelopes.

In most instances, kangaroos tend to flee rather than fight. In fact, they can be panicked easily. Fatalities as a result of fleeing kangaroos looking backward and running head-on into large rocks or trees have been documented. If a kangaroo is cornered or stands its ground, it can put up a good fight. Rearing back on its tail and lashing out with its powerful and clawed hind legs, a large kangaroo can easily disembowel most enemies.

Other types of marsupials include the cuddly looking koala, the burrowing wombat, and the marsupial mole.

**Order Carnivora.** From tundra wolves to rain forest civets and marine otters to desert foxes, the 231 species that compose this order are widely distributed in

Tiger

many habitats and on all continents except Antarctica. They range in size from huge bears and cats to tiny weasels. They hunt in packs or in solitary stealth. Most are terrestrial, but some rarely touch land, living instead in the sea or in trees. Most eat flesh, but some are omnivorous and a few are strictly herbivorous. What, then, does such a large and diverse group have in common? Their common lineage lies in their teeth. The carnivores possess four shearing or carnassial teeth. Only the more predacious species still retain these teeth, and in the vegetarian panda they have reverted to grinding surfaces. Carnivores also share an ancient modification of the limbs—the fusion of bones in the foot.

Wolf

The senses of the carnivores are all acute. Perhaps the most refined is their use of scent to find prey or escape predators and to communicate. Urine, feces, and odorous skin glands convey messages we can only guess about. One type of mongoose can recognize not only the identity but also the status of another mongoose by scent alone.

The order Carnivora has seven families:

- The cat family—35 species including the lion, jaguar, leopard, tiger, cheetah, lynx, ocelot, puma, and domestic cat.
- The dog family—35 species including the wolf, coyote, dingo, jackal, wild dog, fox, and domestic dog.
- The bear family—7 species including the grizzly bear, polar bear, black bear, sloth bear, and spectacled bear.
- The raccoon family—19 species including the common raccoon, coati, olinga, ringtail, kinkajou, and panda. (Controversy surrounds the taxonomic placement of the two panda species, the red panda and the giant panda. Some consider them a separate family, and others maintain the red panda belongs in the raccoon family and the giant panda in the bear family.)
- The weasel family—67 species including the weasel, ferret, badger, marten, wolverine, skunk, and otter.
- The civet family—66 species including the civet, genet, and mongoose.
- The hyena family—4 species including the spotted hyena, brown hyena, striped hyena, and ardwolf.

Fox

Raccoon

**Order Rodentia.** Rodents are distributed worldwide and are found on every continent except Antarctica. They occur from the highest arctic tundra, where some, like the lemming, live under the snow, to the hottest and driest of deserts, where the gerbils live. The flying squirrels and others are aboreal and seldom touch ground; the burrowing mole-rats and others seldom venture above ground. Others, such as the muskrat and beaver, have taken to a semiaquatic life.

The rodents are a large group: Nearly 40 percent of all mammal species belong to this one order. However, rodents show less variation in form than do members of many other mammalian orders. Rodents typically have squat, compact bodies with short limbs, pointed snout, and a tail. Most rodents are small, weighing 100 grams (3.5 ounces) or less. The largest is the capybara, at 66 kilograms (146 pounds). Rodents have characteristic teeth, including a single pair of sharp, often elongated incisors. These teeth allow rodents to gnaw through practically anything. Interestingly, the teeth of a rodent grow continuously, up to several millimeters a week. They are constantly ground down by being rubbed together. If their teeth become misaligned so they do not touch and wear properly, they will grow around and may pierce the skull.

Weasel

Rodents eat primarily a wide range of plant material—leaves, bark, seeds, and fruit. Some will supplement their diet with earthworms, spiders, and insects. A few are specialized predators. The Australian water rat, for example, seldom eats plant material and prefers fish, frogs, and mollusks.

Badger

Skunk

Mongoose

Hyena

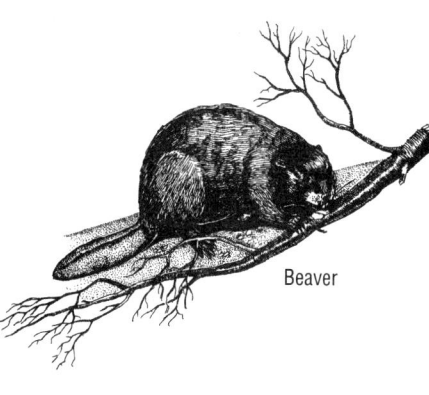

Beaver

Chipmunk

Gerbil

The order Rodentia has 3 suborders, 30 families, and 1,702 species. The following rodent groups are the most familiar:

- From the suborder of squirrel-like rodents:
  - The beaver family—1 species.
  - The squirrel family—267 species including the marmot, chipmunk, ground squirrel, prairie dog, flying squirrel, woodchuck, gray squirrel, and American red squirrel.
  - Also included in this suborder are the families of the pocket gophers, scaly-tailed squirrels, pocket mice, and springhares.
- From the suborder of mouse-like rodents:
  - The rats and mice family—1,082 species and 15 subfamilies including the vole and lemming, blind mole-rat, African pouched rat, African swamp rat, crested rat, African climbing rat, bamboo rat, Madagascan rat, Oriental dormouse, zokor, Australian water rat, hamster, gerbil, Old World rats and mice, and New World rats and mice.
  - Also included in this suborder are the families of dormice, jumping mice, and jerboas.
- From the suborder of cavy-like rodents:
  - The New World porcupine family—10 species including the North American porcupine, South American tree porcupine, and Upper Amazonian porcupine.
  - Also included in this suborder are the families of cavies, capybaras, caypus, pacaranas, pacas, agoutis, chinchilla rats, spring rats, chinchillas, tuco-tucos, cane rats, African rock rats, Old World porcupines, gundis, and African mole-rats.

**The Hoofed Mammals or Ungulates.** "Ungulate" is a term given to all those mammals that have a reduced number of toes and have developed hooves at the tips of those toes.

Ungulates generally have long necks, a head with a long muzzle, and relatively short tails. Their barrel-shaped bodies are carried on powerful legs of roughly equal length. Their skin is thick and covered by a coat of coarse hair rather than soft fur.

The ungulates are terrestrial herbivores that feed on leaves, flowers, fruits, and seeds. Pigs and peccaries are more omnivorous and may include roots, tubers, and small animals in their diet. Ungulates, including the aquatic hippopotamus, feed on land using their lips, teeth, and tongue to take food directly from the plant or off the ground if it has fallen. Ungulate teeth are adapted to grinding, and the back of the mouth functions like a mill to reduce plant materials to small particles.

Ungulates have developed two very different systems for dealing with coarse, indigestible plant material: hindgut fermentation and rumination. In hindgut fermenters, food is completely digested in the stomach and then passes to the large intestine and a pouch called the cecum for fermentation and absorption. Ruminants pass the food into the first stomach chamber (rumen) where it is fermented and then regurgitated to be chewed again. It then passes into the second, third, and finally fourth stomach chamber, where digestion is completed. Nutrients then are absorbed in the small intestine.

*Order Perissodactyla*, the odd-toed ungulates, are distributed from desert to grassland to forest, with 16 species in 3 families:

- The horse, zebra, and ass family—7 species including the African ass, Asian ass, domestic horse, mountain zebra, and plains zebra.

Squirrel

- The tapir family—4 species including Baird's tapir, Malaysan tapir, and mountain tapir.
- The rhinoceros family—5 species including the black rhino, Javan rhino, Sumatran rhino, and white rhino.

*Order Artiodactyla*, the even-toed ungulates, are distributed worldwide on land except for Australia and Antarctica, with 187 species in 10 families:

- The pig family—9 species including the wild boar, pygmy hog, wart hog, and domestic pig.
- The hippopotamus family—2 species including the pygmy hippopotamus and the hippopotamus.
- The camel and llama family—6 species including the llama, alpaca, dromedary (one-humped camel), and Bactrian camel (two-humped).
- The deer family—36 species including the wapiti, Sika deer, mule deer, white-tailed deer, reindeer, moose, and pudu.
- The giraffe family—2 species including the giraffe and okapi.
- The bovine family—118 species including the pronghorn, wild cattle, domestic cattle, spiral-horned antelopes, American bison, duiker, gnu, impala, reedbuck, gazelle, musk ox, domestic goat, mountain goat, bighorn sheep, and domestic sheep.

**Order Cetacea.** The whales, dolphins, and porpoises that make up this order were thought to be fish until 1758, when the Swedish biologist Carolus Linneaus properly recognized them as mammals. The resemblance to fish is apparent but only superficial as cetaceans are definitely mammalian: They possess endothermic bodies, breathe air through lungs, and give birth to live young that are suckled with mother's milk. However, the mammalian characteristic of hair is absent. A thick coat of hair would be a serious impedance in the water in which they live so they have abandoned it in favor of an internal insulating layer of fat.

The largest creature to ever live on this planet is the blue whale. It reaches a length of 24 to 27 meters (80 to 90 feet) and weighs 117 to 135 metric tons (130 to 150 tons). Despite their great size and weight, the cetaceans are very mobile. Blue whales have been observed traveling for 10 minutes at 37 kilometers (21 miles) per hour. Orcas have approached a ship at 56 kilometers (32 miles) per hour and circled around it for 20 minutes at speeds in excess of the ship's speed of 38 kilometers (22 miles) per hour.

The body of a cetacean is smooth and streamlined, and protruding limbs have been modified into fins and a tail. Because of the supporting action of the water, the skeleton of cetaceans does not have to carry their weight and consequently is greatly reduced compared to the skeleton of land mammals.

Air-breathing cetaceans spend nearly all their lives underwater, holding their breath when they dive and coming back up to the surface to breath. The explosive spouting or blowing of spray from a cetacean's blowhole(s) is a widely recognized sign of exhalation.

Cetaceans are distributed throughout the ocean worldwide and are classified into two groups based on how they locate food and what they eat for food:

- The suborder of toothed whales pursue and eat agile fish and squid, which they locate by using echolocation. They emit short, intense pulses of sound in the ultrasonic range. These clicks and other sounds bounce back and give a sound picture of the environment. Included in the suborder of toothed whales are the river dolphin family, the dolphin and orca family, the porpoise family, the white whale family, the sperm whale family, and the beaked whale family.
- The suborder of baleen whales filter plankton or krill from the water for food. Fringed plates (baleen) covered with bristles growing down from

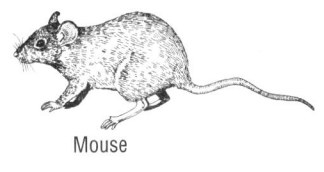

Mouse

Porcupine

Capybara

Zebra

Tapir

Rhinoceros

Wart Hog

Hippopotamus

Camel

Deer

Giraffe

the top jaw act as a sieve. Food organisms are removed from the baleen by the tongue. A 72-metric-ton (80-ton) blue whale can engulf up to 900 metric tons (1,000 tons) of water in a single mouthful. Larger blue whales can eat up to 7 metric tons (8 tons) of food daily, although it should be pointed out that they fast for seven to eight months of the year.

Baleen whales have not yet been shown to use echolocation and may rely on sight to locate the dense swarms of zooplankton on which they feed. Some of them communicate with other individuals by emission of low-frequency sounds that may be audible over tens to hundreds of miles through deep ocean water. Included in the suborder of baleen whales are the gray whale family, the rorqual family, and the right whale family.

**Order Primata.** This order embraces nearly 200 species in 11 families and ranges from animals as primitive as insect-eating shrews to highly complex humans. In the primates, the development of sharp vision and depth perception, grasping hands, and a tremendous brain capacity have given them a unique combination of specialized talents.

Geographically, primates are almost totally confined to the tropical latitudes, although the Barbary macaque is found in northern Africa and the Japanese macaque occurs on both main islands of Japan. Humans, with their cleverness of invention and flair for technology, have managed to dwell or at least visit everywhere on earth, including the greatest depths of the ocean, and have ventured off the planet into space.

Primates are eclectic in their food choices. Most species eat a wide array of foods ranging from insects and other small animals to fruits, flowers, and foliage. However, different species occupying the same habitat differ considerably in the time of feeding, the levels of the forest from which they feed, the type of food eaten, and how far they range to find food.

The shape and structure of the primate body is adapted and suited to its environment. Some walk on arms and legs nearly the same length, and others that brachiate (swing) through the trees have extra-long arms and reduced legs. In humans the arms are short and the legs elongated to accommodate upright bipedal (two leg) locomotion.

The contrast in locomotion is reflected in the shape of the hands and feet. Some brachiating monkeys lack a thumb, but in apes and humans the thumb is well developed and agile to provide a precise but powerful grip. The feet of lemurs are long and narrow, and those of the apes are broader and adept at grasping. Humans have a foot with reduced toes and an arch designed to carry the weight of the body on the heel and the balls of the feet.

The structure and length of the tail varies considerably. Tails are retained in some prosimians such as the lemur but lost in the slow-moving potto and lorises. Tails are present in most monkeys. Some Central and South American monkeys have a grasping (prehensile) tail, but none of the Old World monkeys have such ability. Apes and humans have no tail at all.

One of the most striking characteristics of primates is their sociability. With few exceptions, they band together in groups with complex codes of behavior and communication. Using the power of technology to enhance our incredible abilities of communication, the human species is rapidly taking socialization to its limits—a worldwide human society.

The primates are divided into two groups:

• The suborder of prosimians. These lower primates lead a mostly aboreal existence and tend to have longer snouts, a more developed sense of smell, and smaller brains than the other primates. Included in the suborder of prosimians are the lemur family, the dwarf and mouse lemur family, indri and sifaka family, aye-aye family, bush baby, potto and loris family, and tarsier family.

• The suborder of anthropoids. These higher primates are characterized by flat faces, forward-facing eyes giving a highly developed sense of vision, flexible grasping hands, and exceptionally large brains. Included in the suborder of anthropoids are the capuchinlike monkey family, marmoset and tamarin family, Old World monkey family, great apes family, lesser apes family, and human family.

The class Mammalia also includes the following orders:

| | |
|---|---|
| Pinnipedia—seals and sea lions | Sirenia—dugongs and manatees |
| Scandentis—tree shrews | Dermoptera—flying lemurs |
| Proboscidea—elephants | Hyracoidea—hyraxes |
| Tubulidentata—aardvarks | Lagomorpha—hares and rabbits |
| Macroscelida—elephant shrews | Insectivora—hedgehogs, shrews, moles, and desmans |
| Edentata—anteaters, sloths, and armadillos | Pholiodota—pangolins |
| Chiroptera—bats | |

No other group of animals is so much a part of human history nor as intertwined with our daily lives and needs as are our fellow mammals. Humans have hunted, trapped, domesticated, and in general exploited mammals for their leather, fur, blubber, and flesh for the entirety of human existence. Dogs, donkeys, horses, oxen, camels, and elephants have carried our burdens and plowed our fields and continue to do so in many parts of the world. Many mammals have been trained to race, hunt, stand guard, and guide the sight and hearing impaired.

Mammals have contributed to both human suffering and improving human health. Rats, harboring the flea that carried the bacteria of bubonic plague, contributed to the Black Death that devastated and killed one-third of the people in medieval Europe. Countless monkeys, chimps, dogs, rats, and mice, on the other hand, have lost their lives in the development of medicines, vaccines, and surgical techniques that have relieved human suffering and saved untold lives. Pets such as dogs and cats can give the elderly a sense of purpose and a feeling of companionship and can improve the medical condition of the ill.

Because of their cleverness, large size, and large numbers, mammals affect the environment and the ecology of their habitats like no other animal group. Burrowing moles and ground squirrels alter soil structure and improve soil aeration. Beavers dam streams and create ponds that serve as habitat for other creatures. Grazing mammals disperse seeds far and wide, and fruit-eating bats help pollinate flowers. Whales and walruses stir up the ocean floor in their search for food, adding productive material to sea water. In all habitats mammals are important links in the food web as predator or prey. No mammal has made the widespread and permanent changes to the planet that the bare, upright mammal called human has made. Many domestic and some wild mammals thrive in association with humankind. Sadly, most have not fared well under the unrelenting human pressure to disfigure and dominate the planet.

The plight of our fellow primates demonstrates the peril in which humankind has placed many mammals. The world's rainforests are being felled at an alarming rate for timber and farmland. It has been estimated that the tropical rainforest is being destroyed at a rate of 1 hectacre (2.5 acres) per second—an

Pronghorn

Musk Ox

## The Importance of Mammals

Dolphin

Sperm Whale

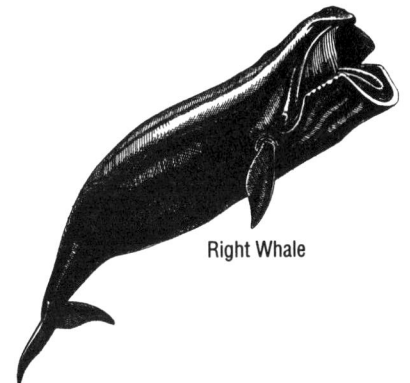
Right Whale

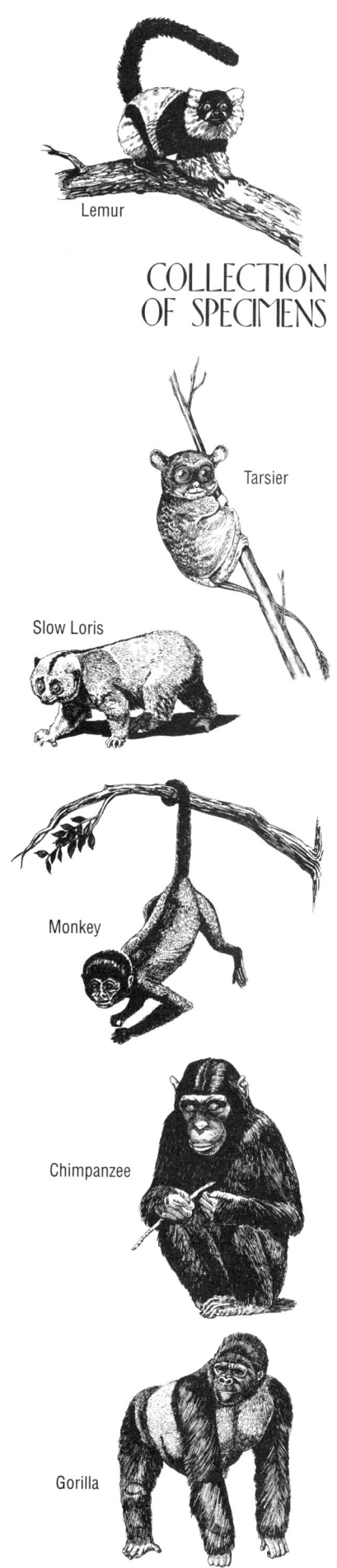

Lemur

# COLLECTION OF SPECIMENS

Tarsier

Slow Loris

Monkey

Chimpanzee

Gorilla

area the size of the state of Colorado every year at least. The populations of forest primates are dwindling fast, and many species soon will be extinct or found only in isolated preserves. Twenty-one species of monkeys in Central and South America, 14 species of Old World monkeys, 4 gibbons, and all the great apes are endangered or threatened. Some species, such as the beautiful golden lion tamarin, are so rare in the wild that only captive breeding programs prevent them from disappearing forever.

The temptation may be great, but wild mammals should not be collected or kept in the classroom. Wild mammals do not adapt well to confined classroom settings, and they may present health and safety problems because of the diseases and parasites they may harbor and the bites and scratches they may inflict.

The definition of wild mammal should also extend to so-called tame mammals such as raccoons, squirrels, and foxes reared by humans. Such creatures retain their natural instincts and may seem tame when young but become increasingly wild as they mature. Tame wild mammals may have a place at school but only for a brief visit—never as classroom residents and only under the handling and supervision of an expert.

Rodents such as mice, rats, hamsters, guinea pigs, and gerbils are the best mammals to keep in classroom settings. Because of their popularity, all of them are likely to be available from local sources such as pet stores, pet centers, or private individuals. Such rodents are descendants of wild stock but have been domesticated for thousands of generations and can be safely handled. Furthermore, they can be cared for with relative ease, are generally free of disease, are adapted to the confines of cage life, and adjust well to the physical conditions of the classroom.

Of all the rodents available and suitable for classroom study, I strongly recommend the gerbil. Since their introduction into this country in the 1950s, gerbils have become well-known and extremely popular pets. Gerbils make outstanding classroom subjects for a number of reasons:

- They are clean and nearly odorless. Gerbils are native to the deserts and dry regions of Asia, Africa, and eastern Europe. Being desert animals, they have physiological adaptations for conserving water. Hence, they produce only dry, hard, nearly odorless fecal pellets and very little if any urine. Other domestic rodents produce large amounts of urine and messy feces and require a great deal of time and care to keep their cages clean and odor free. Most domestic rodents are clean, but gerbils constantly groom and clean themselves.
- They are easy to care for. Being small, they do not require much space; a pair may be kept nicely in a 40-liter (10-gallon) aquarium. They have simple food requirements and adjust well to the physical conditions of a classroom.
- They are not especially susceptible to disease. This is important for everyone—you, the students, and the gerbils. Hamsters are also relatively disease free. Mice and rats are susceptible to respiratory infections, and guinea pigs are quite susceptible to a number of diseases, especially pneumonia.
- They are quite tame and become very docile with frequent handling (some types of domestic rodents often bite and scratch when handled). Gerbils are not aggressive and rarely bite. In fact, they are so charming and likable that students will become quite attached to them.
- They are bright, vital, and extremely curious. These energetic and inquisitive little rodents make excellent subjects for teaching activities and are guaranteed to capture and hold your students' interest.

If you do not want to keep rodents in the classroom but desire to observe and study live mammals, you could ask some of your students to bring their pet dog or cat for a visit. A field trip to a local zoo might show the mammals of your area and some found in other parts of the world. Remember that your students are living mammals, and observations, activities, and investigations later in this chapter make use of that fact.

Aquariums or plastic commercial rodent cages make the best housing for rodents—they are gnaw-proof and easy to clean. Do not use wooden or cardboard boxes to house rodents as the rodents may chew through them. Such containers can become wet with urine and feces, resulting in disagreeable odors. Clean all rodent cages regularly to prevent odor and disease problems.

Due to their large size, rats and guinea pigs require much larger quarters than other rodents. Individuals or a pair of rats may be housed in a commercial rat-sized rodent cage. Such cages are available at pet stores and from the suppliers listed in Appendix B. Aquariums of 60 liters (15 gallons) or larger with a secure screen cover also make satisfactory cages for rats. Guinea pigs should be housed in 80-liter (20-gallon) or larger aquariums or in a screen cage. Individual guinea pigs need at least 60 to 90 centimeters (24 to 36 inches) of floor space, and if two or more are kept together, 0.36 square meters (4 square feet) of floor space is a minimum.

Being smaller, mice, gerbils, and hamsters can be kept in screen-covered aquariums or commercial rodent cages. A pair of these rodents can be housed in a 40-liter (10-gallon) aquarium, but larger sizes are even better.

Hoppers are convenient for dispensing rodent food, but any shallow glass dish will do nicely. It is in the nature of gerbils and hamsters to hide uneaten food, and they will quickly empty a food hopper. Feed gerbils and hamsters in a dish to better regulate the amount of food used and thus prevent waste. Commercial rodent food is available from pet stores, pet centers, or farm supply outlets. These mixtures are specially formulated for the dietary needs of each type of rodent and are relatively inexpensive when purchased in bulk sizes. All rodents will benefit if you supplement their diet with raw vegetables such as potatoes, celery, or carrots and raw fruit such as apples twice a week. To be sure you are providing complete nutrition, you may want to consider adding liquid vitamin drops to your rodents' water bottle.

Provide water with appropriate-sized commercial water bottles. These bottles have ball valves to prevent leaks and covers to prevent gnawing. Such bottles are relatively inexpensive and durable and may be purchased from pet stores, pet centers, farm supply outlets, and the suppliers listed in Appendix B. Fresh water should be provided as needed, and water bottles should be washed and thoroughly rinsed on a regular basis.

There is a misconception that gerbils do not drink water. In their natural desert habitat gerbils can select foods that provide them with adequate moisture, and little if any water is taken in by drinking. However, in a cage being fed only dry rodent food, gerbils can die from lack of water. Provide a balanced diet and a water bottle for gerbils so they can drink if they need to.

Smaller, active rodents like mice, hamsters, and gerbils will benefit from an exercise wheel. A pair of gerbils can run an average of 4.9 to 8 kilometers (3 to 5 miles) in a 24-hour period. Exercise wheels, however, can be noisy and may be distracting in a classroom.

Being especially inquisitive, gerbils will benefit from an enriched environment. Challenging commercial gerbil habitats are available.

The bottom of any rodent cage should be covered with a mixture of wood shavings and cat litter to a depth of around 2.5 centimeters (1 inch) or more. All rodents are gnawing animals that need to wear their teeth down, so place a piece of wood, an egg carton, or cardboard in the cage for them to chew on. Gerbils especially appreciate this and seem to enjoy shredding such materials to create

# MAINTENANCE OF SPECIMENS

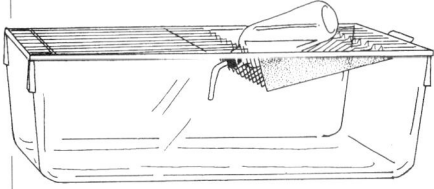
Commercial Rodent Cage

Homemade Rodent Cage

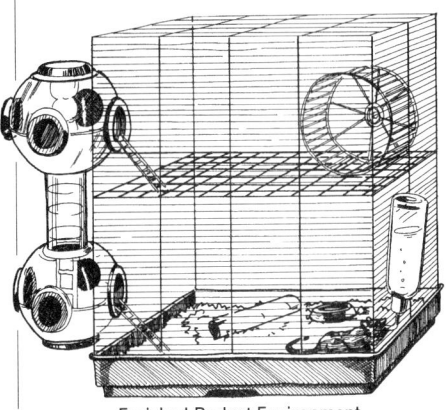
Enriched Rodent Environment

additional bedding. Shredded paper towels may be added for nest materials if you plan on allowing your rodents to breed.

A small wooden box placed in the bottom of the cage gives a sheltered place for the rodent(s) to hide or sleep and may serve as a nest box if they breed.

A special note on rodent reproduction: All rodents breed at a very high rate, and the smaller rodents especially reproduce readily in the classroom. It is said that the most difficult thing about keeping rodents is disposing of their numerous offspring. You can avoid this possibility by keeping only a single animal or by separating males from females (a tricky task with some rodents). If you have an outlet for any young produced, you can let your rodents happily reproduce. For example, I barter my young gerbils to an area pet store for gerbil food, goldfish, and so on. This gives me an outlet for my young gerbils, and we have not had to buy any gerbil food for several years. Whatever your situation, be sure to have a contingency plan for humanely disposing of young rodents *before* you ever bring adult rodents into the classroom.

Rodents can be kept at normal classroom temperatures, and if an adequate supply of food and water is available, rodents can be left unattended over weekends. For longer periods, some arrangements will have to made for their care.

## HEALTH AND SAFETY

### Teachers

Rodents present few health problems or safety risks to you if their cages, water bottles, and food dishes are kept clean and their bedding is changed regularly. As usual, practice good hygiene by thoroughly washing your hands after contact with rodents, cages, water bottles, food dishes, or bedding. Do not keep rodents near areas where food for human consumption is stored, and do not eat or drink while handling rodents, cages, or other apparatus. Reduce your risk of being bitten or scratched by picking up and handling rodents in the proper manner. Consider wearing heavy leather gloves when picking up rodents not accustomed to being handled. As the rodents become used to handling, gloves will not be needed.

### Students

Do not allow students to eat or drink around rodents or rodent apparatus and make sure students wash their hands after contact with rodents, cages, water bottles, food dishes, and bedding. Reduce the risk of bites and scratches by making sure students know and follow the proper techniques for picking up and handling rodents.

### Rodents

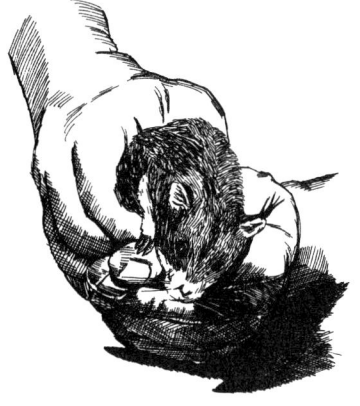

Provide adequate housing, water, and food as outlined in the "Maintenance of Specimens" section of this chapter. Avoid sudden temperature changes and chilling drafts. Clean and wash cages, water bottles, and food dishes often and change bedding regularly to prevent disease and parasite problems.

Proper handling is essential to the safety of the rodent, student, and teacher. Move slowly and calmly, making no sudden moves that might frighten the animal. Move one hand beneath the rodent and cup the other hand around and over it. Do not pick rodents up by their tails as this may cause tail damage, especially in gerbils. Care should be taken not to squeeze or confine the rodent too tightly as they may scratch or bite in defense. Rodents not used to handling may struggle at first and can bite, scratch, and jump from your grasp in an attempt to escape. A fall to the floor can injure or even kill a small rodent, so never lift them more than a short distance above the cage or tabletop. As the rodents become more accustomed to handling, they will become docile and struggling will not be a problem.

## TEACHING ACTIVITIES

Some activities in this section call for the use of students as test subjects. Using humans as subjects for student investigation of mammals has many advantages over the use of other types of live mammals:

- A minimum of preparation and few supplies are needed.
- The subjects walk in the door every day and do not need to be maintained in the classroom.

- The subjects can follow directions and communicate with the investigator, providing valuable data other mammals cannot.
- Students not only learn about mammals in general but also about the working of their own bodies in particular.

However, there are moral, legal, and ethical questions to consider when using humans as test subjects. I used the following guidelines to develop the human investigations in this chapter, and I practice them in my classroom when human subjects are involved in an activity. I strongly urge you to follow these guidelines.

1. Nothing should be done that will harm participants mentally or physically. No one should be hurt or embarrassed. Avoid causing physical pain, encouraging overexertion, administering any drugs, and inducing anxiety or stress through threat or deception. Avoid topics that could cause mental distress—sex, religion, family relations, physical appearance (race, weight, etc.), and achievement level.

2. All activities and investigations should be closely supervised by a qualified adult.

3. Agreement to participate must be obtained from all subjects prior to the beginning of the activity or investigation. All aspects of the activity or investigation should be thoroughly explained beforehand, and any and all questions answered. Use willing volunteers only.

4. Students must have the right to refuse to participate or withdraw from participation at any time during the activity.

5. Information and data collected should be confidential. Participants may not wish to disclose results or information that identifies them individually. Such information should be disclosed only with the participant's full agreement.

**H1.** *Habitats Wanted.* Generate a list of mammal categories from all the major mammal orders. One possible list: platypus, opossum, kangaroo, armadillo, beaver, bat, shrew, mouse, rat, squirrel, chipmunk, prairie dog, rabbit, raccoon, skunk, fox, wolf, coyote, bear, bobcat, lion, puma, deer, antelope, moose, bison, sea otter, seal, dolphin, porpoise, whale, rhinoceros, zebra, and elephant. Be as specific as possible. For example, you might specify the mule deer in the deer category.

Secretly assign individual students or teams of students a particular mammal or group of mammals to work with. No student or team should know what mammals the others have been assigned.

Read students some classified ads from the newspaper for apartments or houses wanted to make sure they understand what such ads are all about. Now challenge the students or teams to write a "habitat wanted" ad for each of the mammals they were assigned. Have them word the ad as if their assigned mammal(s) was actually doing the writing. Encourage them to make each ad as detailed and specific as possible.

Once students or teams have completed their ads, list all the mammals you assigned on a chalkboard or large piece of paper and have students or teams read their ads to the rest of the class. See if students can identify which mammal wrote each ad.

**H2.** *Neighborhood Mammals.* What types of wild mammals are found in your area? Have students draw on their own experiences, use field guides and other appropriate references, and contact local wildlife authorities to determine which specific mammals are found in your area. Assign different students or groups of students different categories of mammals to investigate. Then have students present their findings to the class in whatever

**HABITAT**

manner you deem appropriate. Colored pictures and posters would be an eye-catching and memorable way to present such information.

Taking students on field trips to see local wild mammals in their natural habitat probably will not be very productive. Such trips are great for birds, but you seldom see wild mammals. Instead, consider taking your students to a local zoo or nature center to see wild mammals of your area and perhaps those of other habitats worldwide.

**H3.** *Walk a Mile in My Shoes.* Have students try to put themselves in the mammals' place by having them respond orally or in written form to the question, What specific mammal would you be and why?

**H4.** *This Territory Is Taken.* Begin this activity with a brief discussion of mammal territories and the various ways mammals mark their territories (rubbing against objects to transfer odors from glands, urine marking, and so on). Then divide the class into groups or teams.

Designate an area to serve as a habitat—the classroom and adjacent hallway or a large open area like a gymnasium. Give each team about a dozen cotton swabs and a vial of scent that belongs strictly to that group. Some scents you might use are lemon, maple, vanilla, coconut, root beer, chocolate, cinnamon, and peppermint. The scents will be easier to detect if this activity is done indoors. Challenge each team to develop at least two behaviors to warn other teams away from their territory in case the scent marking doesn't work.

Have the teams draw numbers. Send the team that draws number 1 to the designated habitat area by themselves and unseen by the other student teams. Instruct them to use their cotton swabs and scents to mark out a territory. Caution the first few teams not to mark territories that are unfairly large. Once team 1 has marked its territory, all team members should stand in the middle of their territory. Now send in the next team to establish its territory. The members of each subsequent team will have to use their noses and watch the behavior of other teams to find unoccupied territory. The last team will have the difficult task of finding what little territory is left. This activity can become loud and boisterous. Keep a close eye on territorial disputes that may escalate.

Extend this activity by having students determine their home range. Start by sharing the following information with your students: Mammal territories are places within a larger area called a home range, which is the entire area a mammal may cover to find food, shelter, water, and a mate. A territorial mammal usually doesn't defend its entire home range—only the area it marks out as its own specific territory. The following list shows common mammals and their home ranges in square miles:

| | |
|---|---|
| Common shrew — 0.001 | Male meadow vole — 0.2 |
| Male puma — 15 to 30 | Pack of wolves — 36.0 |
| Female grizzly | Red fox — 2.0 |
| and cubs — 78.5 | Badger — 3.3 |

Now have students make their own personal range maps. On a sheet of graph paper, have each student mark the center square with the letter H to represent the location of the student's home (territory). At the bottom of the paper have students mark the scale:

1/2 inch = 1 mile

1.25 cm = 1.6 kilometers

The top edge of the paper should be marked North, the bottom edge South, the right edge East, and the left edge West.

Challenge students to keep a record of their activities on their range maps for whatever time period—a day, several days, or a week—you decide on. The students should draw and label on their maps where they went and approximately how far and in what general direction each place was from home. Some students may travel far enough that they will need to tape several sheets of graph paper together.

After the students have mapped out all their activities for the time period assigned, have them use rulers to connect the outermost points. These lines represent the boundaries of each student's home range. Using the scale on their maps, have students calculate their home range in square kilometers or miles. Have students compare and contrast the differences in size of range.

**H5.** Challenge: *Habitat Preference in Rodents.* Do rodents prefer sawdust to cedar chips and dim light to bright light? Investigations into these and similar questions can be interesting insights into the habitat preference of rodents.

Such investigations can be conducted in the Quadramod Habitat Chamber. Construct such a chamber by gluing together four identical boxes. Cardboard boxes will suffice as the rodents will be kept there only a short time. For small rodents like gerbils or mice, the dimensions of each box should be about 40 × 40 centimeters (16 × 16 inches). For larger rodents like rats, the dimensions of each box should be about 70 × 70 centimeters (28 × 28 inches). Each box must be the same approximate size and color. Ask students why the Quadramod must be so constructed. (Everything must be kept the same except the variable you are testing. For example, if you are testing light preference, all other factors—temperature and size and color of the boxes—must be as identical as possible.)

On each of the inside walls, cut three or four doorways large enough to allow the rodents you are working with free access to all boxes (mods). Now you are ready to begin investigating specific questions:

a. What bedding materials do rodents prefer? Try a variety of possible bedding materials such as sawdust, cedar chips, sand, gravel, soil, straw, or shredded paper. Avoid the toxic ink of newspaper and irritating resinous wood products. Place an equal amount of each material in a separate mod. Have students predict what they think will happen before they begin.

Instruct students to place one rodent in a mod and, with stopwatches, measure how long it stays in each mod. Use only one rodent at a time so they will react to the test materials and not to each other. Pose these questions to students as they conduct this investigation:

1. After initial exploration, does the rodent remain in one mod only or several mods mainly, or is no preference shown?
2. Does the time of day influence which mod(s) the rodent prefers?
3. Are the results influenced by which mod the rodent is put in to begin with?

Have students keep their data (times spent in each mod) in table form and, when the investigation is complete, graph their data and draw appropriate conclusions.

b. What light level do rodents prefer? Leave one mod unshaded (bright), partially shade another mod (dim), heavily shade the third mod (very dim), and totally cover the fourth mod (dark). Put the same bedding material to the same depth in each mod, or leave all mods bare. Keep all other variables the same. Place one rodent in a mod.

Have students predict what they think will happen before they begin. As before, have students use stopwatches to record the time the rodent spends in each mod. Have students keep their data in table form, make graphs from their data, and draw appropriate conclusions from their graphs.

**H6.** **Challenge:** *What "Habitat" Do Students Prefer?* Have students observe the other students in their school and notice where they tend to congregate before school, during lunch period, or after school. Ask students to keep observational notes about where the other students gather and some of the behaviors they exhibit at these gathering points. After several days of determining the favorite "habitats" of students, have the students survey their fellow students in an attempt to find out why they gather where they do.

Make sure your students understand that the privacy of all individuals must be maintained, that only willing volunteers should be surveyed, and that all notes and data should be kept confidential.

**H7.** *Challenge: Happy Habitats.* Many captive animals are kept in conditions that are minimally adequate (or worse) for normal health and growth. The adverse effects of poor living conditions are well known—but what are the beneficial effects, if any, of enriched living conditions? Behavioral scientists are investigating this question and its applications to some human sociological problems.

Give your students the following problem to solve: What effect does an enriched environment have on the health of rodents? Ideally, your students are familiar enough with experimental design by now to jump all over this as a poorly worded and vague problem. For one thing, you must establish what the phrase "enriched environment" means. Second, what does the word "health" refer to specifically? And last, what species of rodent will be investigated? An enriched environment could be defined specifically as one that contains a variety of things and places for the rodents to investigate and explore, and health could be designated specifically to mean weight gain. Gerbils would be my choice for the test subjects in this investigation because of their natural curiosity.

Now your problem might read: What is the effect of an enriched environment on weight gain in gerbils? Challenge your students to devise a way to test this problem.

One possible design is to set up two different environments using aquariums or animal cages of the same size. One, the deprived environment, should contain a water bottle, food dish, and a thin layer of bedding in the bottom. The other cage, the enriched environment, should contain a water bottle, food dish, a thick layer of bedding, and some playthings such as wooden blocks, small boxes, and tubes.

Place an equal number of weaned litter mates in each container. Carefully weigh each rodent before putting it in its respective environment. Mark individual animals by using food coloring or water soluble dyes. Keep marking fluids away from and out of the rodents' eyes. Provide identical food, water, and temperature for each environment.

Have students predict what will happen before they begin. Have students measure each rodent's weight gain over a set period of time and keep this data in table form. At the conclusion of the investigation, have students calculate the percentage of weight gain for each rodent. This information could then be graphed and appropriate conclusions drawn.

**S1.** *Strange Mammal Contest.* Students see domestic mammals and pets nearly every day, and most are somewhat familiar with the basic body structure of wild mammals. But how familiar are your students with the many variations on the theme? You must admit the playtpus, anteater, giraffe, and manatee, to name a few, are pretty strange mammals. To demonstrate the great diversity of mammals, stage a strange mammal contest.

Have students work individually or in teams to discover what they think is the strangest mammal on earth. Students should consult appropriate references and tap local wildlife authorities. When they have made their selections, have them present and defend their nominations for the strangest mammal to the rest of the class.

After the presentations, select a winner and runners-up. Judge the presentations yourself or invite fellow staff members and local wildlife authorities to serve as a panel of judges. A great way to close this activity is to award gag gifts or mementos relating to mammals.

**S2.** *Mammal Match-up.* Divide your class into three or four teams and give each team a list of 10 to 20 different mammals. Each team should receive a different list, and the contents of the list should not be known by other teams.

Challenge the teams to write descriptions of each mammal on their list. The age and ability of your students will determine how specific and detailed their descriptions should be. Encourage them to be as detailed as possible.

Once the descriptions have been written, have students imagine they are part of a popular television game show called Mammal Match-up. Arrange the room so that the teams face each other. You should take the role of game show host, score keeper, and mediator of disputes. Conduct the game by the following rules:

1. Shouting and screaming are not allowed. Points may be taken off a team's score for rude behavior to other teams, inappropriate comments, and excessive loudness.
2. One group, designated readers, will read one of its descriptions (clue) to the other groups, designated listeners.
3. Once the entire clue has been read, the first team of listeners to signal (by raising hands) gets a chance to name the mammal the readers described.
4. If the listeners are correct, they will be awarded 5 points. If they are incorrect, they will lose 5 points and another group of listeners can attempt to make the match. If the readers stump all the listeners, they get 5 points.
5. Award a 2-point bonus if the listeners can correctly identify the mammal being described and give one additional fact about that mammal that the readers did not include in their description.
6. Groups alternate being readers and listeners.

**S3.** *Biggest, Fastest, Tallest.* In this activity students will learn some amazing facts about mammals and their physical abilities and increase their understanding of how diverse a group mammals really are.

a. Biggest bodies

The largest mammal is the blue whale, which can grow to be more than 30 meters (100 feet) long. Have students measure and mark off this distance to help them better comprehend the size of this mammal. The blue whale may weigh more than 135 metric tons (150 tons). Have students observe cars in the school parking lot and estimate their weights. (For our purposes we will say around 1,350 kilograms (3,000 pounds).

Structure

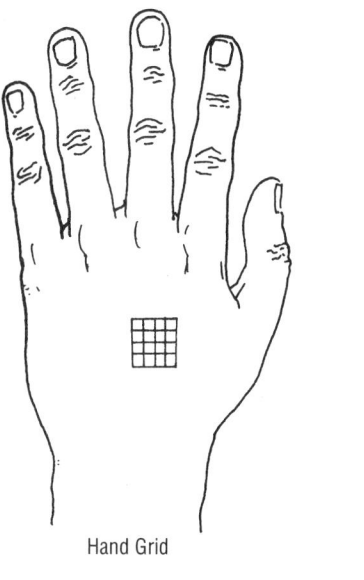

Hand Grid

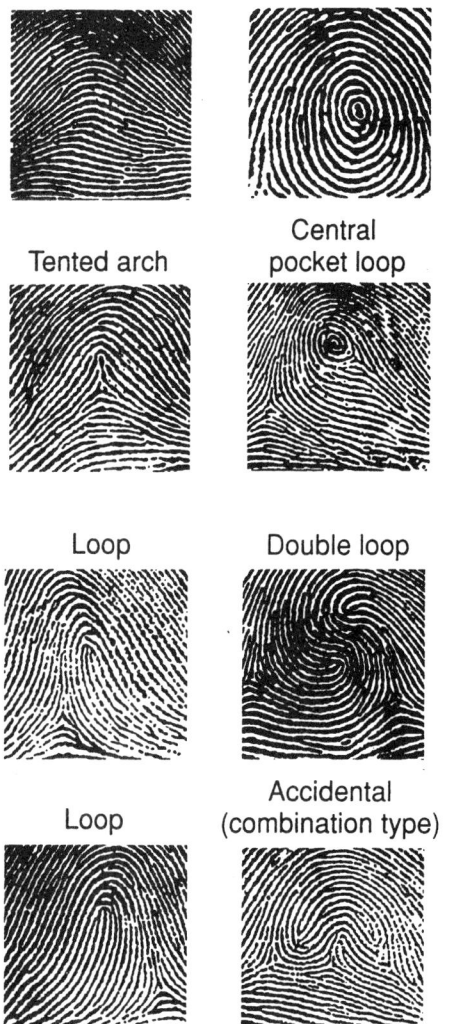

| Plain arch | Plain whorl |

| Tented arch | Central pocket loop |

| Loop | Double loop |

| Loop | Accidental (combination type) |

Fingerprint Categories

Now have students calculate approximately how many cars equal the weight of one blue whale. (About 100 cars).

The heaviest male human ever to live was Robert Earl Hughes (1926-1958), at 481 kilograms (1,069 pounds); the heaviest female human was Ida Maitland (1898-1932), at 410 kilograms (911 pounds). The average adult human male weighs 73 kilograms (162 pounds) and the average adult human female 61 kilograms (135 pounds).

The largest land animal is the African elephant. It may stand more than 3.2 meters (10.5 feet) tall at the shoulder and weigh more than 6.5 metric tons (6 tons), or the equivalent weight of approximately 4 cars.

b. Tallest bodies

The tallest land mammal is the giraffe, which stands 5.6 meters (19 feet) tall. Have students measure their own height and then determine how many students would have to stand on each other's shoulders to make a tower as tall as a giraffe.

The average human adult male stands 173 centimeters (69 inches, or 5 feet 9 inches) tall, and the average adult human female stands 160 centimeters (64 inches, or 5 feet 4 inches) tall. The tallest reliably measured adult human male was Robert Wadlow (1918-1940), at 268 centimeters (107 inches, or 8 feet 11 inches). The shortest recorded adult human male was Calvin Phillips (1791-1812), at 68 centimeters (27 inches, or 2 feet 3 inches) tall. The tallest adult human female was Jane Bunford (1895-1922), at 236 centimeters (95 inches, or 7 feet 11 inches) tall. The shortest adult human female was Pauline Musters (1876-1895), at 56 centimeters (23 inches, or 1 foot 11 inches) tall.

c. Fastest movers

Time each of your students in a 46-meter (50-yard) dash and have them record their own individual time. Now ask them to compare their time to that of the cheetah, the fastest land mammal for short distances. The cheetah could cover the distance your students ran in less than two seconds! Cheetahs may run at speeds of 100 kilometers (60 miles) per hour for 180 to 270 meters (200 to 300 yards). (Note: These figures represent a cheetah's top speed and were not measured from a standing start. To make the comparison more realistic, you may want to have your kids run a 68-meter [75-yard] dash and time them from yard 25 to the end.)

The pronghorn antelope is the fastest land mammal over long distances. They can easily run 55 to 70 kilometers (35 to 45 miles) per hour for 6 kilometers (4 miles), and they reach top speeds of 90 kilometers (55 miles) per hour for shorter distances. The fastest aquatic mammal is the orca, which could cover the 46-meter (50-yard) distance in about 3 seconds. Orcas can swim at speeds of up to 55 kilometers (35 miles) per hour for about 450 meters (500 yards).

The fastest speed recorded for a running human was 45 kilometers (27 miles) per hour briefly during a sprint. The fastest speed recorded for a human swimming was 8.65 kilometers (5.19 miles) per hour briefly during a sprint.

d. Longest and highest jumpers

Stage a long-jump competition and have each student record his or her best leap. Now have them compare their efforts to that of the red kangaroo, which can jump more than 12 meters (40 feet) in one bound. The best high jumper is the puma, which can leap 5 meters (18 feet) high. The longest human jump is slightly over 8.8 meters (29 feet 2 1/2 inches), and the highest human jump is 2.4 meters (8 feet).

e. Best breath holders

Have students hold their breath for as long as they can comfortably. Warn them not to try to hold their breath too long or they may faint. Compare the students' breath-holding abilities to those of the Weddell seal, which can hold its breath for 60 minutes, and the sperm whale, which can hold its breath for 75 minutes.

**S4.** *Mammal Observations.* Have students observe a live mammal such as a rodent, a pet dog or cat, or themselves and answer the questions or do the activities that follow:

a. Skin and hair

1. Mammal skin has well-defined structures within it that can be considered the appendages of the skin. These are hairs and hair follicles, nails, sweat glands, sebaceous (oil) glands, and various sensory nerves and receptors. Have students examine portions of their skin using a hand magnifier, or preferably stereo dissecting microscopes. Have them observe and diagram the appearance of the skin and hair on the back of their hand and observe their fingernails and moles or freckles.

2. As nearly hairless mammals, humans have very sensitive skin. In this activity, students determine the sensitivity of their skin to certain stimuli by making skin sensitivity maps. Have students draw a grid on the back of their hand and draw a similar grid on a piece of paper. Working in pairs, one student (experimenter) should gently press each square in the other's (subject's) hand grid with a toothpick while the subject looks away. When the subject feels pain, mark the squares on the paper data grid that match the squares on the hand where pain was perceived with the letter P. Remind students not to press too hard or to break the skin. The idea is to generate discomfort, not extreme pain. Have students reverse roles and repeat the experiment.

   Now have the experimenter touch each square on the subject's hand grid lightly with a cotton swab. Mark the letter X on the paper data grid in each square where the subject feels the sensation of pressure. Reverse roles and repeat.

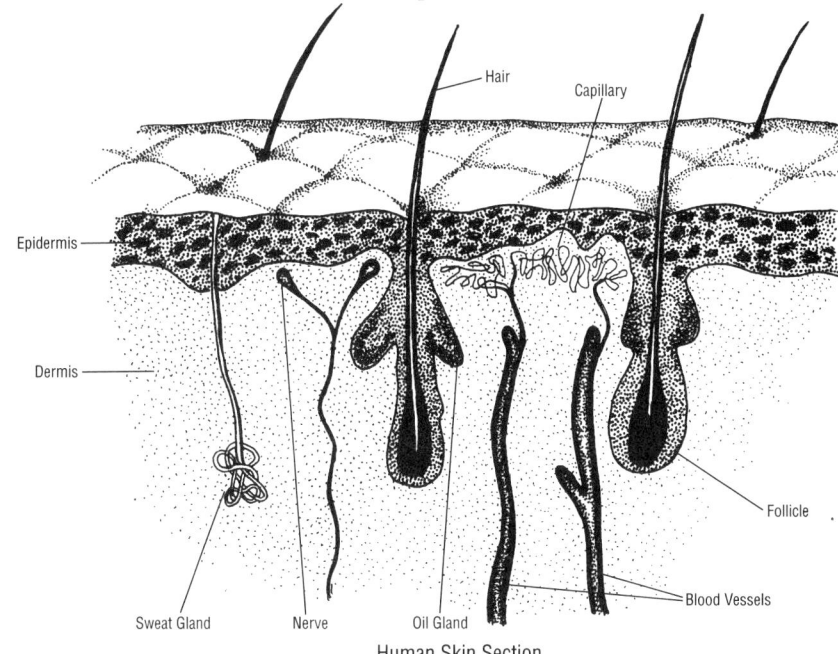

Human Skin Section

*(labels: Hair, Capillary, Epidermis, Dermis, Sweat Gland, Nerve, Oil Gland, Follicle, Blood Vessels)*

My Personal Fingerprint Patterns

| | Right Thumb | Left Thumb | | | | |
|---|---|---|---|---|---|---|
| 4 | 3 | 2 | 1 | | | |

| Total number of sensitive spots | | | |
|---|---|---|---|
| | You | Your partner | Your class |
| Pain | | | |
| Pressure | | | |
| Cold | | | |

Skin Sensitivity Data Table

BEARS

Black Bear

Grizzly Bear

Polar Bear

RABBITS

Black-tailed
Jack Rabbit

Cottontail

Snowshoe
Hare

Pika

Now ask the experimenter to hold the straightened end of a paper clip on an ice cube for several minutes and then touch each square on the subjects's hand grid with the cold paper clip. Mark the letter C on the paper data grid in each square where the subject felt the sensation of cold. Reverse roles and repeat. Have students complete a data table comparing their results to the entire class. If time permits, have students repeat this activity for an area on the palm of the hand.

Once this activity has been completed, have students react to the following questions:

- Does every part of the skin on the back of the hand feel pain, pressure, and cold equally well?
- How are the sensitive spots distributed on the back of the hand?
- How does the distribution of sensitive spots on the palm compare with the back of the hand?

3. Have students examine their fingertips under bright light using a hand magnifier or stereo dissecting microscope. As they observe, ask these questions:

- Can you see ridges on your skin?
- What are these ridges called? (Friction ridges or fingerprints.)
- How are these ridges helpful to us? (They improve our gripping ability and, since each person's pattern of ridges is different, they may be used for identification.)
- Where else on the body would we find such ridges? (On the soles of the feet.)

Have students compare their fingerprint patterns to the basic categories shown on page 240. Have students record the basic pattern of each finger in a table similar to the one shown on page 241.

Once students have determined their own patterns, have them react to these questions:

- Study your patterns. Does each finger on the same hand have a different pattern?
- How does the pattern on the same finger on different hands compare?
- Which pattern type is the most common in class? the least common?

4. One of the most important skin appendages is the sweat glands. Challenge students to explain why sweat glands are so important. (Evaporation of the liquid from these glands off the skin is the main way the body keeps cool.)

Have students map their sweat glands using the following procedure:

a. Mix 1/2 cup water and 2 teaspoonfuls of corn starch. Stir thoroughly. Cut paper into squares about 5 × 5 centimeters (2 × 2 inches). Dip the paper squares into the starch solution and then let the squares dry completely.

b. With the students working in pairs, have the experimenter paint the subject's palm with iodine solution.

c. Have the subject do some form of vigorous exercise such as running in place until he or she breaks a sweat.

d. Have the experimenter press a piece of dry starch paper onto the iodine area of the subject's palm. The sweat glands will appear as dark spots on the paper.

e. Have students reverse roles and repeat.

Once students have mapped the sweat glands of their palms, ask them these questions:

- How does the number of sweat glands in your palms compare to those on other areas of the body?

> (Palms — 370 per square centimeter
> Back of hand — 200 per square centimeter
> Forehead — 175 per square centimeter
> Abdomen and forearm — 155 per square centimeter
> Leg and back — 70 per square centimeter)

- On a hot day you usually feel sweaty, sticky, and uncomfortable. If you fan yourself, you feel cooler. Why? (Fanning increases the rate of evaporation and thus the rate of cooling.)

5. Reptiles have their scales, birds have their feathers, and mammals have their hair. Have students carefully clip hair from various areas of their body and place each type of hair on a labeled circle on a white piece of paper. Instruct students to examine the hairs from each area of the body by placing them on a microscope slide and viewing them under low power through a microscope. Have them observe and diagram the ways in which hair from different parts of the body is similar and different.

Suggest that students carefully clip and microscopically view the hair from various parts of another living mammal, such as a rodent, dog, or cat. Have them compare and contrast human hair with the other mammal's hair.

Once observations have been completed, ask these questions:

- How would you define or describe hair? (Hair is slender outgrowths from the skin of mammals.)
- What is the difference between hair and fur? (All mammals produce hair, but the soft, thick hair covering the entire body of certain mammals is fur.)
- What is the function of hair? (The main function of hair is to provide insulation and conserve body heat. In specialized forms, hair has other roles. For example, the horn of a rhinoceros is actually compressed hair, the quills of a porcupine are rigid hairs, the whiskers of a cat are stiff sensory hairs, and the foot hairs of the water shrew help it run across the water. The color of hair can help attract mates, camouflage the body, and regulate body temperature.)

Propose an explanation for why humans have the thickest growth of hair on their head. (Have you heard the old saying, "To keep your feet warm, put on a hat"? It's true: about 80 percent of the heat lost from the body escapes from the head.)

6. Demonstrate the effect of hair on maintaining body temperature.

Use 4 beakers for this demonstration. Wrap one with several layers of paper, one with cotton cloth, and one with a 100-percent wool blanket or a mammal pelt. Make all materials equally thick if possible. Leave the remaining beaker uncovered.

Pour an equal amount of boiling water into each beaker. Place a thermometer in each beaker and have students record the temperature in each beaker every 5 minutes over a given time period. I suggest you borrow good-quality thermometers from the chemistry

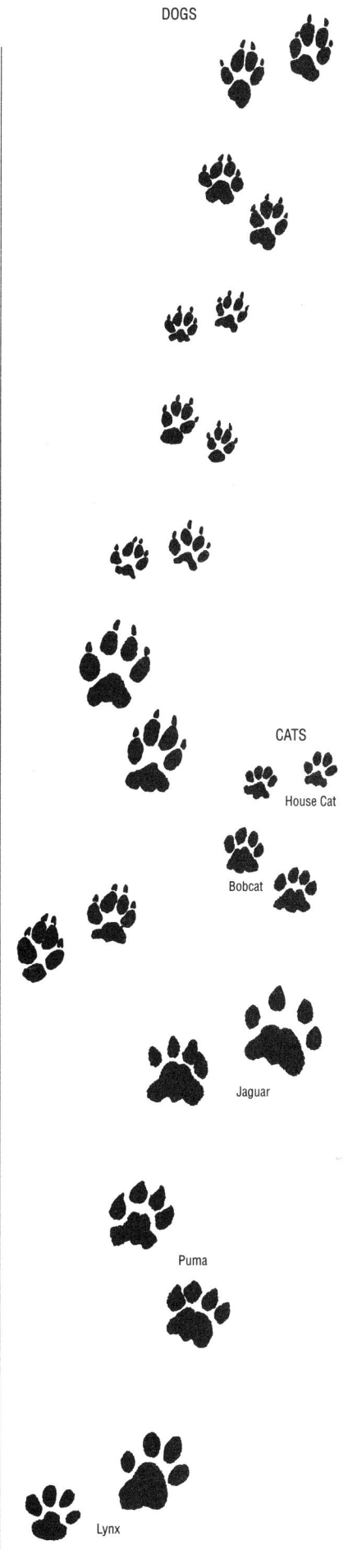

DOGS

CATS

House Cat

Bobcat

Jaguar

Puma

Lynx

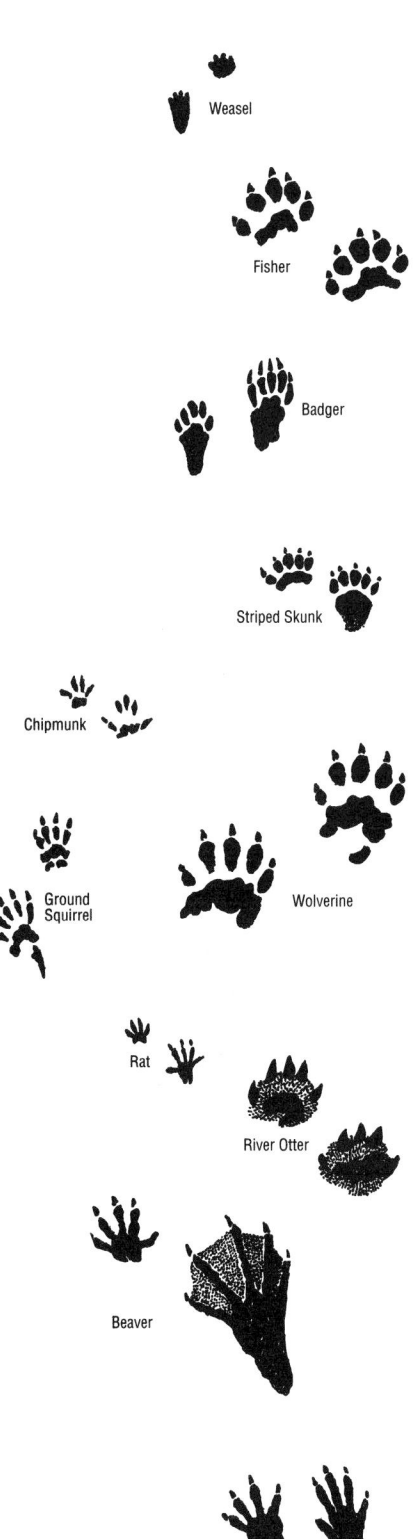

Weasel

Fisher

Badger

Striped Skunk

Chipmunk

Ground Squirrel

Wolverine

Rat

River Otter

Beaver

Muskrat

Porcupine

department. Such thermometers are accurate and are made to withstand the initial high temperature of boiling water.

Have the students keep their thermometer readings in a data table. Once all data has been collected, have students graph their data and use this information to answer the following questions:

- Which beaker had the fastest rate of heat loss? the slowest rate?
- Hypothesize an explanation to account for the different rates of heat loss you observed. (The uncovered beaker should lose heat most rapidly and the one covered by wool or fur most slowly. A reasonable explanation is that the hairs of the mammal trap air, which slows the movement of heat from the beaker to the air.)
- Your aunt has given you a pair of fur gloves to wear during the winter. The gloves are reversible. To keep your hands the warmest, how would you wear the gloves—fur side out and leather side in or leather side out and fur side in, and why? (Fur side in will trap air next to your skin and better slow heat loss.)

b. Limbs and movement

1. Bring in as great a variety of pictures of the limbs of mammals as possible. The limbs should be cut from the body and taped to pieces of paper. Divide the class into groups. Give each group as many limb pictures as possible and challenge them to tell as much as they can about the life of each mammal based on the structure of its limbs.

2. Have students observe the limbs, feet, and toes of a live mammal such as a rodent, pet dog or cat, or themselves. Challenge students to explain how the limbs, feet, and toes of each mammal they observe are perfectly adapted for the life-style of that particular mammal. Have them compare and contrast the limbs, feet, and toes of the various mammals they observe. How are they alike and different?

3. One unique feature of primate limbs is that they have hands with opposable thumbs. Have students view the hands of several common primates and describe as many ways as possible in which the hands of these primates are similar and different.

Ask students: What is an opposable thumb? (It is a digit on the hands [and possibly feet] that sticks out in such a way that it can be wrapped around an object in a grasping fashion.)

Demonstrate how useful an opposable thumb is by taping down your students' thumbs and then having them try to do a variety of timed tasks.

Divide the class into four groups. Group 1: Do not tape any of their fingers. These students will be the experimenters and will tape the others' fingers and record data. Group 2: Do not tape any of their fingers. These subjects represent humans. Group 3: Tape their thumbs to the palms of their hands so their fingers but not their thumb can move. This group represents the spider monkeys, which have no opposable thumb. Group 4: Tape their thumbs to the side of their hands so the only the top joint of the thumb can move. This group represents chimpanzees, which have an opposable thumb that is not very flexible.

After all thumbs are securely taped, have the subjects try to do the following timed tasks:

| | |
|---|---|
| Shell and eat a peanut. | Untie and remove shoes. |
| Put shoe back on and retie. | Put on jacket or coat. |
| Open a door. | Write their name and address. |
| Unscrew a bottle cap. | |

Instruct experimenters to time and record in a data table how long it takes each subject to complete each task.

Once the activity has been completed, have students respond to these questions, basing their answers on data collected:

- Which group completed the tasks most quickly and efficiently?
- Which group took the longest to complete the tasks?
- How does having an opposable thumb help humans? (Our opposable thumb is so important in grasping and manipulating objects that we are nearly helpless without it.)

4. Mammals have feet and toes that often leave distinct marks or tracks. Show students some tracks of common mammals. List the mammals whose tracks are pictured on a chalkboard or large sheet of paper, but do not reveal which mammals made which tracks. Challenge students to match the mammals to their tracks.

Now have students draw a natural setting such as a forest in winter or the muddy margins of a marsh—a place where mammals would leave distinct tracks. Have students draw in appropriate mammal tracks to tell a tale of some event or incident. Mammal field guides typically show tracks for reference. Challenge students to look at each other's drawings and explain what tale the tracks tell.

5. Mammals move because of powerful muscles attached to their limbs. They are capable of great feats of strength and speed but not for extended periods because their limb muscles become fatigued. Demonstrate this process to your students by determining who is the Champion Fatigue Fighter in the class.

Have students hold an object in either hand, palm up. All students should hold objects of identical size and weight (textbooks work well). The arm holding the object should be held up at a right angle to the chest. The free arm cannot be used to hold or prop the arm holding the object. Students may sit or stand but cannot move around (to avoid bumping the object out of another person's hand). The last person left holding the object is the Champion Fatigue Fighter.

Once you have a winner, have students react to the following questions:

- How would you describe muscle fatigue?
- Our limb muscles (skeletal muscles) are powerful but easily fatigued. Is this true of all the muscles in our body? (No. The smooth muscles wrapped around the internal organs are weak but do not tire, and the cardiac muscle that makes up our heart is the best of both types of muscle: powerful but never fatigued.)
- How might sporting events be different if we had cardiac muscle attached to our limbs instead of skeletal muscles?

6. Humans are unique mammals because we are bipedal. That is, we walk on two legs. Bears and apes occasionally rear up on their hind legs but they still are considered to be four-legged animals, and kangaroos need a heavy tail for balance in their bipedal movement.

Show students the illustrations of the skeleton, spine, skull, and pelvis of a human and a gorilla shown on page 246.

Have students observe the differences in body structure and attempt to explain why humans are bipedal and gorillas are not and why this is an advantage to humans. (The shape of the human spine, the way the skull sits on top the spine, the length of the limbs, the attachment point of the legs into the pelvis, and the in-line big toe

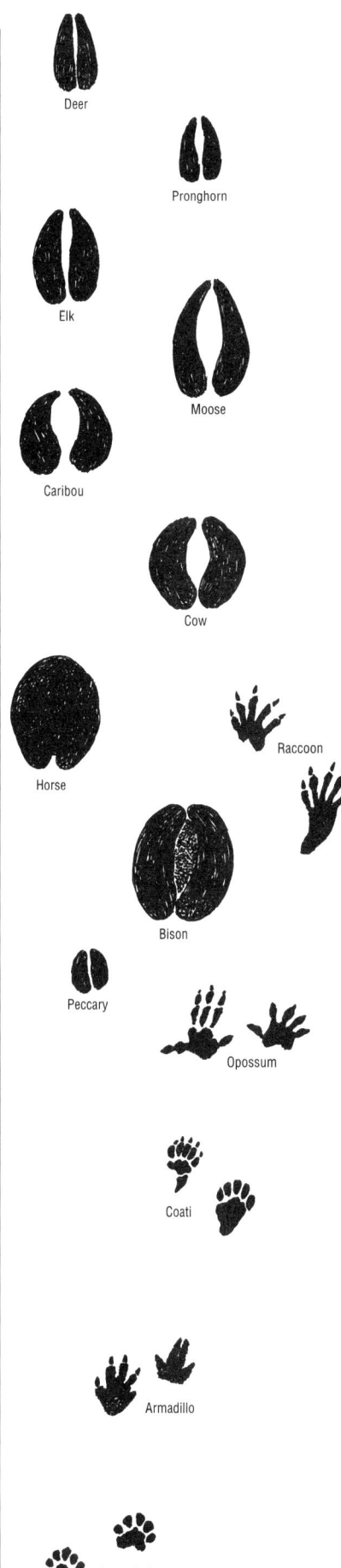

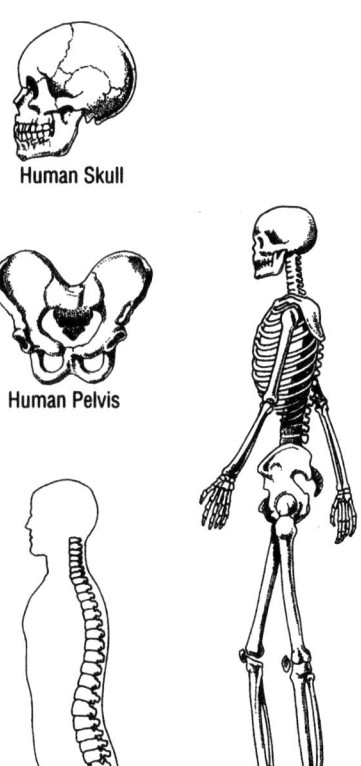

Human Skull

Human Pelvis

Human Spine

Human Walk

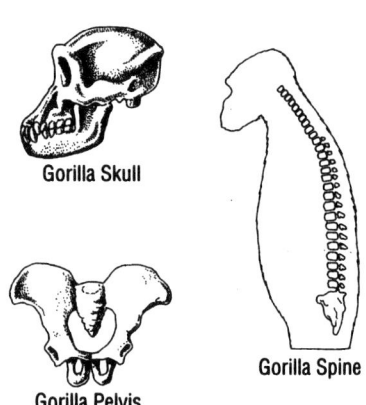

Gorilla Skull

Gorilla Spine

Gorilla Pelvis

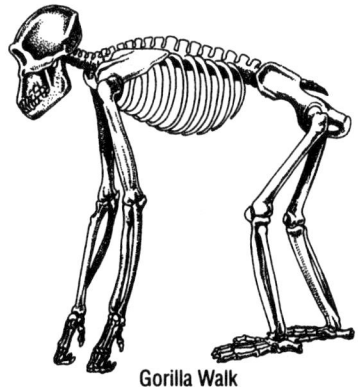

Gorilla Walk

all contribute to making humans bipedal. Being bipedal has given us free use of our forelimbs and hands and a wide range of vision.)

c. Body temperature and heart rate

1. Mammals are endothermic, and most have a constant body temperature. How might mammals be different if they were not endothermic? (Mammals would be more like reptiles and would need to live in warm climes or become dormant during cold weather to maintain their body temperature. They also would move more slowly due to a lower metabolism.)

2. **Challenge:** What is the effect of temperature on oxygen uptake in rodents? Mammals sweat or pant to release heat when the temperature rises, but what do they do when the temperature drops? One answer, of course, is that a mammal's hair provides insulation to prevent heat loss. Endothermic animals also use some of their oxygen to convert energy from their food into body warmth. Therefore, the rate at which a mammal uses oxygen can be an indicator of the amount of body heat that mammal is producing. Given this information, challenge students to devise a way to test this problem.

If you let students brainstorm this problem, they will likely come up with some type of oxygen consumption chamber similar to the one illustrated. To construct such a device, punch two holes in the lid of a jar. Insert two short glass or plastic stems into the holes and seal them in place with epoxy sealer or silicone aquarium sealer. All seals must be airtight or the device will not work. Attach to one stem a short piece of rubber tubing with a clamp on it and to the other stem a longer piece of rubber tubing with a 45-centimeter (18-inch) piece of glass tubing. Have students prepare a data table similar to the one shown. Cover the bottom of the jar with soda lime. The soda lime will absorb the carbon dioxide given off by the rodent that will be placed in the chamber. Your chemistry department may have soda lime, or you can purchase it from the suppliers listed in Appendix B. Cover the soda lime with a layer of cotton and cover the cotton with a screen that fits the entire bottom of the jar. You, your students, and the rodents should avoid contact with soda lime as it could be harmful.

Place a rodent in the jar. Open the air tube clamp. Put the lid on the jar and seal it tightly. Put the long glass tube into a beaker. Fill the beaker with enough water to cover the open end of the tube.

Table 1.  Oxygen Intake at Room Temperature

| | Trial 1 | | | Trial 2 | | Average Oxygen Intake (measured in mm of glass tubing) |
|---|---|---|---|---|---|---|
| Time in Minutes | Water Level (in mm) | Oxygen Intake (in mm of glass tubing) | Time in Minutes | Water level (in mm) | Oxygen Intake (in mm of glass tubing) | |
| 0 | | 0 | 0 | | 0 | 0 |
| 1 | | | 1 | | | |
| 2 | | | 2 | | | |
| 3 | | | 3 | | | |
| 4 | | | 4 | | | |
| 5 | | | 5 | | | |
| 6 | | | 6 | | | |
| 7 | | | 7 | | | |
| 8 | | | 8 | | | |

Putting some food coloring in the water will make it easier to record the movement of water up the tube.

Close the air tube with the clamp and wait one to three minutes for system adjustment. The water level should begin to rise in the tube. After one minute record the level of water under 0 minutes in Table 1. Record the water level each minute for eight minutes. The level should rise constantly. After eight minutes, open the air tube clamp so the rodent can get fresh air. Watch the rodent carefully. If it shows any sign of distress or acts strangely, open the air tube immediately, regardless of how much time has elapsed.

Reset the device and repeat the procedure for another eight minutes. Average the results of both trials and enter this figure in Table 1.

Prepare a second data table similar to the one shown. Reset the device, this time placing the jar with the rodent in it into a shallow pan containing ice and water. Let the jar cool down with the air tube open for three to five minutes before beginning. Add ice as needed during the trial runs to maintain cold temperatures. Close the air tube clamp and repeat the previous procedure conducting two trial runs. Record all data in Table 2 and average results.

Table 2.  Oxygen Intake at a Cold Temperature

| | Trial 1 | | | Trial 2 | | Average Oxygen Intake (measured in mm of glass tubing) |
|---|---|---|---|---|---|---|
| Time in Minutes | Water Level (in mm) | Oxygen Intake (in mm of glass tubing) | Time in Minutes | Water level (in mm) | Oxygen Intake (in mm of glass tubing) | |
| 0 | | 0 | 0 | | 0 | 0 |
| 1 | | | 1 | | | |
| 2 | | | 2 | | | |
| 3 | | | 3 | | | |
| 4 | | | 4 | | | |
| 5 | | | 5 | | | |
| 6 | | | 6 | | | |
| 7 | | | 7 | | | |
| 8 | | | 8 | | | |

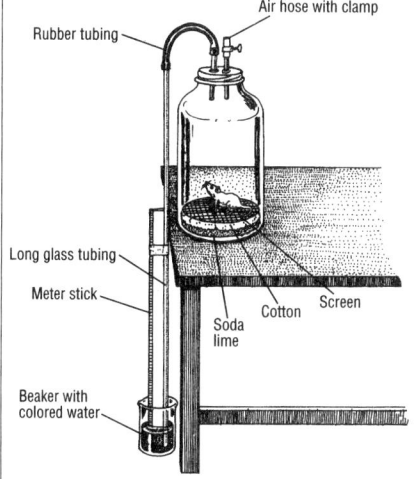

Oxygen Consumption

After the data have been collected, have students graph this information, draw appropriate conclusions, and respond to the following questions:

- How can this device show the relative oxygen consumption of the rodent? (As oxygen is used, air pressure in the jar is lowered. Greater air pressure outside the jar on the beaker pushes the colored water up the tube. Thus, the more oxygen used, the higher the column of colored water in the tube.)
- Why must this device be airtight? (If air leaks in, water will not rise to replace the oxygen used by the rodent.)
- Based on your data, what is the answer to the problem? (As the temperature drops, the rodent's oxygen consumption increases.)
- Why did oxygen consumption go up as temperature dropped? (The rodent attempted to generate more heat metabolically and used more oxygen in the process.)
- Would zookeepers need to buy more or less hay in the winter than in the summer to feed their deer? (They would need more in the winter because the deer will need more fuel and oxygen to generate metabolic heat during cold weather.)

Class Pulse Rates

| Tests | Avg. for men | Range | Avg. for women | Range | Class Average |
|---|---|---|---|---|---|
| at rest | | | | | |
| in bag | | | | | |
| exercise | | | | | |

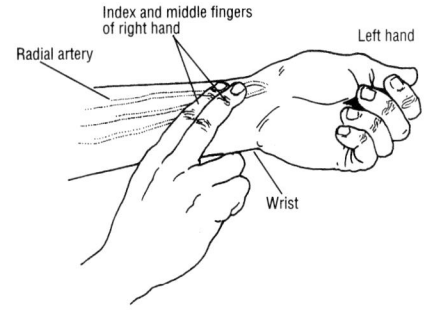

Index and middle fingers of right hand
Radial artery
Left hand
Wrist

My Pulse Rates

| Tests | My Pulse Rate |
|---|---|
| at rest | |
| in bag | |
| after exercise | |

3. The key to endothermy in mammals is an efficient, high-speed circulatory system powered by a high-pressure, pumping heart. In complete coordination and cooperation with the rest of the body, the autonomic nervous system speeds up or slows down the heart on demand.

Have students investigate the variations in their own heart rate by taking their pulse. Instruct students to work in pairs, with one the experimenter and one the subject. Alternate roles after each test.

Have students practice finding each other's pulse. The experimenters should place their right index and middle finger on the thumb side of the left wrist of the subject. Caution students not to use their thumb to take a pulse. The thumb has an artery in it and they may end up taking their own pulse.

Have students prepare a personal data table similar to the one shown. In addition, prepare a class data table on the chalkboard or a large sheet of paper.

Ask students to perform the following tests on each other. Urge students to count quietly as noise is very distracting when taking a pulse.

- Test 1: At rest. Have the subject sit in a chair quietly for 1 minute. Have the experimenter take the subject's pulse at the start of the second minute and take it for 1 full minute. The subject should record his or her pulse rate in a personal data table. Now reverse roles.

- Test 2: In the bag. Have the subject sit quietly and breath into a plastic bag held over the nose and the mouth for 1 minute. Instruct the experimenter to take the subject's pulse (with the bag still in place) at the start of the second minute and take it for 1 full minute. The subject should record his or her pulse rate in the personal data table. Now reverse roles. Some students have difficulty breathing from a bag for two full minutes. Try to get those students to breath in the bag for 30 seconds and then take their pulse for the next 30 seconds. Multiply this pulse rate by 2 to convert to a 1-minute pulse rate.

- Test 3: After exercise. After the subject exercises vigorously for 1 minute, have the experimenter take the subject's pulse rate for 15 seconds. Multiply this rate by 4 to convert to a 1-minute pulse rate. The subject should record his or her pulse rate in a personal data table. Reverse roles.

When the students have completed their personal data tables, use their information to fill out the class data table you prepared. Based on individual and class data, have students respond to the following questions:

- Why don't we use our thumb to take a pulse? (So we aren't counting the pulses of blood in the artery in our thumb and taking our own pulse.)
- What was the purpose of Test 1? (To give us a resting pulse rate as a standard of comparison for the other tests.)
- Who has the fastest pulse rate at rest, men or women? the slowest resting pulse rate?
- What factors other than exercise might increase pulse rate? (Smoking, being overweight, use of prescription drugs, and anxiety.)

4. Have students imagine that the famous mammal heart expert, Dr. Carl Cardiac, has gathered the following actual information about heart rate and mammal size. Have students study the information and respond to the question, From this data, what seems to be the relationship between mammal size and heart rate? (There seems to be an inverse relationship; that is, larger mammals have slower heart rates.)

| Common Name | Weight | Heart Rate Beats/Min. |
|---|---|---|
| European Hedgehog | 500–900 g. | 246 (234–264) |
| Gray shrew | 3–4 g. | 782 (588–1320) |
| Least Chipmunk | 40 g | 684 (660–702) |
| Gray squirrel | 500–600 g. | 390 |
| Harbor porpoise | 170 kg. | 40–110 |
| Mink | 0.7–1.4 kg. | 272–414 |
| Harbor seal | 20–25 kg. | 18–25 |
| Asiatic Elephant | 2,000–3,000 kg. | 25–50 |
| Horse | 380–450 kg. | 34–55 |
| Swine | 100 kg. | 60–80 |
| Sheep | 50 kg. | 70–80 |

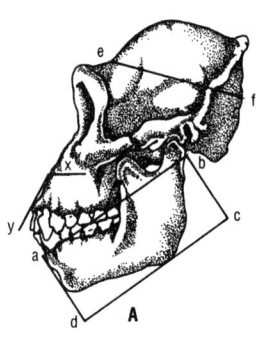

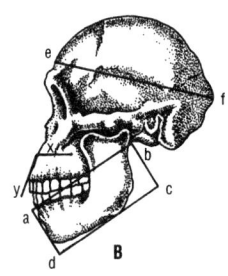

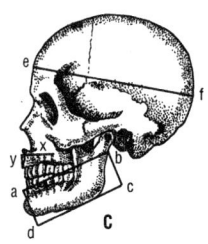

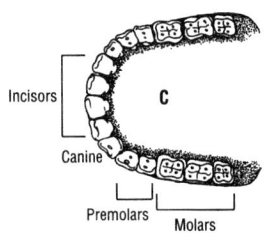

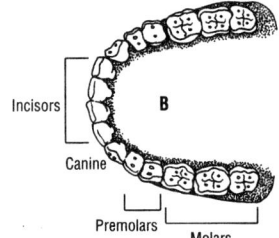

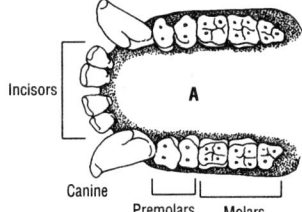

**S5.** *The Brotherhood of Primates.* Biologically speaking, humans are mammals, and the mammals we most resemble structurally are the primates. Help students learn more about the primates illustrated on page 249 by having them construct a branching classification chart similar to the one shown on page 251.

Now have students list the names and numbers of the primates on the lines corresponding to A1 and A2 and write the criteria used to divide the primates into groups. Ask students to choose a trait to divide the primates in A1 and A2 into two more subgroups each. Continue dividing each group until each of the primates pictured is in a group by itself. Have students write the criteria for their groupings as they proceed. The students' charts may contain more or fewer branches than the one shown.

Once students have completed their charts, have them answer the following questions:

- Did everyone group the primates the same way? (Probably not. Students have different perspectives and develop different grouping criteria.)
- What characteristics did you find most useful for classifying primates?
- How does making a chart like this help you better understand primates? (It allows students to see similarities and differences between types of primates.)
- Are humans primates? Are we animals? (This question should lead to some interesting philosophical discussions. We are composed of animal cells and structurally are mammals. However, we humans like to think of ourselves as above the other animals, and we certainly are intellectually, socially, and religiously.)

Have students visualize the following imaginary situation: A man, a chimpanzee, and a gorilla have been killed in the fiery crash of a gasoline tanker truck and the circus train on which they were riding. Fortunately, no other people or animals were injured. All that is left of the man, the chimp, and the gorilla are their skulls and lower jaw bones.

Which is which? The remains are brought to you, famous forensic scientist, Dr. Lester Lemming. You have the following facts available:

- Primates all have the same types of teeth and the same numbers of each type of tooth.
- Gorillas have large, heavy canine and incisor teeth for cutting and tearing coarse plant material. Humans have small canines and incisors, and the chimps are intermediate between the other two.
- The lower jaw length is longest in gorillas, shortest in humans, and intermediate in chimps.
- The lower jaw depth is greatest in the gorilla, least in the human, and intermediate in the chimp.
- The lower jaw area is greatest in the gorilla, least in the human, and intermediate in the chimp.
- The jaw angle is greatest in the gorilla, least in the human, and intermediate in the chimp.
- The cranium (brain case) is largest in the human, smallest in the gorilla, and intermediate in the chimp.

Have students prepare a data table similar to the one shown and make the following counts and measurements:

a. Count the number of each type of tooth in the jaw, noting the relative size of each tooth type. Record this information in the teeth data table.

b. Measure the lower jaw length (*ab*) in millimeters for each jaw. Record in the skull data table.

Comparison of Three Primate Skulls

| Skull | Length of Lower Jaw (mm) (ab) | Depth of Lower Jaw (mm) (bc) | Area of Lower Jaw (mm²) (ab × bc) | Angle of Jaw (xy) | Cranium Diameter (mm) (ef) |
|---|---|---|---|---|---|
| A | | | | | |
| B | | | | | |
| C | | | | | |

c. Measure the jaw depth (bc) in millimeters for each jaw. Record in the skull data table.

d. Measure and compute the lower jaw area (ab x bc) in millimeters for each skull. Record in the skull data table.

e. Use a protractor to measure the jaw angle for each skull. Record in the skull data table.

f. Measure the cranium diameter (ef) for each skull. Record in the skull data table.

Once all measurements and calculations have been made, have students tell which skull and jaw is that of a human, a gorilla, and a chimpanzee and explain how they arrived at that decision.

**B/R1.** *Read a Face, Make a Face.* Mammals, especially the primates, have very expressive faces. One thing we like about primates is the remarkable similarity of their faces and facial expressions to our own.

a. Show the students various chimpanzee facial illustrations. On a chalkboard or large piece of paper write the following list:

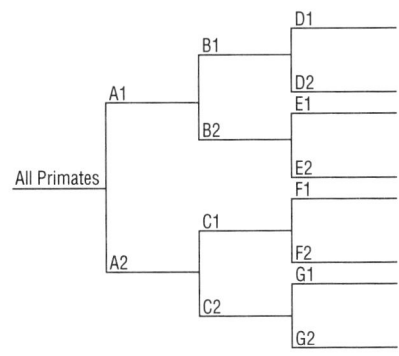

---

fear grin — being approached by a higher-ranking chimp
pout face — begging food
play face — relaxed, open mouth
open grin — intense fear or excitement
display face — showing aggression
whimper face — after being attacked or disciplined

(*Answers: 1—play face, 2—pout face, 3—display face, 4—open grin, 5—whimper face, 6—fear grin.*)

---

Have students match each chimp face to its description and meaning. Then pose this question to students: We must be cautious when trying to interpret what a mammal's face is telling us. Why? (Mammals, including chimpanzees, do not necessarily express their feelings as humans do, and we can draw misleading conclusions. For example, a level stare, innocent to humans, may express hostility in some apes.)

b. Suggest certain situations and have volunteers show how they would express their feelings in each situation using only their face—no talking or sounds. Use situations students can relate to, and keep them humorous and innocuous. For example, "Your best friend has just stepped on your toe," "Someone has just told you that a certain girl (boy) you like likes you too," "You start to pay for something at a store and discover you forgot to bring money," or "Someone with very bad breath is talking directly into your face at very close range."

c. Mammals also use body position and movement (body language) to communicate and express themselves. Divide students into groups and have two of the group members role-play a conflict situation. Have the group observe the role-play and then discuss how body language was

## Behavior/Response

used to communicate the feelings of the participants. Give each group several different conflicts to depict. Give some serious forethought to exactly which conflict situations you devise. Remember, no one should be embarrassed or feel hurt when this activity is over.

**B/R2.** *Investigating Some Mammal Senses*

a. Sight

1. **Challenge**: Do rodents have a sense of depth? Mammals in general have well-developed eyes. Seeing a true three-dimensional view of the world is important for finding food, shelter, water, and mates and avoiding predators or dangerous situations. Depth perception is particularly important for primates swinging through the trees. Do rodents have depth perception? Have your students devise a way to test this problem.

   Gerbils are ideally suited for this activity because they are easily handled and naturally curious. Have students predict what they think will happen before they begin.

   One simple design your students may come up with is to put a rodent on a tower of textbooks and observe its behavior. Start with one textbook on the floor. Put one rodent in the middle of the book and note what it does. (They will usually crawl or jump right off onto the floor.) Keep adding books one at a time and note any changes in the rodent's behavior as the tower gets higher. Have students collect observational data and draw appropriate conclusions.

   Eventually the book tower will become high enough that the rodent will peer over the edge but not jump, crawl, or slide off. From this behavior it seems that they can sense depth (height). Note: Whatever design students come up with, take care that the rodents do not fall or jump from a great height, as such a fall could injure or kill them.

2. Humans have forward-facing eyes that give them good overlapping binocular vision and depth perception. Have students take two pencils or pens, one in each hand, and hold them about 0.6 meters (2 feet) apart at arm's length with the points of the pencil or pen facing each other. Now challenge students to bring the pencils or pens together until the points touch. Have them do this several times. No problem, right? Now challenge them to do it with one eye tightly closed. Usually they will miss by a mile. Have them try it again with the other eye closed. Any difference in results? (Usually not. Most will widely miss the mark regardless of which eye they use.) Now have students respond to this question: Why can you do this stunt with both eyes but not with one eye closed? (You lack binocular vision so that although you can see how far apart the points are, you cannot calculate their relative spatial positions to each other [depth]. The margin for error with targets as small as pencil or pen points is enormous.) However, the human brain and eyes are quite adaptable. The body learns other ways to judge depth when given practice. If the students keep trying to match the points with one eye closed, they eventually get better at it.

   Extend this activity by determining eye preference. Most people have a pronounced eye preference, but few know this or know which eye they prefer. To determine eye preference, the subject, using both eyes, sights a distant object through a 2.5-centimeter (1-inch) hole in the center of a cardboard sheet held at arm's length. The subject must hold the card with both hands and focus on the distant object through the hole without looking at the card. Have the subject gradually move the card up to the face until only one eye can be used. This is the preferred eye. Have students repeat this a number of times and then have them respond to the following questions:

- Which is your preferred (dominant) eye?
- Is your dominant eye on the same side as your dominant hand? Is this true of other class members?

b. Reflexes and reaction time. With their large brain superbly coordinating their highly developed senses and muscular system, mammals are able to react to the environment around them almost instantly. Test your students' reaction times with the following exercise.

Have students construct a data table similar to the one shown. Students work in pairs for this exercise. The subject sits in a chair, and the experimenter stands facing the subject. The experimenter holds the 100-centimeter end of a meter stick at his or her eye level between the thumb and first finger of either hand. The stick should hang vertically. The subject positions the thumb and first finger of either hand at the zero end of the meter stick, but not touching the stick. The subject's thumb and first finger should be about 2.5 centimeters (1 inch) apart with the stick in between.

| Trial | Distance Ruler Falls (cm) | |
|---|---|---|
| | Without Distractions | With Distractions |
| 1 | | |
| 2 | | |
| 3 | | |
| 4 | | |
| 5 | | |
| Average | | |

When ready, the subject says "begin" to the experimenter. Sometime during the next ten seconds, the experimenter drops the stick straight down. The experimenter should vary the time from the "begin" command to the drop within the ten-second period.

At no time during the test should the experimenter and the subject look at each other. The experimenter should look up and beyond the subject and the subject should look only at the stick. The subject should try to catch the stick by moving only the thumb and first finger together as quickly as possible once the stick has been released. When the stick has been caught, the line under the middle of the subject's thumbnail is the mark to read. Record the distance the stick dropped to the nearest tenth of a centimeter in the data table. Repeat the procedure four more times with the same subject, and then reverse roles.

Once students have filled out their data tables, have them average the distance the stick fell. This number represents a relative (not actual) reaction time.

The suppliers listed in Appendix B sell electronic reaction timers. Carolina Biological Supply also carries a less-expensive alternative to the electronic timers called a reaction time ruler. This ruler is marked in such a way that the distance dropped can be converted directly to actual reaction time.

Have students compare their reaction averages and then respond to these questions:

- Why did measuring the distance the stick falls give only a relative reaction time and not an actual time? (The test measured distance and not time. A fast reaction, however, resulted in less distance, so the students with lower reaction averages had the fastest reactions.)
- Why did we do the test several times and then average? (To be as accurate as possible and to eliminate the chance lucky grab.)
- Why do our reaction times vary so much? (Student responses will vary. Accept any reasonable answer.)

Interested, more advanced, or older students could extend this activity even further by asking, for example, Do factors such as time of day, biorhythms, or age affect reaction time?

c. Hearing

1. If possible, bring a dog whistle to class. Tell the class you are going to blow a whistle but do not tell them what type of whistle it is. Blow the whistle and ask if any students can hear it. (Students will not be able to hear it. Some may think you are trying to fool them and are not really blowing on the whistle at all.) Tell the students what type of whistle it is and ask them to speculate about why they cannot hear it. (The frequency, or cycles per second, is too high for their ears to detect—although every dog in the vicinity may react. The human ear has its greatest sensitivity between 2,000 and 4,000 cycles per second, and the dog whistle has a much higher frequency than that.)

2. Pose these questions to students:
   - What mammal "sees" with its ears? (Bats. By using ultra-high frequency sound to echolocate, bats can detect objects or prey around them.)
   - Why can't humans hear most parts of the song of the humpback whale? (The sound in this case is too low a frequency for our ears to detect.)

3. Students now know that seeing with two eyes is important, but is hearing improved by having two ears?

   Sit a subject in a chair, securely blindfold him or her, and plug one ear with cotton or a swimmer's ear plug. Have the experimenter click two coins together at varying points around the subject's head at a distance of approximately 2 meters (7 feet). Vary the time interval between clicks so the subject cannot anticipate when the sound is coming.

   Have the subject point in the direction he or she thinks each sound comes from. The experimenter should record a score of correct or incorrect for 15 to 20 trials. Note: If you have several pairs or groups doing this activity, work in a large open area such as a gymnasium so the subject is not confused by the sounds coming from other groups.

   Keep the same subject, but plug the other ear and repeat the procedure.

   Repeat again with the same subject but with no ear plug.

   If students are working in pairs, reverse roles. Once all trials have been completed, have students compare results and respond to the following questions:
   - Could you locate sound better with one ear or with both ears? (Usually both ears give more accurate results.)
   - Can boys locate sounds better than girls or vice versa? (Results will vary, but there is no gender distinction for sound detection.)
   - Do students who are musically talented have more correct guesses? (Often they will because this ability increases with training.)
   - For a person who is hearing impaired in both ears, would you recommend they use one hearing aid only or one in each ear, and why? (Two hearing aids would give them a much fuller, richer, and accurate sense of hearing.)

**B/R3.** *Observing Some Aspects of Rodent Behavior*

a. Grooming behavior. Small rodents tend to clean and groom themselves frequently. Have students observe this behavior and investigate the following questions:

- Is there a sequence to the grooming pattern of an individual?
- Does the sequence of grooming or the pattern of grooming vary from individual to individual?
- Do rodents groom each other?
- Does a rodent exhibit a different grooming sequence or pattern when it is by itself than it does when it is in a group?

b. Escape behavior. Gently place a small rodent in a small, clean, empty flowerpot or similar container. Have students observe and record how the animal behaves and time how long it takes the rodent to escape. Time should be recorded in a data table. Suggest that students investigate whether the rodent learns to escape more quickly the more times it is put in the container. Have students keep times in a data table, graph the data, and draw appropriate conclusions.

c. Novelty behavior. How does a rodent respond to a new object in its environment? To investigate this question, remove all distracting objects such as water bottles and food dishes from a cage. Place a single rodent in the bare cage, let the rodent adjust for a short time, and then place strange items such as a golf ball, cardboard tube, and wooden block in the cage.

Ask students to consider the following question as they observe the rodent's behavior: What behaviors demonstrate interest or curiosity toward the new object(s)? (Sniffing the object, pushing the object with the head, or putting the front feet on the object all indicate interest.)

Note the length of time a single rodent takes to lose interest in a single new object. Compare that time with the time a group of rodents takes to lose interest in the same single object.

Investigate these questions: Do several new objects hold the attention of a single rodent longer than one new object? Is this true of a group of rodents?

Make sure your students understand that the behavior, intelligence, and memory displayed by caged domestic rodents is not necessarily typical of all mammals in general nor of wild rodents in particular.

**B/R4.** *Observing Some Aspects of Human Behavior*

a. My behavior. Encourage students to think about their own behavior by having them keep a behavior diary. A highly detailed account of each minute of a student's day would not be practical. Instead, challenge students to record in detail three to five things that happen to them each day for a week. The students should record not only the situation but what emotions they felt and how they behaved in each situation. Urge students to look for patterns in their behavior:

- Do they behave a certain way at a certain time of day?
- Do they behave differently according to the day of the week?
- How is their behavior influenced by the age of the people they are interacting with?
- How is their behavior affected by the gender of the people they are interacting with?

This activity should lead students to be more introspective and aware of their own behavior and attitudes. If appropriate, have students share their behavioral insights with the rest of the class.

b. The behavior of others. Without eavesdropping or violating the privacy of others, have students observe human interactions from a distance. Students should note and record the following observations:

- What is the gender mix of the people you observed?
- What is the age mix of the people you observed?

Have students time the interactions and record how many times the subjects shift weight from one foot to the other, look at each other or look away, and move closer or farther apart. As students observe, have them consider these questions:

- What does the distance between subjects indicate about their relationship or the nature of the interaction?
- As the interaction proceeds, do the positions of heads, hands, or legs or facial expressions mirror each other?
- What signals or gestures indicate the interaction is over?

People watching can be very interesting and reveal many facets of human behavior. Have students share some of their observations with the rest of the class. Rules for this sharing should be that all subjects remain anonymous and that compromising situations are off limits. Students may be interested in which couple were locked in a steamy embrace or which student the principal was lecturing in the hall, but such gossip has no place in a serious scientific investigation.

c. The influence of others. People are constantly trying to influence other people to act a certain way, to believe certain things, and to buy certain products by using a knowledge of human behavior.

1. To show how easily people are influenced, arrange the following demonstration: Select several students to be influencers. The day before you want to demonstrate this, instruct these students to look up at a certain point on the ceiling as you are talking about how people are influenced. They should not say anything; they should simply stare at the ceiling and act concerned. Give the students a cue word or phrase that will signal them when to begin staring at the ceiling.

   The next day, give the cue word or phrase and let your influencers do their thing. In a short time everyone in class will be staring at the ceiling and wondering what is going on. Explain to the students how they have been influenced.

2. Have students study commercial advertisements. How effective are advertisements in influencing people to purchase certain products? Have students discuss their reactions to such advertising. What are the reasons they like or dislike certain ads?

3. Challenge students to use their knowledge of human behavior and the likes and dislikes of their classmates to write their own advertisement for some product.

**B/R5.** *Investigating Learning and Memory in Rodents.* A classical and still interesting way to investigate learning and memory in rodents is the maze test. Simple mazes can be constructed from sturdy cardboard. Make the maze walls higher than the rodent can reach and cover the maze with a transparent lid to keep the rodent in. A single alternating T-maze (see illustration) with six or seven turns is suitable. Perhaps your industrial technology department could help construct a maze.

Move the rodent's own cage to the goal end of the maze as a reward for completing the task. Do not use negative reinforcement, such as electrical shocks, for wrong decisions.

Put rodents into the maze one at a time and have students record in a data table the length of time required to complete the maze and the number of wrong turns made. If you use more than one rodent, mark them so individuals can be determined. Have the rodent repeat the maze as many times as needed until it solves the puzzle with no errors (no wrong turns). How-

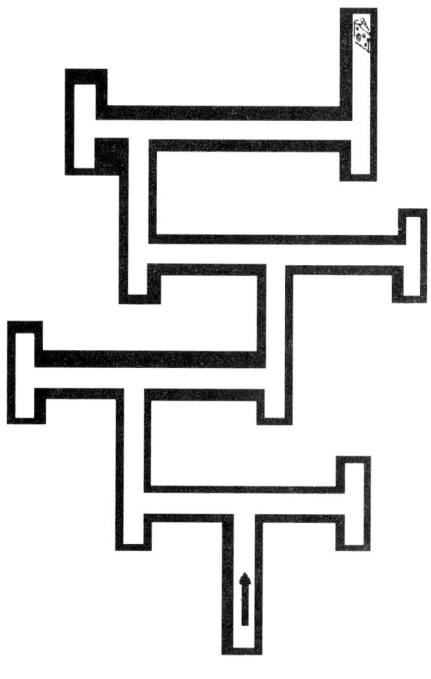

ever, no rodent should repeat the maze more than five times without being given a rest period. Have students graph both the number of trial runs vs. time to solve the maze and the number of trial runs vs. errors made.

Once data have been collected and graphed, have student respond to these questions:

- What is the correlation, if any, between the number of trial runs and the time required to complete the maze? (Usually the time required to solve the maze decreases when more runs are given.)
- What is the correlation, if any, between the number of trial runs and errors made? (Usually the number of errors decreases when more runs are given.)

Interested, more advanced, or older students could extend this activity into the following investigations:

- How long does the memory of how to run the maze last?
- Does age play a role in maze learning? Do young rodents learn the maze faster and/or remember it longer than older rodents?
- Do rodents that have been stroked and petted run the maze faster with fewer errors than those rodents that have not been handled?

**B/R6.** *Investigating Learning and Memory in Humans*

a. Human error. People often view scientists and doctors as highly intelligent, precise, and infallible individuals. However, all humans are fallible and capable of error. Scientists and doctors are trained to keep mistakes and imprecisions to a minimum, but errors can never be eliminated. Discuss human fallibility with students.

To demonstrate the error factor in human activity, give each student a photocopy of the same page of a book. The smaller the type and the more words on the page, the better. Challenge students to accurately count the number of words on the page. Hyphenated words and each letter "a" used by itself count as one word. Have students write their answer on a piece of paper and hand it in.

Tell students the correct answer and then tabulate the answers that were handed in . You might want to graph the results on a chalkboard or large piece of paper. There is usually an enormous range of wrong answers.

b. Human memory

1. Which is easier to memorize: a series of letters, a series of digits, or a mixture of letters and digits? Have students work in pairs to investigate this question. Have the experimenter read a list of ten increasingly large numbers to the subject and then ask the subject to repeat the numbers in order. Read several lists of numbers to the subject. Have the experimenter record the number of errors made by the subject on each list. Now reverse roles.

Repeat the test with letters instead of numbers and then with a mixture of numbers and letters. Reverse roles for these tests as well.

Once the activity has been completed, have students react to this question: In the United States phone codes are all numbers, but in England they are numbers and letters. United State postal codes are all numbers, but in Canada they are numbers and letters. Based on your results from this activity, should the United States change its phone and postal codes to make them easier to remember? Explain your answer.

2. Testing human learning and memory in human-size mazes is not practical, but finger mazes can be used. Construct several finger

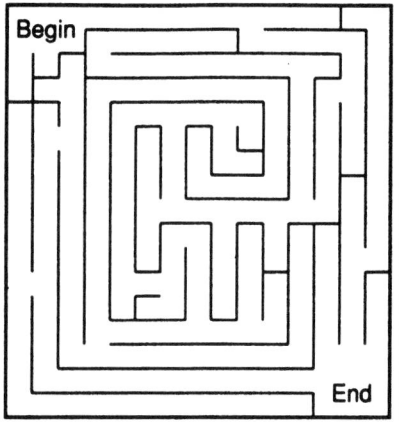

Finger Maze

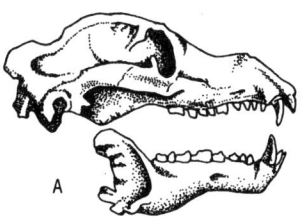

A

B

## Feeding

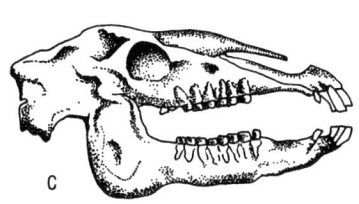

C

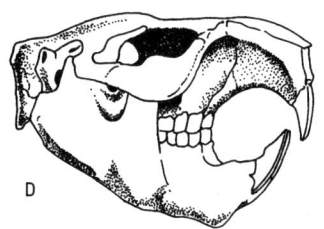

D

mazes similar to the one illustrated by drawing them out on a standard-size piece of paper with a black marker. Remember, students will be using their fingers on these mazes so you must draw them correspondingly larger than a normal pencil maze.

Cut a 6-millimeter (0.25-inch) hole in the center of a card nearly large enough to cover the paper with the maze on it. The subject should never see the entire maze at any time.

Place the hole so the letter S (start) on the maze shows through. On the "go" command, the subject puts his or her finger in the hole and tries to follow the maze to the letter F (finish). As with the rodent maze, time each subject from start to finish and record the number of errors made in a data table. Continue the tests until the subject has made two errorless runs.

Have students graph both the number of trial runs vs. time required to complete the maze and trial runs vs. errors made.

Once data have been collected and graphed, have students respond to the following questions:

- What is the correlation, if any, between the number of trial runs and the time required to complete the maze? (Usually the more runs given, the less time required to complete the maze.)
- What is the correlation, if any, between the number of trial runs and errors made? (Usually the more runs given, the fewer errors made.)

Jigsaw puzzles also can be used to investigate problem solving. Interested, more advanced, or older students might extend this activity to investigate such questions as

- What is the effect of age on problem-solving ability?
- What is the effect of distractions or various types of background music on problem-solving ability?

**F1.** *Feeding a Mammal.* Have students observe and describe the feeding behavior of a rodent. Gerbils make interesting subjects for this activity because after eating, they often bury uneaten food.

**F2.** *What's on the Menu?* Divide the class into teams. Give each team a list of several mammals and challenge them to write a menu for each mammal. For example, the menu for a grizzly bear might read:

> Breakfast: Grub fritters
> Lunch: Berries with honey
> Snack: Apples in sauce
> Dinner: Shredded salmon

**F3.** *Tale of the Teeth.* In birds, the beak determines diet. In mammals, it's the teeth. Mammals have four main kinds of teeth: incisors, canine, premolars, and molars.

Show students the skulls of four mammals without revealing which skull belongs to which mammal. Now share the following information with students: Rodents, like mice, have long, chisel-shaped incisors; no canines; and flat, grinding molars for gnawing and grinding plant material. Hoofed mammals, like horses, have nipping incisors and large, flat grinding molars for nibbling and grinding plant material. Canines, like dogs, have small, pointed incisors; long, sharp canines; and pointed molars for stabbing and tearing meat. Bears have short incisors, long canines, and molars that are intermediate between the dog and horse. Challenge students to determine which skull is that of a horse, dog, bear, and mouse. (Answer: Horse—C, Dog—B, Bear—A, and Mouse—D.)

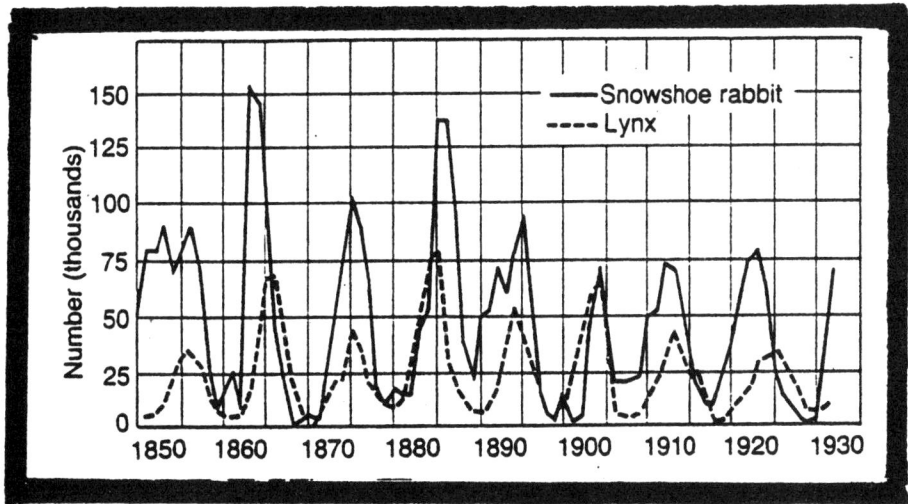

**F4.** *What's the Connection?* Students are usually more familiar with terrestrial (land) food webs than they are with aquatic ones. However, directly or indirectly, aquatic food chains and the mammals involved in them are important to us all. Copy the aquatic food web illustrated here. Cut out each creature from the web. Give the pieces to students and challenge them to reconstruct the food web by taping the pictures onto a piece of paper in their proper position in the web.

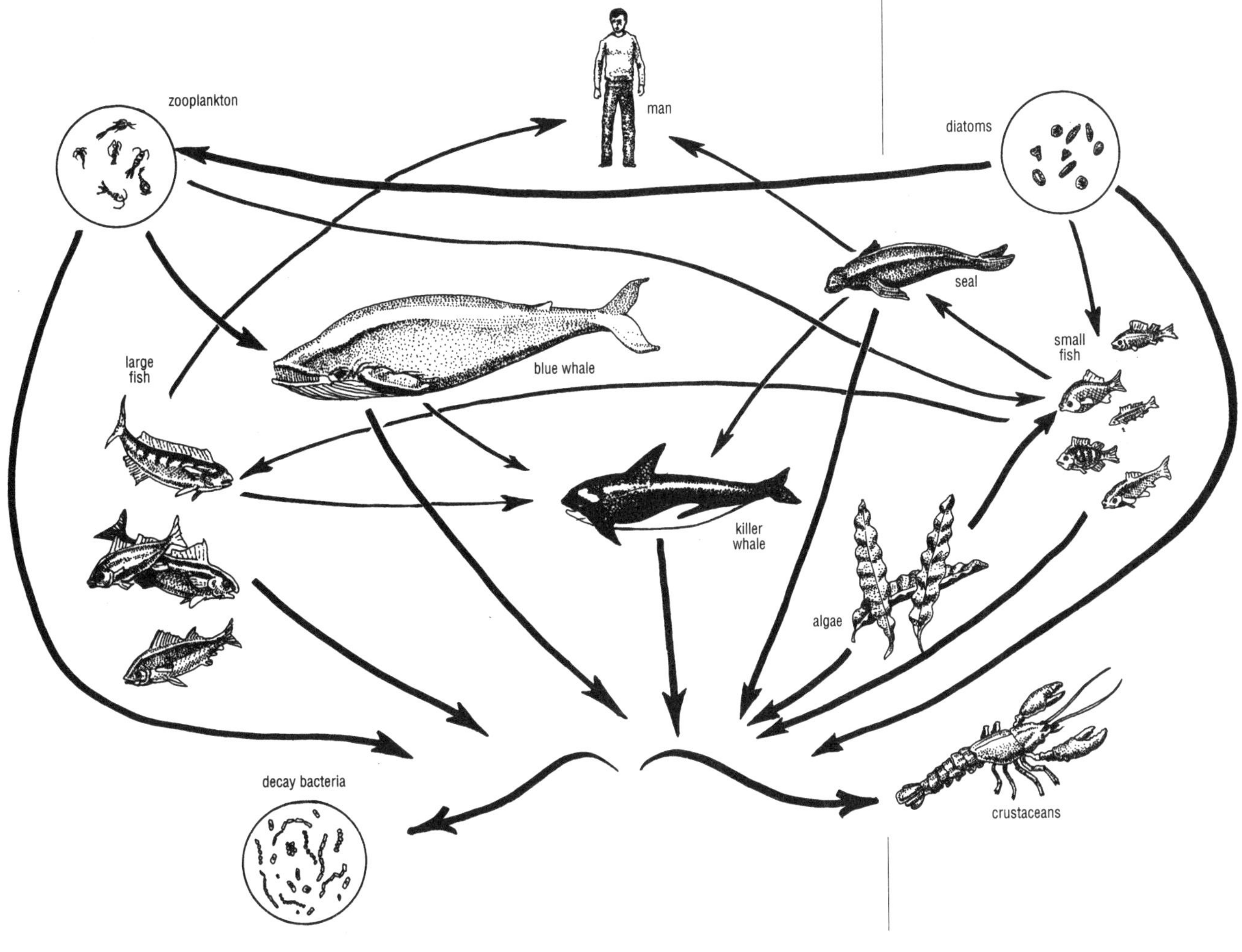

**F5.** *Tooth and Claw.* Have students observe the graph showing the number of pelts (skins) of the lynx and hare taken by the Hudson Bay Company over several decades. After studying the graph, have students respond to the following questions:

a. What does this graph tell you about the relationship between the lynx and the hare? (The population of one influences the population of the other.)

b. Which animal in this graph is the predator and which is the prey and how can you tell? (The lynx is the predator and the hare is the prey. In a stable energy pyramid there must be more prey than predators, and the graph shows far more hares than lynx.)

c. Which population controls the other? (They regulate each other. More hares means more food for the lynx so the lynx population grows and hares decline. But as hares decline there is less food for the lynx, and so the lynx declines. Fewer lynx means fewer predators to eat hares, so the hare population increases, and the whole cycle repeats itself.)

**F6.** *The Kaibab Deer Tragedy.* In 1905 approximately 4,000 Kaibab deer occupied the 727,000 acres making up the Kaibab Plateau on the north rim of the Grand Canyon. Well-meaning but ecologically ignorant people estimated the carrying capacity of the plateau to be 30,000 deer, and in 1907 these people began a campaign to "help" the deer by eliminating their predators. Table A shows the kinds and numbers of predators killed, and Table B shows the estimated number of deer from 1905 to 1939.

Have students use the information in Table B to make a line graph of the deer population from 1905 to 1939. Instruct them to put years on the horizontal axis of the graph and number of deer on the vertical axis. Have them draw a line from the 30,000 point on the vertical axis straight across to the right parallel of the horizontal axis. This line represents the population of deer that was thought to be the carrying capacity of the plateau.

Have students refer to their graph and Table A to answer the questions that follow:

a. What are the natural predators of the deer? (The mountain lion, wolf, and coyote.)

b. Why were the predators killed? (People reasoned that fewer predators meant more deer.)

c. Did removing the predators increase the deer population? (Yes, explosively.)

d. Why did the deer population decline from 1925 on, even though predators were still being eliminated? (Collapse of the habitat resulted in starvation and overcrowding resulted in disease.)

e. Was the actual carrying capacity of the plateau 30,000 deer, as people predicted? How can you tell? (They were not correct or the population of deer would have leveled off and stabilized at around 30,000. The deer population shot past 30,000 on the way up and back down but never remained at that level.)

f. What would have happened to the deer population from 1905 to 1939 if humans had not interfered? (It likely would have remained around 4,000 deer, the population to begin with.)

**F7.** *Fueling the Human Machine.* The following activities and questions should help students appreciate how a mammal's digestive system works and give them a better understanding of their own nutritional well-being.

a. Have students imagine that an educational media company wants to make an animated video explaining the process of digestion to young people (make them younger than your students). Your students have been hired to write the script for a video that explains what happens to

## TABLE A

| | |
|---|---|
| 1907–1917 | 600 mountain lions killed |
| 1918–1923 | 74 mountain lions killed. |
| 1924–1939 | 142 mountain lions killed. |
| 1907–1923 | 11 wolves killed. |
| 1907–1923 | 3,000 coyotes killed. |
| 1923–1939 | 4,388 coyotes killed. |

## TABLE B

| | |
|---|---|
| 1905 — 4,000 | 1927 — 37,000 |
| 1910 — 9,000 | 1928 — 35,000 |
| 1915 — 25,000 | 1929 — 30,000 |
| 1920 — 65,000 | 1930 — 25,000 |
| 1924 — 100,000 | 1931 — 20,000 |
| 1925 — 60,000 | 1935 — 18,000 |
| 1926 — 40,000 | 1939 — 10,000 |

a hamburger, french fries, and a glass of milk as it travels through the human digestive system.

Students do not need to write out the entire script, but they should produce a brief but concise outline including information about what organs are involved and what happens to each nutrient in the food in each part of the digestive system.

b. Why do we eat the things we eat? Give students the following list of foods (add or delete from the list as you see fit):

| | |
|---|---|
| pizza | hamburger |
| snake | eel |
| candy | sushi (raw fish) |
| vegetables | potatoes |
| mushrooms | tripe (the lining of a cow's stomach) |
| steak | hot dog |
| squid | snails |

Ask students if they have eaten or would eat each of the foods on the list. Have them respond in one of three ways for each food listed: "Yes!", "Maybe?", or "Yuck! No Way!" Compile student responses to find out which foods are class favorites. Students could take this list and survey other students and/or adults and see if those surveyed had the same tastes in foods as the class.

Once all responses have been compiled, have students analyze their own responses:

- If they like something, why do they like it?
- Is taste in food a learned part of family life or peer group? Is it part of our national culture?
- Are the things they like to eat healthy and nutritious?
- And what about those "Yuck!" answers? Why wouldn't they try some new and exotic-sounding food?

c. What's in it?

1. Have students prepare a table like the one illustrated. Ask them to examine the nutrition information found on the labels from at least five packaged foods. Once they have completed the table, have students respond to the following questions:

| Information on label | Food item | | | | |
|---|---|---|---|---|---|
| Serving Size | | | | | |
| Grams of Protein | | | | | |
| Grams of carbohydrates | | | | | |
| Grams of fat | | | | | |
| Number of vitamins | | | | | |
| Number of minerals | | | | | |
| Preservatives (yes or no) | | | | | |
| Artificial flavors or colors (yes or no) | | | | | |

## Calories in Common Foods

| Food | Calories |
|------|----------|
| Apple, raw (1 medium) | 75 |
| Potatoes, french fried | 155 |
| Tossed salad | 35 |
| Cheeseburger | 540 |
| Spaghetti with meat sauce | 277 |
| Chicken fried (1 leg) | 160 |
| Chicken baked (1 leg) | 95 |
| Milk, whole (1 cup) | 165 |
| Milkshake (1¼ cup) | 310 |

## Approximate Calories used in Various Activities

| Activity | Calories used per hour |
|----------|------------------------|
| Sedentary<br>sitting, reading,<br>watching TV | 80–100 |
| Light<br>standing up, cooking,<br>washing dishes,<br>walking slowly | 100–160 |
| Moderate<br>walking moderately<br>fast, playing ping<br>pong, mopping a<br>floor, making beds,<br>light gardening | 120–240 |
| Vigorous<br>washing a car,<br>walking fast, bowling,<br>riding a bicycle | 250–350 |
| Strenuous<br>runing, swimming,<br>tennis, dancing,<br>football, skiing | 350 or more |

- Did each product have a complete list of nutrition information?
- Which food on your data table has the most nutritional value? Explain.
- Would any one of the packaged foods on your data table supply a completely balanced diet by itself? Explain.
- Why are laws and regulations being passed requiring food processors to include more complete nutritional information on their labels? (Health-conscious consumers are beginning to demand to know what is in the food they eat.)

2. Students know that to survive they need the nutrients in food. But do they know how much food they need? How do we measure the energy we get from our food? Students have probably heard the word *calorie*. Ask students to define a calorie. (A calorie is a unit of measure for energy.) Show students the table listing the calories in some common foods.

Explain that a person's activity level determines how fast he or she uses calories ("burns food"). Show students the table listing the calories burned at different activity levels. Have students use both tables to do some calorie calculations to determine how long it would take to burn off some common foods at each level of activity. For example, a sedentary person would take over three hours to burn off the calories in one milkshake, and it would take nearly an hour of strenuous exercise to burn off the same milkshake.

Taking in too few calories can result in weight loss, and taking in too many calories can result in weight gain. Have students do some more calorie calculations to demonstrate this. As a general rule, 3,500 calories = 1 pound.

a. Sam Sedentary takes in 1,500 calories more a day than he uses. What effect will this have on his weight at the end of one week? one month? (At the end of one week he will have a calorie sur-

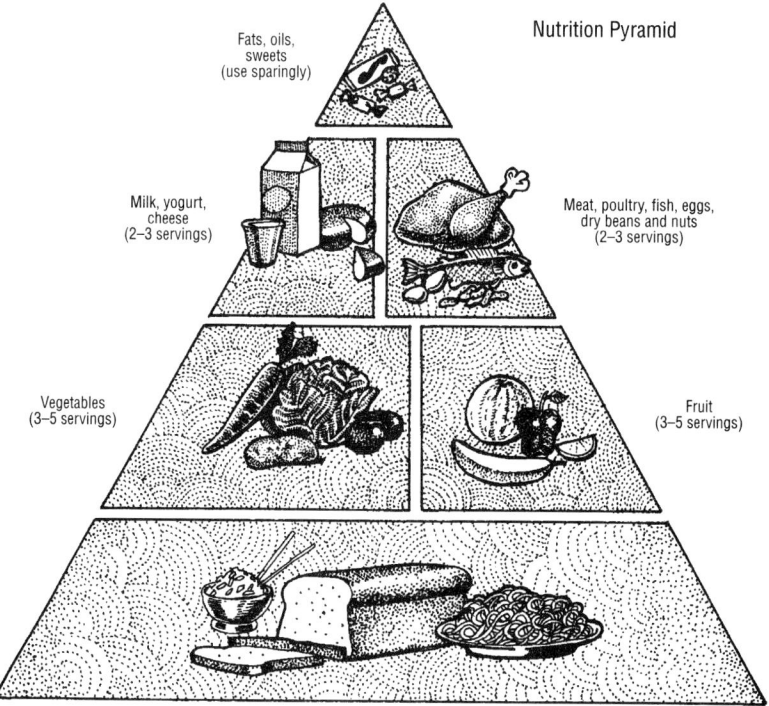

Nutrition Pyramid

Fats, oils, sweets (use sparingly)

Milk, yogurt, cheese (2–3 servings)

Meat, poultry, fish, eggs, dry beans and nuts (2–3 servings)

Vegetables (3–5 servings)

Fruit (3–5 servings)

Grains: Bread, cereal, rice and pasta (9–11 servings)

plus of 10,500 calories. Dividing 10,500 by the 3,500 calories in one pound results in a weekly weight gain of 3 pounds. At that rate, by the end of the month (4 weeks) he will have gained 3 pounds × 4 weeks, or 12 pounds.)

b. Victoria Vigorous burns off 1,000 more calories than she takes in every day. What effect will this have on her weight at the end of one week? one month? (At the end of one week she will have a calorie deficit of 7,000 calories. Dividing 7,000 by the 3,500 calories in one pound results in a weekly weight loss of 2 pounds. At that rate, by the end of the month she will have lost 2 pounds × 4 weeks, or 8 pounds.)

d. A balanced diet.

1. Now that students have some idea about what is in the food they eat and how much food to eat, help them better understand what to eat. Nutritionists have expanded the concept of the four food groups into a nutrition pyramid. Using the pyramid, have students analyze the imaginary students' diets shown.

   - Which student had the most nutritious diet for the day and why? (Student A because the diet filled most of the student's nutrition requirements.)
   - Suggest ways to improve the diets of both Student B and Student C.

2. Challenge your students to write a well-balanced and nutritious plan for themselves that will cover two days. They should plan a healthy breakfast, lunch, snack, and dinner for each day. Instruct students to keep their plans realistic and workable within the framework of their own tastes and the finances of their family.

   Once students have completed their diet plan, encourage them to work their plan and then share the strengths and weaknesses of their plan with the rest of the class. This activity can get kids thinking about what they eat and what they should eat—the first step toward developing life-long nutritional health.

| Student A | Student B | Student C |
|---|---|---|
| *Breakfast* | *Breakfast* | *Breakfast* |
| orange juice | 1/2 grapefruit | none |
| 2 eggs | cold cereal | |
| glass of milk | with milk | |
| toast | glass of milk | |
| *Lunch* | *Lunch* | *Lunch* |
| peanut butter and | fish | cheese sandwich |
| jelly sandwich | spinach | 2 donuts |
| apple | bread | ice cream |
| glass of milk | peaches | soft drink |
| | glass of milk | |
| *Snack* | *Snack* | *Snack* |
| glass of milk | soft drink | candy bar |
| bran muffin | potato chips | soft drink |
| *Dinner* | *Dinner* | *Dinner* |
| sausage pizza | roast beef | hamburger on a bun |
| green beans | rice | carrot and |
| tossed salad | peas | celery sticks |
| glass of milk | gelatin | glass of milk |
| | cookies | chocolate cake |
| | glass of milk | |

**R1.** *Observing Gender Behavior in Rodents.* Does gender influence behavior in rodents?

Mark four to six female rodents so each can be individually recognized. Place one female in a bare aquarium (the larger the aquarium, the better). Add the other females one a time at five-minute intervals. Have students observe and record the rodents' interactions—sniffing, nibbling, nuzzling, or fighting and general behavior toward one another. If serious fighting breaks out, remove the combatants. (Note: It is wise to wear leather gloves when handling fighting rodents.)

As students observe and record, have them consider the following questions:

a. Does behavior change as more females are added? If so, in what ways?

b. Which rodent, newcomer or the one already in the cage, initiates any interaction?

Now place the females together in small groups of two or three only. Have students observe and record their behavior and then change a member or two of the rodent group. Have students note any changes in behavior as group members change. As students observe and record, have them consider the following questions:

a. Does changing the individuals within a group change the behavior of the group?

# Reproduction and Development

b. Does each group have its own unique behavior pattern?

c. Are some females dominant over others? Do the dominant females dominate in all groups or only in certain groups?

Repeat this activity using males. Have students compare and contrast the interactions and behaviors of the males with those of the females.

Repeat the activity once again using a mixed group of females and males. Have students compare and contrast the interactions and behaviors of the mixed group with the all-female and all-male groups.

**R2.** *A Baby Parade.* Begin this activity by showing the class some baby announcements. Then divide the class into groups. Give each group a list of three or four mammals. Make sure each list contains monotremes and marsupials as well as placental mammals. Challenge each group to write a baby announcement for each mammal on their list. Their announcements should contain the following information:

- Who is making the announcement—mother or both mother and father? In many mammals only the female raises the young and in others, both parents do.
- Name of child.
- Time of birth (season of year).
- Place of birth (geographic area or habitat).
- Photo (drawing) of newborn.
- Special baby facts.

Have students draw up their announcements on posters and share them with the rest of the class.

Keep students in the same groups with the same lists of mammals for the next activity.

**R3.** *Family Portrait.* Challenge each group to find out the following information about each mammal on their list:

- Where do the young develop: eggs (monotremes), pouch (marsupials), or uterus (placentals)?
- How long does it take for the young to complete development?
- Size, appearance, and number of young born.
- Who raises the young: mother only, both parents, or other members of their group?
- Where are the young born and raised—den, nest, or in the open?
- What do the young eat after weaning?
- How long does the family group stay together?
- Any unusual facts about the family life of that particular mammal.

Ask each group to share the family portrait of at least several mammals from their list with the rest of the class.

**R4.** *Developmental Diary.* Before using rodents for breeding or development activities, have a plan for a humane way to dispose of surplus animals.

Have students observe the normal growth of young rodents from birth to adulthood. At regular intervals have students measure and record weight, body length (sans tail), and tail length (sans body). Patterns of development can be seen easily if such information is graphed out. Plot measurements on the vertical axis and age of the rodent on the horizontal axis.

**R5.** **Challenge:** *What Effect Does Handling Have on Rodent Growth?* Have students devise a way to test this problem. Before they begin, have them predict what they think will happen.

One design would be to divide one or two litters of rodents into two equal groups immediately after weaning. Weigh and record the weight of each rodent in each group, and then place each group in cages in which conditions are identical. For the next several weeks rodents in the experimental group should be handled affectionately and petted ten minutes every day. Those in the control group should not be handled or touched. Both groups should get identical and adequate amounts of food and water. As the experiment proceeds, have students note any difference in food and/or water consumption between the groups.

Continue this procedure for three to five weeks, and then weigh all the animals in both groups. Compare the total weight with the beginning total weight for each group. Have students draw conclusions from their data and observations.

Interested, more advanced, or older students could extend this activity by investigating the effects of light, temperature, and various kinds of music on the rate of rodent growth.

**In1.** *Writing:*
   a. Challenge students to learn more about mammals by having them do a formal library report on a specific mammal of their choice.
   b. Challenge students to write an essay in which they detail how peoples' lives are enriched by their mammalian pets, friends, and companions.
   c. Have students imagine that they are the attorney for a platypus that has been arrested for impersonating a mammal. Have them write a defense for monotremes as mammals.

**In2.** *Fine Arts:*
   a. Prehistoric humans painted pictures on the walls of their dwellings telling the story of the hunt or other important events. If possible, show students some pictures of prehistoric art of this sort. Then challenge them to draw or paint stylized mammals and symbols in a way that tells a story. You could make this even more challenging by having them use mammal materials such as leather, fur, bone, or antler to paint or draw their story. Hang each student's drawing or painting and see if the others can figure out the story being told on each. If not, have the artist explain the story.
   b. Have students imagine they are genetic engineers in the distant future and challenge them to design and diagram the ideal mammal pet.
   c. Mammals can make some strange and unusual sounds. Have students write a song or compose a poem in which the sounds of mammals, such as the chattering of squirrels or howls of the wolf, are used at appropriate places for emphasis or humor. Initiate this activity by playing recordings of mammal sounds such as the song of the humpback whale. Some record stores and public libraries carry such recordings, as does the Carolina Biological Supply Company listed in Appendix B.
   d. Have students draw a cartoon about the difficulties a common mammal without an opposable thumb—a cow, for example—would have living in our society where such a thumb is vital. How could the cow answer the phone, for example?

**In3.** *Social Studies:*
   a. *History.* As humans moved in and settled, many large mammals, especially predators, were exterminated or driven away. Have students investigate what large predatory mammals used to inhabit your area before human civilization took over.
   b. *Geography.* Play Geography Jeopardy by giving students the name of a specific habitat, country, or continent. Challenge students to determine which mammals are found there. Give them adequate time to do research and make sure their answer is in the form of a question.

Integration
with Other
Subject Areas

**In4.** *Societal/Environmental Issues:*

a. The Whale Adoption Project has adorable humpbacks and the Save the Manatee Club offers cute manatees that you and your students could adopt. The costs for adoption are often inexpensive. As adoptive parents you receive an adoption certificate, a photo of your adoptee, and a newsletter. Adoption fees for both the manatee and the humpback programs contribute to scientific research, public awareness programs, and projects to ensure the species' survival.

Many zoos and aquariums across the country also have adoption programs for a number of different animals. Adoption fees for zoos and aquariums, which usually last for a year, often are higher than the manatee or humpback projects.

Students could donate or you could have a special fund raiser—for example, a "Whale of a Deal Bake Sale"—to raise the money for the adoption fees. Some of the groups that have mammals for adoption are listed here:

*Save The Manatee Club*
1101 Audbon Way
Maitland, FL 32751

*Orca Adoption Program*
Whale Museum
P.O. Box 945
Friday Harbor, WA 98250

*Whale Adoption Project*
634 N. Falmouth Hwy.
Box 388
North Falmouth, MA 02556

*A.D.O.P.T.*
Lincoln Park Zoological Society
2200 North Cannon Drive
Chicago, IL 60614

*ADOPT*
The Philadelphia Zoo
34th St. & Girard Ave.
Philadelphia, PA 19104

*Adopt an Animal*
San Francisco Zoological Society
Sloat Blvd. at the Pacific Ocean
San Francisco, CA 94132

*Adopt an Audubon Animal*
Audubon Zoological Garden
P.O. Box 4327
New Orleans, LA 70178-9986

*Proud Parent Program*
New England Aquarium
Central Wharf
Boston, MA 02110-3309

b. Have students write a position paper on humans and their relationships with mammals. The paper might cover the entire spectrum of human-mammal interactions, from domestication of livestock and pets to hunting, trapping, and whaling, or it might focus more specifically on one aspect of the issue. Explain that this should not be a statement of opinion but a paper in which the student's position is defended with facts and figures.

c. Conduct a role-playing activity concerning mammals similar to the one outlined in Chapter 10, activity In4b.

d. Use the material in Chapter 9, activity In4b, as a model to investigate the problems mammals might be having in your area and what you and your students might do about these problems.

**RELEASE OF SPECIMENS**

If you followed the recommendations in this book, you did not collect any wild mammals, so there are none to release. Do not release domestic rodents into the wild, as they could become established and result in ecological problems.

# APPENDIX A

## A Guide to Classification

The branch of biology that deals with the scientific classification (grouping) and naming of living things is called taxonomy. Modern taxonomists face an enormous and ever-growing challenge. Currently, 1.5 to 2.5 million kinds of living things have been classified and named, but thousands more are discovered yearly. Scientists speculate that there may be as many as 10 to 30 million total different species of living things lurking in every conceivable nook and cranny of earth.

In an attempt to bring order to such a diverse, even chaotic, multitude of life, taxonomists have devised classification systems. This book is based on the five-kingdom classification system used in most textbooks today:

**Kingdom Monera**

The monerans, more commonly known as bacteria, are basically microscopic specks that barely qualify as life. Monerans are cellular but are said to be prokaryotic. That is, they lack an organized nucleus and most other cell structures. The cells that make up the bodies of the creatures in all other kingdoms possess a definite nucleus and numerous cell structures and are said to be eukaryotic. Monerans are the simplest form of life, but they are also the most numerous. They are found in staggering numbers in water, soil, and air and on the bodies of living things.

**Kingdom Protista**

Taxonomists use this kingdom like you would a junk drawer in your home. Any "simple" organism that does not fit well into any other kingdom goes into this kingdom. There are three kinds of protists:

* the animal-like protists called protozoa
* the plant-like protists called algae
* the fungi-like protists called slime molds

**Kingdom Fungi**

Superficially the fungi appear to be plants, and for many years they were classified as part of the plant kingdom. Closer examination, however, reveals that fungi are not green and cannot photosynthesize food. Their bodies are a mass of threadlike cells and they reproduce by spores. Clearly fungi are not true plants and were considered strange enough to warrant their own kingdom.

**Kingdom Plantae**

This group contains those numerous (and often large) nonmoving green organisms we think of as true plants—everything from mosses to roses and ferns to maple trees.

**Kingdom Animalia**

Taxonomists think of animals as multicellular creatures with tissues and organs (except sponges) that ingest their food.

Once an organism is identified as to its proper kingdom, it is placed into progressively smaller and more specific groups in the classification hierarchy based on its physical, biochemical, embryological, genetic, and behavioral characteristics.

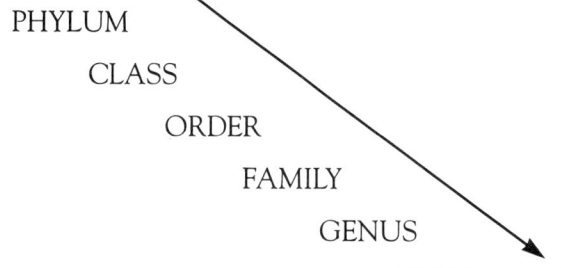

KINGDOM largest group—very general

PHYLUM

CLASS

ORDER

FAMILY

GENUS

SPECIES smallest group—ultra specific

The decreasing size and increasingly specific nature of the classification groups can also be illustrated as an inverted pyramid:

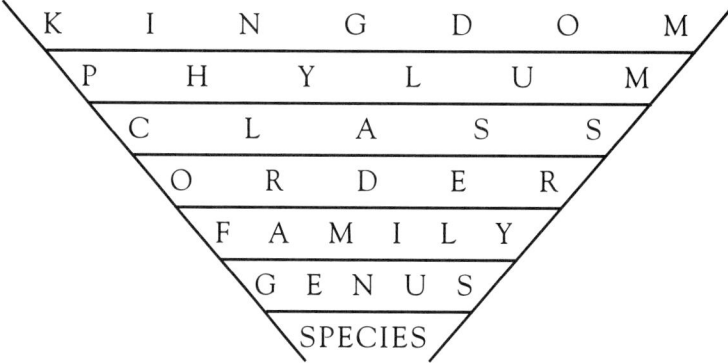

Since this is a book about animals, we will focus in on the animal kingdom hierarchy in more detail. The following simplified overview goes down only to the class or order level and includes only those phyla and classes covered in this book.

## KINGDOM ANIMALIA

Subkingdom Parazoa—animals lacking tissues and organs and possessing no definite symmetry

    Phylum Porifera—sponges

        Class Calcarea—shallow-water sponges with calcerous spicules

        Class Hexactinella—deep-water sponges with siliceous spicules

        Class Demospongiae—large sponges with spongin fibers and/or siliceous spicules

        Class Sclerspongiae—sponges with fibers and siliceous and calcerous spicules

Subkingdom Metazoa—animals possessing tissues and definite symmetry

    Phylum Cnidaria (previously known as Coelenterata)—hollow-bodied animals with stinging tentacles

        Class Hydrozoa—hydra and Portugese man-o-war

        Class Scyphozoa—jellyfish

        Class Anthozoa—corals, sea anemones, and sea fans

    Phylum Platyhelminthes—flatworms

        Class Tubellaria—planarians

        Class Trematoda—flukes

Class Cestoda—tapeworms
Phylum Annelida—segmented worms
    Class Polychaeta—seaworms
    Class Oligochaeta—earthworms
    Class Hirudinea—leeches
Phylum Mollusca—soft-bodied animals, many with shells
    Class Bivalvia (or Pelecypoda)—clams, oysters, scallops, and mussels
    Class Gastropoda (or Univalvia)—snails, slugs, and whelk
    Class Cephalopoda—octopuses, squids, and nautilus
    Class Polyplacophora—chitons
    Class Scaphopoda—toothshells
Phylum Arthropoda—animals with jointed legs
    Subphylum Crustacea
        Class Crustacea—crabs, crayfish, lobsters, shrimps, and pillbugs
    Subphylum Chelicerata
        Class Arachnida—spiders, scorpions, ticks, and mites
    Subphylum Uniramia -
        Class Chilopoda—centipedes
        Class Diplopoda—millipedes
        Class Insecta—insects
Phylum Chordata
    Subphylum Urochordata—sea squirts
    Subphylum Cephalochordata—lancelets
    Subphylum Vertebrata—animals with backbones
        Class Agnatha—lampreys and hagfish
        Class Chondrichthyes—sharks, skates, and rays
        Class Osteichthyes—bony fish
        Class Amphibia—amphibians
            Order Apoda—legless caecilians
            Order Urodela—salamanders and newts
            Order Anura—frogs and toads
        Class Reptilia—reptiles
            Order Rhynchocephalia—tuatara
            Order Squamata—lizards and snakes
            Order Crocodilia—alligators, gavials, caimans, and crocodiles
            Order Chelonia—turtles
        Class Aves—birds (24-34 total orders)
            Order Gaviiformes—loons
            Order Coraciiformes—kingfishers
            Order Pelecaniformes—pelicans and cormorants
            Order Anseriformes—ducks, geese, and swans
            Order Ciconiiformes—herons, ibises, and spoonbills
            Order Falconiformes—hawks, falcons, and vultures
            Order Galliformes—pheasants, turkeys, quails, and partridge
            Order Gruiformes—cranes, coots, and rails
            Order Charadriiformes—gulls, plovers, terns, auks, and puffins
            Order Columbiformes—pigeons and doves
            Order Psittaciformes—parrots, parakeets, and macaws
            Order Cuculiformes—cuckoos and road runner
            Order Strigiformes—owls
            Order Apodiformes—swifts and hummingbirds
            Order Piciformes—woodpeckers, sapsuckers, and flickers
            Order Passeriformes—perching birds

Class Mammalia—mammals (21 total orders)

Order Monotremata—egg-laying mammals—platypus and echidna

Order Marsupialia—pouched mammals—kangaroo and opposum

Order Insectivora—shrews and moles

Order Chiroptera—bats

Order Edentata—armadillos, sloths, and anteaters

Order Rodentia—squirrels, mice, rats, and beavers

Order Lagomorpha—rabbits, hares, and pika

Order Cetacea—whales, dolphins, and porpoises

Order Sirenia—sea cow

Order Proboscidea—elephants

Order Pinnipedia—seals, sea lions, and walruses

Order Carnivora—bears, weasels, and lions

Order Perissodactyla—odd-toed ungulates—tapirs, rhinoceroses, and horses

Order Artiodactyla—even-toed ungulates—camels, deer, giraffes, cattle, and sheep

Order Primata—monkeys, apes, and human

# APPENDIX B

Many biological supply firms advertise live animals for sale but do not actually collect or maintain the animals at their facilities. Often the actual supplier of a specimen is unknown to you and inaccessible to you. Consequently, you cannot verify the species and origins of animals ordered from these companies or know how the animals were treated prior to shipment.

The firms listed here sell and ship live animals from field-collected stocks that are maintained at their facilities. These firms usually can verify the species and origins of the animals they ship and provide firm assurances that the animals were treated humanely prior to shipment. Occasionally due to shortages or to expedite timely delivery, suppliers may substitute. Make sure when ordering that the supplier is aware that you wish to be notified *before* any substitute animal is sent.

Although the firms listed here may be able to offer some general advice on collecting and/or releasing animals in your locale, your state or local wildlife or natural resource officials should always be consulted and regarded as the final authority.

The listing of certain suppliers in this appendix does not represent an endorsement of those companies or a guarantee of their products or services. The information given was provided and verified by company officials.

■ **Carolina Biological Supply Co.**
2700 York Road
Burlington, NC 27215
1-800-334-5551
1-919-584-0381

**Catalog.** A Biology Materials catalog is sent free to schools if requested on school stationery. An individual can purchase a catalog under catalog number 45-1000 at a cost of approximately $18.

**Shipping Requirements.** Recognized educational institutions and full-time teachers may order what they wish with no minimum dollar value involved; terms are 30 days net from the date of the invoice. Individuals must prepay by check, money order, or credit card, with a minimum order of $15. Orders will not be accepted by individuals for chemicals, kits containing chemicals, or liquid-preserved organisms.

**Collection and Treatment of Live Animals.** Most vertebrates are field-collected and a few are reared. Carolina maintains live stocks at its facilities but does drop-ship marine specimens from Florida.

If requested before shipment, Carolina can guarantee the origin and species of a living organism.

According to company officials, "any specimen purchased from Carolina has been ethically and legally acquired by the company, and any animal in their care is handled, housed and treated properly, humanely and in accordance with all applicable laws, regulations and standards."

When necessary, an organism showing signs of illness will be treated. Chemicals and antibiotics are not used as a matter of routine by Carolina except on fish, which receive standard sodium chloride and fungicide treatments, and frogs, which are periodically rinsed with dilute potassium permanganate solution.

Carolina guarantees that their live animals are healthy when shipped and, if they are not healthy upon receipt, they will be replaced at no charge to the customer.

**Company Position on Releasing Commercially Purchased Live Animals.** "Carolina supports an inquiry-oriented observe-and-release program so long as the welfare of the organisms and the local ecology are given full weight in the decision, and so long as it does not violate any federal, state or local regulations."

### ■ Nasco

901 Janesville Avenue
Box 901
Fort Atkinson, WI 53538-0901
1-800-558-9595
1-414-563-2446

**Catalog.** Nasco will supply catalogs free of charge upon request by school officials or private individuals.

**Shipping Requirements.** Orders are shipped on open accounts to schools with good credit. Live materials under $20 are subject to a $2-service charge. Orders can be accepted from private individuals using a major credit card as method of payment. The $20 minimum for live materials also applies to private individuals.

**Collection and Treatment of Live Animals.** The majority of live animal shipments originate from the home facility in Fort Atkinson, Wisconsin, but occasionally live animals are drop-shipped from collecting areas.

All vertebrate stocks except Xenopus laevis are field-collected. Nasco can guarantee the species, but information on origin would be limited to region or state.

Nasco tries to duplicate the natural habitat of the animals it collects and feeds them with natural and processed food when appropriate.

Nasco does not routinely use chemicals or antibiotics. A mild salt solution is sometimes used as an external prophylactic treatment.

Nasco guarantees that it will ship only animals that appear to be disease free based on external visual inspection and guarantees to replace or grant full credit for any live specimens that are not satisfactory on arrival.

**Company Position on Releasing Commercially Purchased Live Animals.** "It would be difficult for Nasco to support an observe-and-release program for commercially purchased live animals, unless teachers or other responsible persons would abide by a decision from local environmental authorities as to whether a specific commercially purchased animal should be released in the local habitat or humanely destroyed."

■ **Connecticut Valley Biological Supply Co.**
Box 326
82 Valley Road
Southampton, MA 01073
1-800-628-7748
1-413-527-4030

**Catalog.** Connecticut Valley will supply catalogs free of charge upon request by school officials or private individuals.

**Shipping Requirements.** No minimum purchase is required of schools, but orders from schools must be accompanied by a purchase order number. Terms are net 30 days. The minimum order for individuals is $10 and these orders must be accompanied by a check, money order, or credit card authorization for the full amount. Connecticut Valley will not sell chemicals to individuals.

**Collection and Treatment of Live Animals.** Most vertebrates are field-collected but live fish, mice, rats, Xenopus frogs, and fertile chicken eggs are bred at their facilities. Connecticut Valley maintains live animal stocks at their facilities and drop-ships specimens "as appropriate."

On request Connecticut Valley can "often provide information" about the species and origin of the live animals they ship. (Officials would not say they could guarantee species and origin of the live field-collected animals they ship.)

Connecticut Valley offers assurances that their live animal stocks are humanely treated.

When shipping aquatic vertebrates, a water conditioner to remove ammonia may be added. They occasionally treat fish with anti-ich medication and frogs and newts with a "dose of tetracycline." Connecticut Valley officials believe that careful monitoring of their live animal stocks enables them to routinely ship healthy, active animals.

The company guarantees to replace or grant full credit for any living specimens that are found to be unsatisfactory on arrival if the company is notified within seven days.

**Company Position on Releasing Commercially Purchased Live Animals.** "We consider a live animal observation program, responsibly handled, to be a valuable and effective educational activity.

"Any organism which is not native to a particular environment has the potential to disrupt that environment's ecological balance if released. Because of this, a live animal should only be released if the release location is known to fall within that animal's native range.

"Before acquiring live animals, it is wise to anticipate the questions that will arise concerning the organisms to be maintained and observed. Preparation through advance reading and research is the best way to avoid problems and ensure a worthwhile learning experience."

# APPENDIX C

## Wildlife and Natural Resource Authorities

All field activities you engage in should comply with federal, state, and local laws. Check with the proper officials of your state wildlife or natural resources department before collecting or releasing. Some states require permits for scientific collectors and certain methods of collection, such as seining, are regulated. Laws have been established to protect animals and ignoring such laws may put you and your school system in an embarrassing situation and set a poor example for your students.

### UNITED STATES

**Alabama**
Director
Division of Game and Fish
Conservation and Natural Resources
64 N. Union Street
Montgomery, AL 36130

**Alaska**
Commissioner
Department of Fish and Game
Box 25526
Juneau, AK 99802

**Arizona**
Director
Game and Fish Department
2222 W. Greenway Rd.
Phoenix, AZ 85023

**Arkansas**
Director
Game and Fish Commission
#2 Natural Resources Drive
Little Rock, AR 72205

**California**
Director
Department of Fish and Game
1416 Ninth Street
Sacramento, CA 95814

**Colorado**
Director
Division of Wildlife
Department of Natural Resources
6060 Broadway
Denver, CO 80216

| | |
|---|---|
| Connecticut | Director<br>Wildlife Division<br>79 Elm Street<br>Hartford, CT 06106 |
| Delaware | Director<br>Division of Fish and Wildlife<br>Natural Resources and Environmental Control<br>Box 1401<br>Dover, DE 19903 |
| Florida | Director<br>Game and Fish Commission<br>Department of Natural Resources<br>620 S. Meridian Street<br>Tallahassee, FL 32399 |
| Georgia | Director<br>Wildlife Resource Division<br>Department of Natural Resources<br>2070 U.S. Highway 278, S.E.<br>Social Circle, GA 30279 |
| Hawaii | Director<br>Land and Natural Resources Department<br>1151 Punchbowl Street<br>Honolulu, HI 96813 |
| Idaho | Director<br>Department of Fish and Game<br>600 W. Walnut<br>Boise, ID 83707 |
| Illinois | Director<br>Department of Natural Resources<br>Lincoln Towers Plaza<br>542 S. Second Street<br>Springfield, IL 62706 |
| Indiana | Director<br>Fish and Wildlife Division<br>402 W. Washington Street<br>Indianapolis, IN 46204 |
| Iowa | Administrator<br>Fish and Wildlife Division<br>Department of Natural Resources<br>Wallace State Office Building<br>Des Moines, IA 50319 |
| Kansas | Supervisor<br>Fisheries and Wildlife Division<br>Department of Wildlife and Parks<br>3300 S.W. 29th Street<br>Topeka, KS 66614 |

| Kentucky | Commissioner<br>Fish and Wildlife Department<br>#1 Game Farm Road<br>Frankfort, KY 40601 |
| --- | --- |
| Louisiana | Secretary<br>Wildlife and Fisheries Department<br>Box 98000<br>Baton, Rouge, LA 70898 |
| Maine | Commissioner<br>Department of Inland Fisheries and Wildlife<br>State House Station #41<br>Augusta, ME 04333 |
| Maryland | Administrator<br>Department of Natural Resources<br>Tawes State Office Building<br>Annapolis, MD 21401 |
| Massachusetts | Commissioner<br>Department of Fisheries and Wildlife<br>19th Floor, Room 1902<br>100 Cambridge Street<br>Boston, MA 02202 |
| Michigan | Director<br>Wildlife Division<br>Department of Natural Resources<br>Mason Building<br>Box 30028<br>Lansing, MI 48909 |
| Minnesota | Director<br>Division of Fish and Wildlife<br>Department of Natural Resources<br>500 Lafayette Road<br>St. Paul, MN 55416 |
| Mississippi | Director<br>Parks and Recreation<br>Department of Wildlife, Fisheries and Parks<br>Box 451<br>Jackson, MS 39205 |
| Missouri | Director<br>Department of Conservation<br>2901 W. Truman Boulevard<br>Box 180<br>Jefferson City, MO 65102 |
| Montana | Director<br>Department of Fish, Wildlife and Parks<br>1420 E. Sixth Avenue<br>Helena, MT 59620 |

| | |
|---|---|
| Nebraska | Director<br>Wildlife Division<br>Games and Parks Commission<br>2200 N. 33rd Street<br>Box 30370<br>Lincoln, NE 68503 |
| Nevada | Administrator<br>Division of Wildlife<br>Conservation and Natural Resources Department<br>1100 Valley Road<br>Reno, NV 89520 |
| New Hampshire | Director<br>Fish and Game Department<br>34 Bridge Street<br>Concord, NH 03301 |
| New Jersey | Director<br>Fish. Game and Wildlife Division<br>Environmental Protection Department<br>501 E. State Street, CN400<br>Trenton, NJ 08625 |
| New Mexico | Director<br>Game and Fish Department<br>Villagra Building<br>408 Galisteo Street<br>Box 25112<br>Santa Fe, NM 87503 |
| New York | Director<br>Division of Fish and Wildlife<br>50 Wolf Road<br>Albany, NY 12233 |
| North Carolina | Director<br>Wildlife Resources Commission<br>512 Salisbury Street<br>Raleigh, NC 27611 |
| North Dakota | Commissioner<br>Game and Fish Department<br>100 N. Bismarck Expressway<br>Bismarck, ND 58501 |
| Ohio | Chief<br>Division of Wildlife<br>Department of Natural Resources<br>1840 Belcher Drive, Building G-3<br>Columbus, OH 43224 |
| Oklahoma | Director<br>Department of Wildlife Conservation<br>1801 N. Lincoln Boulevard<br>Oklahoma City, OK 73105 |

| | |
|---|---|
| Oregon | Director<br>Department of Fish and Wildlife<br>2501 S.W. First Avenue<br>Box 59<br>Portland, OR 97207 |
| Pennsylvania | Director<br>Game Commission<br>2001 Elmerton Avenue<br>Harrisburg, PA 17110 |
| Rhode Island | Director<br>Department of Environmental Management<br>9 Hage Street<br>Providence, RI 02908 |
| South Carolina | Director Wildlife and Marine Resources<br>Box 167<br>Columbia, SC 29203 |
| South Dakota | Director<br>Wildlife Division<br>Department of Game, Fish and Parks<br>523 E. Capitol Avenue<br>Pierre, SD 57501 |
| Tennessee | Executive Director<br>Wildlife Resources Agency<br>Box 40747<br>Nashville, TN 37204 |
| Texas | Executive Director<br>Parks and Wildlife Department<br>4200 Smith School Road<br>Austin, TX 78744 |
| Utah | Director<br>Division of Wildlife Resources<br>Department of Natural Resources<br>1095 W. Motor Drive<br>Salt Lake City, UT 84116 |
| Virginia | Director<br>Department of Game and Inland Fisheries<br>4010 W. Broad Street<br>Richmond, VA 23230 |
| Washington | Director<br>Department of Wildlife<br>600 N. Capitol Way<br>Olympia, WA 98501 |
| West Virginia | Chief<br>Division of Wildlife Resources<br>Department of Natural Resources<br>State Capitol Complex, Building 3<br>Charleston, WV 25305 |

| | | |
|---|---|---|
| | Wisconsin | Director<br>Bureau of Wildlife Management<br>Department of Natural Resources<br>Box 7921<br>Madison, WI 53707 |
| | Wyoming | Director<br>Game and Fish Commission<br>5400 Bishop Boulevard<br>Cheyenne, WY 82002 |
| PUERTO RICO | | Secretary<br>Department of Natural Resources<br>Box 5887<br>San Juan, PR 00906 |
| VIRGIN ISLANDS | | Commissioner<br>Department of Planning and Natural Resources<br>Nisky Center, Suite 231<br>St. Thomas, VI 00802 |
| CANADA | Newfoundland<br>and Labrador | Minister<br>Department of Natural Resources<br>Box 8700<br>St. John's, Newfoundland A1B 4J6 |
| | Nova Scotia | Minister<br>Department of Natural Resources<br>Founder's Square, 2nd Floor<br>1701 Hollis Street<br>Box 698<br>Halifax, Nova Scotia B3J 2T9 |
| | Prince Edward<br>Sound | Minister<br>Department of Environmental Resources<br>11 Kent Street, 4th Floor<br>Box 2000<br>Charlottetown, Prince Edward Island C1A 7N8 |
| | New Brunswick | Minister of Natural Resources and Energy<br>Box 6000<br>Fredericton, New Brunswick<br>E3B 5H1 |
| | Ontario | Minister<br>Ministry of Natural Resources<br>Whitney Block<br>99 Wellesley Street West<br>Toronto, Ontario M7A 1W3<br>M7A 1W3 |
| | Quebec | Minister<br>Ministry of Natural Resources<br>5700 Quatrieme Avenue<br>Charlesbourg, Quebec G1H 6R1 |

| | |
|---|---|
| Manitoba | Minister<br>Department of Natural Resources<br>333 Legislative Building<br>Winnipeg, Manitoba R2C 0V8 |
| Alberta | Minister<br>Department of Environmental Protection<br>Petroleum Plaza, South Tower<br>9915 108th Street<br>Edmonton, Alberta T5K 2G8 |
| Saskatchewan | Minister<br>Saskatchewan Environment and Resource Management<br>3211 Albert Street<br>Regina, Saskatchewan S4S 5W6 |
| British Columbia | Minister<br>Ministry of Environment, Lands and Parks<br>810 Blanshard Street, 4th Floor<br>Victoria, British Columbia V8V 1X4 |
| Northwest Territories | Minister<br>Department of Renewable Resources<br>600, 5102 50th Avenue<br>Yellowknife, Northwest Territories X1A 3S8 |
| Yukon Territory | Minister<br>Department of Renewable Resources<br>Box 2703<br>Whitehorse, Yukon Y1A 2C6 |

# APPENDIX D

Does your state have laws or regulations regarding the use and humane treatment of animals in the classroom? The state agencies listed here should be able to provide you with that information.

**UNITED STATES**

| | |
|---|---|
| **Alabama** | Superintendent<br>Department of Education<br>50 N. Ripley Street<br>Montgomery, AL 36130 |
| **Alaska** | Commissioner<br>Department of Education<br>801 W. 10th Street, Suite 200<br>Juneau, AK 99801 |
| **Arizona** | Superintendent of Public Instruction<br>Department of Education<br>1535 W. Jefferson<br>Phoenix, AZ 85007 |
| **Arkansas** | Director<br>Department of Education<br>Educational Building<br>Capitol Mall<br>Little Rock, AR 72201 |
| **California** | Superintendent<br>Department of Education<br>721 Capitol Mall, Room 524<br>Sacramento, CA 95814 |
| **Colorado** | Commissioner<br>Department of Education<br>201 E. Colfax<br>Denver, CO 80203-1715 |
| **Connecticut** | Commissioner<br>Department of Education<br>165 Capitol Avenue<br>Hartford, CT 06106 |

| | |
|---|---|
| Delaware | Superintendent<br>Department of Education<br>Townsend Building<br>Box 1402<br>Dover, DE 19903 |
| Florida | Commissioner<br>Department of Education<br>The Capitol<br>Tallahassee, FL 32399 |
| Georgia | Superintendent of Schools<br>Department of Education<br>20th E. Tower<br>Martin Luther King Jr. Drive<br>Atlanta, GA 30334 |
| Hawaii | Superintendent<br>Department of Education<br>1390 Miller Street<br>Honolulu, HI 96813 |
| Idaho | Superintendent of Public Instruction<br>650 W. State Street<br>Boise, ID 83720 |
| Illinois | Superintendent<br>State Board of Education<br>100 N. First Street<br>Springfield, IL 62777 |
| Indiana | Superintendent of Public Instruction<br>Department of Education<br>State House, Room 227<br>Indianapolis, IN 46204 |
| Iowa | Director<br>Department of Education<br>Grimes State Office Building<br>E. 14th and Grand Avenue<br>Des Moines, IA 50319 |
| Kansas | Commissioner<br>Department of Education<br>120 E. 10th Street<br>Topeka, KS 66612 |
| Kentucky | Commissioner<br>Department of Education<br>1st Floor, Capitol Plaza Tower<br>500 Moro Street<br>Frankfort, KY 40601 |

| | |
|---|---|
| Louisiana | Superintendent<br>Department of Education<br>Box 94064<br>Baton Rouge, LA 70804-3602 |
| Maine | Commissioner<br>Department of Education<br>State House Station #23<br>Augusta, MA 04333 |
| Maryland | State Superintendent<br>Department of Education<br>200 W. Baltimore Street<br>Baltimore, MD 21201 |
| Massachusetts | Executive Office of Education<br>1 Ashton Place, Room 1401<br>Boston, MA 02108 |
| Michigan | Superintendent<br>Department of Education<br>S. Ottowa Building, 5th Floor<br>Box 30008<br>Lansing, MI 48909 |
| Minnesota | Commissioner<br>Department of Children, Families and Learning<br>550 Cedar Street, 8th Floor<br>St. Paul, MN 55101 |
| Mississippi | Superintendent<br>Department of Education<br>Box 771<br>Jackson, MS 39205 |
| Missouri | Commissioner<br>Department of Elementary and Secondary Education<br>Box 480<br>Jefferson Building, 6th Floor<br>Jefferson City, MO 65102 |
| Montana | Superintendent<br>Office of Public Instruction<br>Box 202501<br>Helena, MT 59620 |
| Nebraska | Commissioner<br>Department of Education<br>301 Centennial Mall S.<br>Lincoln, NE 68509-4987 |

|                 |                                                                                                                                |
| --------------- | ------------------------------------------------------------------------------------------------------------------------------ |
| Nevada          | Superintendent<br>Department of Education<br>700 E. 5th Street<br>Carson City, NV 89710                                         |
| New Hampshire   | Commissioner<br>Department of Education<br>101 Pleasant Street<br>Concord, NH 03301                                             |
| New Jersey      | Commissioner<br>Department of Education<br>225 E. State Street, CN500<br>Trenton, NJ 08625                                      |
| New Mexico      | Superintendent of Public Instruction<br>Department of Education<br>Education Building<br>416 Don Gaspar<br>Santa Fe, NM 87501   |
| New York        | Commissioner<br>Department of Education<br>Education Building<br>89 Washington Avenue<br>Albany, NY 12234                       |
| North Carolina  | Superintendent<br>Department of Public Instruction<br>301 N. Wilmington Street<br>Raleigh, NC 27601                            |
| North Dakota    | Superintendent<br>Department of Public Instruction<br>11th Floor, State Capitol<br>600 E. Boulevard<br>Bismarck, ND 58505      |
| Ohio            | Superintendent<br>Department of Education<br>65 S. Front Street, Room 808<br>Columbus, OH 43266-0308                           |
| Oklahoma        | Superintendent of Public Instruction<br>Department of Education<br>2500 N. Lincoln Boulevard<br>Oklahoma City, OK 73105        |
| Oregon          | Superintendent<br>Department of Education<br>255 Capitol Street, N.E.<br>Salem, OR 97310                                        |

| | |
|---|---|
| Pennsylvania | Secretary<br>Department of Education<br>10th Floor, Harristown Building #2<br>Harrisburg, PA 17120 |
| Rhode Island | Commissioner<br>Department of Education<br>22 Hayes Street<br>Providence, RI 02908 |
| South Carolina | Superintendent<br>Department of Education<br>Rutledge Building<br>1429 Senate Street<br>Columbia, SC 29201 |
| South Dakota | Secretary<br>Department of Education and Cultural Affairs<br>700 Governors Drive<br>Pierre, SD 57501 |
| Tennessee | Commissioner<br>Department of Education<br>710 James Robertson Parkway<br>Nashville, TN 37243 |
| Texas | Commissioner<br>Texas Education Agency<br>1701 N. Congress Avenue<br>Austin, TX 78701 |
| Utah | State Superintendent<br>Office of Education<br>250 E. 500 S.<br>Salt Lake City, UT 84111 |
| Vermont | Commissioner<br>Department of Education<br>120 State Street<br>Montpelier, VT 05602 |
| Virginia | Superintendent of Public Instruction<br>Department of Education<br>Monroe Building, 25th Floor<br>101 N. 14th Street<br>Richmond, VA 23219 |
| Washington | Superintendent of Public Instruction<br>Old Capitol Building<br>Box 47200<br>Olympia, WA 98504 |

| | | |
|---|---|---|
| | West Virginia | Superintendent<br>Department of Education<br>1800 Washington Street, E.<br>Building 6<br>Charleston, WV 25305 |
| | Wisconsin | Superintendent<br>Department of Public Instruction<br>125 S. Weber Street<br>Box 7841<br>Madison, WI 53707 |
| | Wyoming | Superintendent of Public Instruction<br>Department of Education<br>Hathaway Building<br>2300 Capitol Avenue<br>Cheyenne, WY 82002 |
| PUERTO RICO | | Secretary<br>Department of Education<br>Box 190759<br>San Juan, PR 00919 |
| VIRGIN ISLANDS | | Commissioner<br>Department of Education<br>44-46 Kongens Gade<br>St. Thomas, VI 00802 |
| CANADA | Newfoundland<br>and Labrador | Minister of Education<br>Confederation Building<br>Box 8700<br>St. Johns, Newfoundland A1B 4J6 |
| | Nova Scotia | Minister of Education<br>2021 Brunswick Street<br>Box 578<br>Halifax, Nova Scotia B3J 2S9 |
| | Prince Edward<br>Island | Minister of Education<br>Shaw Building<br>105 Rochford Street, 3rd Floor<br>Box 2000<br>Charlottetown, Prince Edward Island C1A 7N8 |
| | New Brunswick | Minister of Education<br>Box 6000<br>Fredericton, New Brunswick<br>E3B 5H1 |
| | Ontario | Minister of Education<br>22nd Floor, Mowat Block<br>900 Bay Street<br>Toronto, Ontario<br>M7A 1L2 |

| | |
|---|---|
| Quebec | Minister of Education<br>1035 De La Chevrotiere Street<br>15th Floor<br>Quebec, Quebec G1R 5A5 |
| Manitoba | Minister of Education and Training<br>168 Legislative Building<br>Winnipeg, Manitoba R3C 0P8 |
| Alberta | Minister of Education<br>Devonian Building<br>11160 Jasper Avenue<br>Edmonton, Alberta T5K 0L2 |
| Saskatchewan | Minister of Education<br>2220 College Avenue<br>Regina, Saskatchewan S4P 3V7 |
| British Columbia | Minister of Education<br>Box 9150<br>Stn. Prov. Govt.<br>Victoria, British Columbia V8W 9H1 |
| Northwest Territories | Minister of Education<br>Box 1320<br>Yellowknife, Northwest Territories X1A 2L9 |
| Yukon Territory | Minister of Education<br>Box 2703<br>Whitehorse, Yukon Y1A 2C6 |

# APPENDIX E

## State Departments of Health

The health and safety of both students and teacher are of prime importance in any science program. The animals recommended for study in this book present little if any risk to students or teacher if proper precautions are followed. However, in certain locales teachers and students may encounter and even collect aggressive animals, poisonous animals, or animals that might transmit diseases to humans. Seek the advice of your state wildlife or natural resource officials (Appendix C) and your state health authorities (listed here) to ensure the health and safety of everyone involved in this program.

**UNITED STATES**

**Alabama**
Director
Department of Public Health
610 E. Patton
Montgomery, AL 36111

**Alaska**
Director
Division of Public Health
Department of Health and Social Services
Box 110610
Juneau, AK 99811

**Arizona**
Director
Department of Health Services
1740 W. Adams Street
Phoenix, AZ 85007

**Arkansas**
Director
Department of Health
4815 W. Markham Street
Little Rock, AR 72205

**California**
Director
Department of Health Services
714 P Street
Room 1253
Sacramento, CA 98514

**Colorado**
Executive Director
Department of Health
4300 Cherry Creek Drive S.
Denver, CO 80222

| | |
|---|---|
| Connecticut | Commissioner<br>Department of Public Health<br>410 Capitol Avenue<br>MS #13 COM<br>Hartford, CT 06134 |
| Delaware | Director<br>Division of Public Health<br>Health and Social Services Department<br>Box 637<br>J. Cooper Building<br>Dover, DE 19903 |
| Florida | Deputy Secretary for Health<br>Health Program Office<br>Health and Rehabilitative Services<br>1317 Winewood Boulevard<br>Tallahassee, FL 32399-0700 |
| Georgia | Director<br>Public Health Division<br>Department of Human Resources<br>2 Peachtree Street, 7th Floor<br>Atlanta, GA 30303 |
| Hawaii | Director<br>Department of Health<br>1250 Punchbowl Street<br>Honolulu, HI 96813 |
| Idaho | Director<br>Department of Health and Welfare<br>450 W. State Street, 10th Floor<br>Box 83720<br>Boise, ID 83720 |
| Illinois | Director<br>Department of Public Health<br>535 W. Jefferson Street<br>Springfield, IL 62761 |
| Indiana | Commissioner<br>State Board of Health<br>1330 W. Michigan Street #4255<br>Indianapolis, IN 46206 |
| Iowa | Commissioner<br>Department of Health<br>Lucas State Office Building<br>321 E. 12th Street<br>Des Moines, IA 50319 |

| | |
|---|---|
| Kansas | Secretary<br>Department of Health and Environment<br>Landon State Office Building, 6th Floor<br>2 North and J Streets<br>Topeka, KS 66612<br>Topeka, KS 66620 |
| Kentucky | Commissioner<br>Department of Health Services<br>Cabinet of Human Resources<br>275 E. Main Street<br>Frankfort, KY 40601 |
| Louisiana | Secretary<br>Department of Health and Hospitals<br>Box 629<br>Baton Rouge, LA 70821 |
| Maine | Commissioner<br>Department of Human Services<br>State House Station #11<br>Augusta, ME 04333 |
| Maryland | Secretary<br>Department of Health and Mental Hygiene<br>201 W. Preston Street<br>5th Floor<br>Annapolis, MD 21201 |
| Massachusetts | Commissioner<br>Department of Public Health<br>250 Washington Street<br>Boston, MA 02108 |
| Michigan | Director<br>Department of Public Health<br>3500 N. Logan<br>Box 30035<br>Lansing, MI 48909 |
| Minnesota | Commissioner<br>Department of Health<br>717 Delaware Street, S.E.<br>Box 9441<br>Minneapolis, MN 55440 |
| Mississippi | State Health Officer<br>Department of Health<br>2423 N. State Street<br>Jackson, MS 39216 |

| | |
|---|---|
| Missouri | Director<br>Department of Health<br>1738 E. Elm<br>Box 570<br>Jefferson City, MO 65102-0570 |
| Montana | Director<br>Department of Public Health and Human Services<br>111 Sanders Street<br>Box 4210<br>Helena, MT 59620 |
| Nebraska | Director<br>Department of Health<br>Box 95007<br>Lincoln, NE 68509 |
| Nevada | Administrator<br>Health Division<br>Department of Human Resources<br>505 E. King Street<br>Carson City, NV 89710 |
| New Hampshire | Director<br>Division of Public Health Services<br>Department of Health and Welfare<br>6 Hazen Drive<br>Concord, NH 03301 |
| New Jersey | Commissioner<br>Department of Health<br>John Fitch Plaza<br>Trenton, NJ 08625 |
| New Mexico | Secretary<br>Department of Health<br>1190 St. Francis Drive<br>Santa Fe, NM 87502 |
| New York | Commissioner<br>Department of Health<br>Empire State Plaza<br>Corning Tower Building<br>Albany, NY 12237 |
| North Carolina | Director<br>Department of Environment, Health and Natural Resources<br>1330 St. Mary's Street<br>Raleigh, NC 27611 |

| | |
|---|---|
| North Dakota | State Health Officer<br>Department of Health<br>State Capitol<br>600 E. Boulevard<br>Bismarck, ND 58505 |
| Ohio | Director<br>Department of Health<br>246 N. High Street<br>Box 118<br>Columbus, OH 43266 |
| Oklahoma | Commissioner<br>Department of Health<br>1000 N.E. 10th<br>Box 53551<br>Oklahoma City, OK 73152 |
| Oregon | Administrator<br>Health Division<br>Department of Human Resources<br>800 N.E. Oregon Street, #21<br>Portland, OR 97232 |
| Pennsylvania | Secretary<br>Department of Health<br>802 Health and Welfare Building<br>Harrisburg, PA 17120 |
| Rhode Island | Director<br>Department of Health<br>3 Capitol Hill<br>Providence, RI 02908 |
| South Carolina | Commissioner<br>Health and Environmental Control<br>2600 Bull Street<br>Columbia, SC 29201 |
| South Dakota | Secretary<br>Department of Health<br>445 E. Capitol Avenue<br>Pierre, SD 57501 |
| Tennessee | Commissioner<br>Department of Health<br>Tennessee Towers, Thea Fl.<br>Nashville, TN 37247 |
| Texas | Commissioner<br>Department of Health<br>1100 W. 49th Street<br>Austin, TX 78756 |

| | | |
|---|---|---|
| | West Virginia | Secretary<br>Health and Human Resources Department<br>State Capitol Complex<br>Building 6, Room B-617<br>Charleston, WV 25305 |
| | Wisconsin | Administrator<br>Division of Health<br>Health and Social Services Department<br>Box 309<br>Madison, WI 53701 |
| | Wyoming | Administrator<br>Health and Medical Services Division<br>Health and Social Services Department<br>Hathaway Building<br>Cheyenne, WY 82002 |
| PUERTO RICO | | Secretary<br>Department of Health<br>Box 9342<br>Santurce, PR 00908 |
| VIRGIN ISLANDS | | Commissioner<br>Department of Health<br>St. Thomas Hospital<br>St. Thomas, VI 00802 |
| CANADA | Newfoundland<br>and Labrador | Minister of Health<br>Box 8700<br>St. John's, Newfoundland<br>A1B 4J6 |
| | Nova Scotia | Minister of Health and Fitness<br>Box 488<br>Halifax, Nova Scotia<br>B3J 2R8 |
| | Prince Edward<br>Island | Minister of Health and Social Services<br>Department of Health and Social Services<br>2nd Floor, Sullivan Building<br>Box 2000<br>Charlottetown, Prince Edward Island<br>C1A 7N8 |
| | New Brunswick | Minister of Health and Community Services<br>Box 6000<br>Fredericton, New Brunswick<br>E3B 5H1 |
| | Ontario | Minister of Health<br>10th Floor, Hepburn Block<br>80 Grosvenor Street<br>Toronto, Ontario<br>M7A 2C4 |

| | |
|---|---|
| Quebec | Minister of Health and Social Services<br>1075 chemin Sainte-Foy<br>Catherine-De Longpre Building<br>15th Floor<br>Quebec, Quebec<br>G1S 2M1 |
| Manitoba | Minister of Health<br>302 Legislative Building<br>Winnipeg, Manitoba<br>R3C 0V8 |
| Alberta | Minister of Health<br>323 Legislative Building<br>Edmonton, Alberta<br>T5K 2B6 |
| Saskatchewan | Minister of Health<br>334 Legislative Building<br>Regina, Saskatchewan<br>S4S 0B3 |
| British Columbia | Minister of Health<br>Parliament Buildings<br>Victoria, British Columbia<br>V8V 4R3 |
| Yukon Territory | Minister of Health and Social Services<br>Yukon Government Building<br>Box 2703<br>Whitehorse, Yukon<br>Y1A 2C6 |
| Northwest Territories | Minister of Health<br>Government of the Northwest Territories<br>Box 1320<br>Yellowknife, Northwest Territories<br>X1A 2L9 |

# APPENDIX F

## Additional Resources

The following materials may prove beneficial to you and your students in the identification of animals for collecting and in the maintenance of animals in the classroom. Many of the materials listed here may be purchased from the suppliers listed in Appendix B, others may be available in aquarium stores and pet shops. The general resources are alphabetized while the specific resources are sequenced to the topics in each chapter.

*Audubon Society Field Guides*. New York: Alfred A. Knopf, 1987-1991.

Behringer, Marjorie B. *Techniques and Materials in Biology*. Malabar, FL: Robert E. Krieger, 1989.

Brown, Vinson. *Amateur Naturalist's Handbook*. Englewood Cliffs, NJ: Prentice-Hall, 1980.

Brown, Vinson. *Investigating Nature Through Outdoor Projects*. Harrisburg, PA: Stackpole Books. 1983.

Camazine, Scott. *The Naturalist's Year*. New York: John Wiley & Sons, 1987.

*Classroom Creature Culture*. Washington, D.C.: National Science Teachers Association, 1986.

Coulombe, Deborah. *Seaside Naturalist*. New York: Simon & Schuster, 1984.

Durrell, Gerald. *Practical Guide for the Amateur Naturalist*. New York: Alfred A. Knopf, 1982.

Garber, Steven. *The Urban Naturalist*. New York: John Wiley & Sons, 1987.

*Golden Guides*. New York: Western Publishing, 1957-1990.

Harrison, George and Kit. *America's Favorite Backyard Wildlife*. New York: Simon & Schuster, 1985.

Headstrom, Richard. *Adventures with Freshwater Animals*. New York: Dover Publications, 1964.

Herberman, Ethan. *The City Kid's Field Guide*. New York: Simon & Schuster, 1989.

Hickman, Mae. *Care of the Wild Feathered and Furred: Treating and Feeding Injured Birds and Mammals*. New York: Kesend Publishing, 1978.

*How To Know Series*. Dubuque, IA: William. C. Brown, 1949-1982.

Katz, Adrienne. *NATUREWATCH—Exploring Nature with Young Children*. Redding, MA: Addison-Wesley, 1986.

Kramer, David C. *Animals in the Classroom*. Redding, MA: Addison-Wesley, 1989.

Margullis, Lynn, and Karlene Schwartz. *Five Kingdoms: An Illustrated Guide to the Phyla of Life on Earth*. New York: Freeman, 1982.

Orlans, F. Barbara. *Animal Care from Protozoa to Small Mammals*. Redding, MA: Addison-Wesley, 1977.

*Petersen Field Guides*. Boston: Houghton Mifflin, 1951-1991.

Simon, Seymour. *Pets in a Jar*. New York: Viking-Penguin, 1975.

Wernert, Susan, ed. *North American Wildlife*. New York: Reader's Digest, 1982.

Wolff, Sonia. *Teaching Nature in Towns and Cities*. Danville, IL: Interstate Publishers, 1985.

GENERAL
RESOURCES

# SPECIFIC RESOURCES

These resources are listed in the same order as the book's contents; that is, from lower invertebrates to mammals.

Shale, David, and Jennifer Coldrey. *The World of a Jellyfish*. Milwaukee, WI: Gareth Stevens, 1986.

Edwards, Ray. *The Nightcrawler Manual*. Eagle River, WI: Shields Publications, 1981.

Edwards. C. A., and J. R. Lofty. *Biology of Earthworms*.
Rochester, NY: Bookworm Publications, 1977.

Knott, Robert. *Earthworms—A Teacher's Guide*. Berkeley: University of California, Lawrence Hall of Science, 1989.

Halton, Cheryl. *Those Amazing Leeches*. New York: Dillon Press, 1989.

Johnson, Sylvia. *Snails*. New York: Facts on File, 1986.

Green, Carl R., and William R. Sanford. *The Octopus*. New York: Macmillan, 1988.

Bliss, Dorothy E. *Shrimps, Lobsters and Crabs: Their Fascinating Life Story*. New York: Columbia University Press, 1990.

Jones, Dick. *Spider: The Story of a Predator and Its Prey*. New York: Facts on File, 1986.

David, Al. *Tarantulas: A Complete Introduction*. Neptune City, NJ: T. F. H. Publications, 1987.

Burton, Maurice. *Insects and Their Relatives*. New York: Facts on File, 1984.

O'Toole, Christopher, ed. *The Encyclopedia of Insects*. New York: Facts on File, 1986.

Headstrom, Richard. *Adventures with Insects*. New York: Dover Publications, 1963.

Nardi, James B. *Close Encounters with Insects and Spiders*. Ames: Iowa State University Press, 1988.

Glenn, George S. Jr. *Ant Rancher's Handbook*. Philadelphia: Running Press, 1990.

Norsgaard, E. Jaediker. *How to Raise Butterflies*. New York: Putnam Group, 1988.

Roberts, Mervin F. *All About Land Hermit Crabs*. Neptune City, NJ: T. F. H. Publications, 1979.

Thompson, Peter. *Thompson's Guide to Freshwater Fish*. Boston: Houghton Mifflin, 1985.

Axelrod, Herbert R., and William Vorderwinkler. *Encyclopedia of Tropical Fishes*. Neptune City, NJ: T. F. H. Publications, 1983.

Schneider, Earl. *All About Aquariums*. Neptune City, NJ: T. F. H. Publications, 1982.

Mills, Dick. *Fishkeeper's Guide to the Tropical Aquarium*. Morris Plains, NJ: Tetra Press, 1984.

Whitern, Wilfred L. *Guppies*. Neptune City, NJ: T. F. H. Publications, 1980.

Friswold, Carroll A. *A Beginner's Guide to Guppies*. Neptune City, NJ: T. F. H. Publications, 1986.

Iwaaski, Noboru. *Guppies: Fancy Strains and How to Raise Them*. Neptune City, NJ: T. F. H. Publications, 1989.

Barrie, Anmarie. *A Beginner's Guide to Goldfish*. Neptune City, NJ: T. F. H. Publications, 1986.

Roberts, Joseph. *Goldfish*. Neptune City, NJ: T. F. H. Publications, 1984.

Schubert, Gottfried. *Fish Diseases*. Neptune City, NJ: T. F. H. Publications, 1987.

Post, George W. *Textbook of Fish Health*. Neptune City, NJ; T. F. H. Publications, 1983.

Zupanc, Gunther. *Fish and Their Behavior*. Morris Plains, NJ: Tetra Press, 1988.

Pyrom, Jay. *Frogs and Toads: A Complete Introduction*. Neptune City, NJ: T. F. H. Publications, 1987.

Mattison, Chris. *Frogs and Toads of the World*. New York: Facts on File, 1987.

Pyrom, Jay. *Complete Introduction to Frogs and Toads*. Neptune City, NJ: T. F. H. Publications, 1987.

Dickerson, Mary C. *The Frog Book*. New York: Dover Publications, 1969.

Bjorn, Byron. *Salamanders and Newts*. Neptune City, NJ: T. F. H. Publications, 1987.

Halliday, Tim, and Kraig Alder, eds. *Encyclopedia of Reptiles and Amphibians*. New York: Facts on File, 1986.

Perkins, Kenneth W. *Reptiles and Amphibians: Care and Culture*. Burlington, NC: Carolina Biological Supply Co., 1981.

Mattison, Christopher. *The Care of Reptiles and Amphibians in Captivity*. New York: Blandford Press, 1987.

Roberts, Mervin F. *All About Chameleons and Anoles*. Neptune City, NJ: T. F. H. Publications, 1981.

Trutnau, Ludwig. *Nonvenomous Snakes*. Hauppauge, NY: Barron's Educational Series, 1986.

Mattison, Christopher. *Keeping and Breeding Snakes*. New York: Blandford Press, 1988.

Perkins, Christopher, and Alex Middleton, eds. *Encyclopedia of Birds*. New York: Facts on File, 1985.

Russo, Monica. *Complete Book of Birdhouses and Feeders*. New York: Outlet Book Co., 1990.

Harrison, George H. *Backyard Bird Watcher*. New York: Simon & Schuster, 1979.

Harrison, George and Kit. *America's Favorite Backyard Birds*. New York: Simon & Schuster, 1983.

Hickman, Pamela. *Birdwise*. Redding, MA: Addison-Wesley, 1988.

Grubb, Thomas. *Beyond Birding: Field Projects for Inquisitive Birders*. Pacific Grove, CA: Boxwood Press, 1986.

Hickey, Joseph J. *The Complete Cage and Aviary Bird Handbook*. New York: Dover Publications, 1975.

Macdonald, David, ed. *Encyclopedia of Mammals*. New York: Facts on File, 1984.

Lawlor, Timothy E. *Handbook to the Orders and Families of Living Mammals*. Eureka, CA: Mad River Press, 1979.

Burton, Maurice. *Warm-Blooded Animals*. New York: Facts on File, 1985.

# LAB NOTES

# LAB NOTES

# LAB NOTES